Praise for
Where the Footprints End: High Strangeness and the Bigfoot Phenomenon Volume I - Folklore

"Impressively, even exhaustively researched, *Where the Footprints End* should give all students of the anomalous serious pause for thought. By documenting both the high strangeness that surrounds Bigfoot sightings, and the deep folklore in which they are embedded, Cutchin and Renner so far broaden the context of Bigfoot encounters that it is no longer possible to credit any single theory or literalistic interpretation concerning their nature. Indeed, we begin to suspect that the reality of Bigfoot is less a problem to be solved than a mystery to dissolve our view of reality itself. Here at last is the book that dear old Bigfoot deserves."

— Patrick Harpur,
author of *Daimonic Reality*

"This book poses a danger to the foundations of cryptozoology. While mainstream Bigfoot investigators would have you believe that people are around the world are merely encountering a lost ape, Cutchin and Renner dig into the details they've swept under the rug, excavating countless Bigfoot reports involving glowing orbs, telepathic communication, and paranormal phenomena that have more in common with tales of ancient gods and alien abductions than they do with primatology. Meticulously researched and backed up with a treasure trove of footnotes, *Where the Footprints End* is poised to do for Bigfoot what *Passport to Magonia* did for UFOs."

— Greg Newkirk,
director of The Traveling Museum of the Paranormal & the Occult
and executive producer and star of *Hellier*

"… what Josh and Tim are accomplishing with their book: it's putting the range of phenomena umbrella-ed under 'Bigfoot' in dialogue with parapsychology and mythology and witch lore and spirit encounters and so on… It's a fascinating catalogue of just how strange your cosmos can actually get when it wants to on the one level—and it's a good read for that —but it will hopefully also assist in further comparative efforts across the various High Strange disciplines… definitely check it out."

— Gordon White,
author of *Star.Ships*
and podcaster at Rune Soup

"For many Sasquatch-seekers, the supernatural Bigfoot is the equivalent of the elephant in the room. But, not for Joshua and Timothy... For me, the most important thing about *Where the Footprints End* is the fact that its authors *do* make a fascinating case for their theory. There is no 'filler' here. The book is written in a coherent, careful fashion; it's definitely not a sensational, over-the-top story for the tabloids at the local store. Rather, the book is filled with not just reports of Bigfoot and high-strangeness, but also with a great deal of history, well-thought-out theories, and an excellent appreciation and understanding of how folklore and reality can blend together in incredible ways... My hope, though, is that everyone who has an interest in the Bigfoot debate will read *Where the Footprints End*, and will dispatch that elephant in the room to pastures new and faraway, and come together. I really think this book has the potential to do that."

— Nick Redfern,
author of *The Bigfoot Book: The Encyclopedia of Sasquatch, Yeti and Cryptid Primates*

"Books like the aforementioned are an integral piece of the puzzle if we ever wish to get to the bottom of what is really taking place on this strange planet of ours, and perhaps what Vallee did for the UFO phenomenon, Cutchin & Renner could do for the Bigfoot Phenomenon. Overall Rating 4 Bigfeet out of 5!"

— Bryce Johnson,
Bigfoot Collector's Club
and Travel Channel's *Expedition Bigfoot*

"... this is not your typical book on the Bigfoot phenomenon. It's simply not from the standard cryptozoological school of thought or presentation that attempts to establish the physical, biological 'missing link' presence of a kind of 'hairy apeman" out there on the global landscape, although the authors aren't denying that such a creature could exist... What these two authors have done in this cryptozoological setting compares with what Jacques Vallee did with the publication in 1969 of his book *Passport to Magonia*, comparing faerie folklore with modern UFO entity encounters... This is a very well-written and thought-provoking volume that bears profound implications for this area of inquiry."

— Brent Raynes,
editor of *Alternate Perceptions* magazine
and author of *John A. Keel: The Man, The Myths, and the Ongoing Mysteries*

Where the Footprints End

High Strangeness and the Bigfoot Phenomenon

Volume Two: Evidence

written by

Joshua Cutchin and Timothy Renner

with illustrations by Timothy Renner

WHERE THE FOOTPRINTS END, VOLUME TWO

Copyright © 2020 by Joshua Cutchin and Timothy Renner.

All rights reserved.

ISBN: 9798580596747

Investigators of apparitions are often frustrated by the way that no apparition exists in isolation. One leads to another. We cannot investigate dogs without cats; cats without fairies; fairies without Bigfoot and lake monsters; any of these without UFOs and aliens. The investigation always broadens to embrace, in the end, all apparitions, as if there were a single principle at work capable of manifesting itself in a myriad of forms. At the same time, the investigation always deepens, pointing to the continuity of apparitions in time, leading us into the past, into folklore and myth... If apparitions cannot be understood in isolation from each other, neither can they be understood separately from the witness who sees them.

- Patrick Harpur,
Daimonic Reality: A Field Guide to the Otherworld

WHERE THE FOOTPRINTS END, VOLUME ONE

DEDICATION

To Patrick Harpur, in whose footprints we follow.

CONTENTS

	ACKNOWLEDGEMENTS	I
	PREFACE by Joshua Cutchin	II
1	MYSTERY LIGHTS by Timothy Renner	1

The Eyes Have It • Spectral Lights • Great Balls of Fire • The Green Flash

2	UFOs by Timothy Renner	26

Momo • The Bell Farm • Bigfoot, White Lights, and a Glowing Bronze Object • Discs in the Sky, Apes in the Van • Strange Entities • The Hovering Light and the Hairy Man • "Something is Seen, But One Doesn't Know What"

3	VOCALIZATIONS by Joshua Cutchin	41

Monkey See, Monkey Do • Mimicry: Animals • Mimicry: Bird Calls • "The Owls Are Not What They Seem" • The Language of the Birds • Mimicry: Other Sounds • Mimicry: Human Voices • Mimicry: Explanations • Samurai Chatter

4	ALTERED STATES by Joshua Cutchin	79

Singing, Infrasound, and Altered States of Consciousness • Mindspeak • Shape Shifting • Cocreation Theory

5	HEX SIGNS by Timothy Renner	115

From the Trees • Bends, Twists, Circles, and Portals • The Upside-Down • When the Bough Breaks • Stick Dolls and Devil Nets • Cryptoanthropology: The Religio-Magical Bigfoot • Hobos Without Bindles

6	TOES by Joshua Cutchin	136

Bidactyl and Tridactyl Footprints • Tetradactyl Footprints • Polydactyly and Other Shapes • Toeing the Line

7   **TRACKWAYS** by Joshua Cutchin   161
    Solitary Footprints • One-Legged Trackways • Nonexistent Tracks • Gliding Bigfoot • Levitation and Speed: The Massless Bigfoot • Where the Footprints End • Thoughts on Abruptly Ending Trackways • Portals

8   **DISAPPEARING EVIDENCE**   201
    by Timothy Renner
    Primary Relics • Disappearing Evidence • Footprints? What Footprints? • Plaid is the New Black • "We Don't Want to Be Hurt" • Threats from the Unknown • Bodies of Evidence • Copies of Copies

9   **THE TRICKSTER** by Joshua Cutchin   228
    The Trickster and Bigfoot • Fake It 'Til You Make It • Make It 'Til You Fake It • Case Study: Rick Dyer • Case Study: The Minnesota Iceman

10 **CASE STUDY: Out of This World**   255
    by Joshua Cutchin
    Premonitions • The Event

11 **CASE STUDY: Under the Owl Moon**   260
    by Timothy Renner
    Murphy is a Bigfoot • A Paranormal, Supernatural Phenomenon • Gifting Exchanges • An Apport • Unexplained Phenomena • Psychic Impressions • Messages from Beyond • It Follows • The Web

AFTERWORD by Timothy Renner   272
INDEX   275

ACKNOWLEDGEMENTS

Edited by Catherine Diehl.

The authors would like to thank—in no particular order, for dozens of different things—Red Pill Junkie, Chad Redding, Tobe Johnson, Chris Woodyard, Jon Darby, Greg Bishop, Tim Grieve-Carlson, Mark Skabs, Ronny LeBlanc, Adam Sayne, Seriah Azkath, Wes Germer, Brother Richard Hendrick OFM, Paul Curtis, Jeff Ritzmann, Aaron Gulyas, TJ Gardner, Ryan Fusco, Wren Collier, Tara Vanflower, Theo Paijmans, Chris Ernst, High on Fire, Rob Blasko, Amy Whedonite, Jason Berg, John Tenney, Vanessa Kindall, Martin Kottmeyer, the ParaManiacs, Lon Strickler, Karen Gulledge, Mike Clelland, Greg Newkirk, Dana Newkirk, Phüntshog, Christopher D. Bader, David Chace, David Bakara, Ron Johnson, Patrick Harpur, David Metcalfe, Dave W., David Williams, Strange Familiars patrons, and all the other friends, family, and colleagues who have supported us and contributed to this volume.

The Yeti copyright 2002, Relapse Records.
Lyrics used with permission from Rob Blasko and High on Fire.

Cover illustration by Timothy Renner with colors by Jesse Heagy.

Preface

Poltergeists… faeries… extraterrestrials… Pagan gods… witches… window areas… ghosts… archetypal Women in White….

Volume I of *Where the Footprints End* illustrates how such topics connect, at least on a mythopoetic level, to contemporary sightings of large, hairy wild men the world over. These subjects all broadly fall under the umbrella of folklore, both modern and ancient. Volume II takes a different approach, primarily examining the way High Strangeness manifests in bigfoot evidence.

This distinction is, of course, something of a misnomer. There is plenty of evidence reported in Volume I; similarly, Volume II is chock-full of folklore. Perhaps a better description of the book in your hands is that it is much more *experiential* than its predecessor.

Volume II catalogues the peripheral oddities reported by bigfoot witnesses—mystery lights, peculiar sounds, stick signs, anomalous footprints and trackways, etc.—and demonstrates why, by-and-large, conventional explanations remain unsatisfactory. We conclude with a pair of case studies, brief sections exemplifying how the messy, disparate topics found in both books can come together in truly baffling encounters.

As noted in the introduction to Volume I, *Where the Footprints End* was conceived as a singular book, only separated for logistical reasons (hence this brief *Preface*, rather than a full-blown *Introduction*). These two volumes are incomplete individually, and should be read together to completely grasp the entire spectrum of High Strangeness and the bigfoot phenomenon.

Finally, as with the last book, a word of caution: those seeking definitive answers will likely be disappointed. No one knows exactly where the footprints end—but Volume II marks the final steps of our journey.

Your beliefs will be the light by which you see, but they will not be what you see and they will not be a substitute for seeing.
- Flannery O'Connor

Mystery Lights

Mystery lights dance around the bigfoot phenomenon like fireflies on a hot summer night. From ubiquitous reports of creatures' eyes glowing —to those pesky UFOs (see Chapter 2) that just don't seem to want to let the sasquatch have the "weird" spotlight all to themselves—strange lights and bigfoot are simply inseparable companions on their nighttime journeys.

The Eyes Have It

In discussing the eyes of bigfoot and other animals—used here in comparison—it is important to note the difference between eye*shine* and eye*glow*. Eyeshine is common in many nocturnal species and is the result of a reflective layer of tissue in the eyes known as the *tapetum lucidum*. The tapetum lucidum is the reason, for instance, that deer eyes seem to light up when your car's headlights catch them. A source of light is required for eyeshine, however—there must be something for the tapetum lucidum to reflect. Eyeglow, on the other hand, refers to eyes illuminating independently, rather than reflecting light from other sources.[1]

Some cryptozoologists prefer to dismiss every example of bigfoot's glowing eyes as simple eyeshine. It is, admittedly, far easier to wrap one's mind around eyeshine than any other possible explanation. We have all seen eyeshine. We know it exists in the natural world. Should anyone ask, "Why do so many bigfoot reports include glowing eyes?"—many flesh-and-blood hypothesis (F&BH) advocates proffer a simple and concise answer: eyeshine.

Doubtless, many bigfoot reports of glowing eyes indicate eyeshine: flashlights, headlights, lanterns, and even campfire flames have all been witnessed as being reflected by the creatures' eyes. It is, however, a bit premature to close the book on glowing eyes, chalk it up to tapetum lucidum, and declare, "Problem solved."

If we take bigfoot to be natural animals—whether your guess is that they are some kind of undiscovered gorilla or a relict hominid—they would undoubtedly fall within the family of great apes (remember: humans, too, are great apes). If this is the case, and bigfoot have a tapetum lucidum, it would make them unique among great apes and, indeed, among the majority of primates. Primitive apes like lemurs have tapetum lucidum, but great apes do not.[2]

Everyone has seen human eyes glowing red in photographs taken by means of flash photography. This does not indicate the existence of a tapetum lucidum in humans. A camera flash is bright enough to reflect off of the retina—the crimson glow is actually the red blood vessels in the eyes reflecting the harsh light of the flash back at the camera.[3]

Finding Bigfoot cast member and longtime bigfoot researcher, Cliff Barackman, posited that Sasquatch eyes might be quite large and thus their pupils open much wider than humans—which could allow for ambient light to be reflected back in much the same way that human eyes reflect camera flashes.[4] It is difficult to imagine ambient light gathering in sufficient quantity to reflect back a steady and consistent glow, but Barackman's hypothesis is still more consistent with great ape morphology than suggestions of a tapetum lucidum present in bigfoot eyes. This concept, however, only explains glowing, *red* eyes in bigfoot creatures, and does little to account for the varied colors of bigfoot eyeglow found in reports: orange, green, white, yellow, and even blue.[5] (Interestingly, bears—which *do* have a tapetum lucidum—exhibit red, green, orange, and yellow eyeshine.)[6]

Short of the presence of a tapetum lucidum in what would be, presumably, a great ape, all of the theories for bigfoot's multicolored glowing eyes fall short of satisfactorily explaining the phenomenon. Even if we imagine bigfoot have highly reflective eyes—by whatever means, known or unknown—there remains a multitude of witnesses insisting they observed creatures with self-illuminated eyes, *not* reflective eyeshine.

That any natural animal could have *glowing* eyes is a biological wonder. While bioluminescence does occur in nature—from fireflies to lanternfish, animals light up for reasons ranging from attracting a mate to self defense—no species possesses glowing *eyes*, and none of them are mammals, much less great apes.[7] With accounts of glowing eyes, we are confronted with, yet again, a major and oft-witnessed bigfoot trait that simply does not align with our current understanding of biology. If bigfoot is a natural creature (part of the recognized mammalian animal class, wherever it falls therein), it is gifted with an astounding number of unique and highly specialized characteristics.

Folklore, on the other hand, provides numerous examples of hairy beings gifted with glowing or *flaming* eyes.

- Peter Asbjørnsen relates this tale of a glowing-eyed creature in his 1883 collection of Norwegian folklore, *Fairy and Folk Tales*: "I went into the stable first to see the horse and found him neighing and waiting for his hay, so I went up to the hay-loft for an armful, but as I put out my hands I caught hold of something hairy, like the ears of a dog, and the next moment I saw two eyes, red as fire, glaring at me out of the darkness." The hairy, fiery-eyed creature in question turned out to be a rather angry *Brownie*, a faerie, who proceeded to kick the farmer out of the barn.[8]

- Asbjornsen reported on another *Brownie's* eyes glaring through the darkness "…I couldn't see my hand before me, but I felt him plainly as now, when I touch you; he was hairy; and didn't his eyes glisten?"[9]

- The *Jack-o-Lantern* light-bearing faeries, known to lead travelers astray, had their American counterpart in the Southern States known as the *Jack-muh-Lantern*, a "hideous creature five feet in height, with goggle-eyes and a huge mouth, its body covered with long hair. and which goes leaping and bounding through the air like a gigantic grasshopper. This frightful apparition is stronger than any man, and swifter than any horse, and compels its victims to follow it into the swamp, where it leaves them to die."[10]

- *A Summer Night in the Norwegian Forest* features an encounter with a wild man on a bridge: "I saw a man coming towards me—he wasn't very tall, but he was terribly big; he was as broad as a barn door across the shoulders, and his hands were nearly a foot across the knuckles. He carried a leather bag in one hand and seemed to be talking to himself. When I came nearer to him, his eyes glistened like burning cinders, and they were as big as saucers. His hair stood out like bristles and his beard was no better; I thought he was a terrible, ugly brute…" On a second encounter, the wild man is noted to have eyes that "sparkled with fire" and a third encounter notes his eyes "flashed like lightning."[11]

- A tale of a headless horseman from Ireland depicts the preternatural jockey holding his own head which bore "a profusion of matted locks of lustreless blackness" and "fiery eyes of prodigious circumference, with a strange and irregular motion" which "flashed like meteors…"[12]

- The *Nains* were a faerie race of hideous beings from Brittany with black hairy bodies and *sparkling* eyes, roughly analogous to the Scottish *Brownie*.[13]

- Though the Devil himself can take many forms, he was often portrayed as half-human, half-hairy-animal with "glowing eyes and saturnine features." A multitude of demons in various guises also bore gleaming or fiery eyes.[14]

- In the Anglo-Saxon epic poem, *Beowulf*, the monster Grendel, the *shadow-cloaked night-walker*, has eyes that produce an "ugly light, most like a flame."[15]

These archetypes extend beyond Western traditions. For example, ancient Persians feared the *Al*, a hairy swamp monster with glowing eyes and an appetite for children.[16] Hindu legend holds that *Rakshasas* were hairy cannibals with fiery eyes known to haunt cemeteries.[17] Sun Wukong, the simian Monkey King of the famous Chinese Buddhist epic *The Journey to the West*, possessed "fiery" eyes which could see great distances.[18]

The above examples amount to but a brief sampling. It would be easy to fill an entire book with tales of folkloric and supernatural creatures which gaze through gleaming eyes—from hairy goblins, ogres, werewolves, and wild-men to hairless river-dwelling frog-men, spectres, vampires, and more. The one thing all of these entities have in common, however, is the tales do not present them as *natural* animals, but rather the *supernatural* Other: faeries, ghosts, demons, giants, the undead, etc.

New World wild men and bigfoot sightings with glowing oculi are as equally pervasive as Old World folkloric accounts of fiery eyes. This phenomenon's ubiquitous nature is expressed in reports separated by hundreds of years and thousands of miles. *Momo*—the town of Louisiana, Missouri's own bigfoot creature—was reported as being a giant bipedal creature, covered in ape-like hair, with a huge, pumpkin-shaped head and orange glowing eyes.[19] Northwest New Jersey's resident bigfoot is actually known variously as *Big Red Eye* or *Old Red Eye*, after its glowing red eyes.[20]

Other examples span the globe:

- **1857 - Oregon:** A wild man reportedly abducts a youth in Oregon. After he is rescued, the young man describes his kidnapper as "a man about twelve or fifteen feet high, of athletic proportions, with glaring eyes which had the appearance of liquid balls of fire."[21]

- **1884 – Georgia:** A wild man haunts Lookout Mountain, described by one witness as being "of giant size and hairy as a Newfoundland dog… about nine feet high" with "an appearance of the most frightful nature and growls equal to the lion." The wild man has "eyes giving light equal to the moon."[22]

- **1890 – California:** A wild man walks into the campsite of some young men on Snow Mountain in September. One of the campers describes it: "… long hair floating in the midnight breezes, his chin resting almost on his sunken chest, his bony fingers bent like a cat's paw when about to spring, and from his eyes shone an unnatural light."[23]

- **1892 – California:** Fresno witnesses see "a naked human being with matted hair, flaming eyes and limbs gnarled with muscles who haunted a few veracious woodsmen and scared them out of their wits…."[24]

- **1896 – Pennsylvania**: In July, a wild man chases berry pickers near Scranton. According to witnesses, "His eyes were flashing fire and he had every appearance of being insane."[25]

- **1911 – Pennsylvania:** The town of Russell is haunted by an "Unknown Monster," "described as being tall, somewhat like a man with large fiery eyes and gives vent to blood curdling shrieks when approached. The appearance of the monster in that quiet neighborhood is causing a great deal of comment and speculation."[26]

- **1947 – Lithuania:** Seven-year-old girl Madesta Stonke is tending cows near Vilnius when one runs off. Madesta follows the bovine over the hills and into a clearing where she sees several tall humanoid figures covered in thick hair. She describes the creatures as "demonic" in appearance, with glowing red eyes. When one of the creatures notices Madesta, she runs from the area.[27]

- **1954 – Nebraska:** Several people in Ravenna report a six-to-eight-foot-tall bipedal "bear" with the face of an ape. The creature has glowing red eyes.[28]

- **1965 – Indiana:** March sees a ten foot tall, green, hairy monster visit French Lick. Known as "Fluorescent Freddie" to the local children, this green giant also possessed orange or red glowing eyes.[29]

- **1966 – Florida:** Four teenagers watch a "smelly" bigfoot creature jump onto the hood of their car near the Anclote River. The creature has eyes which glow green.[30]

- **1974 – Pennsylvania:** In August the community of Monongahela, Pennsylvania is host to a series of bigfoot reports. Along with tales of weird crying sounds heard at night, creatures walking upon the roofs of homes, peeking in windows, and stealing groceries, comes another strange report. Ken R., a man working with Stan Gordon to investigate strange phenomena, visits a man immediately after he reports a strange creature. When he arrives, Ken finds the witness visibly disturbed, holding a shotgun while his wife clutches a Bible. The witness tells Ken that, earlier that night, he investigated the sound of large, heavy rocks thrown at his home. He noticed a loud noise as another large rock—too heavy for the witness to lift—landed on the front of his parked car. The man looked up to see what he called "the devil" in a nearby field: a tall, dark figure with green, glowing eyes. Afterwards, the couple's large German Shepherd refuses to leave its dog house.[31]

- **1975 – New York:** Cliff Sparks sees a bigfoot on a Whitehall golf course in May. It is around 11:00 p.m. when Sparks sees the creature standing in the middle of a green. "It sent the hair bristling on my neck," he says. "It gave the impression of great strength. It had long arms, those glowing red eyes, and ran fast in an odd gait."[32]

- **1975 – Florida:** Vietnam War veteran Jim Spink searches the wetlands for what he calls "the *Yeti*." Spink has taken to living in the swamp, forgoing bathing—even without clothing—for months at a time. "I'm trying to live like the *Yeti*," he says. "I want it to come in my tent, sit down, and let me have a look at it." Spink collects various reports of Florida bigfoot with eyes "glowing hot pink" or "yellow and catlike". One night while crouching on a branch, high in a gumbo tree, Spink claims the Florida *Yeti* comes and sits beside him. Spink is close enough to hear the creature's breathing. "There's no doubt in my mind that he was in the tree with me," Spink reports. "I could see this big, hairy shape, and the glowing eyes. I sat very still, hoping not to scare him away." Spink almost runs into a creature on another night when he crosses a mound, finding himself directly in the path of a bigfoot, its glowing eyes staring him right in the face. Unprepared for the close encounter, Spink turns and runs in terror, cowering in his tent for the remainder of the night.[33]

- **1978 – Pennsylvania:** A man walking his dog near Fawn Grove notices a ten foot tall, hair-covered biped. As the creature walks away, it turns its head to look back and shows shining white eyes.[34]

- **1980 – Kentucky:** Charles Fulton is watching TV in his rural home in Mason County on October 4, 1980, when one of his children comes in the room and tells him someone was turning the knob on the back door of the house. Fulton believes his child is playing some sort of prank and sits the boy down to watch television. "A few minutes later, something liked to have tore my front door off," Fulton later related. He opens the door to see a white-haired bipedal creature, over seven feet tall, running off of his porch. He procures a pistol and, seeing the creature in his back yard, takes aim: "I fired at it twice from about 30 yards away and don't see how I could have missed." The bigfoot turns and flees in what Fulton describes as a "slow motion gallop." Fulton said the creature had "glowing eyes and hair like a horse's mane."[35]

- **1981 – Ohio:** Farmers in Rome experience multiple encounters with bigfoot-like creatures. They display behavior consistent with other such cases: taking and eating animal feed; attacking farm animals; peeking in the windows of the house; and so forth. The creatures—which are observed multiple times by multiple witnesses—almost always display red, glowing eyes.[36]

- **1988 – Pennsylvania:** On May 17, 1988 Sam Sherry is lantern fishing on the Loyalhanna Creek in Sleepy Hollow, PA. After noticing a foul smell and hearing strange noises he likens to "monkey-like chattering" coming from the nearby woods, Sherry shines his flashlight in the direction of the sounds and sees orange eyes gleaming from the dark forest. A huge bipedal creature, almost seven feet tall, appears about 20 feet from Sherry. He is quite stunned, as he did not notice the creature walking from the woods. It has no neck, broad shoulders, and long arms that hang well below the knees when the creature stands erect. The creature appears very aged, bearing patchy skin and sparse hair—as if it suffered from something like mange. The bigfoot has a large head—bigger than a soccer ball—with two golfball-sized eyes, glowing orange. Sherry notes its face is "deeply wrinkled" with "a leather-like appearance" and a large, flat nose (curiously, the creature seemingly sports a Mohawk haircut—its head bare save for a strip of well-kept hair, two inches wide, from the top of its forehead to the back of its skull). It sputters, wheezes, and breathes loudly as if suffering from asthma or another breathing condition. Sherry observes the creature continuously spit saliva as it breathes in and out through puckered lips. When it begins swinging its arms to beat its chest, Sherry calmly walks back to his car, under the impression that the creature is not a threat, but merely putting on a kind of defensive display. Without sound of footfall, the creature suddenly appears alongside Sherry, who thinks it has arrived much too fast to have physically run up to him. The creature brushes up against Sherry, touching his jacket with its hands. Sherry climbs in his car and closes the door, but the bigfoot leans its head through the window, spitting and drooling on Sherry's face as it wheezes, its horrible breath reminding Sherry of "spoiled seafood." Sherry starts his car and drives away, watching the creature stand in place with its right arm extended, as if waving goodbye.[37]

- **1992 – Pennsylvania:** On the night of May 30, a man in Derry hears his dogs barking outside his mobile home. He grabs a rifle and steps outside to investigate, but is confronted by a tall, hairy creature standing on two legs. It turns and walks away into the night. It possessed a pair of glowing red eyes. The man later reports he felt compelled to not shoot at the creature.[38]

- **2000 – Maryland:** During the construction of Arundel Mills Mall in Hanover, workers witness a 12-foot tall creature with glowing red eyes in the woods nearby.[39]

- **2004 – Brazil:** One February night a woman and another family member are washing clothes on a riverbank in Piaui when they notice movement in the foliage. Across the river they see two five-foot tall creatures emerge from the woods. The anthropoids are covered in thick black hair, and both creatures display glowing red eyes. The witnesses flee in fear.[40]

In 2019 Jeremy, a lifelong hunter and Texas resident, appeared on the *Strange Familiars* podcast to discuss his bigfoot encounters. As a teenager, he observed what he believed at the time to be an escaped chimpanzee in the East Texas woods. The creature crossed in front of Jeremy's vehicle, in broad daylight, as he was driving back roads looking for deer. It was quadrupedal, running like an ape, yet would have been about six feet tall had it stood upright—quite large for a chimpanzee.

Despite this early encounter with something simian in the woods of North America, Jeremy remained uninterested in the bigfoot phenomenon until later in life. While recovering from an injury, Jeremy began watching YouTube videos, where he stumbled upon stories of bigfoot. These led him in turn to the *Sasquatch Chronicles* podcast—where he heard more bigfoot stories from East Texas.

Jeremy started visiting areas around Sam Houston National Forest to look for bigfoot. After a number of possible encounters—Jeremy heard loud tree breaks, growls, and what he suspected to be bigfoot mimicking dogs and owls on different occasions—he began noticing a white light in the woods.

From a distance, it appeared to be a single light, but when viewed through binoculars Jeremy determined it was indeed two lights, side by side—like eyes. "They would move back and forth as I looked through binoculars—you could tell there was [sic] two eyes." He was adamant the illumination was eyeglow, not eyeshine. "This was eyeglow—without me shining a light. There was no moonlight. There was no ambient light… I've hunted my whole life. I know what eyeshine is."

Jeremy returned to the location and saw, on multiple occasions, more than one set of eyes glaring from the darkness. "I saw another set of white eyes—and then a set of red eyes," he recalled. "They're all eyeglow. They all move. They all duck. You'll see them up high, maybe seven or eight feet high, then you'll see them down by the ground level, moving back and forth and trying to duck. They realize I'm looking at them."

This eyeglow even changed colors. "That one really bothered me. I've got goosebumps right now talking about it, just thinking about it." Jeremy had driven down some dirt roads in the forest, close to dusk. He stopped in a particularly remote area to pick up firewood for use at his campsite. "I got out of my jeep and something screamed at me." Jeremy decided he should leave the area.

On the way back to his camp, he caught sight of the eyeglow once more.

"Through the trees I could see two sets of eyes—floating. They were moving so fluidly, not even making any noise that I could hear. It was two distinct sets of eyes coming through the woods and then they kinda split up... and then I lost them." Back at his campsite, Jeremy built a fire before relieving himself by the tree line. Looking into the woods he spotted the eyeglow again. "I see these eyes, and they're almost as big as tennis balls. I'm not exaggerating—they were at least nine inches to a foot apart." Jeremy also made out a silhouette of the creature by the light of his headlamp.

> This thing was a monster. It was ten foot [sic]... The size of this thing's head though ... the only thing I can say is this was a monster. I think maybe I pissed this thing off. When I got screamed at—at that area that was real remote—I got followed back to my campsite... This thing's eyes, not only were they far apart, and huge, but they were changing colors from green to blue to white, green to blue to white, green to blue to white.... They were changing fast. I have never seen that before or since. I've never seen anything that big in my life.

Jeremy returned to camp and experienced more activity throughout the night, including what he believes were bluff charges as the creature (or creatures) ran at him from the woods. He spent the remainder of the night in his jeep. "It still shakes me up when I think about what in the hell I saw," he added.[41]

Beyond simple illumination, the eyes of large, hairy hominids sometimes emit *beams* of light. In the summer of 1972, 15-year-old Bianca Ester Cardenas Rain was walking to her grandmother's house on an isolated hillside outside of Huildad, Chile when a 6.5-foot-tall creature climbed from a ditch alongside the road. It was covered in long, black hair and glared at her with large shining eyes. Paralyzed with fear, Bianca stared into the creature's eyes, which seemed to emit a fiery beam of light. She felt an electrical discharge—then began running toward her grandmother's house. The creature followed, making strange leaps and loud screeching sounds. At a clearing near her grandmother's house, the creature finally turned and departed in another direction.[42]

What meaning can we take from these wandering hairy men with fiery eyes? If bigfoot are something Other—something that reflects, in some way, our folklore and mythology and presents itself to us as the *wild man* archetype—then perhaps these glowing eyes take on a symbolic meaning.

In the same way that so many folkloric creatures and Other things, like bigfoot, seem to be fond of walking on roofs—suggesting an *Otherness* to their action (i.e. humans walk on floors, these creatures walk on rooftops); perhaps, then, the glowing eyes are a visual cue that bigfoot possess a kind of inner fire—the same blaze that lit up the oculi of the faeries and ghosts of old.

Fortean researcher and author, John Keel, himself noted that glowing eyes separated the natural from the *un*natural. "Self-luminous eyes," according to Keel, "suggest a paraphysical entity rather than a real animal."[43] Keel defined these paraphysical entities as "…the phantoms that come crashing out of the bushes late at night. They seem to be part of something else."[44]

Jeff, a self-described "bigfoot enthusiast" from York County, Pennsylvania presented a different theory on glowing eyes. Upon witnessing several unexplained lights—which Jeff attributed to bigfoot eyeglow—in an area of repeat High Strangeness code-named "Site 7" (see my book *Don't Look Behind You* for more on this locale), Jeff proclaimed that the bigfoot creatures used their eyeglow to communicate with each other using some sort of code based on the color, intensity, and duration of the lights. Jeff further asserted that one could determine the mood of the bigfoot according to the color. Red glow, Jeff warned, indicated an angry bigfoot.[45]

Red does seem to carry some weight as a warning color in the natural world. Writing for the British Natural History Museum, Katie Provid reports ladybugs sport their bright red wings as a warning to birds who may try to eat them. Many species of ladybug have chemicals within their bodies which make them taste awful. The more intensely red, the fouler the taste. The black widow spider sports a famous red hourglass on its abdomen, warning against its powerful venom. Provid continues, "Studies have revealed that red is associated with aggression and dominance in fish, reptiles and birds."[46]

If bigfoot are natural creatures, are they using the decidedly unnatural feature of eyeglow to communicate warnings to their witnesses? While red, the most commonly reported color of bigfoot eyeglow, has traditional associations of danger and anger (as well as, alternately, love and desire), it seems a leap of logic to ascribe human color symbolism to the eyes of bigfoot creatures. If red glowing eyes express warning, are we to assume that shining green eyes suggest beckoning or safety? What are we to make, then, of the color-changing eyes as Jeremy reported in Texas? (The mystery lights at Site 7 likewise change colors—as witnessed by the author.)

The only true answer, as with so many aspects of the bigfoot phenomenon, is "we don't know."

Spectral Lights

Illuminated eyes aren't the only mysterious lights seen in conjunction with bigfoot. Various reports describe the creatures breathing fire, swinging "lanterns," or—strangest of all—the creatures themselves glowing. Folklore is, of course, fraught with mysterious lights-in-the-night: *Will-o-the-Wisps*, ghost lights, fairy lanterns, witch lights, entities carrying torches, and more populate supernatural tales worldwide. It is unsurprising bigfoot should follow suit. Time-and-again witnesses report sasquatch leading, following, or otherwise accompanying various unexplained light phenomena.

When wild men self-illuminate, witnesses most often describe their eyes glowing. Other facial features, however, exude light as well. The Wild Man of Welsh Mountain in Berks County, Pennsylvania was portrayed in 1885 as "rushing over the rocks and ravines of the mountains on all fours, his eyes glaring wildly, fire blazing from his nostrils, and his mouth foaming with gore and fury."[47] Another wild man, described as a "fearsome apparition," appeared in Claremont, California in early March, 1910. He was noted to be "a raging wild man with a mouth aflame, gloating eyes, and clad in an upholstery of waving hair, who has tormented the minds and inspired the fears of those of the Claremont district."[48]

In rare cases the *entire body* of sasquatch glows. On November 30, 1966 a woman was changing a tire on a rural road near Brooksville, Florida when a gigantic hairy bipedal creature with large green eyes approached her. The entire creature emitted an eerie green glow as well.[49] In another instance, a man named Randall wrote in to *Darkness Radio,* (a paranormal radio program) to report a family of glowing bigfoot. He witnessed the creatures walking out of the woods near his family home in Madison, New Jersey in 1969. According to Randall, the creatures were raiding nearby gardens, and glowed with what Randall called a "radiating energy of a multidimensional nature."[50]

A lantern-carrying spirit is one of the most persistent American ghost story motifs, appearing in seaside lore of the East Coast, tales of railroad hauntings, and phantom car accidents. Surprisingly, the specters of large, hairy ape-men also carry lanterns in local legends. Block Island, off of the coast of Rhode Island, was haunted by its own wild man in 1888: "He appears in the dead of night in a wild, untenanted hollow of the hills, to which the throbbing of the ocean comes as a witch-like murmur; he digs a hole in the brittle peat; the swinging of a spectral light is seen in the drifting mists; the islanders go out to find him; they stumble upon the hole, but the swinging light dances away over the hills with the illusions of an *ignis fatuus*."[51]

Seven employees of the local power company were sent to repair a Middlebrook, Virginia power line one night in late March 1978. They noticed a tall, hairy biped standing in a field rapidly move toward the nearby treeline. The creature appeared to glide across the ground, holding an object to its chest resembling a "red flashlight" before disappearing into the trees.[52]

Lantern-carrying wild men appear internationally: in Australia, three different groups of motorists witnessed a hirsute *Yowie* carrying a lantern. In June of 1975 in Tailem Bend, Australia the witnesses saw the large, hairy biped carrying an illuminated device alongside the road. One group of motorists said they saw the anthropoid carrying a lantern, as well as another light in a nearby field.[53]

Despite these loose trends, anomalous lights associated with bigfoot commonly defy categorization. A handful of the most curious odds and ends:

• In spring of 1975 a woman near San Juan, Puerto Rico heard her guard dogs barking at something in her back yard. She looked out to see a large ape-like creature sitting atop a tall palm tree. The anthropoid glared at the witness with eyes that seemed to emit fire. The creature then began to shrink, assuming a spherical shape in the process, and started glowing. Finally it took the form of an illuminated globe, about the size of a basketball, then slowly floated away into the sky.[54]

• On September 11, 1985 a man was fishing near Shenandoah, Virginia when he saw a seven-foot bigfoot running along the bank. The creature moved faster than any animal the witness had ever seen. The fisherman fired at the creature, hitting it in the chest. The bigfoot stopped and stared at the witness, a blue light shining from the bullet wound. The terrified witness fled the scene.[55]

- One night in October of 1977 in Latrobe, Pennsylvania, a man came home to find his dog killed and hanging by its neck. His house was illuminated by a light from an unknown source. The man then witnessed an eight-foot tall hairy bipedal creature. He shot the bigfoot, but the bullets bounced off, seemingly without effect—after which the creature let out a scream and ran away.[56]

- A mysterious white light accompanied a bigfoot sighting in Trafford, Pennsylvania on January 10, 1980. The light was seen by a group of young boys who also reported a tall creature covered in reddish-brown hair, possessed of red glowing eyes, and smelling sulfurous. The boys watched the creature retreat to the woods where they heard branches breaking. Something—presumably the creature—then threw stones from the woods.[57]

- On the evening of July 20, 1980, witnesses spotted an unusual blue light hovering in a field in Guffey, Pennsylvania. They simultaneously observed a tall, hairy creature in the same area. The creature ran away on two legs, breathing heavily.[58]

- The Sykesville Monster was a bigfoot creature reported around Sykesville, Maryland in the early 1980s. In the Spring of 1982, Willard McIntyre fired upon the creature with no apparent effect. Instead of appearing wounded, the bigfoot turned and hit McIntyre with a ball of light.[59]

- By the early 1980s, Steve Stover—a long-time bigfoot investigator from Maryland—decided the creatures must represent something more than a relict hominid or an undiscovered primate. Specifically, he believed they might be interdimensional beings. While investigating a farm known for recurring activity in Harford County, Stover brought a psychic with him. He asked the psychic to try to contact the bigfoot creature while he observed. During her attempts at dusk, he saw two huge, white, glowing eyes in a dark shape moving down a hillside behind the farmhouse. The (assumed) creature moved into a thicket where Stover lost sight of it. As he scanned the area, trying to find the creature, Stover caught a blinking light and heard a loud hum. He became frightened and asked the psychic to end the experiment. "Bigfoot indicates something far bigger than what we understand at present," Stover later said. "He may be our way into the next frontier… into other dimensions."[60]

• Lugar Penamoa, Spain experienced a wave of animal mutilations in 1985. In September, several witnesses, awakened by their barking dogs, watched multiple six-foot-tall balls of light silently drifting around their property. Small ape-like creatures walked next to the spheres. Though multiple shots were fired at the creatures and the orbs, they displayed no apparent effect.[61]

• In May 1995, a Cascade County, Montana hunter encountered an eight-foot tall bigfoot with glowing red eyes. He fired at the creature, which disappeared in a flash of light.[62]

Great Balls of Fire

A peculiar subset of sasquatch behavior involves their interaction with orbs, sometimes carrying or handling them. At midnight on August 9, 1981 several witnesses camping in the Pamir Mountains region of Kyrgyzstan witnessed a hairy hominid walk silently beside their campsite and disappear into the night, as if it did not notice the campers. The creature held a glowing orb in its hands.[63]

Around 9:30 p.m. on September 27, 1973, two teenage girls witnessed a bipedal creature, covered in white hair, running toward a wooded area of Beaver, Pennsylvania. The creature was between seven and eight feet tall and carried a glowing orb in one hand.

The pair ran to one witness's home and related the sighting to her father, who decided to follow the creature's path into the forest. As he entered the treeline, his daughter observed an object in the sky, which she believed was some type of aircraft. The object moved over the wooded area, projecting some type of beam down into the trees. The girl said her father stayed in the woods for over an hour.

When an investigator interviewed him after the incident, the father denied ever entering the forest that night. He then declared, "There are some things that shouldn't be discussed" and denied the investigator access to the wooded area. He stated he "did not want anyone tramping around" in his woods and refused to discuss his missing hour of time in the forest. The father later began espousing end-times prophecies, predicting that the world would end in six months' time.[64]

Aforementioned East Texas witness Jeremy noticed other anomalous lights in the areas of his bigfoot encounters.

I—almost every time, if not every time—witness the light phenomenon, the balls of light, when I'm having bigfoot activity.

If I'm doubting they're around, if I start seeing the balls of light in the sky, it's like I know they are around and I'll start having activity. Or if I'm having what I think is activity, then I'll start seeing light from the sky or I'll see weird lights in the woods or above the trees. These are the larger orbs and they kind of float around while I'm having the bigfoot activity.

This is just my experience, but I'm almost convinced—with as many experiences I've had - encounters with this phenomenon—there's some kind of correlation between the lights and these creatures... This has happened numerous, numerous times.

From my experience, there's a lot more to these creatures that is on the strange side—that can't be explained—in my opinion they are not just flesh and blood.[65]

Even when not seen in conjunction with bigfoot, orbs or *will-o-the-wisp* lights appear with great frequency in areas thought to be bigfoot hotspots, or to researchers seeking bigfoot.

On an episode of the *Finding Bigfoot* television program, James "Bobo" Fay and Ranae Holland observed two orbs floating through the woods in southern Oregon, while searching for bigfoot. "I can tell you this," Fay said, "whatever we saw was not a person with a headlamp; it wasn't a car; it was much closer than we thought, it was smaller, and not very bright." Holland continued (regarding the orbs), "It just creeps me out... it's weird."[66]

In her book *Backyard Bigfoot*, Lisa Shiel records a laundry list of strange phenomena associated with ongoing bigfoot activity on her property. Game cameras, placed around her horse farm, snapped pictures of orbs with regularity. She wrote, "... the camera keeps filling its memory card with snapshots of orbs, orbs, and more orbs."[67]

While cameras often represent dust particles as luminous balls, on another occasion Shiel witnessed an orb with her own two eyes:

> On the night of June 5, 2005, I was awakened by a flash outside the bedroom window. The light flashed so bright it penetrated the veil of my eyelids. I glanced out the window at

the front yard where the flash had seemed to originate. A line of thirty-foot cedar trees, standing about twenty feet from the deck, screens the house from the driveway. In front of the trees, an orb pulsed. The light was bluish-white with a brighter white rim. The orb glowed for a few seconds, then extinguished. A moment later, another orb (or perhaps the same one, which had moved) pulsed on for several seconds. To the right of where the orbs pulsed, I saw a swarm of fireflies flickering. I estimated the orbs to be similar in size to a basketball, far larger than the fireflies flitting about nearby.[68]

Sasquatch Chronicles podcast host Wes Germer, along with his brothers, was driving a lonesome road near Yacolt, Washington looking for the location of a bigfoot sighting, reported by another witness. The three men witnessed three orb-like lights drifting through the woods. Germer described the lights: "…they were really faint—and they would kind of move around a little bit—not like a headlamp… they would just smoothly kinda just move back and forth and they'd fade out and then fade in. I don't know what it was."[69]

Jimmy B., a man residing in Lewisberry, Pennsylvania was visited by two bigfoot in April of 2018. Jimmy saw the creatures when shining a spotlight across his property while looking for deer. The eight-foot tall, hair covered creatures ducked behind the trees and peeked out at Jimmy, their eyes reflecting in the beam of his spotlight. Both before and after sighting the creatures, Jimmy photographed multiple orbs both inside and around his house.[70]

The Green Flash

A hunting camp in the Sierra Nevada Mountains was made famous by the so-called "Sierra Sounds" recorded by Ron Morehead and Alan Berry. In the early 1970s Morehead, Berry, and a small group of other men heard, and recorded, *something*—presumably bigfoot—emitting a series of strange chants, chatter, growls, and guttural utterances. These voices occasionally appeared to reply and interact with campers. The Sierra Camp, as the site became known, was home to years of bigfoot encounters and evidence in the form of tracks, disturbances around the camp, recorded vocalizations, and rare, fleeting glimpses of sasquatch creatures.

The bigfoot, however, were not the only strange things encountered near the Sierra Camp. One night in August 1974, campers witnessed a bizarre light. One of the men at the camp, a Lewis Johnson, announced, "There's something funny going on, because there was a bright flash from up there that just lit up the whole area." Johnson's brother, Warren, emerged from the shelter just in time to see another flash. "it was like a strobe light," he noted. "It lit up the whole camp scene."

The light, according to Warren, seemed to originate around 15 feet above ground and 30 feet away in the trees. He continued: "To me it seemed like the light source or whatever was round and ball-like, maybe two to three feet in diameter, and it had a bluish cast and a white band around it." The flash was not accompanied by a sound and, curiously, though it lit up the entire campsite, did not affect Warren's night vision or blind him, even momentarily.

A third flash diffused a greenish light which briefly illuminated an area nearly 100 feet in diameter. Warren said it "exploded" from a different area than the previous flashes. The campers watched in amazement as more flashes fired off in the trees around them. Warren started timing the silent "explosions," estimating they occurred at two-minute intervals.

"I walked up to the shelter and back," he noted, "and it seemed like every six to eight feet a light would explode somewhere in the trees overhead." The men realized their shuffling feet in the pine mat covering the ground seemed to somehow activate these light flashes. The proposal that static electricity could have somehow caused the flashes was dispelled by weather conditions, which were not conducive to such a hypothesis. The men also noticed a high-pitched whining noise in the area where they were standing, watching the lights.

The lights eventually tapered off around midnight and the campers went to sleep inside the primitive Sierra Camp shelter. Just after 3:00 a.m. Warren woke to the sound of a mouse scampering near his head. Warren swatted the rodent.

"I nailed him with the palm of my hand and must have knocked him clear across the shelter," he said. "What happened though, was just as I hit him, almost simultaneously, a light flashed inside the shelter, right by the door." The flash was bright enough to wake two of the other men who witnessed, with Warren, "in rapid succession, maybe a second or two apart… five or six more—all intensely bright, greenish flashes. Then they stopped and we saw nothing more. We shined our flashlights around everywhere but couldn't find anything, and there was no sound, nothing at all…."

The next night the light flashes occurred again, similar to the previous evening. The third night the lights intensified and seemed to concentrate on the men at the camp. They flashed over their heads and seemed to follow them, lighting the area up like daylight with each silent burst.

The following morning the men discovered a bigfoot trackway which, like so many others, ended mysteriously. The last track was in the middle of a wide swath of soft, mushy ground with no indication of where the next track landed—even accounting for the creatures' great stride.[71]

This flashing green light, as reported at the Sierra Camp, is repeated in other bigfoot encounters. In 2012 Greg and Dana Newkirk, paranormal investigators and owners of the Traveling Museum of the Paranormal and the Occult, met with Dallas Gilbert and Wayne Burton. The two men had reputations as bigfoot researchers with an... *unusual* approach to the mystery. In fact, Gilbert and Burton were treated as pariahs by many in the bigfoot community. Few of their colleagues had patience for their tales of portals to prehistoric worlds, dimension-jumping bigfoot, and telepathic Sasquatch.

Bigfoot researchers risked their reputation in the community by even associating with Gilbert and Burton, and yet many *did* take the risk—for despite their "crazy" theories—Gilbert and Burton's secret bigfoot hotspot, known as "The Boneyard," produced multiple recordings of unidentified vocalizations, and, sometimes, even close encounters with bigfoot creatures.

The Newkirks accompanied Gilbert and Burton to The Boneyard, somewhere in the wilds of West Virginia. Gilbert taught Dana a special call, a series of "sacred words" supposedly in the bigfoot language. Around the fire that night, Dana issued forth the sacred call.

Her words were still echoing through the mountains when a green flash illuminated the sky above. The flash was followed by loud "booming shrieks" from the woods—first from one side of the campfire, then answered with similar vocalizations from the opposite side. Whatever made the strange cries, there was more than one, and they seemed to be approaching camp.

Though previously somewhat incredulous of Gilbert and Burton's claims, the Newkirks were now faced with the undeniable reality that *something* was indeed out there and, whatever it was, it seemed to respond to Dana's call. Greg recalled, "Frankly, I was terrified. We all were. None of us had heard anything like it before...."

The howls continued for two hours, accompanied by stones thrown into their camp intermittently. On one occasion, something large charged from the tree line, prompting Burton to leap from his chair and run directly at the intruder—which returned from whence it came.[72]

Like so many of these weird anomalies associated with bigfoot, the green flash appears alongside other phenomena. After his night at The

Boneyard, Greg Newkirk looked deeper into the strange viridian lights:

> The more I dug into the green flash phenomena, the more interesting things got. These mysterious lights popped up in loads of reports connected to everything from ghost sightings, to UFO experiences, to, believe it or not, Bigfoot encounters. Most often, the green flash was reported as an afterthought, as if the primary phenomena experienced by witnesses was so stunning that the flash was nearly forgotten in the commotion.[73]

Greg continued:

> I began to go through my own files, realizing that my old ghost hunting team had reported the mysterious green flash several times, often as a precursor to paranormal activity. We weren't alone, either. Fellow investigators had reported ghosts appearing and disappearing in flashes of emerald light, of entire rooms spontaneously illuminating in shades of green, and even glowing, free-floating globules that appeared to have a mind of their own. This phenomena, though, was widely ignored.[74]

Green flashes. Illuminated eyes of various colors. Glowing hairy hominids. Floating orbs. Lights, in various forms both surround and directly inhabit the bigfoot mystery—and indeed, the whole of the paranormal. Seriah Azkath, host of the *Where Did the Road Go?* paranormal podcast wisely noted that if lights are seen within an abandoned house, they will likely be called ghosts, while those same lights seen in the sky will be called UFOs, and seen again in the forest may be attributed to bigfoot.

Their eyeglow may suggest bigfoot is something Other, as Keel noted, but these alternate lights embedded within the bigfoot mystery seem intent on making it more than a suggestion—connecting the creatures to other paranormal phenomena by their visual example. Deepening the mystery, or perhaps, muddying the waters—for, as ever with bigfoot, the more connections we make, the more data we have, we only seem to end up with more questions than answers. Like a silent shadow, bigfoot ambles off into the darkness of the forest, glancing over its shoulder with gleaming eyes and we are left to wonder at the wild man, as generations before us have done.

[1] Renner, T. (2018). *Don't Look Behind You*. Charleston, SC: CreateSpace Independent Publishing Platform.

[2] Nickell, J. (September 28, 2017). Bigfoot Eyeshine: A Contradiction. Retrieved March 28, 2019 from https://centerforinquiry.org/blog/bigfoot_eyeshine_a_contradiction/

[3] Barackman, C. (n.d.). Thoughts on Bigfoot Eyeshine. Retrieved March 28, 2019 from https://cliffbarackman.com/research/articles-2/bigfoot-eye-shine-hypothesis/

[4] Ibid.

[5] Ibid.

[6] Bear. (April 1, 2011). Ask a Bear: What Color Are Your Eyes at Night? Retrieved March 28, 2019 from https://www.backpacker.com/stories/ask-a-bear-what-color-are-your-eyes-at-night

[7] The Ocean Portal Team. (April 2018). Bioluminescence. Retrieved March 29, 2019 from https://ocean.si.edu/ocean-life/fish/bioluminescence

[8] Asbjørnsen, P.C. (1883). *Folk and Fairy Tales*. (H.L. Braekstad, Trans.). New York, NY:cA.C. Armstrong & Son (7th ed.).

[9] Ibid.

[10] Sikes, W. (1880). *British Goblins: Welsh Folklore, Fairy Mythology, Legends and Traditions* (2nd ed.). London, UK: Sampson Low, Marston, Searle, & Rivington.

[11] Asbjørnsen 1883.

[12] Croker, T.C. (1825*). Fairy Legends & Traditions of the South of Ireland Part II*. London, UK: John Murray.

[13] Evans Wentz, W.Y. (1911). *The Fairy-Faith in Celtic Countries*. London, UK: Henry Frowde.

[14] Gunnvör. (August 13, 2020). The Walking Dead: Draugr and Aptrgangr in Old Norse Literature. Retrieved August 13, 2020 from http://www.vikinganswerlady.com/ghosts.shtml

[15] Ibid.

[16] Nunnelly, B. (2017). *The Inhumanoids: Real Encounters with Beings That Can't Exist!* US: Triangulum Publishing (2nd ed.).

[17] Ibid.

[18] Ruzhong Wu Cheng'en, Trans. (n.d.). *The Journey to the West*. Retrieved May 19, 2020 from https://archive.org/details/TheJourneytotheWest/mode/2up

[19] Stokes, B. (April 17, 1983). "Spring Used to Scare Up Good Monster Tales." *The Cincinnati Enquirer (OH)*, p. D-5.

[20] Ash, L. (December 28, 2014). "Bigfoot." *The Daily Record (Morristown, NJ)*, p. A2.

[21] Renner, T. (2018). *Bigfoot: West Coast Wild Men*. Charleston, SC: CreateSpace Independent Publishing Platform.

[22] No author. (February 10, 1884). No title. *The Atlanta Constitution (GA)*, p. 7.

[23] Renner 2018.

[24] Ibid.

[25] Renner, T. (2017). *Bigfoot in Pennsylvania*. Charleston, SC: CreateSpace Independent Publishing Platform.

[26] Ibid.

[27] Kolomiets, I. (n.d.). Case 2. In A. Rosales (Ed.), *1947 Humanoid Sighting Reports*. Retrieved February 5, 2014 from http://www.ufoinfo.com/humanoid/humanoid-1947.pdf

[28] Roth, M.K. (January 26, 1983). "New Nebraska Group Investigates Strange Happenings." *The Lincoln Star (NE)*, p. 17.

[29] Kirkwood, E. (March 22, 2003). "Hairy Hoosier Monster a Freaky Nature Quest." *The South Bend Tribune (IN)*, p. C2(28).

[30] Tomalin, T. (October 31, 1999). "In Pursuit of the Famous Swamp Ape." *The Tampa Bay Times (FL)*, p. 18c.

[31] Gordon, S. (2010). *Silent Invasion: The Pennsylvania UFO-Bigfoot Casebook*. R. Marsh (Ed.). Greensburg, PA: Stan Gordon Productions.

[32] Patton, J. (January 29, 1992). "Monsters of Northwoods: Book Full of Bigfoot Run-Ins." *The Post-Star (Glens Fall, NY)*, p. 1.

[33] Butcher, L. (July 13, 1975). "Yeti Watch." *The Tampa Bay Times (FL)*, p. 190 (p. 14 of Floridian insert).

[34] Renner, T. (2016). *Beyond the Seventh Gate.* North Charleston, SC: Createspace.

[35] No author. (October 9, 1980). "Bigfoot Sighted Again." *The World (Coos Bay, OR)*, p. 3.

[36] Pilichis, D. (1982). *Night Siege: The Northern Ohio UFO Creature Invasion.* Rome, OH: Dennis Pilichis.

[37] Johnson, P.G. (2018). *Chasing the Elusive Pennsylvania Bigfoot.* New Milford, CT: Visionary Living Publishing.

[38] Ibid.

[39] Farentold, D. (October 3, 2004). "East, West, Believers Squabble Over Sasquatch." *The Missoulian (MT)*, p. 7.

[40] UFO Genesis, Brazil. (n.d.). Case 34. In A. Rosales (Ed.), *2004 Humanoid Sighting Reports.* Retrieved February 5, 2014 from http://www.ufoinfo.com/humanoid/ humanoid-2004.pdf

[41] Renner, T. (May 9, 2019). Episode 89: The Eyes of Bigfoot. Retrieved August 13, 2020 from https://www.strangefamiliars.com/home/the-eyes-of-bigfoot

[42] Tabies, A.C. (1980). *Abordaje al Caleuche.* Santiago, CL: Editorial Nascimento.

[43] Keel, J.A. (2002). *The Complete Guide to Mysterious Beings.* New York, NY: Tom Doherty Associates, LLC. (Original work published 1970 as *Strange Creatures from Time and Space*)

[44] Ibid.

[45] "Jeff." (n.d.). Personal correspondence.

[46] Pavid, K. (July 18, 2016). Rainbow Nature: Wildlife in Ravishing Red. Retrieved May 19, 2020 from https://www.nhm.ac.uk/discover/rainbow-nature-ravishing-red.html

[47] Renner 2017.

[48] Renner 2018.

[49] No author. (1988). Case 214. In A. Rosales (Ed.), *1966 Humanoid Sighting Reports.* Retrieved February 5, 2014 from http://www.ufoinfo.com/humanoid/humanoid-1966.pdf

[50] Strickler, L. (November 9, 2016). Daily 2 Cents: 'Glowing' Bigfoot in New Jersey – 'I think they did something to me...' -- Responding to an Asteroid Threat. Retrieved May 5, 2019 from https://www.phantomsandmonsters.com/2016/11/daily-2-cents-glowing-bigfoot-in-new.html

[51] No author. (January 9, 1888). No title. *The Atlanta Constitution (GA)*, p. 5.

[52] Barkley, M. (April 4, 1978). "Bigfoot Reportedly Seen in County." *The News Leader (Stanton, VA)*, p. 1.

[53] Chalker, B. (n.d.). Case 184. In A. Rosales (Ed.), *1975 Humanoid Sighting Reports*. Retrieved February 5, 2014 from http://www.ufoinfo.com/humanoid/humanoid-1975.pdf

[54] Freixedo, S. (n.d.). Case 94. In A. Rosales (Ed.), *1975 Humanoid Sighting Reports*. Retrieved February 5, 2014 from http://www.ufoinfo.com/humanoid/humanoid-1975.pdf

[55] MUFON. (n.d.). Case 130. In A. Rosales (Ed.), *1985 Humanoid Sighting Reports*. Retrieved February 5, 2014 from http://www.ufoinfo.com/humanoid/humanoid-1985.pdf

[56] Johnson 2018.

[57] Ibid.

[58] Ibid.

[59] Opsasnick, M. (n.d.). Case 71. In A. Rosales (Ed.), *1982 Humanoid Sighting Reports*. Retrieved February 5, 2014 from http://www.ufoinfo.com/humanoid/humanoid-1982.pdf

[60] Scarupa, H. (July 11, 1982). "Could Bigfoot Be an Extraterrestrial?" *The Baltimore Sun (MD)*, p. 2 (Baltimore Maryland insert).

[61] Carballal, B.M. (1994). Case 127. In A. Rosales (Ed.), *1985 Humanoid Sighting Reports*. Retrieved February 5, 2014 from http://www.ufoinfo.com/humanoid/humanoid-1985.pdf

[62] Howe, L.M. (1995). Case 117. In A. Rosales (Ed.), *1995 Humanoid Sighting Reports*. Retrieved February 5, 2014 from http://www.ufoinfo.com/humanoid/humanoid-1995.pdf

[63] No author. (n.d.). Case 142. In A. Rosales (Ed.), *1981 Humanoid Sighting Reports*. Retrieved February 5, 2014 from http://www.ufoinfo.com/humanoid/humanoid-1981.pdf

[64] Gordon 2010.

[65] Renner 2019.

[66] Kuhlman, B, Brumels, C., Hammel, C. (Executive Producers). (April 7, 2016). Season Eight, Episode Seven: Squatching on Sacred Ground [Television series episode]. In T. Peyton, D. Jolly, M. Brazie, M. Powers, S. Russell, K. Hoffman, & D. Napierala (Producers), *Finding Bigfoot*. Silver Spring, MD: Animal Planet U.S.

[67] Shiel, L.A. (2006). *Backyard Bigfoot: The True Story of Stick Signs, UFOs, and the Sasquatch.* Lake Linden, MI: Slipdown Mountain Publications LLC.

[68] Ibid.

[69] Germer, W. (February 7, 2016). Sasquatch Chronicles Radio // SC 191: Do not chase strange lights. Retrieved May 19, 2020 from https://sasquatchchronicles.com/sc-ep191-do-not-chase-strange-lights/

[70] J.B., personal communication, October 2018.

[71] Slate, B.A. & Berry, A. (1976). *Bigfoot*. New York, NY: Bantam.

[72] Newkirk, G. (December 8, 2016). Bigfoot is a Ghost: Interdimensional Sasquatch, The Green Flash, and Why We'll Never Find a Body. Retrieved December 1, 2017 from http://weekinweird.com/2016/12/08/bigfoot-is-a-ghost-interdimensional-sasquatch-tulpas-green-flash/

[73] Ibid.

[74] Ibid.

The yeti's feet take flight, upon the tundran ice /
Carries the saucer's key, upon the space bound seed.

- High On Fire, The Yeti, *"Surrounded by Thieves"*

UFOs

(Note: Where the Footprints End, *Volume I, Chapter 4 is an exploration of the bigfoot phenomenon as it intersects with "aliens" and the various strange properties and effects associated with such encounters. Please refer to said chapter for further exploration of the bigfoot/"alien"/UFO connection.)*

While instances of hairy anthropoids seen *inside* Unidentified Flying Object (UFO) craft are covered in Volume I of *Where the Footprints End*, there is no shortage of reports where bigfoot-like creatures are seen outside of UFOs—or of UFOs seen in the same general area around the same time bigfoot creatures have been reported. Many authors have discussed the connection between sasquatch and UFOs *ad nauseum*; for that reason, what follows should not be considered exhaustive, but rather exemplary, of the types of reported encounters.

(For the purposes of this chapter, we separate the idea of "unexplained lights," which may or may not be craft—dealt with elsewhere—from the idea of UFOs. The "O" in UFO—"object"—is emphasized here. These objects could be craft, or things only seemingly physical—as opposed to more ephemeral, possibly amorphous, mystery lights.)

Many F&BH advocates suggest—with a dismissive wave of the hand that betrays a leap from logic to magical thinking—that UFO occupants, whoever they might be, are as interested in bigfoot as we humans are, and that this explains the many, many cases in which bigfoot and UFOs appear simultaneously or in close approximations of time and place.

Bigfoot researcher and author, John Green, said of the bigfoot-UFO connection:

> If they [bigfoot] have been seen near UFOs, I would prefer to consider it a coincidence or to assume that the occupants of the UFO were just looking at the Sasquatch, or vice versa.[1]

This is science-fiction thinking. It is working backward from an unfalsifiable conclusion (i.e. that bigfoot are natural animals) to a bizarre bit of equally unfalsifiable fiction (i.e. that the Ufonauts are interested in bigfoot). We don't really know what bigfoot are, nor do we know who or what UFOs or Ufonauts are.

It remains true that both bigfoot and UFOs are rare and anomalous things. That they would be seen together *even once* is worth noting. That bigfoot and UFOs have ever been seen together, or relatively close to one another multiple times, suggests a connection deeper than mere coincidence. To suggest that bigfoot are aliens—or even, as addressed in Volume I, that bigfoot are the pets of aliens—slips into more fanciful science-fiction speculation.

It is enough to claim that, given reports, there seems to be some connection between bigfoot and UFOs. As there do not seem to be a preponderance of reports of UFOs seen in conjunction with mountain gorillas or orangutans, this suggests there is something *more* to bigfoot—and therefore tips the scale even further away from the F&BH.

As addressed, accounts where sasquatch appear in conjunction with UFOs are far too plentiful to present comprehensively. If readers wish to further explore sightings featuring both UFOs and bigfoot, the work of Stan Gordon comes highly recommended, particularly his book *Silent Invasion*. What follows is a small sample of sightings from across the globe.

- 13-year-old Phillip was walking home from a cinema near Haverigg Beach, England during the summer of 1930 when he, along with a group of others, saw a round "comet" with flames shooting from its rear. The so-called "comet" slowly approached the earth before disappearing. Two days later, Philip was checking his fishing lines when he saw "The Devil": a man-sized creature, covered in red-brown hair, with a silver foil-like material around its waist and feet.[2]

• Emelino Martinez returned from a hunting trip outside Caracas, Venezuela on April 10, 1954. In the nearby bushes, he noticed movement followed by a loud, low utterance. As Martinez ran for his car, he heard an unintelligible shout close behind him. He turned and saw two short creatures, described as half-man, half-monkey, covered with dark-colored hair, pursuing him. Before Martinez could open his vehicle, one of the creatures grabbed him from behind. He dropped the shotgun he was carrying and fell into a ditch, the creature's hands grasping his throat. Somehow freeing himself from the clutches of his hairy-handed attacker, Martinez clambered to the car. The maddened creature once again leapt upon him, screaming and biting. The shocked man grabbed a rock and smashed the creature on its head. It staggered backwards, blood gushing from the wound, while Martinez jumped in his vehicle and locked the door. Undaunted, the two ape-men slammed their fists against the windows, screaming with rage. Martinez made it home, but returned to the site of the attack the following day with friends to recover his shotgun and question local residents about the creatures. The locals told tales of disc-shaped UFOs seen in the area; of missing pets and livestock; and of two farmhands who had disappeared. They also related stories of black, bristly-haired dwarves hiding in caves who abducted both humans and animals.[3]

• Around 8:30 p.m. in early April 1959, David Soucie saw a white, glowing disc land near Kankakee, Illinois. A large ape-like creature appeared in front of the disc and came toward Soucie, who hid as he watched the hominoid pass by. One week later, Soucie and a man named Carl Miller saw a glowing white disc hovering over some railroad tracks. Silhouetted by the light of the disk was a gigantic ape-like creature with no neck and very long arms. It moved about using its arms, like a gorilla.[4]

• A man named Ed claimed to work for United States military intelligence investigating UFOs in Southern California. In 1967, he was called to the scene of a UFO crash at a remote desert location. Ed allegedly saw an oblong object broken in two, and noticed a pungent stench permeating the area around the crash site. The bodies of four creatures answering the description of bigfoot littered the ground. They were nine-feet tall and covered in hair. Their faces, which appeared twisted in pain, presented "Mongoloid features" with broad, flat noses. Their mouths showed fanged teeth. Even more interesting, the beings wore a sort of thick-soled sandal and copper-colored belts with large buckles. The belt buckles housed a series of small buttons. Ed mentioned the belts glowed when activated, but he neither knew nor disclosed their purpose (see *Where the Footprints End* Volume I, Chapter 6 for more belt-wearing bigfoot). As the team examined the creatures, one was found alive. When one of the men offered water, the creature reached up, grabbed his shoulder, gasped, and died.[5]

- On the evening of May 19, 1969, at about 7:30 p.m., George Kaiser crossed the barnyard of his parents' farm outside Rising Sun, Indiana. He noticed a strange, upright figure about 25 yards away. "I'd say it was about five-eight or so," Kaiser related, "and it had a very muscular structure. The head sat directly on the shoulders and the face was black, with hair that stuck out on the back of its head; it had eyes set close together and a very short forehead. It was covered with hair except for the back of the hands and the face." Kaiser stood still, gazing at the creature in amazement. When he finally moved, the creature grunted, turned, leapt over a ditch, and ran off at great speed—leaving strange, four-toed tracks in its wake. The next night, Charles Rolfing, a neighbor of the Kaisers, watched a "greenish-white" glowing object move through the sky above him for eight minutes.[6]

- In the early 1970s Bill Vogel, Staff Fire Control Officer stationed on the Yakima Reservation in Washington state, began collecting reports of strange activity on the reservation. At first this consisted mainly of UFO sightings. Vogel took reports of everything from mysterious lights, metallic cigar-shaped objects, rocket-like craft, and anomalous pillars of fire from members of the Yakima tribe and his own fire lookouts stationed around the reservation. He also heard tales of strange, machine-like rumblings coming from underground, sounds resembling the cries of babies, and horrible screams in the nighttime forest. Along with the UFOs and unusual sounds, other witnesses began finding huge, bare, human-like footprints across the reservation, as well as sightings of giant, foul-smelling ape-like creatures.⁷

• Oxford, England experienced its own bigfoot/UFO encounter in 1971. Linda Milne was strolling near the Wantage Canal when she saw a tall, hairy, bipedal creature walk into the nearby woods. Later, two 14-year-old boys were chased by the same—or a similar—creature in the area. Shortly before their bigfoot encounter the boys observed a "flying disc" in the sky.⁸

• On the night of August 29, 1973, an anonymous witness—wife of a prominent physician—observed a large chevron-shaped object hovering over her Greensburg, Pennsylvania neighborhood. The object appeared to be a solid craft with windows. She also noticed the smell of sulfur permeating the air. Later that same evening, the witness heard gunfire in her neighborhood. The next day she learned the gunfire had come from a nearby residence— the home of another doctor— who, upon walking outside to see what was disturbing his dog, was confronted by a huge, hairy, ape-like creature. The doctor retrieved his rifle and fired multiple rounds at the creature, to no apparent effect. He retreated into his home as the bigfoot ran off.⁹

• Two boys watched a UFO descend to tree-top level around 7:30 p.m. on December 23, 1977, in Trent, Pennsylvania. Later the same evening they saw a tall being covered in brown hair with glowing white eyes. The boys watched as the creature turned and ran, after which the area remained illuminated by a bright white light. Several loud, booming sounds were heard in the region shortly thereafter.¹⁰

• In July 2001 a man walking the woods near Mineral Point, Pennsylvania saw an eight-to-nine-foot tall anthropoid covered in black-brown hair. The creature approached slowly at first, walking on two legs before transitioning to all fours and speeding off into the trees. A short time later the man observed blue lights in a triangular formation hovering a few hundred feet above the woods. The object shot up into the sky and flew away without making a sound.¹¹

Momo

Edgar Harrison became interested in Louisiana, Missouri's Momo monster after it visited his property in summer 1972. A black, hairy creature—six-to-seven-feet tall, splattered with blood and carrying a dead dog under one arm—appeared on the Harrisons' land on July 10, frightening the children. The family's own family dog became ill in the wake of the sighting. The canine's eyes turned red and it vomited for some time after the encounter.

Four days later, Harrison and about a dozen others were talking after their regular Friday evening prayer meeting at the local Pentecostal church when they saw two "fireballs" shoot from Marzolf Hill (an area where Momo was thought to linger). The first fireball was white in color, followed about five minutes later by the second, which was green. Both fireballs descended into the trees behind an abandoned schoolhouse. On the same night, UFOs were seen over the nearby town of New Canton, Illinois.

Harrison's search for Momo compelled him to collect stories from other witnesses. Several reports included a small light which exploded and seemed to leave a foul odor behind; Harrison concluded that the horrible stench accompanying these sightings was meant as some sort of distraction.

On the night of July 26, another "fireball" was seen atop a cottonwood tree near River Road in Louisiana. It shot out two beams of red light before speeding out of sight. On the following three nights, colored lights appeared over a limestone bluff at the north end of River Road. Witnesses from the Shade and Harrison families felt as if the lights were signaling one another. The same evening, the entire Shade family witnessed what Mrs. Shade called a "perfect gold cross on the moon." "The road was lit up bright as day from the cross," said Mrs. Shade.

July 29 found Harrison and some college students standing atop Marzolf Hill. Hearing what sounded like a gunshot from the road below, they hurried down the hill in the direction of the sound. They all heard the phrase, "You boys stay out of these woods" uttered by what sounded like an old man. A thorough search of the area failed to turn up whoever—or *whatever*—issued the warning. The disembodied voices continued on August 5 when a man named Pat Howard, along with an unnamed friend, were camping in Harrison's yard. A voice from nowhere declared, "I'll take a cup of your coffee." Another search failed to yield the speaker.

The following night at 9:00 p.m., a glowing orange UFO with what appeared to be lit windows landed in a thicket atop the same limestone bluff where the colored lights were previously seen. It stayed in place for five hours. Louis Shade then watched the UFO fly away. It "went straight up into the air and disappeared," according to Shade.

Backtracking to August 3: after hearing a high-pitched howl just before dawn, Mr. and Mrs. Bill Suddarth found four three-toed tracks in the mud of their garden. Clyde Penrod, a hunter and friend of the Suddarths, came to make a cast of the prints. He was confused not only by the three-toed structure of the track, but by the trackway itself. The footprints showed no beginning or end— there were only four isolated tracks— with no others discovered elsewhere on the property. "It was 20 to 25 feet from the tracks to anything else," said Penrod. "I can't understand how they were made."[12]

The Bell Farm

Located in Derry Township, Pennsylvania, the Bell Farm was home to both bigfoot and UFO sightings. On the night of September 18, 1973, "Mrs. Bell" (a pseudonym assigned by Stan Gordon) was walking to her vehicle when she saw a dark figure standing upright about ten feet away. The hairy creature took a step toward Mrs. Bell and raised its long arms. Mrs. Bell cried out in fear—and the creature returned a cry, as if mimicking her. Mrs. Bell issued an even louder scream and ran toward her house. Again the creature answered her cries as it fled the scene.

Others had previously sighted bigfoot in the vicinity, and heard weird screams from the woods nearby. Mr. Bell and another man searched for the creature in the surrounding fields but instead found a UFO: large, luminous, and tube-shaped, hovering over the hills behind the farm, its red glow illuminating the ground.

Mrs. Bell, who had also sighted the UFO, said: "I don't know if it has anything to do with this thing, 'the creature,' but every time we see that or hear that, that light is pretty close." The Bells, along with other locals, reported another unusual light: a bright, star-like object would regularly appear in the sky to the Northwest around 10:00 p.m. The light appeared larger than a star or planet and alternated between silver, red, and black.

Barry Clark observed this UFO one night in September 1973. Earlier that same evening Clark heard the cry of what he presumed was bigfoot: "I actually got to hear that thing scream. It was an earth-shattering, scary scream. It started out as a very deep rattling, and then turned into an awful like howl and growl at the same time."

Later, Clark watched the bright light change colors in the sky. He drove to a nearby hilltop where he met others observing the strange light.

The object issued five flashes, each about one second apart, which lit up the sky in descending rings of deep red. Subsequently, the sky was littered with small silver lights gravitating toward the larger light, which had itself turned solid red. The silver lights became red as they approached the larger light, which grew in size and started approaching the ground. The observers fled the area.

This event marked the end of Clark's bigfoot and UFO investigations.[13]

Bigfoot, White Lights, and a Glowing Bronze Object

Jeff Martin was fishing near Galveston, Indiana in October of 1973 when he heard something moving in the foliage behind him. He turned to see a sandy-hued, ape-like creature watching him from around 20 feet away. He called out to the creature, but it turned and quietly sunk back into the woods.

After a few minutes, Martin felt something touch his shoulder and turned to see the creature standing nearby. The bigfoot took off running "like a man on a rope being pulled too fast by a car." Martin pursued the creature, but it easily outran him, leaping over a ditch and disappearing into the woods once more. A short time later Martin observed a "glowing bronze object" rise above the trees and streak into the sky.

Martin returned to the site the next day and did not notice anything out of the ordinary. He returned again the following evening with a group of people, including his fiancée and her father. They claimed their car was followed, for most of the ride to the site, by a glowing white light. The white light disappeared once they reached a nearby bridge. When they arrived at the site, they were surprised to find the bigfoot—as if it was waiting for them.

The creature watched motionless from the weeds, standing eight-to-nine-feet tall. The group exited the car and shone their flashlights at the creature. The beams seemed weaker when they hit the bigfoot—it seemed to *absorb* the light. The creature remained still, emitting a musky odor.

In an effort to get the creature to move, some of the group began throwing stones. They were unable to tell if the stones were hitting the bigfoot, bouncing off, or passing through it—but the creature remained motionless. When an approaching vehicle forced the witnesses to move their car aside, they returned to find the bigfoot gone.[14]

Discs in the Sky, Apes in the Van

Montana Santa, Puerto Rico was host to a series of odd events in 1992. An apparition of the Blessed Virgin Mary was seen in conjunction with colorful disc-shaped objects in the sky. During the incident, Delia Flores, along with several other witnesses, noticed a beige van parked in the same area. The van's occupants were dressed in orange fatigues bedecked with the NASA insignia, and its driver informed Flores that they were transporting some sort of ape-creature, captured in the Caribe State Forest, to a secret primate research laboratory. The witnesses all noticed a covered cage housing something "struggling to get out."

Around the same time, a nearby farmer reported a creature had destroyed a number of his plantain trees, leaving behind huge footprints with a depth suggesting great weight. Others in the area observed a "hairy figure" running about in the darkness.[15]

Strange Entities

Thomas Puzzo was walking through a vacant parking lot in Garden Grove, California during August of 1994 when he noticed a luminous craft hovering in the sky. The UFO noiselessly approached, showing a pulsing white light on its rear portion before abruptly disappearing. Puzzo next witnessed an odd entity emerge from some shrubs: very thin, about five feet tall, wearing a one-piece, light blue, turtleneck spacesuit. The garment was covered in one-inch green squares noted to be otherwise "indescribable." The entity had a "deformed" head, a pointy chin, and holes for ears. It exhibited difficulty walking before stumbling behind a carwash and out of Puzzo's sight. He then heard a sound like a BB-gun firing.

At this point, Puzzo noticed another creature standing behind a nearby air conditioner compressor unit: a five-foot tall simian with huge, hairy forearms, and a "ghostly" appearance. The second entity began walking with an ape-like locomotion. Puzzo recalled the face and head did not look like other "earthly" apes and, frightened, fled the area.[16]

The Hovering Light and the Hairy Man

Second Lieutenant Ranger Hector R. Losa heard a strange buzzing sound one night in October 2008 while keeping watch at a dam near Buenos Aires, Argentina. The television inside his sentry shack had lost signal, which was very unusual, and a short time later he heard a klaxon horn outside, heralding the arrival of a police cruiser and two of his fellow officers. They asked if Losa had seen "the light" above the guard post. Losa had not—he had been inside with the blinds closed. The other rangers reported that, as they headed toward the shack on patrol, they noticed a bright light over the reservoir. As they sped toward the scene, they lost sight of the UFO on one of the turns in the road and could not relocate it.

Elsewhere at the reservoir, a group of fishermen were night-fishing when they heard something emerge from the foliage. Ufologist Scott Corrales reported:

> A group of fishermen had headed to a rather inaccessible part of the lake formed by the reservoir to do some night fishing. They were equipped to spend the night there, carrying with them a battery and a spotlight to dispel the shadows. While they were readying their fishing tackle, they heard sounds emerging from the shrubs, and they turned around to see what it could be. When they were able to focus on the area where the noise was coming from, they were able to see the outline of a very hairy "man," possibly some two meters tall with a very large head and luminous eyes. Without succumbing to panic, one fisherman told another to hook up the spotlight to the battery to get a better look at the "thing," but the man's nervousness kept him from connecting the spotlight to the battery's terminals, and by the time the operation was over, the "stranger" had gone. They didn't wait for it to return: they collected their gear and left immediately.[17]

"Something is Seen, But One Doesn't Know What"

An entire volume could be devoted to bigfoot and UFOs. There exists no shortage of reports, and the selection here is but a small sampling. Though the drumbeat from F&BH advocates for many years has steadily downplayed—or outright denied—the bigfoot and UFO connection, there are simply *too many reports to ignore.*

To accept the word of witnesses who report sightings of giant ape-men on one hand—but throw out accounts by those same witnesses or others when they report UFOs around the same time and place—is disingenuous at best. Self-appointed cryptozoologists fondly invoke the name of *science*, as if it is a shield against ridicule from the mainstream. This selective data-mining is simply unscientific and intellectually dishonest. Either witnesses are to be believed, or they are not. You cannot have it both ways. You cannot pick and choose which elements of a witness's weird story you would like to believe.

Jung may be most prescient in his discussion of the UFO phenomenon in his 1958 essay, *Flying Saucers: A Modern Myth of Things Seen in the Skies*:

> Some time ago I published a statement in which I considered the nature of "Flying Saucers." I came to the same conclusion as Edward J. Ruppelt, one-time chief of the American Air Force's project for investigating UFO reports. The conclusion is: *Something is seen, but one doesn't know what.* It is difficult, if not impossible, to form any correct idea of these objects, because they behave not like bodies but like weightless thoughts.[18]

Many, if not all, of Jung's thoughts regarding the UFO phenomenon seem to apply to bigfoot with such ease that one might simply replace *UFOs, flying saucers*, et al in Jung's text with *bigfoot* and gain much insight into the phenomenon. Jung continued:

> For a decade the physical reality of UFOs remained a very problematical matter, which was not decided one way or the other with the necessary clarity despite the mass of observational material that had accumulated in the meantime. The longer the uncertainty lasted, the greater became the probability that this obviously complicated phenomenon had an extremely important psychic component as well as a physical basis. This is not surprising, in that we are dealing with an ostensibly physical phenomenon distinguished on the one hand by its frequent appearances, and on the other by its strange, unknown, and indeed, contradictory nature.
>
> Such an object provokes, like nothing else, conscious and unconscious fantasies, the former giving rise to speculative conjectures and pure fabrications, and the latter supplying the mythological background inseparable from these provocative observations. Thus there arose a situation in

which, with the best will in the world, one often did not know and could not discover whether a primary perception was followed by a phantasm or whether conversely, a primary fantasy originating in the unconscious invaded the conscious mind with illusions and visions.[19]

Patrick Harpur continued in Jung's wake, writing about UFOs in his absolutely essential volume, *Daimonic Reality*:

> ...the reality of UFOs—and of all apparitions—remains a vexed question. They compel us to ask ourselves what we mean by reality, a very old and knotty philosophical problem. In particular, they ask us to decide whether our encounters with apparitions are subjective or objective—that is, whether a UFO, for example is somehow a product of our minds or whether it exists out there in the world. If it is objectively real, then we have to decide further whether it is physically real or only apparently so; whether, that is, it is material or immaterial (though visible).[20]

Again, Harpur's words could apply just as easily to bigfoot as they do to UFOs.

Are we dealing with, as Jung suggests, a kind of physical phenomenon which triggers, perhaps by its very oddity, a kind of illusion which further heightens or expands upon the already bizarre event (or vice versa)? It is a question we have been asking for the entire history of humanity: what are these things and what is their relationship to us?

Bigfoot and UFOs, whatever they may be, do not seem to be static phenomena, but things that grow and change—viewed through the lenses of culture, folklore, science, and pseudoscience—presenting differently, or interpreted differently (perhaps both), throughout history.

Unidentified Flying Objects have transformed over the centuries, morphing from dragons to flying wheels in medieval times. Hot air balloons from Magonia gave way to steampunk airships in the early 1900s. Art Deco flying saucers and cigar-shaped UFOs began appearing in the 1940s. Large, black triangles flew overhead in the 1980s. The 21st century finds amorphous shapeshifting craft, plasma balls, and floating jellyfish haunting our skies. The phenomenon constantly recontextualizes itself, staying one step ahead of our technology and adjusting to cultural expectations. UFOs are constantly becoming more sophisticated.

Whatever lies behind bigfoot sightings seems to reinvent itself in a similar fashion, albeit with a trend from sophistication to primitivity. To grossly generalize, wild man archetypes in both the Old and New World once positioned large, hairy hominids as sophisticated and intelligent—omnipotent, magically operant spirits in Europe, hairy Indian tribes capable of speech in the Americas. As Darwinism gained popularity, our concept of wild men not only held them as flesh-and-blood animals, but also as more savage. Late 19th and early 20th century bigfoot sightings depict the creatures as aggressive and brutal—yet, often, not without some trappings of civilization like weapons, fire, and clothing. Then (once our reality was fully disenchanted by scientific Materialism) the image of bigfoot took root in modern culture: a brutish primate that can be caught and killed, whose existence can be proven, and who is firmly grounded in our reality.

Which brings us back to Harpur's quote above and the *knotty problem* of what is meant by "reality." If our consensus is based solely in Materialism, UFOs and bigfoot, it seems, shall remain elusive. Seen, but never captured. They leave enough behind to remind us that they are *real* but never enough to prove that they are *here*, twisting the line which holds the physical on one side and the apparitional on the other into a kind of Möbius strip.

Flesh-and-blood apes seem to dematerialize and slip through our fingers like wisps of smoke. Nuts-and-bolts UFO craft refuse to land on the White House lawn, but shoot away at impossible speeds. Clinging to one side of the Möbius strip, we may not notice the twist, but viewed from afar we see the very twist itself allows things to walk on both sides of the loop.

The idea that something can be real—in that most Materialist definition of reality, i.e. *it is physically here* (in terms of sasquatch, for example, able to leave footprints and move things)—and yet completely ephemeral has led to even more "science-fiction thinking." Desperately trying to prove the physical reality of bigfoot, yet faced with all the attendant problems of proving a breeding population exists, bigfoot enthusiasts have turned to explanations as varied as quantum physics, interdimensional travel, or even that bigfoot may themselves be aliens, brought here by the Ufonauts.

It may be more valuable to step back and take a long view. In these mysteries—bigfoot and UFOs—we are confronted with things that force us to consider both sides of the Möbius strip at once. When these things appear together the mystery deepens, but becomes more wondrous at the same time.

It is difficult to draw conclusions from accounts of sasquatch seen with UFOs. The simple quantity of reports establishes an undeniable link between bigfoot creatures and UFOs. The *hows* and *whys* of these connections remain beyond our grasp, currently.

High Strangeness permeates the bigfoot phenomenon, and likewise the UFO phenomenon. When the two are combined, the strangeness multiplies. However, this does not mean that reports of bigfoot in conjunction with UFOs should be ignored or "cherry picked," highlighting only the details confirming sasquatch is some sort of natural, flesh and blood animal. Whatever witnesses report—no matter how strange or unbelievable—should be documented.

Bigfoot and UFOs appear together. Not rarely. Not occasionally. They appear together *often*. The connection between the two is downright weird and defies explanation.

Just like bigfoot.

---

[1] Slate, B.A. & Berry, A. (1976). *Bigfoot*. New York, NY: Bantam.

[2] No author. (n.d.). Case 24. In A. Rosales (Ed.), *1930-1934 Humanoid Sighting Reports*. Retrieved February 5, 2014 from http://www.ufoinfo.com/humanoid/humanoid-1934.pdf

[3] Smith, W. (1975). *Triangle of the Lost*. New York, NY: Zebra.

[4] Keyhoe, D. (n.d.). Cases 45 & 47. In A. Rosales (Ed.), *1959 Humanoid Sighting Reports*. Retrieved February 5, 2014 from http://www.ufoinfo.com/humanoid/humanoid-1959.pdf

[5] Nunnelly, B. (2017). *The Inhumanoids: Real Encounters with Beings That Can't Exist!* US: Triangulum Publishing (2nd ed.).

[6] Clark, J. & Coleman, L. (January 1973). Anthropoids, Monsters and UFOs. *Flying Saucer Review 19*(1), pp. 18-23.

[7] Slate & Berry 1976.

[8] Nunnelly 2017.

[9] Gordon, S. (2010). *Silent Invasion: The Pennsylvania UFO-Bigfoot Casebook*. R. Marsh (Ed.). Greensburg, PA: Stan Gordon Productions.

[10] Johnson, P.G. (2018). *Chasing the Elusive Pennsylvania Bigfoot.* New Milford, CT: Visionary Living Publishing.

[11] Gordon, S. (2015). *Astonishing Encounters: Pennsylvania's Unknown Creatures – Casebook Three.* Greensburg, PA: Stan Gordon Productions.

[12] Clark & Coleman 1973.

[13] Gordon 2010.

[14] Nunnelly 2017.

[15] Corrales, S. (1997). *Chupacabras and Other Mysteries.* Murfreesboro, TN: Greenleaf Publications.

[16] Puzzo, T. (n.d.). Case 187. In A. Rosales (Ed.), *1994 Humanoid Sighting Reports.* Retrieved February 5, 2014 from http://www.ufoinfo.com/humanoid/humanoid-1994.pdf

[17] Corrales, S. (November 26, 2008). Argentina: West of Buenos Aires-Reports, Lights and Strange Beings? Retrieved August 13, 2020 from http://inexplicata.blogspot.com/2008/11

[18] Jung, C.G. (1978) *Flying Saucers: A Modern Myth of Things Seen in the Skies.* Princeton, NJ: Princeton University Press.

[19] Ibid.

[20] Harpur, P. (2003). *Daimonic Reality: A Field Guide to the Otherworld.* Ravensdale, WA: Pure Winds Press.

So, ooh-ooh-ooh, I wanna be like you /
I wanna use that flame just the same you can do
Oh, how magnificus it would be /
A Gigantopithecus like me
Could learn to do like you humans do.

— *King Louie*, The Jungle Book *(2016)*

VOCALIZATIONS

Mimicry is a commonly employed tool in the animal kingdom for a host of reasons, including communication, self-defense, and predation. These imitations need not be sophisticated: the Australian shingleback lizard, for example, has a fat tail which looks strikingly like its head to confuse predators. On the other end of the spectrum, ocean-dwelling cephalopods are among the most complex mimics on the planet, changing not only their skin's color but also its texture to appear as both inanimate and animate objects. The mimic octopus, for instance, has been recorded changing its body shape to resemble lionfish, flatfish, sole, jellyfish, and sea snakes.

Despite the obvious example of parrots, few animals mimic human speech. Apes (though so prone to physical imitation their name is synonymous with mimicry) are cognitively capable of understanding human language, but widely believed incapable of reproducing it verbally due to physical limitations. Even when apes successfully echo human vocal cadences—as a 50-year old orangutan was taught in 2015—the results are not particularly compelling.[1]

If eyewitness testimony is to be believed, however, the world's greatest living mimic is indeed a primate. Countless accounts describe bigfoot imitating a staggering amount of noises, from other animals to mechanical sounds—even human speech.

Monkey See, Monkey Do

Hairy cryptids display uncanny imitation faculties in cultures around the world. According to legend, the *Ebu gogo* (short, hairy bipeds allegedly living on the Indonesian island of Flores) "had their own fairly complex language, and could even mimic—to an eerie degree—the words of the Nage people," according to author Nick Redfern.[2] The much larger *Lae ho'a* also lives on the island and boasts the same ability.[3] Far away in Russia, the *Yagmort* shares many attributes with bigfoot, including a love of swimming, a fondness for horses, and peculiar vocalizations, including the mimicry of human voices.[4]

Testimony from the modern era confirms these legends. Yang Wanchun claimed to observe a wild man in 1977 in Shaanxi province, China, that "uttered 11 or 12 different sounds, which seemed to imitate a sparrow chirping, dog barking, pony neighing, leopard growling, and an infant crying."[5] In another instance from 1948, a bigfoot raiding towns in Tabasco, Mexico wreaked havoc among hunters seeking to kill the beast, allegedly imitating other party members and drawing them to their doom.[6]

Despite how impressive and consistent these similarities appear, they pale in comparison to the abilities reported by North American bigfoot witnesses and First Nations tribes. Elder Otis Frank spoke of the Northern Cheyenne "spirit beings of the mountains": "They are a wild people who keep to the old ways that we had before time was noticed... they whistle to communicate, sometimes they growl like the bear, sometimes they imitate the coyote, the blue jay and the wild dog but we know each of them by their voice."[7]

Stan Courtney, a researcher with a special interest in vocalizations, has claimed to hear a variety of animal sounds during investigations: owls, dogs, turkeys, raccoons, coyotes, and more.

"I myself have heard in Central Illinois in the daytime, during the winter, what can only [be] described as a jungle bird type sound," Courtney wrote. Although none of these sounds were visually confirmed as coming from sasquatch, he added "most occurred in areas that had previous eye-witness [sic] bigfoot sightings," and each call was unnatural in its own way.[8]

"Sometimes they imitate other animals, but not very well," New Mexican researcher Brenda Harris told *Navajo Times*.[9] This "not-quite-right" quality is what often leads witnesses to assume these sounds originate from bigfoot. Birds sound too large and loud. Owls hoot at unlikely times. Human voices in the woods sound as if they are coming from someone with a speech impediment speaking a foreign language: one

Michigan witness described the voices on their property as "sounding like an Amish deaf person."[10]

Bigfoot researchers propose a variety of reasons the creatures display this ability. Some suggest they utilize mimicry to draw in and ambush prey, or the calls represent covert communication between individuals, a technique utilized by military special forces and criminals alike.

"'Contact calls' consist almost exclusively of animal imitations, especially of those animals that make noises at night," wrote 19th century Austrian criminologist Hanns Gross. "Of course, people committing a robbery in the woods or approaching a home for a burglary don't call to each other by name or make any noise that would attract attention. An animal call, especially when well imitated, is never suspected, and when the criminals agree in advance [who will make which animal noise], the calls are as clearly understood as the names themselves."[11]

Mimicry is not restricted to vocalizations. Hairy hominids also reportedly imitate human beings' actions, from pacing witnesses out of their habitats to attempting to build fires, as in Guatemalan *Sisemite* folklore.[12] In June 1999 Colette Alexander and her roommate were picnicking along California's San Lorenzo River when they spotted something peering at them from a large cypress bush 20-30 yards downriver. It appeared to be "a strange cross between human and ape," and was mimicking Alexander as she ate her sandwich. When she slowed her movements, the sasquatch responded in kind.[13]

"It did exactly what Colette did," wrote researcher David Paulides. "The creature even smirked at her, as though it was having fun."[14]

Mimicry: Animals

It is a fool's errand to attempt a comprehensive catalogue of noises imitated by bigfoot, but the following provides some idea of the scope of the creatures' abilities.

- **Deer:** According to Christopher Noël, a Texas habituator once heard a "white-tailed deer bark" from fifteen feet up a tree shortly before "getting hit with infrasound," causing a panic attack.[15] Some theorize this tactic is used to ambush prey: sasquatch attract deer with these vocalizations before incapacitating them with infrasound.[16]

- **Cougars:** Because both bigfoot and large, predatory cats are known for screaming, conflation naturally arises between the two. However, in the 1970s, campers near Wrangell, Alaska heard three "loud screams" along the Stikine River. Though likened to cougar vocalizations, witness Harvey Gross said, "We did not think it was a cougar scream—too loud."[17]

- **Farm animals:** Habituators at a Michigan farm shared audio with investigators from The Bigfoot Field Researchers Organization (BFRO) in 2012. "Immediately on hearing the first few moments of audio I was impressed with what seemed to be out there," wrote investigator Jim Sherman. "I heard what appeared to be communication between multiple vocalizers, mimicry of farm animals, and even interaction between humans and whatever it was in the woods."[18] In another incident Larry Johnson, a colleague of Ron Morehead, described hearing "what he thought was a herd of horses coming down the ridge… He didn't know what to think about that."[19] In May 2015, a witness in Skidaway Island State Park, Georgia noticed grunts, detected foul smells, and "heard a noise that sounded like a person with a very deep and raspy voice was trying to imitate a cow. It went 'moo, moo' twice and then everything was quiet. We thought this was strange because the closest cows were five miles away and this sounded like a creepy imitation of a cow."[20] Another bigfoot tried "to mimic a donkey" in front of a Missouri witness,[21] and some have reported the sound of goats in areas of heavy sasquatch activity.[22]

- **Frogs:** In 1989 a pair of witnesses outside Nevada City, California was sitting beside a lake when they noticed a loud bullfrog call from the reeds. One of them approached the source of the sound, but were surprised to see "a large hairy creature" stand up, run to the beach, and disappear into the woods.[23]

- **Rabbits:** A witness near Ohio's Wayne National Forest noted a variety of strange activity on their property, including agitated dogs. One October night, "I started hearing what I thought was the worst imitation of a wounded or caught rabbit I'd ever heard. I almost laughed…." This was followed by a long, protracted howl. The following New Year's Eve, the witness clearly saw a tall, hairy figure in the yard.[24]

Bigfoot seem especially fond of imitating the long howls of canids. In 2004, campers were driven from a mountain in Colorado's San Juan

National forest when an unseen force agitated their dogs, knocked on trees, and continuously vocalized. "At about midnight, we were winding down when we heard three, two-tone howls to the hill approximately a quarter mile to our north," witnesses told the BFRO. "We knew it was not a coyote but almost sounded like a person trying to imitate a coyote because it had a deeper bass tone."[25]

Campers in Missouri reported a similar account in 2002. "To describe the sound this animal made is difficult," one camper said. "It began the call as a canine type 'howl' followed by a 'whoop' or 'bark' repeated several times. This was NOT a coyote or wolf. The pitch was much deeper and tonal quality gave the impression of something larger than a coyote or wolf... I felt the sound resembled a large human imitating a wolf." The sounds terminated into "very fast, guttural" gibberish "rising and falling in pitch."[26]

"I recorded an unknown howl this spring in Central Illinois," wrote Courtney in 2006. "It has been labeled as either a coyote or wolf. However, I have a Native American friend who reassures me that it is a bigfoot mimicking a coyote."[27] Coyotes and other wild dogs often respond to these calls, setting off a chain reaction of noises difficult to analyze for anomalies. Internet commenters theorize wild canids and bigfoot perhaps employ a symbiotic relationship: the calls function as a sort of "dinner bell" to "proactively employ coyotes to literally digest the evidence of [bigfoot] kills."[28]

Domestic dogs are also regularly mimicked. From North Carolina researcher Tom Burnette:

> Another time I had just got off work, I was tired, and wanted to get in my house after a long day. I walked to the door. I could hear barking on the mountain, approximately two hundred yards behind my home. It was a perfect mimic of Barney, my short-haired Beagle. Barney stood on the porch beside me, raising his ears. He was as puzzled as I was. Something was on the mountain imitating my dog. The damn things can mimic almost anything.[29]

While Burnette speculated bigfoot on his property did this either to convey excitement for his return or jealousy of his dogs' food, the infamously antagonistic relationship between large, hairy hominids and pets casts these reports in an unsettling light. Bigfoot have literally been seen tearing dogs limb-from-limb; Grover Krantz once wrote, "Dogs are universally reported to be terrified when in the vicinity of a sasquatch."[30] Rob Riggs, who co-wrote *Bigfoot: Exploring the Myth & Discovering the*

Truth with Burnette, speculated an even more nefarious motive for bigfoot's hatred of dogs than mere malice.

"Could it be because of the relationship dogs have with human beings that bigfoot go out of their way to kill dogs?" he mused. "Is it because dogs would alarm humans to their presence that they go out of their way to dispose of dogs?"[31] To riff on Riggs's idea: could mimicry—both imitating canids and, as discussed later, their owner's calls—be a method to lure dogs into an ambush?

Mimicry: Bird Calls

One subset of animal mimicry deserves special attention. By far, the most commonly reported imitative bigfoot vocals are bird calls.

Testimony from First Nations informants closely associates bird calls with bigfoot in the lore of certain tribes. A July 15, 1924 newspaper article claimed the Pacific Northwest's *Seeahtik* speak not only "the bear language of the Clallam tribe," but also "the bird language… the *Seeahtik* tribe can imitate any bird of the northwest, especially the bluejay…."[32] Henry Moon, a guide of mixed Modoc and Paiute ancestry, told researcher Bobbie Short he had heard *Yah-yahaas* while bear hunting: "Sometimes it sounded like a bird call, other times it sounded like a two-finger mouth-whistle."[33]

For the Gwich'in of the Yukon Territory, there is little more frightening than hearing a "black giant":

> What scared the Gwich'in… the most? Hearing a whistle, even when friends whistled, they stopped everything. To them, it is the call of a black giant to a female. The Indians also listen to the alarm call of birds and what each alarm call indicated. One bird in their territory is capable of mimicking at least forty other birds; it's the gray catbird. It also mimics the *bushman*, or their *black giant*, and vice versa.[34]

Again, this trend expresses itself worldwide. In Guaraní myth, the South American *Curupira* is a short creature with a "large head like a chimpanzee," covered in reddish hair and known for its "birdlike whistle."[35] Malaysians describe the call of the manlike, hairy *Hantu sikai* as akin to a bird.[36] *Yahoo,* an aboriginal term for the Australian Yowie, is a name synonymous among tribes in Victoria's Snowy Mountains with the Gray-crowned babbler, a songbird.[37] The *Leshy* was especially covetous of this ability: "Don't whistle in the home or in the wood," Slavic lore holds.

"It's only the *Leshy* who whistles."[38]

As indigenous lore goes, so go sightings.

- **1967 – Illinois:** Immediately prior to a harrowing bigfoot encounter in Chicago—covered in Volume I of *Where the Footprints End*—a witness in Schiller Woods hears "a bird whistle, some type of exotic bird I never heard before." The call happens at least four more times, and is also noted by a passing couple.[39]

- **1996-2002 – Virginia:** A variety of dramatic incidents occur at a farmhouse near the North Carolina border over the course of six years, including missing farm animals, house knocks, full-bodied sightings of bigfoot, and vocalizations. The witness hears growls, roars, and a host of vocal mimicry: one night, she awakens to "a front yard full of birds chirping so loudly they woke me up at 2 a.m.!" As a group, the "flock" moves through a pasture and into the forest, "chirping all the way. No humans could copy this."[40] (Note how the faerie host, in some traditions, often made noises "like that of a flock of birds.")[41]

- **2008 – Texas:** A habituator spots a large shape "belly-crawling" through tall grass and shouts, "Oh for Heaven sakes, I *see* you." The shape freezes and crawls out of sight—backwards. Simultaneously, she hears vocalizations from the treeline, including "a bird-whistling so loud it made your eardrums vibrate, so you knew it was no bird on the face of the earth."[42]

- **2010 – Washington:** On September 25, a Skamania County couple notices their dog seems anxious. The same night, they smell a skunky odor outside and hear "three distinct and loud animal calls" like "whoo-up!" They later tell the BFRO: "It sounded like a person trying to imitate a bird call. I have never heard a sound like this ever in my life, and I am familiar with several Pacific Northwest animal sounds."[43]

It is interesting that the world's most skilled vocal mimic, the parrot, is a bird. Perhaps the shared affinity for imitation between parrots and bigfoot provides a clue to the latter's brain structure. In 2015, scientists discovered the first hints to how parrots mimic sounds so well.

"Any bird that's a vocal learner has a part of the brain devoted to this, called the 'song system,'" wrote journalist Ashley P. Taylor for The

Audubon Society. "But in parrots, the song system has two layers—an inner 'core,' common to all avian vocal learners, and an outer 'shell,' which is unique to parrots." Researchers suspect this shell is key to facilitating parrots' mimicry.[44]

Witnesses occasionally identify specific types of bird calls. Alleged encounters describe rooster crows,[45] partridge calls,[46] woodpecker knocks,[47] crow caws,[48] and loon cries[49]—each attributed to bigfoot on account of their vocal quality or proximity to large, hairy hominid activity.

"On the 12 of April, 2005, I went to my local state park," wrote Courtney. "As I was sitting on a log near a large thicket I heard what I thought was wild turkeys clucking. When I turned around to investigate, the sounds stopped and I heard a loud wood knock coming from the top of the hill."[50]

"The Owls Are Not What They Seem"

The birds most commonly imitated by bigfoot are owls.

"When the Indians would go on their hunting and camping trips into the mountains, as soon as they heard an owl screech or hoot, they would stop and listen and try to distinguish if it was an Indian devil imitating the owl or the cry of a wild animal," wrote Klamath River Indian author Lucy Thompson. "The Indians would stop at once, kindle a fire; this was given as a warning to the devils that they were awake and ready to fight them if necessary."[51] Among the Dhegiha-speaking Sioux, a "monkey" called *Inda'cinga* is a large, hairy trickster who hoots like an owl, sometimes appearing as an *actual* gigantic owl.[52]

In Europe, various traditions linked the hooting of owls to the passage of the Wild Hunt, a retinue of fearsome specters—sometimes faeries, sometimes the dead—travelling on a storm led either by a legendary historical figure or a Wild Huntsman, who shares aspects of the wild man archetype. "His approach is heralded by a distant baying or yelping of hounds, while a night-owl, called by the [Saxons] Tutosel (i.e. *Tut-ursel*, tooting Ursula), flies in front of him," wrote Alexander Porteous in *The Forest in Folklore and Mythology*. "This Ursula, was said to have been a nun who, after her death, joined [the Huntsman] and mingled her 'Tu-hu' with his [cry of] 'Hu-hu.' Travelers, when he passes, fall silently on their faces, and lie terror-stricken listening to the barking of the dogs and the huntsman's weird 'Hu-hu.'"[53]

These traditions found a home in the bigfoot community. "If you hear a night owl where there shouldn't be one, it could be a bigfoot," said Mike Rugg, proprietor of Felton, California's Bigfoot Discovery

Museum.[54] A better indicator that "the owls are not what they seem" (to quote the television program *Twin Peaks*) is the volume or incredible bass frequency of the hoot, as noted by one witness in northern Wisconsin.

> ... twice I've seen those straight line trackways in the snow near my home... Can't rule out some bounding animal double tracks but just no evidence of that. Wish I would've taken pictures but I didn't. And although there are plenty of owls around, last year I heard them calling to each other—I figured some mating thing—but the first time I started hearing it, it sounded like grown men making owl sounds. I thought, "Who would be joking around like that middle of the day in gun country?" Crazy-loud, and seemed to be on my property of 15 acres, but just out of range. And I hardly have any neighbors... 800 lb. owl sounds about right. It's an owl-like sound—but you clearly get the feeling that it is imitated. I thought this before I ever heard of bigfoot possibly being associated with it.[55]

There are obvious similarities between the hoots of owls and the hoots of primates. On June 1, 2001, an Oklahoma couple searching near their lake house for a missing cat was inundated without warning by multiple owl hoots of intense volume. Slowly, "some of the calls turned in to jungle noises" similar to "monkeys and toucans." The experience escalated into a crescendo of insane laughter from the forest. All suddenly fell silent, prefacing a loud tree break. The couple returned to their vehicle and rushed down the road, spotting a tall, heavily-muscled figure whose eyes "almost glowed."[56]

Interestingly, the most common contact calls among criminals are owl vocalizations, according to Hanns Gross. Gross even musically transcribed the most commonly imitated owl hoots, and his commentary on their use may provide insight into bigfoot's motivations:

> Owls are everywhere, in the woods, fields, mountains, swamps, in isolated areas, and close to human habitation. No one questions the hoot of an owl early in the evening or before dawn; hunters even use hoots in broad daylight when summoning each other in the woods. Although animals don't fear an owl hoot, men have a superstitious dread of it; on hearing an owl they would sooner stop their ears than watch their pockets. Based on how far apart accomplices are, a Scops Owl or Little Owl hoot is used... The Little Owl is used

for greater distances.[57]

As Gross notes, owls occupy a special role in worldwide folklore. In many cultures they are regarded as messengers from the spirit world, and are closely associated with a variety of paranormal entities, from the child-snatching demoness Lilith to the *Strigoi*, Romanian vampires[58] (in fact, the terms "screech-owl" and "witch" are conflated in parts of Europe).[59] Owls are also increasingly associated with the UFO contact experience, as extensively examined by author Mike Clelland.[60]

Clelland collected a fascinating story combining owls, UFOs, and bigfoot. In 2010 Clelland contacted Susan MacLeod, a witness of partial Mi'kmaq ancestry who sees an inordinate number of owls around her Ontario home. In 2015, MacLeod and her family "were literally surrounded by owls that summer," including a bedroom window visitation on August 14. The following morning, MacLeod underwent a painful medical procedure without anesthesia, but managed the pain after slipping into a meditative state where she experienced visions of Native American imagery and "a beautiful green room with a big golden retriever."[61]

"When the procedure was over, the hygienist said she was amazed that Susan hadn't needed any anesthesia," Clelland wrote. "It was then that Susan shared her visions about the green room and the dog. The hygienist looked shocked and said, 'You just described my bedroom and my dog.'"[62]

That evening, MacLeod went to a small teepee on her property for some quiet reflection and to mourn the recent passing of a dear friend. While drumming and singing, she detected "a strong damp musky odor" and heard something moving outside, brushing against the fabric walls. Unsettled, MacLeod left the teepee for her home—but on the way ran into "two red lights" and "multiple eyes reflecting back at her." It was five large bigfoot, two taller and three smaller individuals, no more than 20 feet away.[63]

MacLeod backed into her teepee, eventually summoning the courage to return home again. On the walk, she saw the bigfoot "family" standing much farther away. Her children met her at the door to her house, frantically rambling about shadowy shapes "flying all through the house." MacLeod calmed her family and, around midnight, visited her partner, who had apparently bivouacked himself in his garage workshop. He claimed to have seen similar figures, including "black shadow beings" peeping in the windows.[64]

Upset and unable to share her bigfoot experience, MacLeod left the garage and stood in the driveway. Clelland described what occurred:

Like that morning in the dentist chair, she again asked for

help. Susan gazed up into the heavens and prayed to God.

She looked up at three bright stars while praying. These points of light all slowly moved together in the sky above her, defining the corners of a giant triangle shape. Initially appearing as three different colors, she watched these stars meld into one beautiful swirling orange-amber-yellow.

She called out to her partner and he came running out to the opening along the driveway. He looked up to see these three colored lights slowly moving apart, but the stars within the triangle were being blotted out by something giant right above them. They both watched as something enormous began forming itself into a semi-solid kind of matter. It was right then that she understood that all these events, the Sasquatch, the shadow beings, and now this giant craft were somehow connected. [65]

The Language of the Birds

If not for contact calls or hunting, why would bigfoot imitate birds? Notably, the "language of the birds" is a longstanding esoteric concept suggesting divine messages are encoded into birdsong, and can be unlocked by the initiated. This belief appears throughout European folklore from Scandinavia to the Mediterranean, even finding its way into the Middle East: in the *Qur'an*, David and Suleiman (Solomon) allegedly "have been taught the language of birds."[66] Given bigfoot's similarity to other paranormal entities—witches, faeries, etc., all of which could transform into birds—this occult connection is intriguing, if inconclusive.

"Classical author E.R. Dodds in his *The Greeks and the Irrational* (1951) noted the role of birds in Greek magical practices," wrote paranormal scholar George P. Hansen. "Birds can be seen as living between the heavens and the earth and as messengers between the realms. Thus birds have a betwixt and between [liminal] quality."[67]

Other bigfoot-bird connections reveal themselves in European art. In Mozart's *Die Zauberflöte*, the protagonist meets Papageno, a bird-catcher of avian appearance, in the woods; when first encountered, Papageno is attempting to lure birds using his whistle. University of California Los Angeles professor Ehrhard Bahr argues Papageno is explicitly a wild man: "He fits the description and definition. Dressed in feathers, he carries a panpipe in his hand, and he is master of the animals..."[68] In the 2006 comedy musical *Tenacious D in The Pick of Destiny*, an entire song dedicated to bigfoot is entitled, *Papagenu (He's My Sassafrass)*.

"The iconographic relationship between simians and birds in mediaeval art is a fairly complicated matter," wrote art professor H.W. Janson. "We often find him next to an owl, who is his counterpart among the denizens of the air... Like the owl, the ape is antagonistic to all other kinds of birds; he is very fond of chasing after small wild birds, such as finches, swallows, etc., but rarely succeeds in catching them. These invariably have a positive symbolic meaning. They are the age-old image of the soul, being pursued by the ape as the symbol of carnal appetite."[69]

Janson explores the ape-bird motif extensively in his book *Apes and Ape Lore in the Middle Ages and the Renaissance*. The origins of the association are unclear, but it is certainly old; Janson speculates it may date to "the hermetic literature of late antiquity."

Regardless of whether life imitates art or vice versa, large, hairy hominids display aggression towards birds (crows notwithstanding, as discussed in *Where the Footprints End* Volume I, Chapter 6). Bigfoot famously raid chicken coops, and Cambodia's wild men, the *Ngoi rung*, allegedly toss stones to kill birds.[70] On one expedition into Texas's Big Thicket, researcher Rob Riggs found a vivisected Cooper's Hawk: "I could think of no natural predators that would even be inclined to attack a fairly good sized hawk, which is itself a predator."[71]

Mimicry: Other Sounds

The benefit of mimicking animal noises is obvious for hunting. It is less apparent why large, hairy hominids would imitate human technology.

"I've had [sasquatch] eyewitnesses that have said it sounded like a forklift backing up," said podcaster Wes Germer. "This one witness I had on the show... he had encounters around his house, he goes out one night and he's like, 'Yeah, it sounds like a forklift backing up... unless that forklift was 20 feet away in the brush.'" Germer asked the witness if there were any warehouses nearby from which the bigfoot could have learned the beeping sound. There were—located 25 miles away.[72]

Beeping bigfoot appear elsewhere. In 1966, two boys riding horseback in Arkansas were surprised when a farmer passing in a tractor warned them of a "monster" lurking in the river bottoms. Undeterred, the pair continued their excursion until their horses refused to travel any farther and they set off on foot. Once they reached a meadow, a peculiar clump of fur suddenly arose from the ground, revealing itself as a nine-foot tall, white, hairy bigfoot with pink skin. "It also emitted a powerful odor, and made a sound like a radio signal as it approached the two boys," D. Douglas Graham wrote in the November 1995 issue of *Fate* magazine. "The signal sounded like 'beep, beep, beep.'" The witnesses fled and a posse was formed, but found only dead livestock.[73]

Robotic and metallic voices are sometimes heard in areas of bigfoot activity. In July 1956, a fisherman in Idaho reported a red-haired, eight-foot tall bigfoot step from the brush onto a road, making "a metallic-sounding laugh as it walked."[74] This peculiar quality finds precedent in lore surrounding the aforementioned Russian *Yagmort*, which natives say has a "high-pitched, metallic laughter"[75] (ptarmigan and porcupines produce a laughing-type noise, but it is neither metallic nor of sufficiently intimidating volume).[76]

Witnesses report bigfoot sounding like helicopters,[77] sirens,[78] mechanical gears,[79] electronic noises,[80] cowbells,[81] running water,[82] gongs,[83] car engines,[84] and locomotives. In one example, a habituator at least a hundred miles from the nearest train tracks shared a bigfoot recording with Germer. "It's not quite perfect—it almost sounds like a mimic of a train whistle—but it's so loud and so powerful, there's no way a human could have done that," he said.[85] Witnesses consistently emphasize the power behind these vocalizations, complaining of eardrum pain and feeling sound waves in their bodies.

"Right outside our shelter, we heard a car door slam—you tell me how that happens," researcher Ron Morehead said of his experiences at the Sierra camp. The camp was "miles back in the wilderness," inaccessible by automobile. "There's certainly no truck outside, there are no cars parked outside, but you hear that slam."[86]

"The two types of audio hallucinations most frequently reported are the sounds of a baby crying and the sound of an unseen car door slamming," wrote John Keel of paranormal activity. "The baby crying phenomenon is common not only among UFO witnesses but among thousands of 'ghost' and monster witnesses as well. We found that the door slamming phenomenon is universal but is rarely reported in print because few investigators bother to collect the necessary background information from the witnesses."[87]

The aforementioned "cowbell" sound is of especial interest, because it not only ties into the underreported phenomenon of music associated with large, hairy hominids (see *Where the Footprints End* Volume I, Chapter 3), but also has precedent worldwide. Citing the work of Dutch Tibetologist Johan van Manen, Dmitri Bayanov noted the appearance of this sound in the Andes, Switzerland, the Himalayas, and

Scotland "where, according to those who tell the tale, there was no possibility of cattle or sheep being present" (this last locale may be a reference to the aural anomalies reported on Ben MacDhui).[88]

Bayanov reprints the testimony of one Yuri Krashnikov, who heard "the sounds of someone walking," rolling stones, and cracking sticks around their camp near Tajikistan's Lake Pairon in late summer 1984:[89]

> When the distance between us and the source of the sounds equaled several meters, the sounds stopped. There was silence. We also kept silent and did not budge. Suddenly, from the place where the movement stopped, came sounds resembling the tinkle of a small bell. The sounds repeated periodically, once or twice a second. And their source began to move around us, counterclockwise, at a distance of several meters. No other sounds, those of steps, for example, were heard... we heard nothing but the tinkling of a bell. Having circled us and returned to the starting point, it stopped. Then we heard the loud sounds of retreating steps.[90]

The following morning, "indistinct marks of big tracks" were found around the camp. Krashnikov recalled the sounds as "TOO clear, so they seemed almost unreal. If I heard them now... I'd sooner describe them as 'computer made' or 'synthesized.'"[91]

While mimicry of machinery is peculiar, it is not unheard of in the animal kingdom. The Australian lyrebird—whose natural songs often exhibit a peculiar metallic quality—has been recorded producing uncanny imitations of trains, whistles, car horns, barking dogs, camera shutters, and chainsaws.[92] However, the replication of man-made sounds has only been observed among lyrebirds in captivity.[93]

Mimicry: Human Voices

It was September 1970, when San Diego Sheriffs Department officer Doug Huse first learned of "Zoobies."

Huse's colleagues pulled over a car during a routine traffic stop, only to find a distressed man at the wheel, a .44 magnum on the passenger's seat. When asked why he was carrying the firearm, the driver —later identified as a psychiatrist, "Dr. Baddour"—mumbled something about "Zoobies."[94]

"That wasn't what the doctor actually called it, I don't believe, but that's what my partner heard and that's how the name got coined," Huse told researcher Matt Moneymaker in a 1992 interview. "He described the Zoobie as a large, upright, walking hairy creature. Dr. Baddour convinced us and later other members of my department, including one of my patrol sergeants, that in truth he'd had three separate encounters with the Zoobies."[95]

Baddour lived in a relatively isolated part of the county, and claimed to have experienced a variety of odd activity (damage to his home, fruit missing from high in trees, four-toed footprints, etc.) before finally seeing a family of the creatures in his yard. One encounter was especially peculiar.

> They had chickens there, and earlier he'd called his wife to say he was going to be late and to remind her to feed the chickens before nightfall, which she did. When the doctor got home he had to exit his car, open the gate, drove through and stopped, then got out of the car again to close the gate behind him. He said that when he went to close the gate that night he heard a very low, very guttural voice say, "Here chicky, chicky, chicky..."
>
> ... It was the doctor's opinion, and we had no reason to doubt him, that the Zoobie had some type of intelligence and the capability of producing sounds like that.[96]

It is extremely unsettling to think of bigfoot imitating human voices, but there is too much evidence to ignore.

- **1972 – Missouri:** Witnesses hear numerous disembodied voices from the woods during the infamous Momo, or Missouri Monster, bigfoot-UFO flap. On July 29, a group of college students detect "an old man's voice saying, 'You boys stay out of these woods.'" The voice seems to come from a small copse of trees, but a search yields nothing. One week later friends enjoying coffee in the vicinity of the sightings hear "someone or something" say "I'll take a cup of your coffee."[97]

- **1977 – Oklahoma:** For weeks, a Stillwell family experiences terrorized pets, lithoboly, giant figures with glowing eyes, "eerie lights in the winter snow, mysterious hoofs clomping across the porch," and "prints of a giant human-like foot in the spring garden." In one instance, a boy in the home sees a luminous bigfoot peering in the bathroom window and hears a voice "from the sky" say, "It won't be stopped, it can't be stopped."[98]

- **1978 – Iowa:** A bigfoot flap hits Ottosen. Among the witnesses is 12 year-old Dawn Henkins, who sees the creature standing under a streetlight. Her screams draw her mother, who hears a man's voice ask, "Does anybody know what time it is?" Looking toward a nearby garage, they see a hair-covered head with eyes "as big as golf balls" peeking around the corner.[99]

- **1995 – Michigan:** Mark Marinelli is sitting by a bonfire when he hears something large on his property. Twigs and acorns begin pelting him, and he shouts, "What the fuck is this?!?" Several high-pitched, rapid voices begin repeating the phrase from the woods. That night in his tent, he is harassed by something and glimpses a dark figure. Marinelli later claims around a dozen bigfoot encounters.[100]

- **2013 – Texas:** A Jasper County hunter hears a call-and-response between what sounds like a coyote and owl before a low, gruff voice says, "Hey you!" According to BFRO investigator Brad Bacon, the area has a history of bigfoot sightings.[101]

When imitating human voices, bigfoot are commonly described as sounding low-pitched, loud, and (distastefully) "like a deaf person trying to speak."[102] These descriptions are at odds, however, with accounts of creatures sounding more like children. In autumn 2002, a Minnesota witness with recurring bigfoot encounters heard a voice like "a four-year-old child attempting to mimic words" on his property. Perhaps a juvenile bigfoot was vocalizing—after all, the witness "had the impression that he was [standing] between an adult and a child"—but only one large bigfoot was observed.[103]

As noted in *Where the Footprints End* Volume I, bigfoot screams are commonly compared to those of women and babies, raising the question whether these are imitations as well. During an expedition in September 2004 to northern New Mexico, a female BFRO investigator had her screams closely mimicked by a voice in the woods.[104] Some researchers suspect these feminine cries are an attempt to lure people into forests.

"One of the lesser known aspects of the bigfoot phenomenon is the reported ability of the creatures to mimic the distressing cries of a human baby," wrote Nick Redfern. "Almost certainly, this is done to try and lure concerned people deep into the woods."[105] (Bears, however, are capable of making sounds similar to a sobbing child as well).[106]

As discussed by Keel, disembodied baby cries occur in nearly every reported paranormal category, from hauntings to UFO sightings, and human beings are hard-wired to respond to crying children.

"The sound of a baby cry captures your attention in a way that few other sounds in the environment generally do," said Katie Young, leader of a 2012 University of Oxford study examining the effect of infant cries on human brains. Sounds of babies in distress generated more intense reactions in participants' brains when compared to other noises. The study implies humans process baby cries differently than other sounds, and "[tag them] important even before our brains have had a chance to fully process them," activating fight-or-flight instincts. Results were identical even in non-parents.[107]

If imitating infants or women is a potential lure, calling names is almost certainly a trap. A salmon surveyor near Raymond, Washington, was examining a fish habitat in April 2001 when she heard a voice from the forest. "I got out of the truck to pour myself some coffee when I heard this loud scream," she reported to the BFRO. "I heard it twice and it sounded almost like my partner was calling my name: 'Con-nie!'" The sound then devolved into animalistic cries and the noise of clacking rocks and crashing brush. After finding her partner, he confirmed he had never yelled—he was too busy examining a freshly killed deer carcass ripped in half.[108]

A North Carolina habituator told Christopher Noël that the bigfoot on her property "imitate my son, and say, 'Mom!' loudly, they can sound just like him."[109] At a Kansas farm plagued by regular bigfoot activity and sightings in 2016, the daughter of a witness came rushing to her father after hearing his voice.[110] "It was a mimic of a call in my own voice that I use to let the kids know it is safe to approach when I am out shooting in the belt," he wrote. "My daughter knew I had no intention of going hunting that day so she came running straight to me in the house to let me know what happened."[111]

At the Washington location known to researchers as "Devil's Creek"—a site yielding copious footprints, audio evidence, gift exchanges, and at least one bigfoot sighting—names shouted in the night are commonly recorded, despite the home's isolation. Audio was also captured of a deranged-sounding voice clearly calling the owners' dog, Layla, from the woods, in one instance saying, "Is there Layla?"[112]

Since dog owners must often call their pets inside, it comes as little surprise that bigfoot allegedly repeat dog names; there are ample opportunities to hear them repeated. The aforementioned Virginia witness not only heard anomalous bird calls on her property, but also "a strange voice bellowing from the barn in the woods that sounded like someone trying to copy my calling of my little dog 'Muffin.'" The voice was deep but unclear.[113]

Retired police deputy Jim Akin—discoverer of the Elkins Creek cast, arguably the best bigfoot print found east of the Mississippi—was repeatedly called out to a rural home in Pike County, Georgia, in 1994. The owner complained of something knocking on his home in the night, and ripping his barn door off its hinges. The behavior escalated when the witness's livestock and dogs disappeared.[114]

"He had a little dog he kept in the house, and he had a couple of bigger dogs that had been out in the yard," said Akin. "The bigger dogs were gone." The house dog was a Chihuahua named Peanut.

"That son-of-a-gun, he's making fun of me," the witness told Akin, assuming it was a human. "He's whispering Peanut's name through the wall."

"I said, 'What?'" Akin recalled. "'He's whispering your dog's name?'" The witness explained how someone with a low voice stood outside his bedroom window at night calling, "Peanut… Peanut…."[115]

During the dramatic "Siege of Honobia," where large, hairy hominids allegedly terrorized an Oklahoma family, witnesses regularly heard voices calling from the woods. One, Mike, told Wes Germer:

> "Wes, one time I had left for work and my brother and my dad were out there… Every night I call for my dogs, to have my dogs come in. My brother and my dad are out there, and they hear me calling for my dogs out in the woods. They hear my voice, out there calling for the dogs…" [Mike's] brother kind of felt like it was a little bit of a trap, too, to get them to come out towards the woods… it sounded just like Mike calling for his dogs.[116]

Mimicry: Explanations

The logical assumption is that bigfoot create this array of sounds with their voices. Indeed, acoustic analysis of the Sierra camp vocalizations suggests a biological origin.[117] In 1977 electrical engineer R.L. Kirlin and graduate student Lasse Hertel examined the recordings and averaged the largest creature's vocal tract length as 20.2 cm. "This is significantly longer than for a human male," and, utilizing human ratios, "gives height estimates [of the speaker] of between 6'4" and 8'2"."[118]

"The range that doctor Kirlin shows on his graph in the book *Manlike Monsters on Trial*… shows their vocal ability, pretty much… and how they compared to a human," Morehead said. "They go way above, inside, and way below what we can do, which shows me—and tells me—their vocal mechanism is much superior to ours, and they can probably have the ability to mimic just about anything."[119] These analyses provide reason to believe a primate could generate some of the more organic noises attributed to bigfoot, but pure speculation enters the discussion when trying to account for inorganic noises.

"How do they make the metallic sounds I hear?" asks Morehead, who postulates these anomalies may indicate the presence of multiple vocal cords. "If they're doing that with their vocal mechanism, they pretty much have to have more than two vocal cords... if they have several vocal cords they could maybe make these metallic sounds."[120] Currently the only land mammal known to possess an additional set of vocal folds is the koala, whose organ—while useful in producing extremely low frequencies—does not aid in mimicry.[121] In fairness, a lack of primate precedent does not rule out the possibility of multiple vocal cord sets in bigfoot, but it certainly casts doubt.

"Examples of mimicry of speech in non-human mammals are, however, vanishingly rare, probably, in part, because the vocal apparatus of other mammals differs significantly from that of humans and also because the sounds are relatively complex," wrote Laura Kelley and Susan Healy in *Current Biology*.[122] If bigfoot does indeed represent an unknown primate, perhaps this firmly places them in the "apelike human," rather than "humanlike ape" category.

Spanish cryptozoologist Jordi Magraner wrote of the *Homo neanderthalensis* vocal apparatus:

> A deeper study of Neanderthal cranial ontogenesis, substantiated by knowledge recently acquired in dentofacial orthopedics, enables us to propose an outline reconstitution of the vocal tract of the last Europeans who lived before *Homo sapiens* took their place. It shows a wide supra-laryngeal cavity and prompts us to conclude that these hominids were able to communicate over long distances, like animals, by uttering loud cries... and that they could also imitate animals. As a result, one may wonder to what extent these hominids had reached a clear mental distinction between an animal and a non-animal identity.[123]

We find no better explanation, but perhaps additional insight, at the peculiar intersection of neurology and folklore. Many cultures believe a retreat from civilization into the wilderness can feralize human beings both behaviorally and physically. Those rejecting communities to live in the bush become savage, bestial creatures covered in hair. While this belief has zero demonstrable scientific basis, there does seem to be a psychological precedent: Jumping Frenchmen Syndrome (JFS).[124]

First appearing in the 19th century among groups of lumberjacks in Maine, this disorder remains poorly understood, but manifests in an amplified startle reflex, where individuals are easily and dramatically alarmed. Other JFS symptoms include uncontrollable yelling, hitting, preternatural strength, echopraxia (mirroring the movements of others) and echolalia—vocal mimicry—all of which are found in bigfoot stories. [125]

None of this demonstrates a connection between bigfoot and this syndrome. But lumberjacks are a living embodiment of the wild man archetype, and may acquire JFS from their isolation in the wilderness, according to professors M.H. and J.M. Saint-Hilaire. Just as living in the forest was once believed to physically change men into bestial, hairy monsters, similar conditions may contribute to erratic behavior in isolated human populations—behavior reported identically in some bigfoot encounters.[126]

Unlike most behavior attributed to large, hairy hominids, bigfoot's love of vocal imitation lacks a strong archetypal antecedent; it simply does not appear to be a hallmark of wild men in myths and legends. It is, however, as noted in Volume I of *Where the Footprints End*, a common trait in poltergeist, faerie, demon, and witch folklore. The anomalous sounds "mimicked" at bigfoot sites seem to share more in common with hauntings, where anomalous noises—including "echoes" of people, machinery, and events long past—are commonly reported.

If there is a connection between the wild man archetype and bigfoot's mimicry, perhaps it lies in the former's ability to shape shift. Most of folklore's supernatural beings display the ability to literally transform their appearance into a person, animal, or inanimate object; wild men are no exception. Though there are accounts of bigfoot literally shape shifting in front of witnesses—addressed in Chapter 4—perhaps their greatest talent is the ability to *vocally* "shape shift."

Samurai Chatter

After so much discussion of uncanny imitation, it is almost quaint to suggest bigfoot use language. Just as wild men were liminal, half man, half beast creatures, bigfoot straddle a division between animal and human vocalizations.

In addition to mimicry, a number of other noises are attributed to bigfoot: growls, roars, screams, grunts, whoops, laughter, whistles, and words spoken in an unknown language. Although bigfoot whistles do share an overlap with the topic of mimicry—in one case, a habituator claimed to have taught a bigfoot to whistle *Amazing Grace* and a melody from the film *Kill Bill*[127]—non-human primates can produce all except the last of these. Ergo, since it is an anomaly among apes, language is our primary focus.

Even after eliminating all comparatively mundane vocalizations, it is still impossible to comprehensively address the topic of bigfoot speech, which could fill an entire volume. As touched upon throughout this book, Ron Morehead and Al Berry made an invaluable contribution to the topic with their recording of the infamous Sierra Sounds, which depict multiple voices speaking with a depth and rapidity that many experts believe humanly impossible. After studying the vocalizations at length and participating in fieldwork with Morehead, retired United States Navy crypto-linguist Scott Nelson is convinced of the recordings' authenticity.

"Immediately I recognized that there was language there," Nelson said, citing morphemes, phonemes, and syntax indicating intelligent communication. According to Nelson, non-human primates "don't have the apparatus to communicate with the articulations that are on the Berry-Morehead tapes."[128]

Despite the building blocks of language present in the Sierra Sounds, those who have heard these vocalizations firsthand commonly describe them as "nonsense," "gibberish," "jabber," "chatter," or "speaking backwards." One bow hunter used the term "incoherently intoxicated" to describe voices heard in Michigan.[129]

Comparisons of bigfoot vocalizations to backwards speech are prescient. A variety of medieval witch rituals, including the Black Mass, were purportedly recited backwards. In Germanic folklore, powers of sorcery were unlocked by reading a black book from the devil. "Its magical powers were released by reading it forward and backward," wrote Rosemary Ellen Guiley. "If anyone failed to read the book backward, the Devil was able to take control of him or her. Once activated, the book enabled people to acquire great wealth and do terrible things to others without punishment."[130] Given the wild man's medieval categorization as a demon, this association is unsurprising, but it is interesting to see reflected in modern reports.

Researcher, magician, and blogger Wren Collier noted that recordings of alleged sasquatch speech are reminiscent of "barbarous words," language employed in magical rituals. These speech patterns are—from a linguistic standpoint—nonsensical, yet still possess a cadence and façade of logic inherent in glossolalia (speaking in tongues).

"Some words are clearly just transliterated Hebrew, sometimes corrupted through copier error," wrote Patrick Dunn in *Magic, Power, Language, Symbol: A Magician's Exploration of Linguistics*. "But many other words are not Hebrew at all, nor any other language... More likely, these 'barbarous words' are meaningless in a strict sense... they had an inherent strangeness that made them salient and 'weird.' In some spells, the magician even claims to be speaking languages like Persian, when really he or she is reciting nonsense (from our perspective) syllables."[131]

In folklore, the tongues of both faeries and wild men were commonly unintelligible. From anthropologist Roger Bartra:

> The wild man did not have language, but took words by storm in order to express the murmurings of another world, the signals that nature gave to society. The wild man spoke words that did not have literal meaning, but were eloquent in communicating sensations that civilized language could not express. His words were devoid of sense, but expressed feelings. Spenser described this discordance between the expression of natural passions and the articulation of a rational language...[132]

In Edmund Spenser's *The Faerie Queene*, a wild man only communicates via gestures and looks, because:

> ... other language he has none, nor speach,
> But a soft murmure and confused sound
> Of senseless words, wich nature did him teach
> T'expresse his passions, wich his reason did empeach.[133]

This arcane language is also comparable to the speech of faeries, in both the Old and New Worlds. Circa 86 B.C., Roman general Sylla was returning after sacking Athens when he encountered a *satyr* (a faerie with direct ties to the wild man archetype, as discussed in Chapter 6, Volume I of *Where the Footprints End*) who "uttered nothing intelligible; his accent being harsh and inarticulate, something between the neighing of a horse and the bleating of a goat."[134]

According to Lynn King Lossiah, the *Yûñ'wĭ Tsunsdi'*, a subset of Cherokee Little People, "speak in an ancient *Tsa-la-gi* dialect. Some of the elders today can understand this strange dialect and know what they are saying. Some say it is *Elati*, a *Tsa-la-gi* language now extinct."[135]

Lossiah adds:

> The Elders say that if you stop and listen to the small voices while in the woods, the voices will sometimes come to you. They will circle all around you with their laughter and singing, their whistling and chanting. You will find them watching you from behind old stumps and rotting logs, peering out from tree branches and piles of leaves. When this happens, they are the ones who decide when and how you leave. You can't run.[136]

In his book *The Rebirth of Pan*, author Jim Brandon compares the nonsensical jabbering of the Sierra Sounds to electronic voice phenomena (EVPs) collected in ghost hunts. In these examples, disembodied voices not heard at the time of the recording are audible on playback. To underscore this comparison, Brandon cited the work of "one of the leading researchers, the Latvian psychologist Dr. Konstantin Raudive" who "lists as typical [EVP] traits (1) multilingual vocabulary, (2) stilted, often confused grammar, (3) awkward, telegram-like sentences, (4) use of many neologisms, or seemingly made up words with an otherworldly ring."[137]

Disembodied voices in forests are commonplace throughout folklore. Certain Malaysian traditions whisper of the *Orang Buni*, or "voice-folk," whose vocalizations are "said to be very similar to the human voice in distress." According to Alexander Porteous, "Tales are often told of those who under this impression have answered the call and proceeded towards the voice, but having once done so, they could not retrace their steps. The unfortunate one is lured ever farther on into the dark recesses, until at last the Voice-Folk become visible to him, and his doom is to become one of them and invisible to man, only his voice betokening his presence."[138] This sounds not only like Celtic tales of being *pixie led*, but alarmingly similar to the Kwakiutl *Buk'wus*, "who tries to tempt humans into eating ghost food and therefore becoming *Buk'wus* themselves."[139]

Occasionally witnesses liken bigfoot speech to the cadence of known languages. By far the most common comparison is Japanese, leading some to dub sasquatch speech "Samurai chatter" because of its speed and guttural quality. In the late 1980s, a sense of dread fell upon a lone hunter in Sweden Valley, Pennsylvania, just before he heard what he believed were people "talking to each other loudly. But what they said made no sense. It sounded like the Japanese language played backwards." The voices ascended 200 yards up a steep hill in around 15 seconds, and several minutes later the witness spied a seven-foot tall figure stepping behind a small cluster of trees from which it never emerged. "Keep in mind these trees were spaced about a foot apart and were maybe eight inches in diameter," he wrote. "The odd thing was you could not see any hair between the trees or movement even through my scope."[140]

Others describe the vocalizations as similar to indigenous North American languages, Chinese,[141] or Russian—in one instance, a professor hiking in the United States stumbled upon two bigfoot tearing down trees in a forest, jabbering in what he thought was "a Siberian dialect" unfamiliar to him.[142] Texas resident Zollie Owens spotted bigfoot on numerous occasions near his cornfield, and even recorded the creatures, which were described as "Hebrew or Oriental language speeded up like Donald Duck sounds."[143] Floridian witnesses found tracks in autumn 2009 near the Escambia River, having a few days earlier heard "a low, guttural vocalization that sounded almost like a Native American dialect, only in a much lower range than most people would speak in."[144]

"I have been awakened in the night and heard the Cherokee dialect being spoken outside of my home in the mountains," wrote Burnette. "Call it ghost sound or whatever from the past, but I hardly think so. Could it be that the creatures have had enough contact with the Cherokees to understand their language, and they sense me being part Cherokee and are trying to communicate with me?"[145]

Even if they cannot speak human languages, some tribal lore suggests sasquatch can at least understand them. "It's a common belief among many of the tribes in this area that if you confront a Bigfoot that you should talk to it in your native tongue, tell it to stay calm and then slowly back your way out of the area," wrote Paulides of indigenous belief in Northern California. "The Natives believe that Bigfoot understands their Hoopa language."[146]

Sasquatch language remains indecipherable, however. "I've played the tapes for—I mean, at real time and slowed them down for—everyone from colleagues who were native Japanese speakers to Persian to Russian to Native American," Nelson said. "The problem with that is that no matter who it is that's listening to it, picks up bits and pieces that they recognize as part of their own language."

Nelson attributes this to pareidolia, our natural tendency to create order out of chaotic patterns. "They might have morphemes or phonemes that sound exactly like English or Spanish or Cherokee or Persian or Russian or 'Acadian,' but there's no way we can, you know, take the language as a whole and say, 'Oh, they're speaking ancient Acadian.' That's impossible—first of all, 'Acadian' is a dead language. Nobody knows what it sounded like."[147]

With the exception of Native American dialects, witnesses compare bigfoot vocals exclusively to Asian languages. Many researchers believe bigfoot may be relict *Gigantopithecus,* a massive species of Asian ape. While *Gigantopithecus* seems a poor fit for bigfoot—it seems much larger, less mobile, and more apelike than modern reports—it is still entertaining to think large, hairy hominids with their own Asiatic language may have migrated to the Americas alongside *Homo sapiens* via the postulated Bering land bridge.

If bigfoot is capable of language, are vocalizations in English mimicry or fluency? A handful of cases suggest the latter. In the September 24, 1972 issue of *The Daily Colonist*, T.W. Patterson reported "an Indian, hunting and following a buck, came across an animal that he believed to be a big bear. To his astonishment, upon taking aim at the animal, the creature looked up and spoke to him in his own tongue." The hunter then realized he was staring down a seven-foot tall, hairy "man."[148]

Other, more specific examples:

- **1978 – Wisconsin:** Two brothers hunting near Shawano separate. One sees what he believes is a large "stump" rise up to reveal itself as a bigfoot. An intense snowstorm begins. The hunter raises his firearm but hears a voice say, "Don't shoot." He becomes paralytically "frozen in time" until his brother appears, who has been tracking the creature. Both watch the bigfoot for a time before fleeing.[149]

- **1985 – Washington:** A "bear-like animal" attacks a couple camping in the Greenwater area on July 6. The eight-foot tall creature, "ugly and smelly, with curly brown hair," speaks to them in a "high-pitched voice," asking their names and whether they have permission to camp. They respond in the affirmative, but the creature tells them to leave immediately and begins pelting them with rocks.[150]

- **1991 – California:** Two hunters leaving Jackson Demonstration State Forest hear loud screams, piquing their curiosity. Returning to their hunting site, one witness sees "a heavily hairy man" eight to nine-feet tall and approaches him at gunpoint. At 15 feet the creature makes weird noises before mouthing, "No danger" and pointing at itself. The hunter lowers his rifle and the beast walks into the trees.[151]

Bigfoot seem incredibly adept at mimicry. In an echo of European wild man tradition, this talent even extends to altering their appearance; while many flesh-and-blood cryptozoologists believe they can appear as trees, stumps, or logs (no mean feat), other, stranger accounts describe bigfoot fully transforming into other forms altogether.

Continuing these themes, the next chapter not only explores shape shifting, but also altered states of consciousness and—perhaps the most taboo cryptozoological subject of all time—sasquatch's alleged ability to telepathically "mindspeak" to witnesses.

---

[1] New Scientist staff and Press Association. (July 27, 2016). Orangutan learns to mimic human conversation for the first time. Retrieved January 16, 2019 from https://www.newscientist.com/article/2099090-orangutan-learns-to-mimic-human-conversation-for-the-first-time/?utm_source=NSNS&utm_medium=SOC&utm_campaign=hoot&cmpid=SOC%7CNSNS%7C2016-GLOBAL-hoot

[2] Redfern, N. (2016). *The Bigfoot Book: The Encyclopedia of Sasquatch, Yeti and Cryptid Primates.* Canton, MI: Visible Ink Press.

[3] Forth, G. (2008). *Images of the Wildman in Southeast Asia: An Anthropological Perspective.* Abingdon, UK: Routledge.

[4] Eberhart, G.M. (2002). *Mysterious Creatures: A Guide to Cryptozoology.* Santa Barbara, CA: ABC-CLIO, Inc.

[5] Bord, J., & Bord, C. (1989). *Unexplained Mysteries of the 20th Century.* Lincolnwood, IL: Contemporary Books.

[6] Rivera, E. (n.d.). Case 19. In A. Rosales (Ed.), *1948 Humanoid Sighting Reports.* Retrieved February 5, 2014 from http://www.ufoinfo.com/humanoid/humanoid-1948.pdf

[7] Short, B. (n.d.). The De Facto Sasquatch. Retrieved January 18, 2019 from https://static1.squarespace.com/static/596c0bae4c0dbfa1d26e86be/t/5b9bff06562fa7cfcdf1bfc8/1536950038606/The+de+facto+Sasquatch+premier+installment.pdf?fbclid=IwAR3763B1leKUEQofPRbPvzAItNH5K-RUVoKU-vOLW_iXvSTkdKSg4o4xBXw

[8] Courtney, S. (December 10, 2006). Vocal Mimicry. Retrieved January 16, 2019 from https://stancourtney.com/vocal-mimicry/

[9] Yurth, C. (January 26, 2012). Bigfoot's stomping grounds: There's more to Upper Fruitland than Northern Edge casino. Retrieved January 16, 2019 from http://navajotimes.com/entertainment/2012/0112/012612bigfoot.php

[10] Sherman, J. (May 31, 2015). Ongoing activity and possible vocalizations recorded near Detroit Metro Airport. Retrieved January 16, 2019 from http://www.bfro.net/gdb/show_report.asp?ID=48824&PrinterFriendly=True

[11] Ackermann, A.M. (August 19, 2015). Hoots, Crows, and Whistles: Criminals Using Animals Calls as Secret Signals. Retrieved January 18, 2019 from https://www.annmarieackermann.com/animal-calls-as-secret-signals/

[12] Prince-Hughes, D. (1997). *The Archetype of the Ape-Man: The Phenomenological Archaeology of a Relic Hominid Ancestor.* USA: Dissertation.com

[13] Paulides, D. (2009). *Tribal Bigfoot.* Blaine, WA: Hancock House.

[14] Ibid.

[15] Noël, C. (2009). *Impossible Visits: The Inside Story of Interactions with Sasquatch at Habituation Sites.* Bloomington, IN: Xlibris Corporation.

[16] Teal [screen name]. Wood knocks. Retrieved January 16, 2019 from https://sasquatchchronicles.com/topic/wood-knocks/

[17] Alley, J.R. (2007). *Raincoast Sasquatch.* Blaine, WA: Hancock House. (Original work published 2003)

[18] Sherman, J. (February 3, 2012). Farmers record interesting vocalizations west of Clare. Retrieved January 16, 2019 from http://www.bfro.net/GDB/show_report.asp?ID=32981&PrinterFriendly=True

[19] Germer, W. (October 21, 2017). Sasquatch Chronicles Radio // SC EP: 371 Sasquatch Language? Retrieved January 16, 2019 from https://sasquatchchronicles.com/sc-ep371-sasquatch-language/

[20] Germer, W. (November 22, 2017). Tomorrow Night's Show: Sighting Of Bizarre Animal. Retrieved January 16, 2019 from https://sasquatchchronicles.com/strange-sighting-of-bizarre-animal-last-night-in-georgia/

[21] Cryptozoology News. (n.d.). Researchers Encounter 'Bigfoot' in Missouri, say it Made Donkey Sounds. Retrieved January 16, 2019 from http://cryptozoologynews.com/researchers-encounter-bigfoot-in-missouri-say-made-donkey-sounds/

[22] Paulides 2009.

[23] Germer, W. (February 8, 2016). A large hairy creature stood up and ran. Retrieved January 16, 2019 from https://sasquatchchronicles.com/a-large-hairy-creature-stood-up-and-ran/

[24] Germer, W. (March 15, 2017). Tonight's Show: Nothing can prepare you to see it. Retrieved January 16, 2019 from https://sasquatchchronicles.com/nothing-can-prepare-you-to-see-it/

[25] The Bigfoot Field Researchers Organization. (July 19, 2004). Campers driven off mountain by unseen intruders. Retrieved January 16, 2019 from https://www.bfro.net/GDB/show_report.asp?ID=9018&PrinterFriendly=True

[26] Courtney, S. (October 21, 2002). Loud calls, rock/boulder throwing disturbs campers. Retrieved January 16, 2019 from http://bfro.net/GDB/show_report.asp?id=5123

[27] Courtney December 10, 2006.

[28] Bigfoot Evidence. (September 7, 2013). Today I Learned That Bigfoots Are Best Friends With Coyotes. Retrieved January 16, 2019 from http://bigfootevidence.blogspot.com/2013/09/today-i-learned-that-bigfoots-are-best.html

[29] Burnette, T., & Riggs, R. (2014). *Bigfoot: Exploring the Myth and Discovering the Truth.* Woodbury, MN: Llewllyn Publications.

[30] Krantz, G. (1992). *Big Footprints.* Boulder, CO: Johnson Books.

[31] Burnette & Riggs 2014.

[32] Rick. (July 3, 2013). Earliest documented Bigfoot Sighting in Pacific Northwest. Retrieved January 8, 2019 from http://hamell.net/earliest-documented-bigfoot-sighting-in-pacific-northwest/

[33] Short n.d.

[34] Ibid.

[35] Eberhart 2002.

[36] Ibid.

[37] Ibid.

[38] Bayanov, D. (2011). *Bigfoot Research: The Russian Vision.* C.L. Murphy (Ed.). Blaine, WA: Hancock House Publishers.

[39] Godfrey, L.S. (2016). *Monsters Among Us: An Exploration of Otherworldly Bigfoots, Wolfmen, Portals, Phantoms, and Odd Phenomena.* New York, NY: Tarcher Penguin.

[40] Powell, T. (2003). *The Locals.* Surrey, CA: Hancock House Publishers Ltd.

[41] MacDougall, J. (1910). *Folk Tales and Fairy Lore in Gaelic and English.* G. Calder (Ed.). Edinburgh, UK: John Grant.

[42] Noël, C. (2014). *Our Life with Bigfoot: Knowing Our Next of Kin at Habituation Sites* [Kindle edition]. US: CreateSpace Independent Publishing Platform.

[43] Taylor, S. (September 27, 2010). Couple hear strange vocalization at their cabin near Carson. Retrieved January 18, 2019 from http://www.bfro.net/GDB/show_report.asp?id=28307

[44] Taylor, A.P. (August 6, 2015). Why Do Parrots Talk? Retrieved January 21, 2019 from https://www.audubon.org/news/why-do-parrots-talk

[45] Germer, W. (December 4, 2016). Strange vocals captured. Retrieved January 18, 2019 from https://sasquatchchronicles.com/strange-vocals-captured/

[46] Parsons, E.C. (1925). "Micmac Folklore." *Journal of American Folklore 38*(55), pp. 55-113.

[47] Germer October 21, 2017.

[48] Cryptozoology News. (n.d.). Alabama Minister Captures 'Baby Bigfoot' Sounds. Retrieved January 18, 2019 from http://cryptozoologynews.com/minister-captures-baby-bigfoot-sounds/

[49] Charles R [screen name]. (December 28, 2016). North Florida Howl. Retrieved January 18, 2019 from https://sasquatchchronicles.com/north-florida-howl/

[50] Courtney December 10, 2006.

[51] Thompson, L. (1991). *To the American Indian: Reminiscences of a Yurok Woman*. Berkeley, CA: Heyday Books.

[52] Roth, J. E. (1997). *American Elves: An Encyclopedia of Little People from the Lore of 380 Ethnic Groups of the Western Hemisphere*. Jefferson, NC: McFarland & Company, Inc.

[53] Porteous, A. (1928). *The Forest in Folklore and Mythology*. New York, NY: The Macmillan Company.

[54] Beck, D.L. (December 12, 2004). On the trail of Bigfoot in Santa Cruz Mountains: Museum Focuses On Sightings Of Sasquatch. Retrieved January 18, 2019 from http://www.bfro.net/GDB/show_article.asp?id=433

[55] Germer, W. (April 6, 2017). Then it proceeded to urinate on our campfire. Retrieved January 18, 2019 from https://sasquatchchronicles.com/then-it-proceeded-to-urinate-on-our-campfire/

[56] Higgins, A. (March 19, 2002). Wooded, rural, lake house scene of late night encounter. Retrieved January 18, 2019 from http://woodape.org/reports/report/detail/391

⁵⁷ Ackermann 2015.

⁵⁸ Clelland, M. (2015). *The Messengers: Owls, Synchronicity and the UFO Abductee*. New York: Richard Dolan Press.

⁵⁹ Russell, J. B. (1972). *Witchcraft in the Middle Ages*. Ithaca, NY: Cornell University Press.

⁶⁰ Clelland 2015.

⁶¹ Clelland, M. (2018). *Stories from the Messengers: Owls, UFOs and a Deeper Reality*. New York: Richard Dolan Press.

⁶² Ibid.

⁶³ Ibid.

⁶⁴ Ibid.

⁶⁵ Ibid.

⁶⁶ Marzluff, J.M., & Angell, T. (2007). *In the Company of Crows and Ravens*. New Haven, CT: Yale University Press.

⁶⁷ Hansen, G.P. (2001). *The Trickster and the Paranormal*. Bloomington, IN: Xlibris Corporation.

⁶⁸ Bahr, E. (1972). Papageno: The Unenlighted Wild Man in Eighteenth-Century Germany. In E. Dudley & M.E. Novak (Eds.), *The Wild Man Within: An Image in Western Thought from the Renaissance to Romanticism* (pp. 249-258). Pittsburgh, PA: University of Pittsburgh Press.

⁶⁹ Janson, H.W. (1952). *Apes and Ape Lore in the Middle Ages and the Renaissance*. London, UK: The Warburg Institute – University of London.

⁷⁰ Short n.d.

[71] Riggs, R. (2001). *In the Big Thicket, On the Trail of the Wildman.* New York, NY: Paraview Press.

[72] Germer October 21, 2017.

[73] Nunnelly, B.M. (2011). *The Inhumanoids: Real Encounters with Beings That Can't Exist.* Woolsery, UK: CFZ Press.

[74] Ibid..

[75] Eberhart 2002.

[76] Alley 2007.

[77] Burnette & Riggs 2014.

[78] Amy H [screen name]. (October 31, 2018). Siren in the Woods. Retrieved January 23, 2019 from https://sasquatchchronicles.com/topic/siren-in-the-woods/

[79] Slate, B.A. & Berry, A. (1976). *Bigfoot.* New York, NY: Bantam.

[80] Germer October 21, 2017.

[81] Ibid.

[82] Noël 2014.

[83] Paulides 2009.

[84] Ibid.

[85] Germer October 21, 2017.

[86] Ibid.

[87] Keel, J. (1972). Medical Aspects of Non-Events. *Anomaly* 8, pp. 139-142, 145.

[88] Bayanov 2011.

[89] Ibid.

[90] Ibid.

[91] Ibid.

[92] Young, W. (2014). *The Fascination of Birds*. Mineola, NY: Dover Publications, Inc.

[93] Taylor, H. (February 2, 2014). Lyrebirds mimicking chainsaws: fact or lie? Retrieved January 23, 2019 from http://theconversation.com/lyrebirds-mimicking-chainsaws-fact-or-lie-22529

[94] Moneymaker, M. (June 30, 1992). An Interview with a San Diego Sheriff's Sergeant Regarding a Series of Incidents after the Laguna Fire of 1970. Retrieved January 23, 2019 from http://www.bfro.net/gdb/show_report.asp?id=2782

[95] Ibid.

[96] Ibid.

[97] Clark, J. & Coleman, L. (January 1973). Anthropoids, Monsters and UFOs. *Flying Saucer Review 19*(1), pp. 18-23.

[98] Pilichis, D. (1982). *Night Siege: The Northern Ohio UFO Creature Invasion*. Rome, OH: Dennis Pilichis.

[99] Santiago, F. (August 6, 1978). Town has Hairy Time with "Monster." Retrieved January 23, 2019 from https://www.bfro.net/GDB/show_article.asp?id=57

[100] Cundiff, V. (November 7, 2016). Bigfoot Eyewitness Episode 12. Retrieved January 23, 2019 from http://bigfooteyewitnessradio.libsyn.com/bigfoot-eyewitness-episode-12

[101] Bacon, B. (November 5, 2013). Hunter's possible encounter near Kirbyville. Retrieved January 23, 2019 from http://www.bfro.net/GDB/show_report.asp?id=42473

[102] Germer, W. (May 24, 2016). High-pitched voice theory – Neanderthal. Retrieved January 25, 2019 from https://sasquatchchronicles.com/high-pitched-voice-theory-neanderthal/

[103] P., A. (May 24, 2002). Two witnesses have a daylight encounter in their camp near Spring Valley. Retrieved January 25, 2019 from http://www.bfro.net/GDB/show_report.asp?id=4379

[104] Si, M., Moskowitz, K., Higgins, A., & Moneymaker, M. (2004). The Northern New Mexico Report. Retrieved January 23, 2019 from https://www.bfro.net/news/roundup/expNM2004_report.asp

[105] Redfern, N. (October 24, 2017). Bigfoot: A Deadly Mimic? Retrieved January 23, 2019 from https://mysteriousuniverse.org/2017/10/bigfoot-a-deadly-mimic/

[106] Alley 2007.

[107] Jha, A (October 17, 2012). Why Crying Babies are So Hard to Ignore. Retrieved January 23, 2019 from https://www.theguardian.com/science/2012/oct/17/crying-babies-hard-ignore

[108] Brandenburg, K. (June 28, 2011). Salmon surveyor has unusual experience near confluence of Fall River and Boss Creek. Retrieved January 23, 2019 from http://bfro.net/GDB/show_report.asp?id=29700

[109] Noël 2014

[110] Paul A [screen name]. Activity Update 2 Years Later. Retrieved January 23, 2019 from https://sasquatchchronicles.com/topic/activity-update-2-years-later/

[111] Ibid.

[112] Renner, T. (September 3, 2018). Strange Familiars Episode 45: A Dip in Devil's Creek. Retrieved January 23, 2019 from https://www.strangefamiliars.com/e/episode-45-a-dip-in-devils-creek/

[113] Powell 2003.

[114] Germer, W. (November 15, 2015). Sasquatch Chronicles Radio // SC EP: 165 Calling 911 and reporting a Sasquatch. Retrieved January 23, 2019 from https://sasquatchchronicles.com/sc-ep164-calling-911-and-reporting-a-sasquatch/

[115] Ibid.

[116] Germer, W. (February 22, 2017). Sasquatch Chronicles Radio // SC EP: 11 The 'Siege' at Honobia. Retrieved January 23, 2019 from https://sasquatchchronicles.com/sc-ep11-the-siege-at-honobia/

[117] Berry, A. (1998). The Bigfoot Recordings [CD and cassette]. Mariposa, CA: Sierra Sounds.

[118] Kirlin, R.L. & Hertel, L. (1980). Estimates of Pitch and Vocal Tract Length from Recorded Vocalizations of Purported Bigfoot. In M.M Halpin & M.M. Ames (Eds.), *Manlike Monsters on Trial* (pp. 274-290). Vancouver, BC: The University of British Columbia.

[119] Germer October 21, 2017.

[120] Ibid.

[121] Cell Press. (December 2, 2013). Koalas' low-pitched voice explained by unique organ. Retrieved January 24, 2019 from https://www.sciencedaily.com/releases/2013/12/131202121445.htm

[122] Kelley, L.A., & Healy, S.D. (January 11, 2011). Vocal Mimicry. In *Current Biology 21*(1), pp. 9-10.

[123] Magraner, J. (n.d.). Oral Statements Concerning Living Unknown Hominids: Analysis, Criticism, and Implications for Language Origins. Retrieved January 24, 2019 from http://www.bigfootencounters.com/biology/jordi.htm

[124] Renner, T. (January 17, 2019). Strange Familiars Episode 65: The Jumping Frenchmen. Retrieved January 24, 2019 from https://www.strangefamiliars.com/e/episode-65-the-jumping-frenchmen/

[125] Saint-Hilaire, M.H., Saint-Hilaire, J.M., & Granger, L. (September 1986). Jumping Frenchmen of Maine. *Neurology 36*(9), pp. 1269-1271.

[126] Ibid.

[127] Noël 2014

[128] Germer October 21, 2017.

[129] Sherman, J. (June 4, 2012). Bow hunter remembers possible intimidation behavior near Grand Rapids. Retreived January 25, 2019 from http://www.bfro.net/gdb/show_report.asp?id=35671

[130] Guiley, R.E. (2009). *The Encyclopedia of Demons & Demonology.* New York, NY: Facts on File, Inc.

[131] Dunn, P. (2008). *Magic, Power, Language, Symbol: A Magician's Exploration of Linguistics.* Woodbury, MN: Llewllyn Publications.

[132] Bartra, R. (1994). *Wild Men in the Looking Glass.* (C.T. Berrisford, Trans.). Ann Arbor, MI: University of Michigan Press.

[133] Bernheimer, R. (1970). *Wild Men in the Middle Ages: A Study in Art, Sentiment, and Demonology.* New York, NY: Octagon Books. (Original work published 1952)

[134] Bayanov 2011.

[135] Lossiah, L.K. (1998). *The Secrets and Mysteries of the Cherokee Little People.* Cherokee, NC: Cherokee Publications.

[136] Ibid.

[137] Brandon, J. (1983). *The Rebirth of Pan: Hidden Faces of the American Earth Spirit.* Dunlap, IL: Firebird Press.

[138] Porteous 1928.

[139] Native Languages of the Americas. (2015). Native Languages of the Americas: Kwakiutl Indian Legends (Kwakwaka'wakw). Retrieved January 31, 2019 from http://www.native-languages.org/kwakiutl-legends.htm

[140] Betz, C. (July 30, 2008). Man remembers hearing strange vocalizations and seeing a hairy, upright figure while hunting in Sweden Valley. Retrieved January 25, 2019 from http://www.bfro.net/GDB/show_report.asp?id=24301

[141] Noël 2014

[142] Azkath, S. (December 22, 2018). Bigfoot: Terror in the Woods. Retrieved January 25, 2019 from https://www.wheredidtheroadgo.com/show-archive/2018/item/565-bigfoot-terror-in-the-woods-dec-22-2018

[143] Barnett, J. (1978). Flying Saucers and Bigfoot are Related! *UFO Review 1(1)*, pp. 6-8.

[144] Smykal, K. (November 30, 2009). Hunter and daughter hear chatter and find possible tracks near Escambia River. Retrieved January 25, 2019 from http://www.bfro.net/gdb/show_report.asp?id=26947

[145] Burnette & Riggs 2014.

[146] Paulides, D. (2008). *The Hoopa Project: Bigfoot Encounters in California.* Blaine, WA: Hancock House.

[147] Germer October 21, 2017.

[148] Bayanov 2011

[149] Lapseritis, J. (1998). *The Psychic Sasquatch.* Mill Spring, NC: Wild Flower Press.

[150] Bord & Bord 1989.

[151] Strickler, L. (October 1, 2018). Sasquatch Speak… 'No Danger.' Retrieved January 25, 2019 from https://www.phantomsandmonsters.com/2018/10/sasquatch-speaksno-danger.html

JESSUP: If I come out of that tank anthropoid, I'll be in a very primitive state, and impossible to relate to, so sedate me while I'm still in the tank... otherwise you'll have to chase me around and subdue me.

PARRISH: Okay... (I'll tell you this, if he comes out of that tank looking like an ape, I'm going straight over to Mass Mental to commit myself.)

- Altered States *(1980)*

4 Altered States

"Modern technological society idealises and is monopolistically focused on only one state of consciousness—the alert, problem-solving state of consciousness that makes us efficient producers and consumers of material goods and services," wrote journalist and alternative historian Graham Hancock. "At the same time our society seeks to police and control a wide range of other 'altered' states of consciousness on the basis of the unproven proposition that consciousness is generated by the brain."[1]

When mankind first began pondering our role in the universe, we sought contact with the Otherworld. Sometimes this unknown country bled unbidden into our reality; other times, we yearned to seek it out ourselves. For that reason, *Homo sapiens* began experimenting with ways to alter our consciousness, to access dreamland without slumber.

It is a destination accessible by many paths. Some of us arrive passively through sleep. Spiritual traditions, particularly in the east, refined the art of meditation, a slow climb to the mountaintop of spirituality. In shamanistic cultures *entheogens*, psychedelic substances, were employed to "release the inner god," granting access to the spirit world. These medicines come in a variety of forms: *psilocybin* mushrooms, *ayahuasca*, peyote, *Amanita muscaria* (fly agaric), iboga, etc.

The theory that altered states of consciousness may serve as a vector for nonhuman contact has become quite popular in most Fortean disciplines (Ufology, faerie studies, parapsychology, etc.) in the past few decades, but has been practically ignored by cryptozoologists. This was understandable in an era where psychedelics were taboo, but recent research supports such substances have profound medical and psychological value.[2]

Unfortunately—even in the face of overwhelming research by institutions as prestigious as Johns Hopkins University—some still dismiss these substances as harmful "drugs." They are unable, or perhaps unwilling, to abandon the unscientific and unseemly connotations drilled into western culture for the past century. While it is true psychedelics may be abused, they can also be extremely useful, and modern society has ignored their benefits at its peril. They also represent a truly untamed frontier.

"You know, people tend to complain there's no adventure left in the world, the world is devoid of challenge," said lecturer and psychonaut Terence McKenna. "I say to you: five grams [of dried *psilocybin mushrooms*] in silent darkness in the confines of your own apartment on a rainy Sunday evening and you'll feel that Ferdinand Magellan should take a back seat."[3]

Psychedelics may represent a separate reality, normally inaccessible from our own but no less objectively genuine. It is widely believed Francis Crick discovered the double-helix structure of DNA under the influence of lysergic acid diethylamide (LSD);[4] while that may not be entirely accurate, fellow Nobel Prize winner Kary Mullis wholeheartedly believes revelations while taking "acid" allowed him to develop the polymerase chain reaction method, by which DNA is copied in laboratories.[5] Anecdotes abound of visions shared between separate psychonauts, experiences which, according to the current Materialist model —the dominant philosophical doctrine of science, wherein matter is the fundamental constant of reality and all other phenomena, including human consciousness itself, are illusory byproducts of matter—should be entirely subjective and internal. Those in altered states sometimes even learn information they should not be able to access: in a famous story from anthropologist Kenneth Kensinger, six Amazonian *ayahuasca* drinkers informed him his grandmother had died—two days before he received the news via radio.[6]

This is not to say every psychedelic trip is a revelation, or every vision is true. Some are meaningless. Still—given the possibility that experiences during altered states of consciousness may have an external reality—what are we to make of reports where entities are encountered under the influence of psychedelics?

New Mexico School of Medicine professor Rick Strassman

obtained multiple such accounts in laboratory sessions using N, N-dimethyltryptamine (DMT), a psychoactive substance contained within the human body. In his experiments, many of Strassman's subjects reported beings similar to angels, faeries, and Grey aliens, leading some researchers to suggest DMT might function as a way for humans to interact with beings from other realities.[7]

Though none of Strassman's subjects reported interactions with large, hairy hominids under the influence of DMT, other substances can produce similar visions. Canadian researcher Robert Milner collected an account where bigfoot was seen under the influence of *psilocybin* mushrooms.[8] Psychonaut Jon Hanna has seen a number of entities during his varied experiences; on ketamine, a medication used in anesthesia and depression treatment, Hanna encountered "a pygmy shaman, proto-human ape-like creatures, and some tentacled cephalopods."[9]

In his book, *Where Bigfoot Walks: Crossing the Dark Divide*, Robert Michael Pyle muses on *Sehlatiks*, bigfoot of the Yakama:

> Various cultures have employed the alkaloids of the *Amanita muscaria* mushroom—toxic, but highly mind-altering if you survive ingestion—in shamanic or religious rituals. Mythologist Robert Graves suggests that Greek *Satyrs* and *Centaurs* were inspired by pantheistic or Dionysian humans who ingested *A. muscaria* to enhance their sybaritic lifestyle with heightened sensations, strength, and sexual powers. I don't know whether the fly agaric was used by Cascades Indians, but if it gave a connection to Pan, why not to *Sehlatiks*?[10]

Singing, Infrasound, and Altered States of Consciousness

Bigfoot singing and infrasound have already been covered in *Where the Footprints End* Volume I, Chapters 3 & 4 vis-à-vis their relationship to faeries and witness paralysis. What follows is an elaboration upon those ideas, and how they might actually facilitate altered states of consciousness.

Referring to Berry's description of singing at the Sierra site, we find comparisons to "a chant" from "a Japanese monastery" that "welled out of the gut" and "droned on and on," comprised of "umms, ahhs, and ohs." This is surprisingly congruent with overtone singing, wherein a singer establishes a stable fundamental pitch and the vocal cords are manipulated to produce additional pitches above the drone. The Mongolian/Siberian variant of this is known as Tuvan throat singing, although the technique is used in a variety of cultures. Overtone singing is practiced in Tibetan Buddhism and, until 1976, was practiced among Japan's Ainu.[11] While the human vocal apparatus is obviously capable of overtone singing, the technique would be much easier, and perhaps more elaborate, with additional vocal cords, an aspect of bigfoot physiology proposed by some researchers.

On Episode 29 of the *Strange Familiars* podcast, Timothy Renner captured what sounds uncannily like overtone singing during an interview with a bigfoot witness at his encounter site. "To me it sounds like something or someone moaning, or doing like a Tuvan throat singing, or something in the background," Renner said. "I don't know what this was, and I didn't notice it while we were there."[12]

Constant, uninterrupted drones are found in indigenous music worldwide, often used to induce altered states of consciousness and contact the spirit world.[13] Some Australian aboriginal cultures believe the didgeridoo (a tubular wind instrument perhaps predating all other musical instruments) allows them to access "the dream time," the Otherworld. The sound of a didgeridoo is very similar to overtone singing: the player's buzzing lips create a drone, over which additional pitches are hummed or sung with their vocal cords.[14]

One witness was on an overnight expedition with several bigfoot researchers near the Klamath River when his seven-year old son broke off from the group. Rushing to follow, the witness watched in horror as his son froze and collapsed, almost as if having a seizure. The boy's eyes were glazed over when his father, now at his side, noticed a sensation of nausea and a loss of focus. There was a sound—almost felt, more than heard—coming from the tree line.[15]

"The closest thing I could compare it to… it's an instrument played by the Australian aborigines," the witness said. "It's called a didgeridoo. It makes a very, very weird, distinct sound." The witness then noticed a dark, hairy figure 15 yards away in the forest: the "shoulders and the head of a very, very large person." With "every ounce of concentration and focus," the witness discharged his firearm into the air then into the creature's knee. As howls filled the forest, the witness immediately evacuated to the hospital, where he claimed his son suffered a bear attack. The boy recovered quickly, but remained traumatized.[16]

Witnesses believed the boy's seizure was caused by infrasound. But are researchers conflating the physiological effects of infrasound with altered states of consciousness? Recall the experience of researcher Scott

Carpenter (see Chapter 4, Volume I of *Where the Footprints End*), who, when he finally saw a bigfoot, was compelled to nonchalantly walk away —almost certainly an altered state of mind.

"The Sasquatch's ability to hypnotize and change forms in order to trick people tends to be a recurring theme in many Native legends," wrote Bobbie Short.[17] Like so many anomalies associated with bigfoot, the notion of large, hairy hominids possessing the power to induce altered states enjoys strong precedent in Native American lore. Tribes of the Puget Sound expressly equated the effects of hypnosis with what modern researchers would call infrasound, claiming the *Seeahtik* "kill their game entirely by hypnotism."[18] The Salish believed giant Stick Indians, the *Tsiatko*, played pranks on humans "such as removing their clothes and tying their legs apart... made possible by a sort of hypnotic helplessness engendered by the sound of the giants' whistle."[19] In Quinault legend, the giant *Glue-keek* possessed powers of hypnotism,[20] as did the *Nakani* of the American northeast.[21]

A Spokane informant told anthropologist Ed Fusch:

> [He] reported having ascended a hill in the early hours of the morning as it was just beginning to become daylight. He was immediately aware of a strong *S'cwene'y'ti* odor and saw a shadow, as of a huge man, a short distance away. He remembers absolutely nothing that occurred the rest of the day. When awareness returned, it was late afternoon and he found himself walking back down the same trail and route that he had gone up that morning. He believes that he had been under a sort of hypnosis.[22]

This anecdote finds resonance with notions of missing time (UFO experiencers, faerie witnesses, and psychonauts all regularly report time dilation as well). Hairy hominids elsewhere in the world, like Central Asia's *Gul* and Siberia's *Kheyak*, allegedly posses similar hypnotic abilities, as do a variety of other cryptids... to say nothing of faeries, witches, and demons.[23] Indeed, researcher Dmitri Bayanov draws comparisons between large, hairy hominids and the *domovoy*, a Russian faerie who, according to lexicographer Vladimir Dahl, "can be seen on Good Sunday's night in the cattle-shed; he is shaggy, but nothing else can be remembered because he knocks out memory."[24]

Many psychedelic experiences (and, by extension, altered states of consciousness) are preceded by a strong, overpowering buzzing noise, often compared to a swarm of bees or hornets. While profound silences are commonly reported before sightings, alien, faerie, and bigfoot witnesses also report similar humming sounds. Late alien abduction researcher John Mack found that "an odd buzzing or humming sound" indicated "an abduction [was] about to occur" among his subjects.[25] The famous faerie abduction of Anne Jeffries was accompanied by a sound "as if a thousand flies were buzzing around her" (refer to Chapter 3, Volume I of *Where the Footprints End*).[26] Moreover, buzzing noises are regularly reported in Marian apparitions,[27] out-of-body experiences, and near-death experiences (OBEs and NDEs).[28]

A Norwegian folktale describes a young adventurer overnighting in the forest who, during a rainstorm, encountered a curious set of anomalies: "a hollow, metallic sound, like the croaking of the frog and a penetrating whistling and piping" and "a buzzing sound, as if from a hundred spinning wheels." Fearing faeries, the boy ran, hearing "the heavy tread of some one [sic], who moved over the crackling branches of the underwood." The source was "a dark shape, which approached... with a pair of eyes shining like glowing stars." Calling out, he received a growl in response-interpreted as coming from a "bear."[29]

Late bigfoot researcher Rob Riggs noted a trend of "strange humming sounds frequently heard in ghost light and wild man sightings."[30] One researcher was "bigfoot scouting" in Washington when he "heard a weird sound like a large bumblebee or fly" darting around his head, though nothing was visible.[31] A handful of varying stories feature similar sounds:

- **1934 – Canada:** Mrs. James Caufield of Harrison, British Columbia hears "a buzzing sound similar to that made by a humming bird" while washing clothes in the river. Turning, she sees "a big man covered with hair from head to foot" and hides her eyes, for fear of bigfoot's alleged hypnotism. She screams and faints, but her cries draw her husband near. The creature flees.[32]

- **1976 – Washington:** A 14-year old Pierce county witness is retrieving clay pigeons when a bigfoot over eight feet tall rises from behind a tree. He simultaneously experiences tunnel vision, time dilation, paralysis, and a "buzzing feeling" in his head as they lock eyes. He turns to run and never sees the creature again.[33]

- **1977 – Colorado:** A rancher sees a landed flying saucer and two fair, blond-haired people in tight fitting, color-changing suits. Nearby, a box sits on the ground, buzzing. Suddenly, a bigfoot appears and walks toward the box, which changes tone. The creature falls to the ground and the witness returns home posthaste.[34]

- **1981 – Washington:** A witness sleeping over at a friend's house awakens "to the sound of a loud grumbling/humming type noise, hard to describe and unlike anything I had ever heard before." Looking out the window—which sits seven to eight feet off the ground—he sees a figure cupping its hand as if trying to peer in. The witness is unable to rouse his friend, but after a time the shape leaves, resuming its "deep singsong type humming sound."[35]

"All of a sudden he was feeling like there was this buzzing sound of, like, bees, you know, and it was lulling him into almost a trance," said researcher Brenton Sawin of an Oklahoma witness who had seen bigfoot near his property. "As soon as he recognized it and shook his head and started to ask, 'Do you hear that?' something roared at him, and he said this roar shook him to the core." The witness grabbed his little brother and took off for the house, but another friend several yards ahead of them claimed to never hear the vocalizations.[36]

If altered states of consciousness play a role in bigfoot sightings, sound could be one of several possible vectors for initiating interaction. After all, a buzz could easily be described as a drone, or vice versa.

Smells may also initiate altered states of consciousness. In 1995, a fisherman in Fresno County, California flagged down a compatriot, drawing his attention to an eight-foot tall, reddish-haired creature on a hill. The sighting was accompanied by an overpowering, "wet, moldy, animal musk."[37]

"I tried to follow it, but again I felt an almost hypnotic sensation overtake me, and my partner later told me he felt the same way," the fisherman later wrote. "I couldn't move, we watched it go right up to the top [of the hill] and over it.... I felt very overwhelmed...." The witness said the odor made him feel "almost hypnotized or drugged," and retained profound emotions from the event that caused him to cry whenever he remembered the sighting—not unlike the strong psychological breakthroughs experienced in some psychedelic trips.[38]

The idea that smells could create altered states of consciousness is central to the thesis presented in my book *The Brimstone Deceit*, which examines all variety of smells attributed to large, hairy hominids. Notably, hydrogen sulfide—the characteristic "rotten egg" odor found in so many paranormal encounters, including bigfoot sightings—can produce a state of suspended animation in mammals.[39]

A handful of hypotheses spring to mind, all fantastical but, as thought experiments, quite parsimonious. Perhaps flesh-and-blood bigfoot have harnessed these powers of hypnosis, and all of their supernatural behavior (disappearing, invulnerability to bullets, phasing) is merely illusory. More skeptically, perhaps these altered states of consciousness are induced by natural environmental factors, causing a shared set of consistent-yet-artificial hallucinations (i.e. enormous wild men) among witnesses.

Or... perhaps an inhuman Other, wishing to interact in this reality, lures witnesses into an altered state of consciousness. This Other may be physical, interdimensional, spiritual, or something in-between; the large, hairy wild men seen by witnesses may be its true face, or one of a dozen masks, interchanged with faeries, aliens, witches, and ghosts.

Mindspeak

As noted, altered states can also be induced via meditation. Jim Mangano, a 17-year old witness, was hiking in the Angeles National Forest with six friends in October 1974 when he sought a quiet spot to gather his thoughts. He found a large rock by a stream and sat down. After a while, he found himself in a deep trance, and remained at the rock for an hour before returning to the campfire.

"I was like in a blank trance," Mangano later said. "I couldn't pull myself out of it. I kept waiting... for something to enter my mind... waiting for *something* which I couldn't figure out." He found himself drawn back to the rock, but the once serene forest now felt "weird." This second visit only lasted 15 minutes, he believed, but a friend at camp told him he had been absent for two hours.

Unnerved, Mangano tried to sleep, but the evening was punctuated by five screams "like a kid was being murdered." In the morning, a single, three-toed footprint 19 inches long was discovered by the large rock.

Some time later, Mangano revisited the site, this time in the company of bigfoot researchers who monitored his meditation. After a time, he said, "They... want me to come to them." Mangano insisted "they" wished for him to come alone, but the researchers refused, and everyone turned in for the night. Screams and a dangerous shower of stones from a nearby cliff rendered sleep impossible.

On January 15, 1975, Dr. Robert Jordan hypnotically regressed Mangano to recall his initial encounter. Memories surfaced of a large, dark brown figure approaching Mangano while he meditated, placing a warm and "powerful" hand on his shoulder. Using its eyes, the mysterious being communicated its purpose for contacting Mangano. "He called me with his mind to help him get out," he murmured. "The hunters... people keep him in." The session concluded with a vision of "a bunch of them standing, looking down on me. I must be sitting on the ground."⁴⁰

Mangano clearly described receiving telepathic messages from bigfoot, a phenomenon most commonly known as "mindspeak." While the concept has been co-opted by the New Age movement, even rational, grounded witnesses report the phenomenon. For many researchers, this concept is a proverbial line in the sand: paranormally-inclined researchers feel it is disingenuous to ignore such reports, while flesh-and-blood hypothesis (F&BH) advocates think the very concept is nonsense.

"Science is the anchor which holds the *S.S. Cryptozoology* in place in the midst of the storms created by the wannabelievers," wrote John Kirk. "All cryptids are, of necessity and factuality, biological entities. There is not one shred of evidence to the contrary. They don't communicate telepathically with 'chosen ones,' cannot dematerialize or change shape, do not shift between dimensions and do not have disciples as some have claimed. No evidence that these things occur has EVER been adduced."⁴¹ This is a shockingly unambiguous, confident statement from someone in a field characterized by ambiguity and doubt.

Cryptozoologists like Kirk are extremely hasty to dismiss bigfoot's paranormal aspects—aspects occurring in countless reports—when one of the central pillars of cryptozoology is eyewitness testimony. F&BH advocates in one breath decry the closed-mindedness of the zoological establishment, yet in the very next sentence dismiss witnesses as liars, hoaxers, or insane should they bring up mindspeak with bigfoot.

"The BFRO [Bigfoot Field Researchers Organization] has been notorious for 'throwing out' any accounts of sasquatch activity that also feature things like UFOs, aliens, other sorts of cryptids, or telepathic communication," wrote Kirk Sigurdson in 2013. "I joined a BFRO web board several years ago and was summarily expelled from the site within days for mentioning the fact that my experience with sasquatch involved mild telepathic exposure (a phenomenon that I have never experienced in any other context)."⁴²

Many cryptozoologists erroneously reject telepathy as "unscientific," a bias demonstrating their willful ignorance of modern consciousness studies. Researchers like Dean Radin, Pim van Lommel, Lynne McTaggart, Rupert Sheldrake, Raymond Moody, Ian Stevenson, Penny Sartori, and scores of others are constantly redefining our understanding of human consciousness, often in peer-reviewed scientific journals.

For example, in 2010 Cornell University professor Daryl Bem published a paper suggesting intense emotions may facilitate presentiment, the ability to intuit the future. In Bem's research, more than 1,000 subjects exhibited greater aptitude in guessing the location of erotic images over neutral images (53.1% versus 49.8%—statistically significant).[43]

This field of research strongly suggests consciousness is not an epiphenomenon of the human brain, but may well have a non-locality untethered from our physical world. If true, this idea fundamentally breaks the Materialist paradigm. When data does not fit the Materialist model, it is not inherently unscientific; we can retain scientific data obtained under a Materialist doctrine, but the model must expand to accept the non-physical.

(To use a metaphor, the addition of a single color to a black-and-white film eliminates neither black nor white—but the film can no longer be referred to as "black-and-white movie." Similarly, the nonphysicality of consciousness, if proven, would not negate the incredible, hard-fought victories won under the banner of Materialism… but the Materialist paradigm itself would be falsified.)

For years, Western culture waited for spirituality to learn from science; now, we wait for science to learn from spirituality. Indigenous belief systems worldwide, however, have long accommodated metaphysics.

"Clara Pearson described a Tillamook Indian's telepathic experience with the wife of a giant Indian named Thunder," wrote Henry James Franzoni. "The Indian describes how Thunder's wife knew what was in his mind without him saying anything. Today we would call that mind reading or telepathy."[44] A Choctaw informant told researcher Rob Riggs bigfoot "are very simple in speech type" and primarily choose to communicate with humans via "headspeak."[45]

Coast to Coast AM guest host Connie Willis was on an expedition to an undisclosed location when she suddenly awoke in a completely alert state. Something forcefully hit the side of the pop-up camper, but her tent mate "had not moved and was sleeping, they were out cold."[46]

> My body was frozen solid and then I realized something was standing at the end of where my feet were on the other side [of the tent canvas]. I felt what I believe were two big beings standing right outside where I was. I then heard what I later learned was called Mindspeak, "Well, here you go. This is what you came to see." Yes, I heard that. I now knew what was inches away from me, my chance to see the legendary bigfoot, and not just one but two. All I had to do was unzip the window and I would see them. I could feel them actually waiting for me to make my decision to do it. Then I did, I made my decision. I didn't want to see them. I was not prepared to look directly into the souls of their existence, as I was not ready for them to look back at mine. I knew that I

knew now they were real and they existed, that was all I needed. I did not need to see their faces haunting me for the next ten years. I needed some prep for that, heck I just got there and I was already quite terrified. After I made that decision it's as if they heard my thought, I felt them "understand" and they were no longer there.[47]

Note the unrousable sleeper, as addressed in Chapter 4, Volume I of *Where the Footprints End*, a common feature of alien and faerie encounters. Willis was also in an altered state of consciousness (sleep) when she made initial contact. Of course, accounts like Willis's are not exactly evidence of mindspeak—the voice she heard could have easily been her own inner monologue.

In fact, researcher Tom Burnette wrote, despite embracing the weirdness surrounding bigfoot, "I refuse to go out into the woods and try to project thoughts and hopefully get answers telepathically in my mind from a monster that may or may not even exist. One reason is that I believe the subconscious mind will answer the questions we have for us by placing little voices in our heads."[48]

Television personality Les Stroud has experienced what he believes is mindspeak on a handful of occasions. The first time was while filming in Tennessee. A storm moved in around sunset, and Stroud was walking back to camp when his hair stood up on the back of his neck. He sensed, but did not see, two presences on a nearby hill.[49]

"I'd never experienced this before in my life," he later said. "It was like it was right in the middle of my head, right inside my brain: the strongest-ever voice that was not my own." The voice said, "If you want to meet us, stay the night. We're over here on the hill, but you have to stay." Terrified, Stroud replied in thought: "I'm not ready for this… I can't." The experience was so convincing Stroud sought professional help, but was given a clean bill of mental health.[50]

If mindspeak exists, altered states of consciousness like meditation appear to be powerful tools to initiate communication with bigfoot, as in the Mangano incident. Burnette's coauthor Rob Riggs encountered an individual who claimed multiple contacts in Texas's Big Thicket while meditating. The creatures would appear whenever the witness "entered a profound state of peacefulness."[51]

"Let me tell you something," the witness told Riggs. "These creatures are psychic. If you go in there with guns with the intent to shoot one to prove that they exist, you'll never see one. They'll pick up on you before you even get there."[52] This closely corresponds to what Bayanov was told by informants regarding the Russian *almasty,* which are capable of "mind reading": "As soon as you leave Moscow for the Caucasus, he already knows it."[53]

Keri Campbell, partner to Ron Morehead, offers interesting testimony of this psychic ability. While visiting friends, Campbell was looking at the landscape through binoculars when she spied a "shimmery, pixelated image" with the stature and build of a sasquatch.[54]

"I thought, in my head, 'In order for me to believe what I'm seeing, you're gonna have to move,'" she recalled.[55] Following this mental command, the figure "turned, side to side, and I felt this overwhelming sense of gratitude."[56]

There are simply too many accounts of bigfoot mindspeak to ignore. While the sources are not unimpeachable—few if any in Forteana are—this can at least in part be laid at the feet of orthodox cryptozoology which, as illustrated time and again, actively seeks to repress any outliers challenging the F&BH.

- **1975 – Washington:** Researchers on the Lummi Indian Reservation see a bigfoot disappear in front of their eyes, leaving behind deep footprints simply ending at a barbed wire fence. During another investigation they discover large, bare footprints in the snow, which, over the course of 200 feet, "slowly morphed into human boots, ending at a house. Nobody home." In another experience, they try calling out to sasquatch but receive a booming voice in their heads: "Get out of here." They also interview two alleged bigfoot abductees. "One experienced telepathy, from him to them, and later, he found they answered his questions into his head, without he [sic] having to speak in words."[57]

- **1975 – Florida:** A Miami motorist swerves to avoid striking an enormous apelike creature. She pulls off the road and the two watch each other, leaving the witness with the telepathic impression it was hungry.[58]

- **1976 – Pennsylvania:** Two high school students skip class to squirrel hunt on private property in Levittown. One of them stumbles across a red-haired bigfoot lazily chewing leaves. When his friend arrives, he takes aim with his bow, but the primary witness hears in his head, "If you hurt me I am going to kill you both." Startled, the pair flees.[59]

- **1979 – Pennsylvania:** Four Amish youths working in a field spot a peculiar "man" bounding toward them like a kangaroo.

They realize it is covered in hair, and as it draws nearer, one of the witnesses experiences "a stabbing sensation, like an electrical jolt." He feels as though something is controlling him, making him shout odd words, similar to the foreign tongue the creature yells before retreating into the woods.[60]

- **1981 – Pennsylvania:** Frank Simpson hears something shuffling though the woods, receiving a strange message repeated in his head: "Come back down the gas line." Compelled, Simpson encounters a 12-foot tall bigfoot before running away. Three toed footprints are discovered the following day.[61]

- **1984 – Oregon:** Lynda Kennedy spots a bigfoot while camping near Mt. Hood. She is terrified until a voice in her head says, "I am not going to hurt you, and you're not going to hurt me." The creature then runs into the bush.[62]

- **1990 – Utah:** After collecting an odd bone adjacent to an apparent bigfoot trackway, Dave and Sharon Oester are pelted with rocks. The projectiles' sizes increase as the assault drags on until Sharon intuits: "Dave, the bone, they want us to leave the bone." They replace the object and the shower of stones immediately ceases.[63]

- **1992 – Oregon:** Screams in Rooster Rock State Park draw a couple's eyes to a ten-foot tall sasquatch across the river. Despite the creature's fiery red, luminescent eyes, the husband receives a message of peace and non-aggression. He then packs up and leaves his wife behind in a sort of daze, only to reunite later.[64]

- **1996 – Oregon:** A woman camping with her family detects a revolting odor and sees a shaggy biped with one fist in the air mere feet from her tent. The tan-haired being telepathically tells her he is part of a peaceful race from another dimension who call themselves "Melkoy." The beings are on Earth to investigate human emotion and reproduction. When her family returns to the camp, the creature departs.[65]

- **1999 – Puerto Rico:** A red-eyed bigfoot appears in a lover's lane near Ponce, telepathically encouraging a woman to jump off a nearby cliff. She obeys, but thankfully survives.[66]

- **1999 – California:** Julie and Allen Bradley report numerous bigfoot sightings and activity on their 50 acre property near Willow Creek. Their fruit trees are regularly raided by something leaving behind humanlike teeth marks. One summer, Allen examines a half-eaten apple and feels "that something with intelligence was telling him they were being watched and 'we could take more any time we want, but we will leave some for you.'"[67]

- **2000 – Russia:** Sasha Fitiev allegedly mindspeaks with a bigfoot claiming to be from a parallel world. According to the creature, his people once lived alongside humans until we became violent, hence their relocation to an alternate dimension. Since bigfoot are prohibited from interacting closely with humans, the creature abruptly ceases communication and disappears in a shimmer.[68]

- **2001 – Oregon:** A hunter raises his camera to snap a photo of bigfoot but receives a warning in his mind: "If you take my picture I will kill you." The creature disappears, then rematerializes on his opposite side. The witness nearly soils himself before running away.[69]

- **2007 – Oklahoma:** A couple in the Ouachita National Forest encounters an "obviously male" large, hairy hominid. Though terrified, their minds are filled with a soft, feminine voice saying, "Do not be afraid. You will not be harmed. Do not come closer." The couple describes the sensation as if they "were thinking the words, but listening to them, too." When one of them moves to take a picture, the voice sternly says, "Do not" three times. The being moves within ten feet of the witnesses and mindspeaks, "You will not be hurt and you need not fear. Go. One more time I shall see you." The couple musters their courage and runs away.[70]

- **2017 – New York:** As he pulls into his patient's driveway, a home healthcare worker hears "in his head, not in the ears" a voice say, "Look for me over here." Near the treeline, he sees "a dark shadowy mass." Doing his best to ignore it, he retrieves his equipment from his car and looks up again, only to see "a big sasquatch" replacing the shadow. The creature is "blacker than black," with a conical head, pronounced brow ridge, and black leathery skin. He watches the massive ("nine feet tall, maybe four feet across") creature for around 45 seconds before it "bows," never breaking eye contact. Its movement is erratic and jerky. Feeling no threat, the witness attends to his patient, and the creature is gone when he leaves. "Every visit after that I always scanned the treeline as well as the treeline across the street," he writes in 2020. "I believe it was the fourth patient visit after my encounter, I heard a female voice in the center of my head tell me, 'Don't waste your time looking for us. We show ourselves when we want to.'"[71]

As noted in Chapter 3, bigfoot are sometimes reported speaking English to witnesses. If a reality lies behind mindspeak, it begs the question of whether bigfoot are speaking, or projecting sentences into the minds of witnesses. This is not always the case, however; as exhibited in one fascinating, little-known encounter, the creatures sometimes directly convey imagery and emotions.

A community in rural Tennessee called upon famed, controversial paranormal investigator Lorraine Warren for help with a large, hairy creature that had attempted to abduct a two-year-old child. Though disinterested in bigfoot, Warren embarked on what she believed might, at worst, be a refreshing expedition to the great outdoors.[72]

After a full morning of hiking, Warren and her party encountered "a clearing where the tall grass was mysteriously beaten down, as if something very heavy had rolled over it again and again." Shortly thereafter, the mindspeak began.[73]

> … Lorraine's mind suddenly offered her a picture of a curious creature. He did, in fact, appear to be a fusion of man and ape, a tall slope-shouldered animal with very long arms that were covered with almost shaggy hair. His face was flat with a protruding bony shelf above the eyes. Two things about him were especially disturbing—first, his eyes, which shone with intelligence, compassion, and fear. Second, his ability to project images telepathically into Lorraine's mind. No so-called dumb animal is able to accomplish such projections.[74]

Images and emotions washed over Warren: caves, rivers, a family of sasquatch, isolation, pain. She learned that the creature was injured and feared he could not return to his people, and that he had approached the human child only because "he felt he could perhaps explain himself to the child just as he was explaining himself to Lorraine."[75]

Eager to help, Warren intuitively started pushing through the brush. She was greeted with "an almost acrid odor," the sasquatch's scent, but before she could reach the beast, another member of the party—"a rather flip student with a battery-operated bullhorn that he used excessively as a joke"—frightened the creature, whose telepathic imagery became violent and terrified. The bigfoot ran away, but not before leaving behind "blood of a type both redder and more viscous than human blood," which Warren tracked "all the way to the edge of a cliff."[76]

It is worth comparing sasquatch mindspeak to the messages telepathically received in the alien contact experience. From alien abduction researcher David Jacobs:

> During the entire abduction experience, communication between aliens and abductees is telepathic. The abductee either "hears" the communication or receives an impression in her mind. She knows she is being addressed and what the Beings want from her. The alien's communication to her is almost always reassuring. For instance, she may ask, "Why are you doing this?" and the answer might be, "We are not going to hurt you" or "You will be all right."[77]

In addition to assuaging fears, the messages relayed by aliens and sasquatch are also similar in content. According to bigfoot contactee (and associate of Jack "Kewaunee" Lapseritis) "SunBôw True Brother," the creatures have a deep concern for the planet and are upset that human beings are not better stewards of the environment.[78] While SunBôw's work —transcribed from conversations with bigfoot "Elder Kamooh"— is viewed skeptically, it nonetheless strongly resonates with messages from alleged extraterrestrials, particularly the contactee movement of the 1950s and 1960s, where warnings of nuclear war and strong pro-environment messages were commonplace.

A variation upon mindspeak may be witnesses' inability to fire upon bigfoot. Stories from countless hunters—even those who are convinced they sighted a flesh-and-blood primate—end with bigfoot walking away unharmed. In some instances it is because the creature appears too human for the hunter to pull the trigger. A deer hunter near Whitney, Ohio noticed the forest was oddly silent just before a seven-foot tall, dark haired, bipedal creature appeared. "As I'm watching it walk I had my pistol aimed at it," he told the BFRO. "I was about to pull the trigger, when something in my head told me not to."[79]

Other times, gunmen are mysteriously compelled to lower their weapons. Richard Davis believed he was confronting a prowler outside his

Cape Coral, Florida home at 2:00 a.m. on February 2, 1975, but instead encountered a nine-foot tall bigfoot. He fired once with his revolver and the bullet ricocheted off the creature's chest; he wished to empty the remaining five rounds into the creature but "found that he was mentally unable to pull the trigger again." The bigfoot grunted and ran off.[80]

This implies bigfoot are not only telepathic, but can control people with their minds, an unsettling prospect. Al Berry collected the story of a California witness who smelled something like "sewage or spoiled apples" coming from a bush shaking outside his home.

> "I'm not the scary type, but I made a beeline for the house in no uncertain terms!" the veteran said. Now within the safety of the duplex, he put on the kitchen lights, pulled up the blinds, and looked out. There was nothing except the big bush, which was no longer moving.
>
> "So I thought to myself, it's as plain as day. I'm losing my marbles!" Bailey said. "I started to let the blinds down when something grabbed me mentally. I don't know what it was—it's beyond description, but it was literally hypnotizing me! I'm not a dramatic person, or an imaginative one. You could say I'm about as down-to-earth as a doorknob, but I felt like something alien and outside myself was trying to control me."
>
> As the Palmdale man stood transfixed at his window, unable to move a muscle and being commanded mentally from somewhere in the courtyard to continue looking, he saw it. There, standing motionless and relaxed next to the telephone pole in the center of the yard some fifty feet away was a nine-foot black, hairy form. While shadows obscured the giant's face, Bailey felt it was looking directly into his eyes, somehow telepathically, hypnotically urging him to come to it.
>
> Then abruptly, as if tired of the game, the hairy figure strode away across the courtyard....[81]

Shape Shifting

"As far back as ancient Rome, poet Virgil described in his *Aeneid*, book six, how the great wild nature god Pan disported himself and caused *panic* among those who would capture him, with his many monstrous guises, including wild beasts and demoniacal apparitions," wrote author Jim Brandon in *The Rebirth of Pan*.[82] Given the wild man's archetypal roots in depictions of Pan and other *Satyrs/Fauns*, it is no surprise they—and by extension, bigfoot—are ascribed transformative properties.

Author W.J. Sheehan collected a story from John Murray, a western Pennsylvania witness, who spotted a bigfoot while racing all-terrain vehicles with a friend. As they came around a bend "a huge, fur-covered monster" crossed the trail, turning its head to look at them. They reached where the creature had entered the forest and decided to loop around, hoping to catch it as it exited the patch of woods on a parallel path.[83]

The maneuver took about five minutes. "Ahead of us, leaning against a tree, was a man wearing nothing but a white t-shirt, blue jeans, and a pair of white canvas boat shoes with no socks," Murray said. "It was early October, and late in the day, with the temperature being in the upper 40s and windy. The forest was damp and the trails were somewhat loose and muddied from rain in the morning." Despite these conditions, the man appeared undisturbed by the chill, and his shoes were immaculate.[84]

As they stopped to greet him, Murray was overwhelmed by the odor of "cheap aftershave and hair tonic." The man, who resembled a 1950s "greaser" character, denied having seen anything unusual and lit a cigarette—which neither smelled nor burned down. He claimed to live nearby, but was otherwise not particularly talkative. Murray took his eyes off the man for just a moment… and he vanished, without leaving so much as a footprint. The pair were baffled, and returned to the site of their initial sighting, where they failed to find any tracks.[85]

While the connection between the greaser and bigfoot is more implied than overt in Murray's story, other witnesses tell similar stories. From radio journalist Dave Scott, who grew up on the lower mainland of British Columbia.

> This lake is called Davis Lake, and two fisherman got chased out of that lake by a sasquatch in 2006 [according to reports online]. And we were out geocaching there one day and my daughter looks over to the left side of the lake… and probably 200 yards away from us she watches this boy in swim trunks jump into the lake. There are no vehicles at this lake—you have to four-by-four in, like we had to ATV into this lake… There's one road in, one road out… There was no splash… and he never came up. And so my daughter was, like, "Dad… dad, there was just somebody who jumped into the water off

that big rock over there, and they haven't come up, and there was no splash..." She was just, like, "I'm scared, can we go?"[86]

Like the bigfoot greaser, there is nothing in this story to suggest that bigfoot morph into boys wearing swim trunks... but we must look, as argued in Volume I of *Where the Footprints End*, at the company these phenomena keep. If everyone is to be believed, the *least correlated scenario* is that bigfoot lurk around an area where there is a swimming ghost boy. For our purposes, perhaps bigfoot—*or whatever lies behind bigfoot*—adopted the form of a swimmer.

Stories of shapeshifting bigfoot can be found worldwide. Antonio Blanco collected a 1978 case from Italy, of all places. A family travelling between Milazzo and Santa Lucia del Mela were passing an abandoned house when a bright light allegedly descended from the sky, stopping just above the ground to release a cloud of gray smoke. Out of the cloud came a naked, hairy being with sharp teeth and large round eyes. As the beast bounded along the road it transformed into a human being with long, brown hair, dressed in light colored pants and a dark jacket.[87]

This "mystery cloud" appears in other stories where bigfoot changes appearance. In 2014 Anthony Padilla claimed to have seen a sasquatch "living on an ancient Indian burial ground" on his Michigan property. Padilla told interviewers:

> I tried to speak to it... and I couldn't spit it out. And not that I wasn't scared, he wouldn't let me! He started getting, like, blurry, fuzzy, like a mist... like a spirit, like... and then I seen some antlers evolve. Like, they say they move like the ninja—that part is true. He turned around... Bam! Gave me a vision of white deer's tails [and] two hooves jumpin' away from me to try and make me forget what I'd seen.[88]

"Wildmen of both European folklore and late mediaeval culture possess a greater number of fantastic, or seemingly 'spiritual,' attributes..." wrote University of Alberta anthropologist Gregory Forth. "Their strength is unearthly and, like spirits everywhere, they are able to change shape."[89] This trend is shared with witches, ghosts, faeries, and demons, all of which, as illustrated elsewhere, have significant ties to the bigfoot phenomenon. For example, a Mr. & Mrs. Lew Lister were sitting in a parked car near Point Isabel, Ohio when they saw a bigfoot "change shape, then vanish."[90]

The aforementioned propensity for Alien Black Cats to appear in close temporal and geographical proximity to bigfoot sightings, coupled with the frequency with which creatures of myth and legend shape shifted into panthers, begs the question of whether or not these are actual felines being observed. In at least some cases, bigfoot have been "misidentified" as panthers. During a highly localized 1979 bigfoot flap in Byhalia, Mississippi, residents opened fire on a large, black cat stalking outside a chicken coop.[91]

"Your uncle said when he went out there how it reminded him of a panther on its belly—that's kind of how they move when they're on all fours," podcaster Wes Germer told the primary witness. "They move more like a cat when they're on all fours than they do... like a great ape, or a monkey. They move more like a feline, when they're on all fours." Either way—bigfoot or ABC—the creature dropped several stolen eggs, implying hands.[92]

"Some witnesses believe they have documented trackways that simply stop, leading some to wonder if bigfoot may be 'interdimensional'—whatever that means—or have the ability to 'shapeshift' into another form," wrote The Oregon Bigfoot group. "Some witnesses have indicated that bigfoot can 'turn into' a rock or a stump or become invisible. It is unclear whether these reports are simply misidentifications of the creature's ability to camouflage themselves in their surroundings and hold very still. Native American stories of 'skinwalkers,' which were shape-shifters, have been attributed to Sasquatch."[93]

A variety of Native American bigfoot analogues, including the Tlingit *Kushtakaa*, are ascribed shape shifting abilities as well.[94] Some Kootenai elders claim bigfoot can transform into wolves,[95] while the Cherokee "Stone Coat" (*Nun'yunu'wi*) "could assume human form or make itself invisible."[96] Willie Charlie, a Chehalis tour guide, told *The Toronto Star* that "Sasquatch is a *slalocum*. These supernatural beings can shapeshift into anything. Sasquatch has the ability to walk the two realms, both the physical and spiritual."[97]

Again, these beliefs may extend beyond the Americas. In India, the *rakshasas* of Hindu tradition are demons, often depicted as fanged, clawed, hairy man-eaters with flaming red eyes and the ability to assume any form. In fact, an episode of the popular mid-1970s television show *Kolchak: The Night Stalker* featured a *rakshasa* that targeted its victims by taking on the appearance of people they trusted most.[98]

"In Australia's Western Desert, an unlucky person may come across the path of a *Mamu*, a cannibalistic humanoid that typically lives underground or in hollowed-out trees," wrote John B. Kachuba, author of *Shapeshifters: A History*. "It has a hairy body, bulbous eyes and sharp, pointed teeth capable of stripping off the flesh from its victims. It may appear human-like, or it may transform into a sharp-beaked bird, a dog or even a falling star."[99] (This last guise has obvious implications vis-à-vis mystery lights and UFOs seen in conjunction with large, hairy hominids.)

In his 2008 book *The Hoopa Project: Bigfoot Encounters in California*, researcher David Paulides spoke with numerous indigenous informants from northern California who regularly saw not only bigfoot, but also *Kamoss*, "a snake-like creature that has a head the size of a horse and presumably eats river fish."[100]

During his investigations, Paulides began to suspect that, given the creatures' aforementioned affinity for swimming—while outright ignoring their physical description—bigfoot might actually be mistaken for *Kamoss*. ("Several of the tribal people gave me strange looks and stated, 'Possibly,'" he later wrote.)[101] Paulides, of course, assumed simple misidentification, that tribes were seeing a swimming hominid and ascribed it serpentine attributes.

It is tempting, if unfounded, to speculate an alternative conclusion: perhaps bigfoot can shape shift into river monsters? This possibility finds Old World precedent in the Scottish *Kelpie*, or water-horse, which, as mentioned in *Where the Footprints End* Volume I, appeared as a water-dwelling horse monster, a beautiful lady, or a large, hirsute man.[102]

"In human form the *kelpie* is a rough, shaggy man who leaps behind a solitary rider, gripping and crushing him," wrote James MacKillop in his *Dictionary of Celtic Mythology*. "Some stories depict a human-form *kelpie* as tearing people apart and devouring them."[103]

Even F&BH advocates believe bigfoot has abilities shockingly close to shape shifting. To these researchers, bigfoot are able to freeze so perfectly they blend in with the landscape, appearing as oversized stumps, logs, or trees. While this activity has certainly been explicitly observed during unambiguous bigfoot sightings, it has also led to an entire subculture where bigfoot is "seen" hiding in completely unremarkable photographs.

"In the thousands of sighting reports I have read, numerous witnesses stated that they saw a large black stump or ball on a hillside, they looked at it momentarily and after a few seconds it started to move," wrote Paulides. "This is a recurring theme in sighting reports..."[104]

This tree-sasquatch connection appears in some indigenous lore.

> According to Ojibwe legend, a long time ago a very hungry man was stumbling through the woods in the spring, and he grew so weak that he collapsed. Thinking that he might die, he offered tobacco and begged the Creator for help. Looking

up, he saw a tall, hairy being that the Ojibwe called *Misaabe*. The *Misaabe* held a large knife and used it to cut his own leg. As the wound started to bleed, the *Misaabe* transformed into a giant tree and his blood turned into maple sap, which began to flow from the tree trunk. The hungry Ojibwe man tasted the sweet liquid. It worked like medicine, making him feel strong again.[105]

In one humorous anecdote, Bob Strain was on an investigation in the south central United States with the North American Wood Ape Conservancy (NAWAC) when he experienced bigfoot disguised as logs. During his search, Strain peered inside a thicket but noticed nothing remarkable, save a few large logs on the ground. The following day, investigators could not find the logs.[106]

"It's our belief that the logs were actually apes that were prone, that were laying there, pretending to be logs," said Brian Brown of the NAWAC. "We have a slogan: shoot all the logs," he joked. "Stopping and freezing and pretending to be a tree... not moving, is something that has been observed time-and-again."[107] Sasquatch mistaken for trees are found in a plethora of reports.

- **1963 – Washington:** Paul Manley and two passengers driving through Satus Pass see a tall, hairy "tree stump" step from out of a ditch as their car passes.[108]

- **1983 – Washington:** Four girls and one boy are playing jump rope when one of them spots "a tall black thing on two legs" jumping across a creek. Scanning the area, the primary witness notices "a black stump under a tree, which I could not recall being there before. I kept looking at it thinking, 'Is that a stump or something else?' The shape looked like a tall black figure standing upright, leaning forward with very long arms down to its knees. The head was turned looking directly at us. However it was so still I thought it had to be a burnt stump." When the children scream, the figure flees.[109]

- **1999 – Colorado:** A youth leader at a Bible camp near Grand Junction is playing with his students one evening when he sees a bigfoot emerge from the bushes. Hearing children's voices, the creature spins and crouches, appearing identical to "a large stump." It remains in position until the children leave, then continues on its way.[110]

- **2018 – Kentucky:** A couple driving near Sandy Hook see a tall figure "the color of a tree" standing by the road. It crosses the road in a few steps. "She described it as a walking tree," wrote BFRO investigator Jack Smarr.[111]

Some contend sasquatch grow algae or moss on their coats, further enhancing their vegetal appearance. While possible from a biological standpoint—sloth fur can house "a wide variety of organisms, ranging from moths, beetles, and cockroaches to ciliates, fungi, and algae"—it also finds precedent in folklore.[112] "Some Nordic giants from the harshest climatic zones sprouted bushes and trees in their body hair for additional protection and camouflage," wrote Sarah Teale. "Camouflaged giants could have hours of fun with the unwary. There are few more disconcerting discoveries than to find oneself astride a giant's big toe or kneeling on his upper lip peering up his nose...."[113]

Bigfoot do not *literally* turn into logs… according to most reports. One exception comes from a Washington witness who allegedly spotted a large, hairy hominid outside her home. As she approached the creature, it "abruptly walked a short distance into the woods, lay down on the ground, and, in full view, *turned into a log*." The witness allegedly "dragged the log back into her home" where she "used it as a coffee table for years."[114] This is easily one of the most unbelievable stories ever recorded, even in a book about peculiar bigfoot sightings.

It is certainly true bigfoot's fur could make them difficult to see in the wild—after all, witnesses commonly compare the creature's coat to a ghillie suit, the shaggy outfits used by special forces to obscure the human form. Burnette related a story from the late 19th century where a girl watched a bigfoot lie next to a pile of debris and deliberately cover itself with detritus—twigs, leaves, dirt, etc.—to conceal itself from hunters.[115]

"Nature might have designed bigfoot's long, shaggy hair to serve a similar purpose to the ghillie suit," he wrote with Riggs. "Indeed, a good-sized man wearing a ghillie suit seen from even a short distance in heavy woods bears a striking resemblance to a hominid with long, shaggy hair."[116]

Perhaps the most peculiar shape shifting story was collected by Ufologist Don Worley. A hitchhiker travelling through Texas in November 1964 was down on his luck and began walking along the highway. After a time he heard movement from the bush and saw three glowing, red orbs in the sky. The lights were dispelled momentarily by a passing car, but shortly returned and the sound of movement escalated.[117]

Unnerved, the witness turned to walk in the opposite direction but was confronted by eight tall, dark, simian figures with glowing yellow eyes blocking the road. They followed the witness as he backed away slowly, fading out as cars approached and rematerializing once they passed. He kept an eye on the beasts for around half an hour until a motorist finally stopped. As the witness entered the car, the apparition changed.[118]

"A large glowing red ball of light began to turn black in places and there formed an off pattern of luminous black lines on its surface, or near its surface from within," wrote Albert Rosales, who collected the encounter for his humanoid database. "These black lines began to rotate clockwise, slowly at first and the longer he looked at them the faster they got. They had a strong hypnotic effect on the witness." He felt an odd sensation of pressure between his eyes, and his glasses began to fog.[119]

The driver, who said the witness was cold to the touch, had also spotted the red spheres and tall, apelike creatures. "They were able to join their bodies together into twos, fours, or all eight and then separate," and apparently lacked hands and feet. The creatures, however, were never overtly hostile throughout the encounter.[120]

Cocreation Theory

What are we to make of ape-men who share more with the imaginal realm than our reality?

"To me that appears to firmly be an impossibility," said Fred Beck, witness of the famed Ape Canyon Incident, when asked of bigfoot's physical existence. Beck, along with several other miners, allegedly had their cabin besieged by a group of at least six bigfoot in 1924. Beck was told by an Indian informant that bigfoot were "not like a man and not like a spirit, but in between." Beck wrote:

> Material things usually make a big splash in the material world, and spiritual things often do not make a ripple there. Why? We can give proof of a phenomenon, but its nature is immersed in the Spiritual and can only be explained by laws of the spiritual...
>
> The Abominable Snowmen are from a lower plane. When the condition and vibration is at a certain frequency, they can easily, for a time, appear in a very solid body. They are not animal spirits, but also lack the intelligence of a human consciousness. When reading of evolution we have read many times conjecture about the missing link between man and the Anthropoid Ape. The Snowmen are a missing link in

consciousness, neither animal nor human. They are very close to our dimension, and yet are a part of one lower. Could they be the missing link man has been so long searching for?

The Human Soul once dwelled in a spiritual body, and eventually incarnated, at the fall of man, into bodies like we have now. The beings we call Abominable Snowmen were not of the necessary high development to incarnate in human form. They had not reached that scale of spiritual evolution.

They are the easiest beings materialized as evidenced by the many reports of their appearances to more people in recent years. In fact, if the vibratory influence right for them is present they can manifest without any human being present at all. This accounts for the many tracks being seen along the mountain ranges of the West Coast and Canada...

All life has some order of consciousness. Someone might call the Snowmen a delayed race, awaiting for [sic] the highest expression of consciousness. That is the human consciousness. They seem to be curious about human beings more than anything else; and I think it possible, as time passes, they will manifest farther and farther away from the mountain ranges (which has been their natural, attractive habitat) and the time may come when you hear stories from cities of people seeing strange hairy like creatures. This is a distinct possibility. Just four days ago, I received a letter from a friend from Seattle, Washington, and in it she told me of a lady who just recently had seen an Abominable Snowman right on the outskirts of Yakima, Washington. And as the letter stated, "it was in or near her yard."[121]

Many of Beck's ideas—especially the oblique references to man's role in manifesting sasquatch—call to mind the Co-Creation Hypothesis proposed by author Greg Bishop. While his model has strong antecedents in all anomalous studies, Bishop is actively attempting to bring the concept into the 21st century, combining the concept with Information Theory and other cutting edge scientific hypotheses. Of UFO encounters featuring High Strangeness—the nonsensical details around which much of this book is structured—Bishop says:

These cases evince almost none of the normal elements of a

supposed abduction or what we have become used to as the standard "alien," but they are only very rarely mentioned in surveys and research, mainly because they both don't make any sense and because they don't fit comfortably into a standard narrative.

Many UFO researchers would be tempted to say that these accounts are either faulty recollections (that would fit a humanoid narrative if given enough questioning) or screen memories imposed by aliens, but perhaps extra-human consciousness has no need or method to impose any mind control on us. We have our own built-in screen memories that function quite well in earthly situations such as childhood trauma. How much do we bring to the dance during a paranormal encounter? In other words, how much of the UFO experience is the result of our subconscious minds trying to make sense of unexpected, startling, and/or frightening input, and leaving us with an insane placeholder when it can't decide on anything else?[122]

Bishop conceived this idea in a Ufological context, primarily as a new means of thinking about nonsensical UFO encounters and "screen memories," a process where false memories are allegedly implanted by alien abductors to prevent witnesses from fully recalling their experiences (e.g. an alien might be remembered as an owl, an alien medical examination as a dentist's visit, etc.). The Co-Creation Hypothesis is equally useful when considering old faerie tales of *glamour*, the folkloric ability to appear, or make other things appear, completely different than their true nature. In this fashion, faeries effectively shape shifted dank, dreary caves into beautiful Faerie Palaces, or presented twigs, worms, and dirt as delicious food.

In Bishop's model something, a non-human Other, appears to witnesses, and our own preconceptions and biases shape what we see. This concept finds strength in other paranormal disciplines: it is not uncommon (if underreported) for—out of a group of, say, five individuals—three people to see a UFO in the sky while the other two see nothing. Equally problematic are sightings where all five witnesses see a bright light in the sky, yet they disagree on crucial aspects, such as the object's behavior or color. This strongly indicates individual sensitivities, perceptions, etc. are at play in every numinous encounter.

This discrepancy appears in the mid-1990s sighting of a witness named Gage near Hillsboro, Oregon. As a young man, Gage and two friends were traipsing through the woods near their home when they noticed a foreboding sensation pervading the forest. The sky visibly darkened—perhaps only a cloud, perhaps something more sinister—and the area fell deathly silent. Rounding a bend in the trail, the trio saw a fallen tree, upon which sat a "big, white thing." An errant beam of sunshine broke the clouds and shone upon the creature, which jumped from the highest point of the log to the ground, prompting them to flee.[123]

Gage later described "the beast" as tall and covered in medium-length hair, with "creamy tan" skin. It was built "like a bodybuilder," and appeared somewhere between a man and a gorilla. He and his friends got the impression that the being was not natural, but more supernatural. However, one of Gage's friends later claimed he "never saw it," while the other witness—described as living a troubled home life at the time of the incident—reached out to Gage in 2019 with another discrepancy: not only did he interpret "the beast" as a malevolent "wood spirit," but he said the creature was "black, dark, dark black." Both remain steadfast in their descriptions.[124]

Faulty recall, wracked by two decades of rewritten memories? A disagreement in a shared lie by three kids, whose narrative has begun to unravel into adulthood? Or is the appearance of the paranormal—as obliquely suggested by such physics theories as the observer effect—dependent upon the witness?

How can we ever hope to measure phenomena that defy our eyes, our most trusted means of navigating reality? If our eyes can be deceived, can our trusted scientific instruments be fooled as well? Writes chaos magician and author Gordon White:

> Could you measure the tidal flow of Sydney's harbour mouth in your kitchen sink? With the right (expensive) equipment, you could potentially measure the Moon's impact on gravity influencing a tiny rise in your water and then blow those numbers up to an estimated volume of the harbour that evening and subtract the difference between your high and low estimates.
>
> Sounds fucking horrible, right? Welcome to psi research.
>
> What you should actually do is have a team at the harbour mouth with some far cheaper equipment. It is an *in field* experiment. The tide happens to a harbour, not a sink. And anyone wishing to criticise your results will say so.[125]

When seeking the truth behind paranormal phenomena, perhaps our most useful tool remains—as it has always been—our consciousness. This is certainly the message passed down to us through time, a position championed by every culture from the Australian aborigines to the Celtic Fairy Faith to New Age channelers. It is only our modern culture, the industrialized, Materialist, reductionist, western world, smothered in concrete, glass, and steel, that has ever actively sought to discredit and disregard this crucial method of interrogation.

This is admittedly uncomfortable territory for anyone seeking to validate their view of sasquatch as a large, undiscovered primate. Yet despite reductionist opinions to the contrary, High Strangeness persists unabated in the bigfoot phenomenon, a perennial thorn in cryptozoology's side.

---

[1] Hancock, G. (November 4, 2013). The Consciousness Revolution. Retrieved January 26, 2019 from https://grahamhancock.com/the-consciousness-revolution-hancock/

[2] Pollan, M. (2018). *How to Change Your Mind: What the New Science of Psychedelics Teaches Us About Consciousness, Dying, Addiction, Depression, and Transcendence.* New York, NYL Penguin Press.

[3] The Constellating Image. (May 1, 2008). Edge Material. Retrieved January 26, 2019 from https://constellatingimage.blogspot.com/2008/05/

[4] Roberts, A. (May 4, 2015). Francis Crick, DNA & LSD. Retrieved January 26, 2019 from http://realitysandwich.com/314873/francis-crick-dna-lsd/

[5] Watts, M. (2017). *Psychedelic Healing for the 21st Century.* USA: Michael Watts.

[6] Stafford, P. (1993). *Psychedelics Encyclopedia* (3rd ed). Berkeley, CA: Ronin Publishing.

[7] Strassman, R. (2000). *DMT: The Spirit Molecule.* Rochester, VT: Park Street Press.

[8] Pyle, R.M. (2017). *Where Bigfoot Walks: Crossing the Dark Divide.* Berkeley, CA: Counterpoint (Original work published 1995).

[9] Hanna, J. (November 2012). Aliens, Insectoids, and Elves! Oh, My! *Erowid Extracts 23*, pp. 8-21.

[10] Pyle 2017.

[11] Van Tongeren, M.C. (2004). *Overtone Singing: Physics and Metaphysics of Harmonics in East and West*. Delft, NL: Eburon Academic Publishers.

[12] Renner, T. (March 29, 2018). Episode 29: The Michaux Roar. Retrieved January 26, 2019 from https://strangefamiliars.darkhollerarts.com/episode-29-michaux-roar/

[13] Fachner, J. & Rittner, S. (2011). Ethno Therapy, Music and Trance: An EEG Investigation into a Sound-Trance Induction. In D. Cvetkovic & I. Cosic (Eds.), *States of Consciousness: Experimental Insights into Meditation, Waking, Sleep, and Dreams* (pp. 235-256). Berlin, DE: Springer.

[14] Mannes, E. (2011). *The Power of Music: Pioneering Discoveries in the New Science of Song*. New York, NY: Bloomsbury.

[15] Germer, W. (December 2, 2018). Sasquatch Chronicles Radio // SC EP: 495 Don't Look Behind You. Retrieved January 26, 2019 from https://sasquatchchronicles.com/sc-ep495-dont-look-behind-you/

[16] Ibid.

[17] Short, B. (n.d.). The De Facto Sasquatch. Retrieved January 18, 2019 from https://static1.squarespace.com/static/596c0bae4c0dbfa1d26e86be/t/5b9bff06562fa7cfcdf1bfc8/1536950038606/The+de+facto+Sasquatch+premier+installment.pdf?fbclid=IwAR3763B1leKUEQofPRbPvzAItNH5K-RUVoKU-vOLW_iXvSFkdKSg4o4xBXw

[18] Rick. (July 3, 2013). Earliest documented Bigfoot Sighting in Pacific Northwest. Retrieved January 8, 2019 from http://hamell.net/earliest-documented-bigfoot-sighting-in-pacific-northwest/

[19] Rennard, A. (June 18, 2000). Pre-Columbian and Early American Legends of Bigfoot-like Beings. Retrieved January 26, 2019 from https://www.bfro.net/legends/salish.htm

[20] Short n.d.

[21] Eberhart, G.M. (2002). *Mysterious Creatures: A Guide to Cryptozoology*. Santa Barbara, CA: ABC-CLIO, Inc.

[22] Short n.d.

[23] Eberhart 2002.

[24] Bayanov, D. (2011). *Bigfoot Research: The Russian Vision*. C.L. Murphy (Ed.). Blaine, WA: Hancock House Publishers.

[25] Mack, J. (1994). *Abduction: Human Encounters with Aliens.* New York, NY: Charles Scribner's Sons.

[26] Hunt, R. (1903). *Popular Romances of the West of England: The Drolls, Traditions, and Superstitions of Old Cornwall.* London, UK: Chatto and Windus (3rd ed.).

[27] Hancock, G. (2007). *Supernatural.* New York, NY: The Disinformation Company, Ltd.

[28] Bladon, L. (2007). *The Science of Spirituality.* Lulu.com.

[29] Asbjørnsen, P.C. (1883). *Folk and Fairy Tales.* (H.L. Braekstad, Trans.). New York, NY: A.C. Armstrong & Son (7th ed.).

[30] Riggs, R. (2001). *In the Big Thicket, On the Trail of the Wildman.* New York, NY: Paraview Press.

[31] Mac M [Screen name]. August 22, 2016. Oddball sounds. Retrieved January 26, 2019 from https://sasquatchchronicles.com/topic/oddball-sounds/

[32] Coleman, L. (April 7, 2006). Sasquatch 1934. Retrieved January 26, 2019 from https://cryptomundo.com/cryptozoo-news/sasquatch-1934/

[33] Taylor, S. (February 1, 2011). Memory told of close encounter with a sasquatch while picking up clay pigeons near Sumner. Retrieved January 26, 2019 from http://www.bfro.net/gdb/show_report.asp?id=28788

[34] Rife, P.L. (2000). *Bigfoot Across America.* Lincoln, NE: Writers Club Press.

[35] BFRO. (January 5, 2001). Northeast Washington resident sees a bigfoot looking in the window. Retrieved January 26, 2019 from https://www.bfro.net/GDB/show_report.asp?ID=1113&PrinterFriendly=True

[36] Germer, W. (August 15, 2016). Webcast: Mysteries to Search. Retrieved January 28, 2019 from https://sasquatchchronicles.com/webcast-mysteries-to-search/

[37] BFRO. (January 2, 2001). Two fisherman have daytime sighting above Huntington Lake. Retrieved January 27, 2019 from http://www.bfro.net/GDB/show_report.asp?id=1068

[38] Ibid.

[39] Cutchin, J. (2016). *The Brimstone Deceit.* San Antonio, TX: Anomalist Books.

[40] Slate, B.A. & Berry, A. (1976). *Bigfoot*. New York, NY: Bantam.

[41] Kirk. J. (September 3, 2014). The Science of Cryptozoology. Retrieved January 28, 2019 from https://cryptomundo.com/cryptozoologists/the-science-of-cryptozoology/

[42] Sigurdson, K. (April 18, 2013). Can't We All Just Get Along? Retrieved January 28, 2019 from http://www.bigfootlunchclub.com/2013/04/cant-we-all-just-get-along.html

[43] Bem, D.J. (2011). Feeling the future: Experimental evidence for anomalous retroactive influences on cognition and affect. *Journal of Personality and Social Psychology 100*, pp. 407-425.

[44] Franzoni III, H.J. (2008). *In the Spirit of Seatco.* Deer Island, OR: Ste Ye Hah Publishing.

[45] Burnette, T., & Riggs, R. (2014). *Bigfoot: Exploring the Myth and Discovering the Truth.* Woodbury, MN: Llewllyn Publications.

[46] Willis, C. (November 6, 2012). Bigfoot is Real. Retrieved January 28, 2019 from https://www.huffingtonpost.com/connie-willis/bigfoot_b_2084099.html

[47] Ibid.

[48] Burnette & Riggs 2014.

[49] Germer, W. (December 21, 2018). Sasquatch Chronicles Radio // SC EP: 500 Survivorman Les Stroud. Retrieved January 29, 2019 from https://sasquatchchronicles.com/sc-ep500-survivorman-les-stroud/

[50] Germer December 21, 2018.

[51] Burnette & Riggs 2014.

[52] Ibid.

[53] Bayanov 2011.

[54] Boxleitner, K. (2019, March 6). Sequim man describes Bigfoot encounters. Retrieved April 5, 2020 from https://www.ptleader.com/stories/sequim-man-describes-bigfoot-encounters,60131

[55] Megargle, A., Meyer, R.C. (Producers), & Megargle, A., Meyer, R.C. (Directors). (2020). *The Bigfoot Alien Connection Revealed.* USA: Centre Communications, Inc.

[56] Boxleitner 2019.

[57] Cornet, S.E. (May 22, 2005). Vanishing Bigfoot and Anecdotal Accounts: Implications and Challenges for Researchers. Retrieved May 11, 2019 from https://www.nabigfootsearch.com/vanishing_bigfoot.html

[58] Berry, R. (1993). *Bigfoot on the East Coast.* Harrisburg, VA: Campbell Copy Center.

[59] No author. (n.d.). Case 119. In A. Rosales (Ed.), *1976 Humanoid Sighting Reports.* Retrieved February 5, 2014 from http://www.ufoinfo.com/humanoid/humanoid-1976.pdf

[60] Rife, P.L. (2001). *America's Nightmare Monsters.* Lincoln, NE: Writers Club Press.

[61] Gordon, S. (n.d.). Case 144. In A. Rosales (Ed.), *1981 Humanoid Sighting Reports.* Retrieved February 5, 2014 from http://www.ufoinfo.com/humanoid/humanoid-1981.pdf

[62] No author. (n.d.). Case 88. In A. Rosales (Ed.), *1984 Humanoid Sighting Reports.* Retrieved February 5, 2014 from http://www.ufoinfo.com/humanoid/humanoid-1984.pdf

[63] Steiger, B. (2019). The Rise of the Planet of the Bigfoot. In R.E. Guiley (Ed.), *FATE Presents: Planet Bigfoot.* (pp. 129-136). New Milford, CT: Visionary Living Publishing.

[64] Crowe, R. (n.d.). Case 147. In A. Rosales (Ed.), *1992 Humanoid Sighting Reports.* Retrieved February 5, 2014 from http://www.ufoinfo.com/humanoid/humanoid-1992.pdf

[65] Peak, N. (n.d.). Case 219. In A. Rosales (Ed.), *1996 Humanoid Sighting Reports.* Retrieved February 5, 2014 from http://www.ufoinfo.com/humanoid/humanoid-1996.pdf

[66] Corrales, S. (n.d.). Case 27. In A. Rosales (Ed.), *1999 Humanoid Sighting Reports.* Retrieved February 5, 2014 from http://www.ufoinfo.com/humanoid/humanoid-1999.pdf

[67] Paulides, D. (2009). *Tribal Bigfoot.* Blaine, WA: Hancock House.

[68] Kolomiets, I. (n.d..) Case 33. In A. Rosales (Ed.), *2000 Humanoid Sighting Reports.* Retrieved February 5, 2014 from http://www.ufoinfo.com/humanoid/humanoid-2000.pdf

[69] No author. (n.d.). Case 246. In A. Rosales (Ed.), *2001 Humanoid Sighting Reports*. Retrieved February 5, 2014 from http://www.ufoinfo.com/humanoid/humanoid-2001.pdf

[70] Redfern, N. (April 30, 2013). Sasquatch Speaks and Strangeness Strikes. Retrieved January 29, 2019 from https://mysteriousuniverse.org/2013/04/sasquatch-speaks-and-strangeness-strikes/

[71] Anonymous. (2020, June 12). Personal communication.

[72] Warren, E., Warren, L., & Chase, R.D. (1989). *Ghost Hunters: True Stories from the World's Most Famous Demonologists*. New York, NY: St. Martin's Press.

[73] Ibid.

[74] Ibid.

[75] Ibid.

[76] Ibid.

[77] Jacobs, D. (1993). *Secret Life*. New York, NY: Simon and Schuster.

[78] SunBôw True Brother. (2016). *The Sasquatch Message to Humanity: Conversations with Elder Kamooh*. Chewelah, WA: Comanche Spirit Publishing.

[79] Kovalski, J. (April 6, 2015). Memory told of being startled by a large biped while scouting for deer during the day near Whitney. Retrieved January 29, 2019 from http://bfro.net/gdb/show_report.asp?ID=48372&PrinterFriendly=True

[80] Bord, J., & Bord, C. (2006). *Bigfoot Casebook Updated: Sightings and Encounters from 1818 to 2004*. Enumclaw, WA: Pinewinds Press.

[81] Slate & Berry 1976.

[82] Brandon, J. (1983). *The Rebirth of Pan: Hidden Faces of the American Earth Spirit*. Dunlap, IL: Firebird Press.

[83] Azkath, S. (December 22, 2018). Bigfoot: Terror in the Woods. Retrieved January 25, 2019 from https://www.wheredidtheroadgo.com/show-archive/2018/item/565-bigfoot-terror-in-the-woods-dec-22-2018

[84] Ibid.

[85] Ibid.

[86] Scott, D. (March 17, 2020). March 17/20 - Spaced Out Radio live with Joshua Cutchin. Retrieved March 19, 2020 from https://www.youtube.com/watch?v=RXO-PdZAyUA

[87] Blanco, A. (n.d.). Case 405. In A. Rosales (Ed.), *1978 Humanoid Sighting Reports*. Retrieved February 5, 2014 from http://www.ufoinfo.com/humanoid/humanoid-1978.pdf

[88] Riddle, T. (January 15, 2014). Midland Man Says Bigfoot is a Psychic Shape-Shifter Living On 'Ancient Indian Burial Ground.' Retrieved May 20, 2020 from https://banana1015.com/midland-man-says-bigfoot-is-a-psychic-shape-shifter-living-on-ancient-indian-burial-ground/

[89] Forth, G. (2007, December). Images of the Wildman Inside and Outside Europe. *Folklore 118*(3), pp. 261-281.

[90] Cornet 2005.

[91] Germer, W. (February 9, 2019). Sasquatch Chronicles Radio // SC EP:514 Encounters On The Property. Retrieved February 25, 2019 from https://sasquatchchronicles.com/sc-ep514-encounters-on-the-property/

[92] Ibid.

[93] Dark Mountain Productions (2016). What is Bigfoot? Retrieved January 30, 2019 from http://www.oregonbigfoot.com/what-is-bigfoot.php

[94] Alley, J.R. (2007). *Raincoast Sasquatch*. Blaine, WA: Hancock House. (Original work published 2003)

[95] Strickler, L. (n.d.). The Bigfoot Paradox. Retrieved December 26, 2018 from https://www.phantomsandmonsters.com/p/near-end-of-overnight-appearance-of.html

[96] Camuto, C. (1997). *Another Country: Journeying Toward the Cherokee Mountains*. Athens, GA: University of Georgia Press.

[97] Fletcher, K. (September 6, 2007), Hot on the trail of the elusive Big Foot. Retrieved May 20, 2020 from https://www.thestar.com/life/travel/2007/09/06/hot_on_the_trail_of_the_elusive_big_foot.html

[98] Kachuba, John B. (2019). *Shapeshifters: A History*. London, UK: Reaktion Books Ltd.

[99] Ibid.

[100] Paulides, D. (2008). *The Hoopa Project: Bigfoot Encounters in California.* Blaine, WA: Hancock House.

[101] Paulides 2009.

[102] Steiger, B. (2013). *Real Ghosts, Restless Spirits, and Haunted Places* (2nd ed.). Canton, MI: Visible Ink Press.

[103] MacKillop, J. (1998). *A Dictionary of Celtic Mythology.* Oxford, UK: Oxford University Press.

[104] Paulides 2008.

[105] Treuer, A. (September-October 2012). Ojibwe Lifeways. *Minnesota Conservation Volunteer,* pp. 39-47.

[106] Breedlove, S. (2015, June 7). Episode 52: with Daryl Colyer and Brian Brown. Retrieved September 8, 2017 from http://saswhat.podbean.com/e/episode-52-withdaryl-colyer-and-brian-brown/

[107] Ibid.

[108] Bord & Bord 2006.

[109] Brandenburg, K. (November 5, 2011). Woman recalls afternoon sighting as a child near Port Angeles. Retrieved January 30, 2019 from http://bfro.net/GDB/show_report.asp?id=31009

[110] Pfohl, D. (April 26, 2006). Night time sighting by a youth leader at a bible camp near Grand Junction. Retrieved January 30, 2019 from http://bfro.net/gdb/show_report.asp?id=14503

[111] Smarr, J. (October 19, 2018). Passenger has a possible evening sighting in Sandy Hook. Retrieved January 30, 2019 from http://bfro.net/GDB/show_report.asp?id=61097

[112] Horne, G. (April 14, 2010). Sloth fur has symbiotic relationship with green algae. Retrieved May 11, 2019 from https://blogs.biomedcentral.com/on-biology/2010/04/14/sloth-fur-has-symbiotic-relationship-with-green-algae/

[113] Teale, S. (1979). *Giants.* New York, NY: Harry N. Abrams, Inc.

[114] Nunnelly, B. (2017). *The Inhumanoids: Real Encounters with Beings That Can't Exist!* US: Triangulum Publishing (2nd ed.).

[115] Burnette & Riggs 2014.

[116] Ibid.

[117] Worley, D. (1982). Case 135. In A. Rosales (Ed.), *1964 Humanoid Sighting Reports.* Retrieved February 5, 2014 from http://www.ufoinfo.com/humanoid/humanoid-1964.pdf

[118] Ibid.

[119] Ibid.

[120] Ibid.

[121] Beck, R.A. (1967). I Fought the Apemen of Mount St. Helens, WA. Retrieved January 30, 2019 from http://www.bigfootencounters.com/classics/beck.htm

[122] Bishop, G. (2017). The Co-Creation Hypothesis: Human Perception, The Informational Universe, and the Overhaul of UFO Research. In R. Graham (Ed.), *UFOs: Reframing the Debate* (pp. 189-208). Hove, UK: White Crow Books.

[123] Renner, T. (April 23, 2020). Strange Familiars Episode 163: The Beast. Retrieved June 21, 2020 from https://www.strangefamiliars.com/home/the-beast

[124] Ibid.

[125] White, G. (August 15, 2016). Details and the Devil. Retrieved June 21, 2020 from https://runesoup.com/2016/08/details-and-the-devil/

Some folks call them bird traps. Old aunty told us that they were "devil nets." You put 'em around the bed, catch the devil before he gets too close.

- Minister,
True Detective Episode 1, Season 1:
"The Long Bright Dark"

Hex Signs

    Some bigfoot believers, both modern and ancient, have offered a rather idealistic view of the creatures as *Guardians of the Forest*—a somewhat ironic title for entities that inflict so much damage to trees, both assumed and witnessed. Multiple witnesses have reported bigfoot creatures snapping or twisting trees and limbs (presumably in anger or as a show of strength) as they walk through the forest. Of course there are also the powerful wood knocks, presumed to be bigfoot smashing limbs, rocks—*something*—against trees. Last, but not least, there are the enigmatic tree structures which tend to show up in areas where bigfoot activity has also been reported.

    Because of their alleged affinity for breaking, bending, and knocking trees, bigfoot's arboreal association is a foregone conclusion. Our wild men, whatever forms they have taken, have always lived in the dappled shadows of the forest. At some point in our evolution, man chose savannah over trees, building villages in clearings, cutting down trees to make open spaces. Were we trying to escape The Other that dwells within the deep, dark wood? Or did The Other move beyond the tree line when man chose the fields? Whatever the reason, the forest became a place of mystery... and danger. Within forests dwell—besides lions, and tigers, and bears (oh my!)—trolls, elves, witches... and, of course, bigfoot.

From the Trees

Medieval depictions of wild men blend with the forest itself. Artistic representations of the Green Man and some *Wodwose* illustrations appear wholly comprised of branches and leaves. In modern times, bigfoot are commonly reported with sticks, leaves, and moss in their hair; this detail strongly reflects indigenous Native American traditions such as the Cherokee *Nun'yunu'wi* ("Stone Coats") or the Seneca *Genoskwa* ("Stone Giants"), legendary cannibal giants with impenetrable skin. Some researchers equate these creatures with bigfoot, suggesting the creatures roll in mud (or mud and gravel) which only gives them the *appearance* of stone skin.[1]

Bigfoot researcher Bob Garrett gathered similar testimony suggesting bigfoot use mud to attach leaves to their hair for camouflage.[2] A similar theory proposed by Daniel Dover, author of *Evidence Sasquatch Camouflage Themselves*, suggests the scaly, bipedal South Carolina Lizardman—which allegedly harassed the Bishopville swamps circa 1988 — may have in fact been a bigfoot with dried mud, algae, and other detritus caked into its hair.

Dover asserts dried and cracked mud could impart the appearance of scales.[3] The Honey Island Swamp Monster, a large, hairy hominid from the bayous of Louisiana, is sometimes reported with weeds entangled in, or possibly an algae bloom on, its hair (something commonly seen in the coats of sloths—as noted in Chapter 6, a relict giant sloth has been posited as the culprit behind South America's *Mapinguary* sightings).[4]

Other encounters, covered extensively in Chapter 3, describe bigfoot mimicking tree stumps, rocks, and logs. For example, Brian "Duke" Sullivan, a bigfoot investigator and podcast host from Montana, told of a 2015 incident in which he saw a bigfoot "pretending to be a stump." Sullivan noticed what he thought was a stump with a peculiar face-like pattern on it. He reached for his video camera, intending to document the stump as an example of pareidolia, when he noticed the face's expression had changed. At this time he realized the "stump" was in actuality a bigfoot creature, which appeared rather upset at the prospect of being filmed. Sullivan decided to move along, rather than deal with an angry stumpsquatch.[5] Similarly, a witness in Benzie County, Michigan in the mid-1980s reported seeing a large boulder in a field which, after a time, proceeded to stand up. It had the shape of a person, but the witness said it looked to be two feet taller than the average man, with arms hanging down to its knees.[6]

Kevin Jones, a 16-year old hunter in the Blue Mountains of

Washington, observed a bigfoot creature for 45 minutes through his rifle scope. At some point, two other hunters walked by the creature which turned, curled its body, and took on the appearance of a stump. The hunters walked within 15 feet of the creature and seemed to look directly at it. Jones noted that the hunters seemed startled at first, but quickly seemed to lose interest, and simply walked away.[7]

The color most associated with the forest is perhaps green. Green bigfoot, as alluded to in *Where the Footprints End* Volume I, Chapter 3, are more common than traditional cryptozoologists would have us believe.

Additional reports of green bigfoot:

• The infamous "the two brothers" from *Where the Footprints End* Volume I, Chapter 8 have allegedly seen numerous bigfoot, including a large creature with green hair.[8]

• Toad Road in York County, Pennsylvania is an area fraught with strangeness—in addition to reports of winged entities, ghosts, and mystery lights, witnesses have also reported bigfoot. In 1973, a "green haired monster" attacked a witness in the area.[9]

• Jeff Beaudoin was camping atop a mountain in Maine with his cousin. After the two heard several tree breaks, Jeff's cousin witnessed a bigfoot with a green face looking at them from *above* a ten-foot spruce tree. The rest of the night the two men experienced several hallmarks of bigfoot encounters... including some stranger aspects, such as the sounds of a woman singing and an ATV, neither of which were noticeably present.[10]

• "Fluorescent Freddie" was a ten-foot tall monster seen in the region of French Lick, Indiana in March of 1965. While some cryptozoologists report that "Freddie" gained the title "Fluorescent" due to his glowing red eyes, they usually omit the strange fact that the same witnesses stated "Freddie" was covered with emerald green fur.[11]

• Millrace Park, Indiana residents reported multiple encounters with a "Green Haired Monster" in November 1974. In one incident, a resident heard strange noises before discovering the monster in a garage. He locked the creature inside, but when police were called nothing was found (of course).[12]

Some bigfoot aficionados—admittedly, those who tend to dwell on the opposite side of the spectrum from the F&BH folks—have even suggested that bigfoot somehow live *inside* trees—or use trees as some sort of means to enter our reality.

In an episode of his television series *Survivorman - Bigfoot*, survivalist, musician, and filmmaker Les Stroud visited northwest California in search of answers to the bigfoot mystery. Deep in the forest, accompanied by a Hupa guide named Inker, Stroud found his electronic equipment and cameras malfunctioning in strange ways. They heard wood knocks... then, sitting by a large cedar, noticed knocks that seemed to issue from *inside* the tree. Stroud noted that cedars can be hollow from top to bottom, large enough that "anything large could live inside."

After attempting—and failing—to build a fire several times (a skill Stroud can execute expertly), Stroud wondered aloud, "I don't know if they want us here"... "they," presumably, being the local sasquatch. With a wet snow falling, and all available kindling soaked, the men nearly abandoned hope of a fire when suddenly, a mere 50 feet away, a tree fell, revealing a fresh supply of dry wood. Using this kindling, Stroud lit their campfire at last.

The wood knocks continued during this process, sounding to Stroud as if emanating from inside the tree, at seemingly deliberate intervals, until the moment the fire was lit—at which point they ceased. "I started out looking for what I was told was a big ape," said Stroud. "Now I'm not so sure anymore." Stroud has since experienced a number of harrowing encounters, covered throughout these volumes.[13]

A small but persistent set of cases also describe wood knocks coming from inside trees. The author of the *Bizarre Bigfoot* blog detailed an expedition where researchers Russell Accord and Adam Davies experienced knocking noises that seemingly emanated from a large double tree. From the blog entry:

> Stopped about twenty feet from the knoll, with my video camera recording I heard two distinct thumps. "Whump whump"... with Davies just behind me, he said, "Did you hear it?" And I replied, "Twice," in soft voice, absolutely surprised.
>
> I was puzzled, but strove to remain calm and as Adam climbed the small knoll, happy to get results so quickly, JB arrived to acknowledge that he too heard the strange thumps. What the hell was this?
>
> I held my recorder as still as possible while Davies spoke to the tree, "Hi Big Guy!!... we're so glad to know you're here!"

The author of the blog notes that one member of the expedition considered the tree itself a conscious entity, something more than your average tree, while Davies was "fully convinced that a creature lives inside or underneath the big double tree."[14]

One of the most controversial personalities in the bigfoot community is Dr. Matthew Johnson. Johnson has made some truly bizarre claims, including that he helped migrate 23,542 bigfoot "souls" from their dying planet to Earth. According to Johnson, these bigfoot souls come to Earth in the form of orbs, but then become trees. Johnson claims a bigfoot named Zorth told him bigfoot do not knock on trees, but create the sound, somehow, from *inside* trees. According to Johnson, Zorth said, "We are inside the trees during the day..."[15]

There is an incredibly strong folkloric precedent for strange creatures of all shapes and sizes living in trees. Setting aside all other ephemeral spirits—tree-residents such as fae folk, dryads, little people, wood nymphs, and sundry winged things—here is a small sampling of bigfoot-like critters said to make their homes inside trees:

- The King of the Forest was said to inhabit the oldest, most gnarled trees of each wood in Northern Europe. Depictions of his woodland majesty always show him holding an uprooted fir tree. (Belsnickel figures from the Pennsylvania German country often show the Christmas wild man holding an evergreen tree.)[16]

- In Scandinavia, ash trees were thought to be homes for ogres or, sometimes, *actual* ogres themselves, cloaked in a sort of glamour to appear as trees (as discussed later in this chapter, Yggdrasil, the Norse world-tree, was sometimes depicted as an ash tree—see also *Where the Footprints End* Volume I, Chapter 5).[17]

- The *Norg*, a sort of demon from Norway, made its home in trees.[18]

- "Forest Demons" in Denmark hid themselves in old cherry trees.[19]

- West Africa's Senagambia is home to a "tree demon" with long hair.[20]

- A Russian proverb states that either owls or *devils*—a descriptor inextricably linked to Bigfoot lore, as covered throughout these volumes—dwell in all old trees.[21]

There are stories too, where trees themselves become animate. A wonderful example comes from Scottish folk musician and storyteller Robin Williamson. Williamson relates *The Battle of the Trees*, a writing attributed to the bard Taliesin. In this story the magician Gwydion calls to life all the trees of Britain to battle with an army from the Otherworld.[22] A variation on this concept appears when Shakespeare's Macbeth sees his doom in the form of an entire forest moving against him. While Birnam Wood was felled and moved by the hands of the invading force come to dethrone Macbeth, it was those old friends of bigfoot, the witches (see *Where the Footprints End* Volume I, Chapter 6), who prophesied:

> Macbeth shall never vanquish'd be until
> Great Birnam wood to high Dunsinane hill
> Shall come against him.

In *The Lord of the Rings* trilogy, Tolkien wrote of the *Ents* (*ent* being an Old English word for "giant"), a population of ancient, wise—but easily angered—forest guardians who took the form of enormous animated tree-beings. The Ents, according to Tolkien lore, were trees "awakened" by the magic of the elves in an earlier age.[23]

Bends, Twists, Circles, and Portals

Bent stick structures and glyphs are attributed to Bigfoot worldwide, though no one has actually *seen* a bigfoot creature making these designs: combinations of broken trees, deadfall, and living trees bowed, twisted, and wedged into various shapes like arches, teepees, lean-tos, and more. For the most part, bigfoot researchers believe these represent some sort of sign system, perhaps trailway markers. Though some suggest they are hunting blinds or even shelter, most of these structures (with very few exceptions) are open to the sky and would very poorly serve that purpose.

Assuming these structures are markers of some sort—and that they mean *something* to their makers—we will generally refer to them as "stick signs." These stick signs tend to fall into two general categories: stick structures and glyphs.

Stick structures tend to be built up from leaning or interlocking trees and branches, or sometimes by driving uprooted trees or larger limbs into the ground in order to keep them upright. Glyphs are subtler and are arrays of sticks or other material placed on the ground, boulders, logs, benches, etc. Often there are rock cairns and other structures composed of both found (i.e. manmade) and natural items (bones, feathers, acorns, et. al.), all of which are incorporated into the stick signs or used on their own. Gifting—the act of Bigfoot exchanging food and other items with humans, either in return for other things, or as a sort of present—is addressed in *Where the Footprints End* Volume I, Chapter 5. Instead, our interest here lies with the idea of meaning or communication imparted in these glyphs. Unlike other subjects covered in these volumes, there is not an abundance of folkloric precedent for entities communicating via sticks. There are some notable exceptions.

While not broken sticks *per se*, the Western European idea of the "faerie ring" does involve The Other manipulating nature for its own unknown purposes. Faerie rings are often circles of mushrooms, but can take the form of patches of grass, greener than that around it, or other circles of vegetation somehow set apart from the landscape. To step into the faerie ring was always a dangerous proposition— for one could be entranced or otherwise *taken* by the fairies merely by entering the ring.[24] (See *Where the Footprints End* Volume I, Chapter 1 for a faerie ring appearing in an area known for multiple bigfoot sightings.)

In Russian folklore the *Leischi* were a sort of tutelary forest genii thought to inhabit groves and, especially, birch trees. One could summon the Leischi by making a sort of magic circle of young birch trees. The trees were cut and arranged in a circle with the points facing inward. Entering the circle, the summoner would call upon the Leischi, at which point the spirit would appear. It was important to then face East, place one's foot on one of the birch stumps, bend at the waist, and, while speaking through one's own legs, implore the Leischi to take a friendly shape: "Uncle Lieschi, ascend thou, not as a grey wolf, not as an ardent fire, but as resembling myself." All the leaves were said to tremble as the Leischi took human form, and, provided the summoner promised his soul to the spirit— the Leischi would then offer its services.[25]

In other legends, it was said the Leischi themselves "engaged in fierce skirmishes" and "pulled out trees by the roots." It is particularly noteworthy that artistic representations of the Leischi and its Slavic variants—*Leshy, Lesnik, Lesovik, Lesovoi*, etc.—commonly appear as archetypal *satyrs* or wild men: tall, bipedal, and hairy.[26]

Another folk magic practice originating in the United Kingdom used sticks to form a sort of "spirit portal." This arrangement of sticks was accompanied by a "peculiar vocalization" (tying into the odd sounds attributed to bigfoot). The resultant portal, with practice, is said to allow efficient communication with the spirit world.[27] Other folk magic practices from Europe involved tying knots in tree branches as a kind of transference of sickness or pain (that of a toothache, for instance).[28] In other cases, charms for various purposes were inserted in holes bored in tree trunks, which were then plugged with a piece of wood.[29]

Similar signs and shapes occur in a variety of bigfoot encounters. The author, in the company of eyewitness Geof—whose bigfoot experience is detailed in *Where the Footprints End* Volume I, Chapter 8— saw knotted branches in trees beside the boulder field at White Rocks, Pennsylvania.

The Upside-Down

The haunted Hexenkopf Rock, located in Williams Township, Pennsylvania has enough folklore associated with it to fill a book of its own. (Indeed, a book has been written on the topic: Ned D. Heindel's *Hexenkopf: History, Healing, and Hererei*.) The name *Hexenkopf* is translated as "witch's head," and the list of oddities associated with the landmark reads like a dizzying catalog of the folkloric and supernatural motifs covered at length in both volumes of *Where the Footprints End*. While it is most closely associated with powwow—a folk magic practice originating with the Pennsylvania Germans—other oddities reported around Hexenkopf Rock include tales of buried treasure; a gigantic, ghostly figure dressed in white; the spirit of a headless man and his companion, a similarly headless black dog; strange lights in the form of fire balls—often accompanied by sulfurous fumes; a Wild Hunt-like "spectral troop of headless Continental soldiers who, with the rock as their headquarters, rode out to patrol the township on dark and moonless nights"; and disembodied voices in the form of "moanings of the dead and the softly preached words from old funeral rites."[30]

Hexenkopf Rock is also closely located to Lenape Indian burial mounds in the vicinity, supposedly plowed over in the 1890s, and the area boasts tales of a witch who requested—and received— gifts of meals from local farmers. This witch was said to cause illness in people and to braid the manes of horses, a behavior often attributed to bigfoot.[31]

Another entity associated with Hexenkopf is a woman-in-white spirit. The practitioners of Urglaawe, a pagan tradition based in Pennsylvanian German beliefs and heritage, meet at Hexenkopf each April. The Urglaawe believers see this woman-in-white as the goddess Holle, a figure closely associated with Perchta (see *Where the Footprints End* Volume I, Chapters 5 and 8 for more on Perchta).[32]

Urglaawe adherents have also claimed to witness *upside-down trees* scattered around Hexenkopf.[33] Trees inverted and impaled into the ground with their roots facing skyward are sometimes attributed to bigfoot.

Sasquatch Investigations of the Rockies (SIR) reported one finding of a tree, impaled roots-up on a ridge in Northern Colorado, "adjacent to an area of known [bigfoot] activity in the past."[34] Of these inverted trees, SIR noted, "This is Sasquatch related activity mainly found in the West, Canada and Alaska."[35]

In the early 1990s a series of cedar trees—jammed top-down, roots-up, "thirty yards apart, into a muskeg in perfectly vertical fashion"—were found in Alaska north of Klawock Lake, Prince of Wales Island. This "discovery" was in actuality preceded by longstanding indigenous awareness of trees "jammed into the soft muskeg by huge two-legged creatures as markers" in the area.[36]

The trees themselves are harrowing to behold: between nine-and-twelve-feet tall, devoid of bark, without a machined mark upon them. Their perfect verticality rules out timber accidentally dropped from helicopters, as, according to sasquatch researcher J. Robert Alley, "logs from helicopter 'dropped turns' are invariably set into the ground at an angle."[37] Alley quotes from researcher Al Jackson's interview with indigenous informant H.M.:

> My uncle also told me that Old-Man Albert Brown had warned them that, 'whenever hunting above the lake on Klawock Mountain, you have to watch out for those big black gorillas that live up there. They mark their territory by driving blown-down trees into the ground, upside down, with the root wads up in the air.' Of course, people thought he was making up stories, until they built the logging roads up there forty years later and found the trees.[38]

"Survivorman" Les Stroud inspected another upside-down tree on an episode of his Survivorman Bigfoot series. Stroud determined the tree was not hammered into the ground, nor was its hole machine-dug. While not outright declaring a bigfoot creature drove the tree into the ground, Stroud did rule out human hoaxing as the source of the oddity.[39]

Back in Pennsylvania, another upside-down tree was found in February of 2017—forming part of an X-structure along the mysterious Toad Road.[40]

When the Bough Breaks

The tale *A Summer Night in a Norwegian Forest*—which is itself really a collection of stories-within-stories, as so many folktales are—features some tree-related strangeness. One man tells a story of his father who was transported on a strange journey after cutting a "withered fir" surrounded by other withered firs. The woodcutter was taken to what seems to be a sort of faerie hall, only to be returned to the withered trees after refusing to consume their food and drink. Scattered throughout this tale are other interesting details hinting at the bigfoot/wild man archetype: large, wide footprints that, after followed for a distance, seemingly end; a bear with glowing eyes; and, most interestingly, a man "broad as a barn door" with hands "nearly a foot across at the knuckles." This man also had saucer-sized eyes like "burning cinders" with bristly hair and beard.[41]

Elsewhere in Scandinavia, the Danish forest of Rugaard was said to have, within its borders, a leafless tree. Though this tree appeared like other trees, it was, in fact, an elf disguised as a tree (see bigfoot tree mimicry). After nightfall this "tree" ambled through the forest. Great harm was said to befall any who tried to cut or harm this elf-tree.[42] Similarly, the Norwegian *Niagiusar* was a sort of goblin said to inhabit trees of the Faroe Islands. It was considered unwise to cut down certain old trees, as this is where the Niagiusar made their homes.[43]

Wood-Wives, elusive female forest spirits of Germany, were the quarry of the Wild Hunt (detailed further in *Where the Footprints End* Volume I, Chapter 8). If a Wood-Wife could reach a tree with a cross on it, however, she would be safe from the Huntsman and his horde. For this reason, woodcutters often carved three crosses into trees and stumps.[44]

Such folklore recurs internationally. India's *Maruts* were storm gods, but echo The Wild Hunt in their rampages: they would shake all beings and, like bigfoot with their reported tree breaks, could "chew up the forests like elephants."[45] In the Fan region of the Congo, heaps of branches could be found in the forests. Leafy limbs were laid in piles by forest travelers as a sort of offering to demons—or perhaps as an act of sympathetic magic. Placing a branch on the heap insured one would not be hit by a falling limb or tripped up by the roots of trees on his forest passage.[46]

The Japanese *Kodama* were forest spirits inhabiting ancient trees and protecting the forests. The *Kodama* could appear as ghostly figures or as orbs of light (orbs are, of course, often seen in areas associated with bigfoot and sometimes even *alongside* bigfoot). Felling a *Kodama's* arboreal residence could result in a powerful curse, condemning an entire community to ill fortune.[47]

Multiple folk stories relate, for one reason or another, tree-breaking or cutting taboos. While not a folkloric explanation for bigfoot tree breaks or stick signs, these tales suggest tree-breaks hold significance for indigenous peoples worldwide, and a suggestion that humans should avoid such practices.

Stick Dolls and Devil Nets

Pop culture provides clearer echoes of the bigfoot stick sign thanks to the hairy, scary Blair Witch. In *The Blair Witch Project*, cairns, bundles of sticks, and the iconic "stick dolls" were all left as signs to the tormented characters.

More recently, the first season of HBO's *True Detective* television series delivered a powerful and bleak combination of Southern Gothic and Lovecraftian dread. Amongst other occult symbols found around the program's various crime scenes were *bird trap* fetishes—or *devil nets*—creepy assemblages of sticks bound into rough teepee or pyramid-like structures. *True Detective* also happened to feature what was, by a child's description in the series, a "green eared spaghetti monster." The composite sketch by the police artist appeared very much like the Green Man.

Artist Lee Brown Coye utilized recurring lattice-like stick and board motifs in his drawings, published in a variety of magazines such as *Weird Tales*. In the spring of 1938, Coye stumbled onto a very strange property while fishing at Mann Brook in central New York. He had followed a series of cairns and stones set in arcane patterns on the ground to an abandoned farmhouse. According to Coye, this property was surrounded by lattice structures, primarily sticks and boards fastened together by means of wire and nails.

"The lawn and trees and even the house were covered with these structures," Coye stated. He entered the house to find the walls covered with "fantastic murals" of abstract design. Coye said these images appeared to have been drawn with charcoal.[48]

As Coye explored the basement of the house, a hand reached out from the darkness and grabbed him (shades of the hairy hand phenomenon as covered in *Where the Footprints End* Volume I, Chapter 7). He hit this unseen assailant with an iron frying pan and beat a hasty retreat from the abandoned house. Coye later returned to Mann Brook in 1963 to look for the strange property but was unable to locate the house. He later wrote it had been washed away due to flooding.

Coye's tale of finding the lattices and abandoned farmhouse was fictionalized into Karl Edward Wagner's 1974 short story *Sticks*. Bringing our pop culture discussion of stick structures full circle, many cite *Sticks* as the original inspiration behind both *The Blair Witch Project* and *True Detective*.[49]

Cryptoanthropology:
The Religio-Magickal Bigfoot

Interestingly—despite the overwhelmingly *supernatural* purposes of stick structures in art—most bigfoot researchers attribute nothing but mundane purposes to stick signs. Everything from trail or territory markers to hunting blinds and even warnings for humans to "keep out" has been suggested. (Attributing the "Keep Out" message to two trees crossed in an "X" formation in the woods is such a gross anthropomorphization of the bigfoot phenomenon that this leap in logic itself seems almost paranormal.)

In his book *A Field Guide to Sasquatch Structures*, author Christopher Noël documented 50 different types of common stick formations attributed to bigfoot. Noël believes such structures are mundane signage that simultaneously meet the emotional/psychological needs of these creatures—akin to traits found among autistic populations—and satisfy a desire for intense focus and the orderly arrangement of objects.[50] (Most bigfoot stick structures do not appear very orderly, but perhaps the author is applying a human personification of "order," while the builders of the structures exhibit the concept differently.)

Another, far more complex, order to the structures is suggested in *The Vertex Correlation*, a short documentary film examining a series of stick structures in Florida. The filmmakers cast the mundane aside as they suggest these structures represent an *asterism*—a pattern of stars. The filmmakers plotted three tree structures using GPS devices and found each to be five miles from the others, forming a shape corresponding to the Winter Triangle, an asterism including the stars Sirius, Betelgeuse, and Procyon.

Not only did the position of the structures geographically correspond to the Winter Triangle, but their triangular shape matched the same angles. At least one of the structures aligned with the constellation Orion—of which the Winter Triangle is a part—as it moves through the night sky. The filmmakers assert the structure's builders possess some ability to "look down" upon the earth from a higher vantage point and, likewise, note that, "The builders are geniuses—whoever they are."[51]

Adjusting our view of stick signs, and looking past the mundane, we must wonder if there isn't an entirely overlooked possibility: could stick signs go beyond simple communication and suggest religion, or even magical practice? Could they be idols of unknown bigfoot gods? Fetishes, not unlike gigantic versions of the devil nets from *True Detective*? Altars for strange ceremonies? A kind of spiritual "Keep Out" sign, akin to the hex signs placed on the barns of Pennsylvanian Germans?

In occult practice, sigils are a kind of graphic spell. A symbol, created by the magician, is "charged" or imbued with power by various means (usually intense concentration or physical exhaustion). It isn't difficult to imagine stick signs as a sort of three dimensional sigil—left in the woods for purposes known only to their makers.

Lisa Shiel documented a series of glyphs left around her Texas home by what she presumed was bigfoot—she also found footprints, animals killed in strange ways, mysterious scat, and large urine stains. Along with the bigfoot signs came other weird phenomena—UFOs and other mystery lights, black panthers, and a presumed-to-be-extinct red wolf—phenomena inextricably joined to Bigfoot sightings, as illustrated in these volumes. It is worth noting that, when Shiel moved from Texas to Michigan, the glyphs and other phenomenon began appearing at her new residence.[52]

The glyphs left for Shiel included all manner of shapes and symbols created from sticks (mostly), stones, feathers, and found objects. The various glyphs Shiel photographed range from seemingly random collections of sticks, to "V" and "X" shapes, and arrow designs. Shiel also documented a circle of sticks, bringing to mind not only faerie rings and the Leischi tradition, but also *magic circles* in general. Magic circles are used in many occult traditions as a means of marking out a sacred space, containing spirits and other entities, or providing a kind of protective border for the magician.

One of the most striking glyphs Shiel discovered and photographed was what she described as "a long stick with a V-shaped stick crossed over it a few inches from the end". Though Shiel did not make this connection, this description is identical to the *elhaz* rune from the *Elder Futhark*. The Elder Futhark, commonly called "runes," is a runic alphabet once used by Germanic peoples.

The *Norns*, the three *wyrd* women of Norse mythology, shaped the fate of all things by carving runes into Yggdrasil, the World Tree. The great ur-wild man, Odin himself, received these runes after nine days of self-sacrifice: he pierced himself with a spear, fasted, and hanged himself from Yggdrasil. At the end of Odin's nine day ordeal, he could perceive both the meaning and power of the runes. The runes are recognized not only as a writing system, but also as a divination method and a means of imbuing power. The elhaz rune specifically is believed to perhaps represent Yggdrasil and, therefore, the mystical power of the universe.

The same symbol is alternately known as the *drudenfuss*, *drudenfuß*, or "witch's foot." "Witch's foot" is an incredibly interesting name for the symbol given bigfoot's connection to witches. Likewise, it is interesting that the witch's foot, according to this symbol, looks like a three-toed track or bird footprint —both of which have significance to tridactyl bigfoot prints.[53]

Even the random sticks documented by Shiel and others may have a magical purpose. *Cleromancy* is the magical system of casting lots for divinatory purposes. Sticks (also, bones, dice, and other objects) are cast and, depending on their position and relation to each other and/or their surroundings, can offer magical insight of some sort.

The upside-down trees too, may hold some spiritual or occult symbolism. Generally, inverted symbols in the occult are interpreted as having an opposite and sometimes negative meaning. If trees represent life, their branches reaching toward the heavens, could upside-down trees be symbols of death? (Volume I, Chapter 7 includes an exploration of bigfoot's relationship with death and the dead.) Given our hairy wild man's connection to Christmas (see Volume I, Chapter 5), it is worth noting that in the Middle Ages fir trees were hung upside down to represent the Trinity.[54]

It may seem outrageously bizarre to think of bigfoot creatures casting lots, making sigils, or building star maps in the woods, but this is only because bigfoot researchers have, in a sense, animalized our wild men. In an effort to force the square peg of bigfoot into the very narrow round hole of "natural creature" it has become nothing more than a "damned dirty ape." Cryptozoology by its very definition is a study of *animals*. The cryptozoologist searches for unknown or disputed animals. When looking at wild men, we instead require a sort of *cryptoanthropology*.

Of late the trend, even amongst ardent F&BH bigfoot believers, is to refer to these creatures as relict hominids—rather than mere apes. The theory that bigfoot is just an evolution of *Gigantopithicus blacki*—a prehistoric giant ape—has fallen out of fashion. Even the most practically-minded bigfoot enthusiasts have begun entertaining the idea that these creatures may be genetically closer to humans than has been considered for a very long time. The bigfoot community is putting away ideas of giant gorillas and dusting off our old archetypal forest friend (or fiend), the wild man.

Is it so outrageous to imagine, then, a wild man with some form of spiritual belief? It wasn't so long ago that we considered a hominid from which many modern humans still carry DNA, Neanderthal man, to be nothing more than a dumb savage. Recent discoveries of cave paintings, body adornments,[55] and musical instruments[56] have changed these notions of Neanderthals as club-wielding savages into a race of fellow humans with, it seems, *culture*: music, art, and, even rituals—a recently discovered grave site of a Neanderthal child suggests ritual, and possible ceremony, used in the burial.[57]

Likewise circles, comprised of broken stalagmites, were found within a Neanderthal cave site.[58] Could these be the first magical circles? At another Neanderthal site, seven bear skulls were discovered, all facing the same direction, and a human skull on a stake, in a ring of stones.[59] These, taken with cave paintings, suggest Neanderthal man possessed the capacity to grasp symbolic thought. It isn't a far leap from symbolic thought and/to ritual to/and magic.

If Neanderthals—hominids but not *Homo sapiens*—had culture and magic, then is it so bizarre to think that bigfoot, a possible relict hominid, could have cultivated similar beliefs? On the other hand, if bigfoot is not a hominid but *something else*—something *Other*—a creature unlike anything else on the planet, or a creature very much like the folkloric things that have always haunted humanity—then who is to say of what it is capable?

Some First Nations tribes pass down stories of bigfoot as magical practitioners. In an example from Episode 507 of the *Sasquatch Chronicles* podcast, eyewitness Ned described a tale from the Lakota Sioux regarding the origins of bigfoot. Ned stated:

> A tribe of what they [the Lakota] considered to be a type of people... a certain tribe turned itself toward black magic and consuming human flesh in a time of starvation... and they became evil and it actually caused some sort of change... Due to this, an evil tribe of natives arose that were basically what a lot of them consider to be sasquatch or bigfoot.[60]

Practicing witch and author Vanessa Kindell has contemplated the idea that bigfoot creatures may be a race of shamans with highly developed magical skills. Whereas humans chose to focus on material technology, Kindell suggests bigfoot might have, instead, focused on a kind of magical technology.[61]

Could bigfoot creatures be master wizards?

Hobos Without Bindles

Another possibility is that bigfoot-associated stick signs could be some kind of symbolic language, not unlike "hobo signs." Starting in the late 1800s, a transient American population known as hobos (grossly generalized, homeless traveling workers) began developing a system of symbols known as "hobo signs." These simple graphic codes relayed information about the area and who, or what, may be living there. For instance, hobo signs related whether a camp was safe or dangerous, if a kind woman lived in a nearby house, or there were threats like men with guns or angry dogs, etc.[62]

Hobo signs were not only made by individuals to remind themselves about the locality, but also as a sort of kindness to other itinerant persons, provided they understood the code. Perhaps it isn't difficult to imagine a transient population of bigfoot moving hither and thither across the countryside, leaving various signs for themselves and their fellow hairy brethren to give some indication about the resources or dangers in the area.

What may be harder to imagine, perhaps, is bigfoot making their way across the country by hopping trains, like so many hobos of America's past. Perhaps the reader is far enough in this book to guess what is coming next: yes, bigfoot creatures allegedly hitch rides on freight trains!

Stan Courtney, along with other researchers, noted the propensity for sasquatch to appear around railroad tracks and train yards. In 2012 Courtney related a tale of meeting another bigfoot researcher named Mike in southern Illinois. Mike had several bigfoot sightings along the railroad tracks which passed through wooded sections in the area. He told Courtney he thought the creatures were hopping trains. Bigfoot riding trains!

Courtney was dubious, having never heard of such a thing. His doubt soon turned to amazement, however, when he and Mike were leaving the area, and Courtney stood close to the tracks to get a good view of a passing freight train. Courtney looked at the cars, one by one, as they passed. Somewhere around the middle of the train he caught sight of something strange indeed:

> It was one of those trains carrying large cargo carriers, double-decker style. It was traveling at perhaps 30 mph. In between each car is a good size area. About half way through the train I saw a very large hair covered animal sitting down with its back towards the container. I only could see it for a couple of seconds and then it was gone. I was in shock and awe. It was almost surreal. It did not look at all like Patty from the Patterson-Gimlin Film. This had five inch long dark brown hair covering it down to where I could see, it's [sic] waist. I couldn't make out any facial details and it was looking down and not directly towards me.[63]

It is a strange, circuitous trackway of footprints leading from primal forests to railroad yards, a trackway that leaves signs and symbols of unknown meaning in its wake. A trackway that has taken us from faeries to wild men to gorillas and back again...

Where, indeed, do these footprints end?

[1] Anonymous. (June 12, 2016). Native American legends as Bigfoot evidence: issues and concerns. Retrieved February 1, 2019 from https://apesoftheuncannyvalley.wordpress.com/2016/06/12/native-american-legends-as-bigfoot-evidence-issues-and-concerns/

[2] Dover, D. (June 2014). Evidence Sasquatches Camouflage Themselves. Retrieved February 1, 2019 from http://sasquatchresearchers.org/blogs/bigfootjunction/2014/11/09/evidence-sasquatches-camouflage-their-hairy-coats/

[3] Ibid.

[4] Renner, T. (2016). *Beyond the Seventh Gate*. North Charleston, SC: Createspace.

[5] Renner, T. (May 25, 2018). Patron Episode 16: The Windigo and Other Sightings. Retrieved August 13, 2020 from https://www.strangefamiliars.com/home/the-windigo-and-other-sightings

[6] Kimball, T.L. (September 21, 2008). Report #24776 (Class A): Near Bendon, woman and daughter recall their daylight sighting from automobile. Retrieved August 14, 2020 from https://www.bfro.net/GDB/show_report.asp?id=24776

[7] Sandsberry, S. (July 3, 2012). Yakima Washington Newspaper Shares Local Bigfoot Stories. Retrieved February 1, 2019 from http://www.bigfootlunchclub.com/2012/07/yakima-washington-newspaper-shares.html (Original article published in *The Yakima Herald-Republic* as *Giant in the Crosshairs*)

[8] Germer, W. (July 22, 2016). Sasquatch Chronicles Radio // SC EP: 237 We Need Help! Retrieved July 19, 2019 from https://sasquatchchronicles.com/scep237-we-need-help-members/

[9] Renner 2016.

[10] Monson, G. & Corson, S. (April 17, 2017). Monster X Radio presents Eyewitness Encounters: A Bigfoot Encounter of the Strange Kind. Retrieved August 14, 2020 from https://www.youtube.com/watch? v=Hu7kcSVhBNw

[11] Kirkwood, E. (March 22, 2003). Hairy Hoosier Monster a Freaky Nature Quest. *The South Bend Tribune (IN)*, p. C2(28).

[12] The Indianapolis Star. (November 10, 1974). Elusive Monster Remains on Prowl. *The Indianapolis Star (IN)*, p. 33.

[13] Stroud, L. (Writer & Director). (April 8, 2015). Season 6, Episode 2: Where the Myth Began [Television series episode]. In L. Stroud & B. Farrell (Producers), *Survivorman*. Huntsville, ON: Les Stroud Productions, Inc.

[14] S.A.R. (November 23, 2018). Bigfoot is the One Who Knocks. Retrieved February 2, 2019 from http:// bizarrebigfoot.blogspot.com/2018/11/bigfoot-is-one-who-knocks.html

[15] S.A.R. (May 15, 2017). Channeling Bigfoot. Retrieved February 2, 2019 from http:// bizarrebigfoot.blogspot.com/2017/05/channeling-bigfoot.html

[16] Porteous, A. (2002). *The Forest in Folklore and Mythology*. Mineola, NY: Dover Publications. (Original work published 1928)

[17] Ibid.

[18] Ibid.

[19] Ibid.

[20] Ibid.

[21] Ibid.

[22] Williamson, R. (1994). The Battle of the Trees. On *Songs of Love and Parting/ Five Bardic Mysteries* [CD]. The Music Corporation.

[23] Shippey, T. (2001). *J.R.R. Tolkien – Author of the Century*. Boston, MA: Houghton Mifflin.

[24] Hartland, E.S. (1891). *The Science of Fairytales: An Inquiry into Fairy Mythology*. London, UK: Walter Scott.

[25] Porteous 2002.

[26] Ivantis, Linda J. (1992). *Russian Folk Belief.* M.E. Sharpe, Inc. Armonk, New York.

[27] Dickerson, C. (January 28, 2019). Personal correspondence.

[28] Porteous 2002.

[29] Renner, T. (2019). Personal field work.

[30] Heindel, Ned D. (2009). *Hexenkopf: History, Healing, and Hexerei.* Easton, PA: Northampton County Historical and Genealogical Society.

[31] Ibid.

[32] Merlin, M. (October 31, 2016). Haunted Hexenkopf Rock Legends Live on in Technology, Religion. Retrieved May 15, 2020 from https://www.mcall.com/news/local/mc-hexenkopf-rock-haunted-halloween-2016-20161030- story.html

[33] Ibid.

[34] Sasquatch Investigations of the Rockies. (March 2011). Sasquatch Research Oddities. Retrieved May 15, 2020 from https://sasquatchinvestigations.org/bigfoot-research/sasquatch-oddities/

[35] Ibid.

[36] Alley, J.R. (2007). *Raincoast Sasquatch.* Blaine, WA: Hancock House. (Original work published 2003)

[37] Ibid.

[38] Ibid.

[39] Stroud, L. (Writer & Director). (April 22, 2015). Season 6, Episode 4: Giants of the Forest [Television series episode]. In L. Stroud & B. Farrell (Producers), *Survivorman.* Huntsville, ON: Les Stroud Productions, Inc.

[40] Renner, T. (2018). *Don't Look Behind You.* Charleston, SC: CreateSpace Independent Publishing Platform. Independent Publishing Platform.

[41] Asbjørnsen, P.C. (1883). *Folk and Fairy Tales.* (H.L. Braekstad, Trans.). New York, NY: A.C. Armstrong & Son (7th ed.).

[42] Porteous 2002.

[43] Ibid.

[44] Ibid.

[45] Ibid.

[46] Ibid.

[47] Meyer, M. (n.d.). Kodama. Retrieved May 18, 2020 from http://yokai.com/kodama/

[48] Hanley, T.E. (January 26, 2015). Lee Brown Coye (1907-1981)-Part Two. Retrieved January 31, 2019 from https://tellersofweirdtales.blogspot.com/2015/01/lee-brown-coye-1907-1981-part-two.html

[49] Hanley, T.E. (February 23, 2015). Lee Brown Coye (1907-1981)-Part Four. Retrieved January 31, 2019 from https://tellersofweirdtales.blogspot.com/2015/02/lee-brown-coye-1907-1981-part-four.html

[50] Noel, Christopher. (2016). *A Field Guide to Sasquatch Structures*. Scotts Valley, CA. CreateSpace.

[51] Connor, C. (Producer). (2018). *The Vertex Correlation* (motion picture). USA: The Trail to Bigfoot.

[52] Shiel, L.A. (2006). *Backyard Bigfoot: The True Story of Stick Signs, UFOs, and the Sasquatch*. Lake Linden, MI: Slipdown Mountain Publications LLC.

[53] Austin American Statesman. (March 25, 1971). Peace Symbol. *Austin American Statesman (TX)*, p 5.

[54] Mafie, C. (February 18, 2020). Exploring the Upside-Down Christmas Tree Phenomenon. Retrieved August 28, 2020 from https://www.thespruce.com/upside-down-christmas-trees-1976407

[55] Clark, L. (March 12, 2015). Neanderthal Jewelry Is Just as Fiercely Cool as You'd Imagine. Retrieved February 2, 2019 from https://www.smithsonianmag.com/smart-news/neanderthal-jewelry-just-fiercely-cool-you-imagine-180954553/

[56] Schuster, R. (December 15, 2016). Neanderthals Turned to Faith When Confronting Death, New Evidence Suggests. Retrieved February 2, 2019 from https://www.haaretz.com/archaeology/did-neanderthals-believe-in-god-1.5473681

[57] Ibid.

[58] Barras, C. (May 25, 2016). Neanderthals built mystery underground circles 175,000 years ago. Retrieved February 2, 2019 from https://www.newscientist.com/article/2090183-neanderthals-built-mystery-underground-circles-175000-years-ago/

[59] Dann, J. & Dozois, G. (2007). Preface. In J. Dann & G. Dozois (Eds.), *Wizards* (pp. ix-x). New York, NY: Berkley Books.

[60] Germer, W. (January 18, 2019). Sasquatch Chronicles Radio // SC EP: 507 Stalked in the Woods. Retrieved January 19, 2019 from https://sasquatchchronicles.com/sc-ep507-stalked-in-the-woods/

[61] Kindell, V. (October 2018 - February 2019). Personal correspondence.

[62] Lehner, E. (1950). *Symbols, Signs, and Signets*. Mineola, NY: Dover Publications.

[63] Courtney, S. (March 28, 2012). Railroading Sasquatches. Retrieved February 2, 2018 from https:// stancourtney.com/railroading-sasquatches/

Four toes don't make a foot.

- Anthony T. Hincks

Toes

    Footprints occupy a unique place in supernatural studies, providing physical evidence of phenomena that, if not wholly intangible, are transient at best. While feet and footprints seem less important to Ufology as a whole—that particular discipline is more obsessed with physical effects of "spacecraft" on environments—paranormal researchers like John E.L. Tenney have noted how the longstanding tradition of placing powder on floors to capture ghost footprints is mirrored in cryptozoology, where bigfoot tracks are coveted forms of evidence.

    Mankind held anomalous footprints in reverence long before enterprising 'squatchers began examining and collecting 18-inch casts in the Pacific Northwest. An enormous print embedded in rock on the banks of Moldavia's Tyras River is reputedly the footprint of the mythological hero Heracles; Herodotus described similar impressions of a three foot long print "like a man's" in Scythia, dimensions corresponding to the size of Perseus's sandals. Paleontologists and geologists have satisfactorily explained these natural formations, but legends, as they are wont, endure.[1]

    "In antiquity, heroes of myth were visualized as giants, yes, but they were not necessarily completely human," wrote historians Adrienne Mayor and William Sarjeant. "Heroes and giants could have animal attributes, extra limbs, and so on."[2]

    Though larger-than-life heroes were gifted equally magnificent extremities, by the 16th century some associated oversized feet with a life in the wilderness. Linnaeus called these individuals—supposedly raised by animals—*homo ferus*. Swiss physician Conrad Gessner described a boy trapped in a Salzburg forest:

> Of a reddish color, verging on blond; of a marked savagery, fleeing from men, and, when able, hiding in darkness. Because keeping him in captivity was not feasible because of his need to eat, he died a few days later. His back feet were different to his front ones and considerably larger—he was captured in the year of grace 1531.[3]

Anomalous footprints are unquestionably the most common and compelling physical evidence for bigfoot's existence, and few have done more to further their study than Dr. Jeffrey Meldrum, Professor of Anatomy and Anthropology at Idaho State University. Meldrum and his colleagues convincingly argue at least some portion of alleged bigfoot tracks are *not* hoaxes: they exhibit unique, difficult-to-reproduce features such as dermal ridges (whorls on the feet similar to fingerprints), underlying bone structures, or drag patterns only attainable from a biological foot.[4]

Specific casts, like the Bossburg, Washington (aka "Cripplefoot") tracks, even present specific podiatric injuries arguing against fraud. "It is very difficult to conceive of a hoaxer so subtle, so knowledgeable—and so sick—who would deliberately fake a footprint of this nature," said Dr. John Napier. "I suppose it is possible, but it is so unlikely that I am prepared to discount it."[5]

Footprints even suggest regional bigfoot subspecies. In the American southeast, where tales of slightly shorter, more simian "skunk apes" abound, tracks sometimes exhibit the fifth digit set at a 90° angle from the foot, akin to a human hand. This conforms to a typical pongidae (great ape) foot configuration.[6]

These encouraging findings make it all the more disappointing that an active effort seems determined to discredit or ignore footprints deviating from the accepted norm. In some sense, this is understandable; the study of these tracks is by far the most respectable and scientifically defensible reason to suspect bigfoot's objective reality—why sully it with three-toed footprints, one-footed trackways, or trails abruptly ending in the center of snow-laden fields?

From late, esteemed researcher John Green's foreword to Slate and Berry's 1976 book *Bigfoot*:

> In all, research in the area where I have been active has

roughed out the picture of a creature that presents no real problems except how to collect one. I am aware, however, that other people have found other things.

There are, for instance, footprints apparently made by feet with only three toes. These tracks have been reported, photographed, and cast both in southern California and in the eastern United States. I must confess that my attitude toward them is similar to that of my scientists toward the five-toed prints. I haven't seen one, and knowing no acceptable explanation for them, I'd just as soon forget them.[7]

Green added, "But the Sasquatch, as I know them, fit very logically among the other creatures of Earth—far more so than does man himself. If they have been seen near UFOs, I would prefer to consider it a coincidence or to assume that the occupants of the UFO were just looking at the Sasquatch, or vice versa." Though Green, to his credit, asked readers to read Slate and Berry's book full of High Strangeness with "full and fair consideration," his unwillingness to engage this outlying data is frustrating.[8]

More extreme resistance from the cryptozoological old guard came from Rene Dahinden. According to author Robert Schneck, Dahinden was examining a trackway of footprints dead-ending in the center of an open field when "someone suggested, jokingly perhaps, that the bigfoot flew away... Dahinden turned and left without saying a word."[9]

(Dahinden's aversion to High Strangeness is well-documented. When asked about the metaphysical encounters of Kewaunee Lapseritis, Dahinden exclaimed, "He had 235—or 500 by now—Sasquatch encounters... in his mind! I'm not interested in Sasquatch in his goddamn mind. I'm interested in Sasquatch in the bush on the ground. How many Sasquatch he has in his mind, I don't want to hear about it!")[10]

It is telling that Green and Dahinden—famously at odds with each other, so much so their rivalry was fictionalized as two opposing bigfoot hunters in the film *Harry & the Hendersons*—would find unity in a shared rejection of the paranormal. This trend continues to this day, though more researchers are slowly accepting High Strangeness in sasquatch reports.

"I know there are groups in the bigfoot community that believe any number of toes other than five on a foot is a hoax; I disagree," wrote researcher David Paulides. "There have been many legitimate sightings where four-toed prints were found. I don't have an explanation as to why some feet have different numbers of toes."[11]

While more dramatic topics are covered shortly, one topic rarely covered is the depth footprints exhibit. From the author of the Bizarre Bigfoot Blog:

> Firstly, as a layman, armchair researcher I am not seeking to roil anyone, but only want better explanations for why a creature that is ostensibly larger and heavier than a standing Grizzly bear, leaves footprints in soft soils or mud that do not correspond with a height/weight ratio for that animal. Let's pick an average of 8 feet tall and 350 lbs. to begin. Any engineer or math person will tell you that that a bipedal foot track for human weighing in this neighborhood, in soft soil or mud will sink to a much more noticeable degree than that of a more normal 200 lb. clothed human.
>
> Yet in photo after photo we find these tracks to be nearly equal in depth. The footprints of the surveyor is [sic] usually indistinguishable from that of the purported cryptid, except for its length and to a lesser degree, its breadth. [12]

Other oddities abound. Henry James Franzoni contends tracks are sometimes "too deep, even for a 1,500 lbs. [sic] animal… The deep footprints are always explained away as 'soil compression.'"[13] Footprints might appear rigid, static or "fake," even when coupled with convincing eyewitness testimony.[14]

In her final work *The De Facto Sasquatch*, Bobbie Short wondered, "Primates are not physically built to withstand sub-zero temperatures, which is why finding footprints left by the Sasquatch traversing miles and miles of deep snow mystify me; how is that accomplished without some manner of foot protection? Why don't their feet and ankles freeze?"[15] (F&BH advocates will correctly counter that Japanese macaques are well adapted to the cold, so this may not be all that unusual).[16]

These peculiarities pale in comparison to the truly bizarre characteristics of some bigfoot tracks.

Bidactyl and Tridactyl Footprints

"All primates have five toes," wrote Barton Nunnelly in his book *The Inhumanoids: Real Encounters with Beings That Can't Exist*. "There are no exceptions. Yet many of the footprints left by these creatures clearly show three, four, five, or even six or more toes on each print."[17]

Nunnelly is correct. While South American spider monkeys, woolly spider monkeys, and African colobus monkeys present missing or atrophied *thumbs*, all primates have five *toes*.[18] Generally speaking, the number of a mammal's toes is inversely related to how fast it can run (think of hooved animals, toed ungulates, canids, and finally man, on a rough spectrum of fastest to slowest).

Most sasquatch footprints presenting three toes do not appear as though the digits have been lost due to trauma. Generally speaking, these tracks depict three equally sized toes, or a larger, longer center toe flanked by two smaller ones. The heels, though rarely remarked upon, either taper to a point or appear much narrower than in "normal" five-toed prints.

Setting hoaxes aside—which are covered shortly—what could naturally account for three-toed, or tridactyl, tracks? F&BH advocates commonly cite syndactyly, a birth defect where multiple digits are fused. While common in certain mammals, it is considered rare in humans. Current estimates place incidence at one in 2,000-3,000 births.[19]

To be fair, it is certainly possible bigfoot may present this defect more commonly. The siamang, an arboreal gibbon native to Southeast Asia, derives its scientific name (*Symphalangus syndactylus*) from the webbing between the third and fourth digits of its feet and hands. Even so, syndactyly is not a common feature or deformity in great apes.[20]

Beyond possible syndactyly, tridactyl footprints are odd for other reasons. Their overall aspect is peculiar; with few exceptions, they do not have the appearance one associates with a typical bigfoot print. In these cases, the elongated heels and foot shape appear oddly avian—in a word, the entire affair looks *silly*, almost as though faked, or formed as an afterthought. As one Dr. Roth of the Baltimore Zoo astutely joked to Berry and Slate, "Perhaps if [sasquatch are] constructing and deconstructing and reconstructing themselves, they forgot to put on the rest of the toes!"[21]

It is a widespread misconception that tracks with odd numbered toes are confined to a single region. This is simply untrue. The idea comforts F&BH advocates because it preserves the notion bigfoot are undiscovered primates: since an estimated 10-40% of human syndactyly cases are inherited, it stands to reason—if syndactyly causes tridactyl tracks—the condition would occur within an isolated population in a specific region, perhaps due to inbreeding.[22]

Outliers are not confined to one single area, however. "Here in North America, three-toed tracks have been found in Pennsylvania, Oregon, Mississippi, and Florida," wrote Thom Powell in *The Locals*.[23] Tridactyl footprints are even attributed to Australian Yowies.[24]

Berry and Slate handily addressed this fallacy as early as 1976. "Stan Gordon, in his assessment of the Uniontown incident and others of the continuing Pennsylvania UFO-creature flap, argues that the bigfoot of West Coast tradition and the Pennsylvania variety could not be one and the same, chiefly, it seems, because the former usually has five toes and the latter only three," they wrote. Yet "three-toed (and four-toed) creatures have been reported out West, in fact, and descriptions otherwise are usually much the same."[25]

The below list of selected tridactyl footprint discoveries supports this assertion.

- A family near Albuquerque, New Mexico had several encounters with a blank-faced, man-sized figure roaming their backyard in October 1966. It cried like a baby and, in one instance, incapacitated a young witness. Peculiar prints shaped like a "fork" were found nearby.[26]

- Beginning in May 1972 a tall, hairy creature began prowling Cole Hollow Road near Peoria, Illinois, earning it the nickname "the Cole Hollow Road Monster," or "Cohomo." The nine-to-ten-foot tall, whitish-haired beast was responsible for more than 200 phone calls to the police department. Cohomo's "very unusual tracks showed that it had only three toes on each foot."[27]

- Numerous sightings from the 1973-1974 Pennsylvania UFO-bigfoot flap featured prints with three toes, so many it birthed the erroneous assumption that *only* Pennsylvania bigfoot are tridactyl.[28] Three *fingered* sasquatch were also spotted during this time: a Monongahela witness saw from her second story window a large, hairy arm with three claws dangling from the roof, and a print left on the side of a McChesneytown residence outlined a similar hand.[29]

- Louisiana's famed Honey Island Swamp Monster stalks the bayou, famously leaving behind "pointed three-toed footprints." Though descriptions vary, it is regularly described as a large, hairy hominid.[30]

- Witnesses in a Gibsonia, Pennsylvania mobile home spotted a bigfoot peeking through their window in July 1975. Claw marks were later found on the screen door, and tridactyl footprints were discovered in a nearby tunnel.[31]

- In 1976, indigenous people living near Poplar River,

Manitoba regularly observed a large, hairy creature around eight feet tall peeking in their doors and windows. The being was covered in grey-white fur and left behind three-toed tracks.[32]

- North Carolina's Chatham County boasted numerous sightings along the Cape Fear River in 1976. The bigfoot was approximately seven feet tall, ran with "a slumping gait," and would frequently scream. Tridactyl tracks, each measuring 18 inches, were found in the area.[33]

- A trio of children discovered large, three-toed footprints while playing in Somerset Hills, New Jersey in 1976. They also heard a loud knock and caught a glimpse of a bigfoot. Local newspapers claimed a flap of "hairy and scary giants" were terrorizing Rockaway and Chatham Townships. In neighboring Morris County, beasts "said to be nine feet tall… supposedly left 18-inch footprints, always with only three toes."[34]

The northern Ohio UFO-bigfoot sightings of 1981 are not often discussed, but featured a number of notable peculiarities. Witnesses on a rural farm in Rome, Ohio not only saw nine-foot tall, bulletproof bigfoot, but experienced close encounters with a variety of light phenomena, including glowing objects in the sky. They also spotted dark "shadow people" on the property; had automobiles mysteriously shutdown; discovered 1,200 lb. test parachute cords snapped to steal bait from traps; fired at something either shape shifting into (or projecting) a simulacrum of the family horse; and documented footprints displaying three and five toes.[35]

In his self-published book *Night Siege,* Dennis Pilichis—who witnessed much of the activity—described tridactyl prints found on the farm the morning after a June 25, 1981 encounter:

> Sure enough, we started finding a trail of prints left by the creature. They were large, circular footprints with three toe-like extensions. They were seven inches wide by eight inches long. From the way these prints were in the ground the middle "toe" appeared to sink in deeper then [sic] the side "toes." There were at least 40 or so of these impressions, starting from the side of the house and across the plow field up to the oil and gas wells west of the property. The trail was unusual in that there would be a few places where no prints appeared at all, then continued on the other side of this "void." There

was a six foot stride between prints (not all) and it appeared whoever or whatever made them, that is [sic] was walking on two legs.[36]

Even more puzzling than the tridactyl prints was a curious whorl pattern Pilichis noticed around another set of tracks. The 18-inch footprints, found early on July 6, seemed to retain the morning dew for a full 12 hours, and Pilichis observed that "the field grass was swirled around the footprint impressions in a clockwise direction. It was one of the strangest things I had ever seen." Nothing else in the field—neither tractor marks, nor the tridactyl prints and "big hoofmarks of some sort" found in the vicinity—displayed this effect. Though speculative, one's mind inevitably turns to crop circles, which display a similar whorl writ large around their designs.[37]

Even more peculiar than three-toed tracks are *two-toed* (bidactyl) tracks, recorded in a handful of other cases. Explorer James Alan Rennie stumbled across "a set of large, bear-like, two-toed tracks, spaced equally in a single line" traversing a frozen lake in northern Canada. Though no hairy creatures were observed, Rennie believed they belonged to a *Windigo*, a Native American entity sometimes synonymous with bigfoot (this belief was dispelled—or confirmed?—when Rennie saw the tracks *materializing in front of him*).[38] Recall also the Traverspine Gorilla (see Chapter 6 in Volume I of *Where the Footprints End*) which also left hooflike, cloven tracks (in some ways, bidactyl tracks are easier to dismiss than tridactyl tracks, as they are easily rationalized as misidentified ungulate footprints).

For those arguing tracks with anomalous numbers of toes are generally confined to the eastern half of the country, some of the most infamous bigfoot cases in history feature three-toed tracks—all west of the Mississippi River. Footprints collected in the wake of the Fouke Monster flap (beloved in the bigfoot community and immortalized in the 1972 cult film *The Legend of Boggy Creek*) presented three toes. Primary witness Smokey Crabtree wrote of several hundred tracks he found:

> There were only three toes and there wasn't all that much difference between the size of the first toe and the third toe. There was no place for other toes. It was not like his little toes had been burned off in a fire or frozen off. His foot was designed for three toes only.[39]

Other tridactyl footprints found west of the Mississippi—if only barely—include those from the Missouri Monster, or "Momo" sightings (see Chapter 2). Beginning in 1972, a hairy, bipedal creature appeared in the small community of Louisiana, nestled along the banks of the river. Momo killed animals... in one instance it was seen with a dead dog under its arm. Three days later, Louisiana residents leaving church spotted "two 'fireballs' soaring from over Marzolf Hill and descending into the trees behind an abandoned school across the street." One was green, the other white. (This is just one example out of a plethora of unexplained aerial phenomena, including "a perfect gold cross on the moon," during the Momo flap.)[40]

Tracks discovered on the farms of Freddie Robbins and Bill Suddarth in late summer all depicted three toes, including a set of prints 20-25 feet "away from anything else." "They began abruptly in the center of the garden and ended just as mysteriously," wrote author Troy Taylor. "It looked as if the three-toed creature had just appeared in the center of the garden and then vanished. No tracks were found anywhere else on the property and there was no sign any prankster could have made them either."[41]

Despite the popularity of stories like the Momo flap, some in the bigfoot community still dismiss their accompanying physical evidence, embracing eyewitness testimony while condemning the tracks as fake. This is not only intellectually dishonest, but illogical: why would a hoaxer create footprints with *three toes?*

"If you were going to create a hoax and you wanted to fool your local authorities for even a day or two, would you not put five toes in your fake footprint?" cryptozoologist Loren Coleman asked in *Mothman and Other Curious Encounters*. "After all, most so-called bigfoot tracks do show five toes. Why would a hoaxer leave such any [sic] obviously strange series of prints behind? It defies logic."[42]

Coleman is correct, and instead suspects three-toed tracks might represent a bigfoot subspecies or an entirely different type of large, hairy animal:

> E-mail lists and websites appear to be reinforcing the notion that everything huge and hominid, literally around the globe, is only some form of bigfoot or Sasquatch. Besides being extremely ethnocentric, typically American, and shortsighted, I think it's downright wrong. Such a view completely ignores the diverse spectrum of animals with which we are dealing. Take, for example, one variety—the three-toed, manlike animals (yes, a few researchers like me think there are more than one "type")...

> Sadly, bigfoot is the first frame of reference for news reporters, police officers, zoo keepers, and college professors —often the "first responders" who are called upon when anything big and unknown is seen or an unusual footprint found...
>
> ... To suggest that perhaps a different kind of animal, one with three toes, exists in some of America's swamps is just asking too much from some of these folks.[43]

Coleman's speculation is informed by firsthand experience. While the UFO-bigfoot flap rocked Pennsylvania in 1973, Coleman was investigating sightings in Albany, Kentucky. Two large "monkeys"—for they had long, bushy tails, a feature exceedingly rare in bigfoot reports— and a juvenile were seen on numerous occasions. The creatures, which alternated between two legs and all fours, could rear up to six feet in height and had a flat face, a cross between a human and an ape. One witness told Coleman how the animals wiped out two herds of pigs, and lived in an abandoned mine nearby. The creatures left tridactyl footprints, although in at least one case, nine toes were recorded.[44] Green and Dahinden had investigated sightings of similar creatures four years prior in British Columbia, where three toed tracks were discovered.[45]

"If there were just five-toed tracks and three-toed tracks and each type was of consistent shape, I would accept that as a clear indication of two different species," said Green. "Since there are four-toed tracks as well, and the three-toed kind are very inconsistent in shape, I don't think such a conclusion would help much."[46]

Separating five-toed sasquatch from tall, hairy hominids with fewer toes is a stance championed by Fortean author Jerome Clark, who pioneered the concept of Hairy Bipeds, or HBs. Clark coined the term to differentiate between the hairy, apelike humanoids seen in the Midwestern and eastern United States and more typical bigfoot creatures from the Pacific Northwest. A primary feature of HBs is their lack of distinguishing facial characteristics, as hair often obscures their faces.[47]

Perhaps the defining difference between bigfoot and HBs is their number of toes, which range from two to six. Writes George M. Eberhart in *Mysterious Creatures: A Guide to Cryptozoology:*

> All primates have five toes. Any Hairy biped that leaves clear imprints showing anything less than five toes constitutes an extreme evolutionary anomaly. Pentadactyly (having five fingers or toes) is a common and primitive feature of reptiles

and mammals. However, it is not an essential requirement, and many animals have modified the plan: frogs only have four digits, cows have two, horses have dropped all but one, and snakes have gotten rid of legs altogether. Most birds get by walking on only four (three in front and one behind), while the Ostrich (*Struthio camelus*) only has two. If three-toed, humanlike bipeds really exist as flesh-and-blood creatures and are not paranormal apparitions, it would be most interesting to find out more about their foot structure. Perhaps three toes is [sic] better than five when you've chosen a swamp or wetland as your habitat.[48]

Note how none of the examples given are closely related to primates.

"Anyone who has taken a basic course in biology would understand that such a departure from basic pentadactyly is approximately as likely in a supposed higher primate as a reversion to egg-laying," wrote Jim Brandon in *The Rebirth of Pan*.[49]

With all due respect, the subspecies or HB hypotheses comes off as yet another attempt to distance bigfoot sightings from High Strangeness, even though Coleman and Clark have written extensively on the paranormal, UFOs, synchromysticism, etc. The ideas also feel as if they unnecessarily multiple variables while simultaneously working backwards from an assumption: "Bigfoot are flesh-and-blood and always present five toes, therefore any deviation must be something other than bigfoot."

Bigfoot? Hairy Bipeds? Big monkeys? "A Sasquatch by any other name would smell as awful." This is to demean neither these researchers nor their literally invaluable contributions to cryptozoology, but rather to turn a critical eye on certain foregone cryptozoological conclusions.

The subspecies hypothesis is unpalatable even among respected cryptozoologists. John Napier wrote, "It is unthinkable that Sasquatch of north-western America, if it exists at all, should consist of two distinct families or even genera. The only alternative to such a travesty of evolutionary principles is that one of the two sasquatch footprint types are man-made artifacts."[50]

Nothing about bigfoot is proven or disproven, and it seems more parsimonious, if unacceptable in Materialist circles, to suggest we are seeing multiple manifestations of a singular wild man archetype, rather than positing elaborate taxonomies of flesh-and-blood primates. Surely the Rome, Ohio sightings—where both pentadactyl and tridactyl footprints manifested—suggest as much. Moreover, such a drastic divergence in foot structure, while not unheard of, is a significant morphological deviation for a primate subspecies to possess.

Indigenous lore yields a suitable precedent for tridactyl footprints. The Cheyenne *Maxemista* is a shy and retiring creature "somewhat like the Sasquatch or bigfoot of the Northwestern tribes, only with birdlike feet."[51] Bird tracks, of course, typically look three-toed, with the fourth toe either not presenting or appearing like an elongated heel. A Kwakiutl *Buk'wus* variant is described as a monkeylike, "half-bird child with a hooked nose and head feathers" which "cries like a bird or whistles"; it is unclear whether these avian features extended to the beings' feet.[52]

Three-toed bird tracks appear associated with wild men beyond the shores of the Americas. In European folklore, the *Wodewose* was occasionally depicted "astride a large bird," as in an illustration from *Dyson Perrins Folio*.[53] Other illustrations found in Tibetan Buddhism show *bamros*, attendants of *Shingkyong* protector spirits, as monkey-bodied beings walking upon their bird-clawed hands.[54]

Some Native American bigfoot analogues could detach their digits, providing an indigenous (if fanciful) explanation for the existence of two- and three-toed footprints. In Seneca myth the *Genonsgwa*, or stone skins, possesses "an animate finger that it uses to locate people who are hiding." A folk tale describes a wily elk hunter who craftily steals one *Genonsgwa*'s finger. The creatures, weeping across a river, beg the hunter to return the digit.

"The young hunter places the finger on his palm and stretches his hand over the stream toward the women as far as it will go," wrote Sam Gill and Irene Sullivan in their *Dictionary of Native American Mythology*. "When [the *Genonsgwa*] reach for it, they lose their balance and fall into the stream, sinking to the bottom."[55]

Tetradactyl Footprints

Unlike bi- or tridactyl footprints, tetradactyl (four-toed) bigfoot tracks are easier to explain through deformities or trauma. The overall shape of these four-toed prints is much more consistent with typical five-toed tracks. Like tridactyl tracks, four-toed prints appear worldwide: in Australia in 1912, Sydney Jephcott found tetradactyl tracks in the area of a Yowie sighting, remarking, "A striking peculiarity was revealed in the footprints; these, resembling an enormously long and ugly human foot in the heel, instep, and ball, had only four toes—long (nearly five inches), cylindrical, and showing evidence of extreme flexibility."[56] Similarly, North Central Nepal's *Nyalmo* are allegedly hairy giants standing 20 feet tall, and leave behind tetradactyl tracks.[57]

A few examples of tetradactyl tracks:

- **1902 – Idaho:** An eight-foot tall, hairy "boogie man" is spotted near Chesterfield on January 14. It wields a large club and leaves behind 16-inch tetradactyl footprints.[58]

- **1969 – Indiana:** The day after a neighborhood blackout, George Kaiser walks through his family farmyard on May 19 and sees a muscular, roughly five-foot tall figure covered in dark hair. Upon spotting him, the figure grunts, leaps over a ditch, and disappears down the road. Kaiser finds tracks the following morning of "a foot with three toes plus a large big toe that stood out like a thumb" (i.e. a pongid configuration, albeit missing a digit).[59] The family and neighbors had also noticed "mysterious lights" moving along a nearby ridge around the same time.[60]

- **1975 – New York:** On January 21, night nurse D. Daly nearly hits "a large bipedal creature covered with long black hair" as it walks in front of her car. Slamming the breaks, she stops within six feet of the beast, which stands just under six feet tall. Two tetradactyl footprints are found in the snow the following morning.[61]

- **1980 – Ohio:** Off-duty policeman Ray Quay stumbles upon a seven-foot tall bigfoot in his barn while unloading pigs in June. Quay steps forward to publicly share his story, which his colleagues investigate. They find "a number of clawed, four-toed prints" 16 inches long and four inches wide.[62]

- **1980 – California:** Prospector Dave Bishop and his wife are roused by something on two legs while camping near Red Cap Creek in August. The following day, Bishop finds one enormous, partial footprint with four toes.[63]

- **1997 – California:** A "monkey monster" chases children in Hesperia. The creature stands over six feet tall, is covered in dark brown hair, and runs "with bent knees in a non-human way." A single 14-inch track is found (an anomaly in itself, as discussed later) sporting four toes.[64]

- **2006 – California:** Roger and Sheila Huntington are driving home from Grants Pass, Oregon when they decide to stop near Eight Dollar Mountain. The family dog immediately leaps from the car and begins barking and running in the direction of a nearby creek. After a few seconds, several ten-pound rocks are thrown in its direction. Though no sasquatch is seen, Roger investigates the creek bank and discovers three prints, each with four clearly-defined toes.[65]

One of the earliest discoveries of four-toed tracks in North America comes from the journals of David Thompson, renowned surveyor, trader, and explorer who pioneered nearly 2.5 million square miles of the western United States and Canada. In an 1811 entry, Thompson wrote of a track discovered in six inches of snow: "I saw the track of a large animal, has four large toes, 3 or 4 inches long and a small nail at the end of each." The track measured 14 inches long and resembled a bear track (this, along with the reality that tracks melt and change shape in snow, may provide a mundane explanation, though Thompson's indigenous guides denied the possibility).[66]

Four fingers are also present in a handful of sasquatch sightings. Slate and Berry talked to Andrew Stone, a witness who observed a nine foot tall bigfoot peering in through his window, noting "the creature's immense hand, placed on the screen, revealed only four fingers with black claws."[67]

Numerous footprints of what cryptozoologist Mark A. Hall dubbed "true giants"—any hairy hominid more than nine feet tall—display only four toes. Hall argued this "shows us the result of the evolution of the primate foot to carry the size of True Giants… The fifth toe has become vestigial and is not prominent or might even be absent in some tracks." On the subject of tridactyl tracks, Hall further argues these prints only *appear* to have three toes "because three of the toes have become so small and bunched that they appear to be almost one toe." How these conclusions were arrived upon without a specimen remains unclear.[68]

Tetradactyl feet feature in indigenous art and lore. Amerindian petroglyphs found in Ledford Hollow, Kentucky depict large, four-toed prints; the lack of a characteristic "hour glass shape" suggests a representation of bigfoot, rather than human, feet.[69] Four toes are also found in rock art overseas, appearing in Europe—the mysterious Cochno Stone, unearthed in 1887 near Clydebank, Scotland, is dated to 3000 B.C. and features "an incised pre-Christian cross set within an oval, and two pairs of carved footprints, each foot only having four toes."[70]

Unlike tridactyl tracks, it is much easier to assume four-toed footprints result from a defect in the media, e.g. a five-toed foot slips and gives the *impression* of one less toe. A trackway discovered outside Evarts, Kentucky in 2008 suggests this possibility: after spotting what they initially assumed was a "large black bear," three friends found 15-inch footprints which presented "one big toe, and there were sometimes three other toes, and on one track there was [sic] four toes, or what looked like the slight imprint of a fourth toe" in "slippery mud."[71] Another set of tracks from 1997 in Chaffee County, Colorado was discovered in muddy snow and showed three, four, and five toes, although some were separated by a distance of 100 yards.[72]

Another rational explanation for tetradactyl prints is clinodactyly. This condition describes a digit curving inward. In feet, a toe may skew above or underneath another toe, obscuring its presence and giving the false impression of a missing digit in a footprint.[73]

Polydactyly and Other Shapes

While tridactyl and tetradactyl tracks represent a majority of the anomalous footprints associated with bigfoot, researchers have found even stranger shapes.

- A six-foot tall, gray haired, shaggy biped allegedly assaulted Law Chiu in March 1955 in Hong Kong. The villager fought off the creature, which ran away on all fours after Chiu punched it in the stomach. Large, triangular prints were supposedly found in the dirt, entirely dissimilar to any ape or human tracks.[74]

- Multiple witnesses in Presque Isle, Pennsylvania were left in hysterics after a metallic object descended onto the beach around 9:30 p.m. on July 31, 1966. They watched from their car as the UFO beamed strange lights through the trees. Within moments an "upright, gorilla-shaped" six-foot-tall creature shuffled toward them and scratched their vehicle.[75] "The next day quantities of silicon were found at the landing site," wrote John Keel, "along with some peculiar cone-like indentations in the sand" leading from the landing site to where the automobile had parked.[76]

- On July 17, 1974, three witnesses watched a "torpedo-shaped" UFO hover above a valley near Palmdale, California, and jettison "numerous dark masses" which fell to the ground. Though it was difficult to perceive details, the "blobs" each had two glowing eyes and dispersed into the forest. According to author Peter Guttilla, all three witnesses displayed "symptoms of sunburn and eye irritation the next day." Researchers following up on the sighting discovered 18-inch long tracks bearing "all the characteristics of the typical five-toed bigfoot prints, but with marked peculiarity. The foot was twisted and displayed a strange contraction of the toes in clusters, almost as if fusing together." The middle toes were enlarged, the fourth/fifth and big/second toes fused together, respectively.[77]

Other bigfoot exhibit what may be polydactyly—more than five digits. In 2010, North Carolina resident Tim Peeler claimed a 10-foot-tall, blonde-haired bigfoot wandered onto his Cleveland County property. "Peeler told authorities he thought the creature might be menacing his dogs," *The Charlotte Observer* reported, adding he saw "six fingers on each hand." More than three decades earlier, witnesses claimed to have sighted a large, hairy hominid dubbed "Knobby" around Carpenter's Knob, a nearby mountain.[78]

In summer 2008, witnesses in northwestern Ontario spotted an "upright, human-like" creature covered in black fur. "A large, six-toed footprint was found in the area 140 miles northeast of Winnipeg shortly afterwards," papers reported.[79]

Many of the fabled "giants" rumored to have once inhabited America—whose skeletons were discovered and purportedly confiscated by the Smithsonian Institution as part of a massive conspiracy—allegedly had "six fingers on each hand, six toes on each foot and a double row of sharp teeth."[80] According to contemporary newspaper articles, numerous specimens were exhumed from indigenous earthworks during the 1800-1900s, a claim supported by the strong precedent for depictions of polydactyl hands and feet in Native American rock art, particularly in the Southwest's Four Corners area.[81] Hard evidence for these skeletons is scarce, however, leaving most skeptics to level charges of "yellow journalism" deployed to inflate circulation.

Toeing the Line

The subject of hoaxes vis-à-vis oddly-toed footprints has been addressed. It would simply be a mind-bogglingly poor choice to fake tridactyl bigfoot tracks if the goal is to have them accepted as genuine.

While syndactyly and clinodactyly are attractive to F&BH advocates wishing to explain peculiar footprints, these remain unsatisfactory explanations for one primary reason: neither condition consistently manifests between both feet in clinical studies. Plenty of syndactyly cases in humans only appear on one hand or foot, and clinodactyly is even less likely to be identically mirrored on both sides, given its association with trauma. Exceedingly few trackways present fewer toes on one foot than the other; ergo, if bi-/tri-/tetradactyl prints are from a primate, they are much more likely to represent a subspecies than a deformed pentadactyl foot.

One popular explanation holds three-toed footprints are misidentified alligator tracks. In fairness, footprints left by alligators' rear feet do appear similar to tridactyl bigfoot tracks in the right medium, but their front feet are clearly tetradactyl. Moreover, alligator feet are also *much* smaller than the average sasquatch footprint—though, in the interest of honesty, prints may enlarge on a slippery, muddy riverbank. Even if alligators are responsible for anomalous footprints in the southern United States, three-toed tracks have been found in locations where alligators would be just as rare as large, hairy hominids.

Precedence exists for tridactyl feet among mammals, including the rhinoceros, kangaroo—important to later discussion—and, of course, sloth. There are four species of three-toed sloth and two species of two-toed sloth (which, in truth, have three toes and two *fingers*).[82] For this reason, some researchers speculate that the bigfoot leaving behind two and three-toed prints may represent some type of sloth or other related species. One popular candidate is *Megatherium*, a 20-foot long, four ton giant ground sloth presumed extinct for 10,000 years.[83]

Suffice to say, most bigfoot witnesses do not describe anything remotely resembling a gigantic sloth. There are, however, a handful of compelling exceptions, most notably the *Mapinguary*, a large, hairy beast from the Amazon rainforest. Depending on which tribe you ask, the *Mapinguary* "is tall, seven feet or more when it stands on two legs, [and] emits a strong, extremely disagreeable odor… it has thick, matted fur, which covers a carapace that makes it all but impervious to bullets and arrows." The creature can allegedly hypnotize victims.[84]

While all of these features resonate strongly with bigfoot lore, some cryptozoologists suspect informants might be describing a relict *Megatherium* specimen. One Peruvian tribesman told a researcher he saw a *Mapinguary* depicted in Lima's natural history museum—an institution which has a diorama of a giant ground sloth.[85]

It is difficult to scientifically account for primates with oddly numbered toes. But a variety of entities from myth and legend exhibit peculiar foot features, including tridactyly. Recall the number of witches, faeries, and spirit familiars with birdlike feet—as alluded to in Chapter 5, the *drudenfuss*, or witch's foot, is a runic symbol appearing similar to three-toed bigfoot prints. The mobile, magical, bipedal hut housing the infamous Russian witch *Baba Yaga* tramped through the forest on fowl's legs. Australia's Kamilaroi people tell stories of the *Dhinnabarrada*, a tribe of monstrous people with human bodies and "the legs and feet of emus."[86]

The *Shedim,* offspring of a succubus and a man, possessed rooster's feet in early Hebrew lore;[87] in later traditions, they became "hairy, wild demons who lived in the woods and danced."[88] A union with the child snatching, bird-footed demoness Lilith could also spawn *Shedim.*[89]

Another curious connection appears in Middle Eastern *Djinn* lore. *Djinn* can safely, if grossly, be generalized as Muslim analogues to faeries in Christian tradition—like the fae, they ate detritus, stole human children, employed changelings, inhabited ancient ruins, and could shape shift.[90]

"Even when they appear in beautiful human form, Djinn are said to still have a physical flaw that exposes their true identity," wrote Rosemary Ellen Guiley in *The Djinn Connection*. "Most common are hairy legs and hoofed feet." This obviously resonates with western images of Satan, devils, *Fauns,* and *Satyrs*, but also with the aforementioned zoologist's comment that bigfoot maybe "forgot to put on the rest of the toes"—in both instances, a crucial aspect of the entity is presented as malformed, or an afterthought.[91]

Tridactyl footprints appear in modern encounters with a wide variety of unknown beings, from UFO occupants to cave goblins in Kentucky to Puerto Rico's *el Chupacabras* to the Lizardman of Bishopville, South Carolina. Such tracks are so common, in fact, it almost seems as if the three-toed print is a calling card of the Otherworld; indeed the number three and its multiples are of paramount numerological importance in a variety of occult and spiritual traditions around the world. Three is a heavenly number to the Chinese, three magi visited Jesus in Bethlehem, Christianity is built around the trinity, Noah had three sons, Buddhists take refuge in The Three Jewels, three Gunas define the Samkhya Hindu philosophy, etc.

With this in mind, perhaps tridactyl prints, like glowing eyes, indicate bigfoot's supernatural origins—some of the strangest cases share this detail. The 1981 "bear scare" of Hackney, England began on December 27 when four boys walking through a marsh happened upon "three-clawed footprints" in the snow. One of the witnesses decided they were bear prints, a fact confirmed by a mysterious couple who told them "to keep away because it was dangerous" and tossed snowballs at the youths to frighten them away. Undaunted, the boys soldiered onward until they encountered "a gigantic great growling hairy thing" which sent them running. Not only is England devoid of bears, but the tracks discovered by authorities "started and finished abruptly, and were surrounded by virgin snow."[92]

This, however, does not represent the full extent of the oddities surrounding bigfoot prints. Stranger things lurk where the footprints end.

---

[1] Mayor, A. & Sarjeant, W.A.S. (2001). The Folklore of Footprints in Stone: from Classical Antiquity to the Present. *Ichnos 8*(2), pp. 143-163.

[2] Ibid.

[3] Bartra, R. (1994). *Wild Men in the Looking Glass*. (C.T. Berrisford, Trans.). Ann Arbor, MI: University of Michigan Press.

[4] Meldrum, J. (2006). *Sasquatch: Legend Meets Science*. New York, NY: Forge Books.

[5] Loxton, D. & Prothero, D.R. (2013). *Abominable Science! Origins of the Yeti, Nessie, and Other Famous Cryptids*. New York, NY: Columbia University Press.

[6] Coleman, L. (2003). *Bigfoot! The True Story of Apes in America*. New York, NY: Paraview Pocket Books.

[7] Slate, B.A. & Berry, A. (1976). *Bigfoot*. New York, NY: Bantam.

[8] Ibid.

[9] Schneck, R.D. (2014). *Mrs. Wakeman vs. The Antichrist*. New York, NY: Jeremy P. Tarcher/Penguin.

[10] McLeod, M. (2009). *Anatomy of a Beast: Obsession and Myth on the Trail of Bigfoot*. Berkeley, CA: University of California Press.

[11] Paulides, D. (2009). *Tribal Bigfoot*. Blaine, WA: Hancock House.

[12] Bizarre Bigfoot. (August 3, 2011). The Trouble with Tracks. Retrieved February 12, 2019 from http://bizarrebigfoot.blogspot.com/2011/08/trouble-with-tracks.html

[13] Franzoni III, H.J. (2008). *In the Spirit of Seatco*. Deer Island, OR: Ste Ye Hah Publishing.

[14] Slate & Berry 1976.

[15] Short, B. (n.d.). The De Facto Sasquatch. Retrieved January 18, 2019 from https://static1.squarespace.com/static/596c0bae4c0dbfa1d26e86be/t/5b9bff06562fa7cfcdf1bfc8/1536950038606/The+de+facto+Sasquatch+premier+installment.pdf?fbclid=IwAR3763B1leKUEQofPRbPvzAItNH5K-RUVoKU-vOLW_iXvSFkdKSg4o4xBXw

[16] Hamada, Y. & Yamamoto, A. (2010). Morphological Characteristics, Growth, and Aging in Japanese Macaques. In N. Nakagawa, M. Nakamichi, & H. Sugiura (Eds.), *The Japanese Macaques* (pp. 27-52). New York, NY: Springer.

[17] Nunnelly, B.M. (2011). *The Inhumanoids: Real Encounters with Beings That Can't Exist.* Woolsery, UK: CFZ Press.

[18] Encyclopaedia Britannica. (2019). Primate (Mammal) – Hands and feet. Retrieved February 13, 2019 from https://www.britannica.com/animal/primate-mammal/Hands-and-feet

[19] Ahmed, H., Akbari, H. Emami, A., & Akbari, M.R (November 2017). Genetic Overview of Syndactyly and Polydactyly. *Plastic Reconstructive Surgery Global Open 5*(11), pp. 1-8.

[20] Delson, E., Tattersall, I., Van Couvering, J.A., & Brooks, A.S. (2017). *Encyclopedia of Human Evolution and Prehistory* (2nd ed.). New York, NY: Routledge.

[21] Slate & Berry 1976.

[22] Boston Children's Hospital. (2019). What are the different forms of syndactyly? Retreived February 13, 2019 from http://www.childrenshospital.org/conditions-and-treatments/conditions/s/syndactyly/symptoms-and-causes

[23] Powell, T. (2003). *The Locals.* Surrey, CA: Hancock House Publishers Ltd.

[24] Emmer, R. (2010). *Bigfoot: Fact or Fiction?* New York, NY: Chelsea House Publishers.

[25] Slate & Berry 1976.

[26] Coleman, L. (n.d.). Case 178. In A. Rosales (Ed.), *1966 Humanoid Sighting Reports.* Retrieved February 5, 2014 from http://www.ufoinfo.com/humanoid/humanoid-1966.pdf

[27] Taylor, T. (2005). *Weird Illinois.* M. Moran & M. Sceurman (Eds.). New York, NY: Sterling Publishing Co.

[28] Gordon, S. (2010). *Silent Invasion: The Pennsylvania UFO-Bigfoot Casebook.* R. Marsh (Ed.). Greensburg, PA: Stan Gordon Productions.

[29] Brandon, J. (1983). *The Rebirth of Pan: Hidden Faces of the American Earth Spirit.* Dunlap, IL: Firebird Press.

[30] Coleman, L., & Clark, J. (1999) *Cryptozoology A to Z: The Encyclopedia of Loch Monsters, Sasquatch, Chupacabras, and Other Authentic Mysteries of Nature.* New York, NY: Fireside.

[31] Johnson, P.G. & Jeffers, J.L. (n.d.). Case 203. In A. Rosales (Ed.), *1975 Humanoid Sighting Reports.* Retrieved February 5, 2014 from http://www.ufoinfo.com/humanoid/humanoid-1975.pdf

[32] Bord, J., & Bord, C. (2006). *Bigfoot Casebook Updated: Sightings and Encounters from 1818 to 2004.* Enumclaw, WA: Pinewinds Press.

[33] Ibid.

[34] Coleman, L. & Hallenbeck, B.G. (2010). *Monsters of New Jersey.* Mechanicsburg, PA: Stackpole Books.

[35] Pilichis, D. (1982). *Night Siege: The Northern Ohio UFO Creature Invasion.* Rome, OH: Dennis Pilichis.

[36] Ibid.

[37] Ibid.

[38] Rickard, B. & Michell, J. (2007). *The Rough Guide to Unexplained Phenomena* (2nd ed.). London, UK: Rough Guides Ltd.

[39] Crabtree, S. (2011). *Smokey and the Fouke Monster: A True Story.* Sudbury, MAL eBookIt.com

[40] Clark, J. & Coleman, L. (January 1973). Anthropoids, Monsters and UFOs. *Flying Saucer Review 19*(1), pp. 18-23.

[41] Taylor, T. (2013). *The Big Book of Missouri Ghost Stories.* Mechanicsburg, PA: Stackpole Books.

[42] Coleman, L. (2002). *Mothman and Other Curious Encounters* (3rd ed.). New York, NY: Paraview Press.

[43] Coleman 2002.

⁴⁴ Nunnelly 2011.

⁴⁵ Coleman & Clark 1999.

⁴⁶ Redfern, N. (November 14, 2016). The Mystery of Bigfoot's Big Feet. Retrieved February 14, 2019 from https://mysteriousuniverse.org/2016/11/the-mystery-of-bigfoots-big-feet/

⁴⁷ Eberhart, G.M. (2002). *Mysterious Creatures: A Guide to Cryptozoology*. Santa Barbara, CA: ABC-CLIO, Inc.

⁴⁸ Ibid.

⁴⁹ Brandon 1983.

⁵⁰ Napier, J. (1973). *Bigfoot: The Yeti and Sasquatch in Myth and Reality*. New York, NY: E.P. Dutton.

⁵¹ Native Languages of the Americas. (2015). Legendary Native American Figures: Maxemista. Retrieved February 14, 2019 from http://www.native-languages.org/maxemista.htm

⁵² Roth, J. E. (1997). *American Elves: An Encyclopedia of Little People from the Lore of 380 Ethnic Groups of the Western Hemisphere*. Jefferson, NC: McFarland & Company, Inc.

⁵³ Sanderson, I.T. (2019). Wudewasa: The Furry Men of Europe. In R.E. Guiley (Ed.), *FATE Presents: Planet Bigfoot*. (pp. 35-43). New Milford, CT: Visionary Living Publishing.

⁵⁴ Watt, J. (September 2017). Buddhist Protector: Shingkyong Yab-Yum (& Bamro Yab-Yum). Retrieved June 21, 2020 from https://www.himalayanart.org/search/set.cfm?setID=1198

⁵⁵ Gill, S.D. & Sullivan, I.F. (1992). *Dictionary of Native American Mythology*. Santa Barbara, CA: ABC-CLIO.

⁵⁶ Admin, A. (April 23, 2006). The Murphy File Newsletter #8 18-04-06. Retrieved February 15, 2019 from http://yowiehunters.com.au/blog/75-bigfoot/1016-the-murphy-file-newsletter-8-18-04-06

⁵⁷ Hall, M.A., & Coleman, L. (2010). *True Giants: Is Gigantopithecus Still Alive?* San Antonio, TX: Anomalist Books.

⁵⁸ Orchard, V. (1902). Idaho Has a Boogie Man. Retrieved February 15, 2019 from http://www.bigfootencounters.com/articles/vo.htm

[59] Steiger, B. (2011). *Real Monsters, Gruesome Critters, and Beasts from the Darkside.* Canton, MI: Visible Ink Press.

[60] Clark & Coleman 1973.

[61] Warth, R.C., Zumwalt, S., & Clement, H. (1975). HUMCAT – 1975 Addenda. Retrieved February 14, 2019 from http://www.cufos.org/HUMCAT/HUMCAT_Index_1975.pdf

[62] Redfern, N. (2016). *The Bigfoot Book: The Encyclopedia of Sasquatch, Yeti and Cryptid Primates.* Canton, MI: Visible Ink Press.

[63] Paulides, D. (2008). *The Hoopa Project: Bigfoot Encounters in California.* Blaine, WA: Hancock House.

[64] Bord & Bord 2006.

[65] Paulides 2009.

[66] Ibid.

[67] Slate & Berry 1976.

[68] Hall & Coleman 2010.

[69] Coy, Jr., F.E., Fuller, T.C., Meadows, L.G., & Swauger, J.L. (1997). *Rock Art of Kentucky.* Lexington, KY: The University Press of Kentucky.

[70] Holloway, A. (September 8, 2016). Will the Secrets Behind the 5000-year-old Cochno Stone Finally Be Solved? Retrieved February 15, 2019 from https://www.ancient-origins.net/news-history-archaeology/will-secrets-behind-5000-year-old-cochno-stone-finally-be-solved-006607

[71] Benny, H. (January 2, 2009). ATV riders find possible tracks outside Evarts. Retrieved February 15, 2019 from http://www.bfro.net/GDB/show_report.asp?id=25257

[72] Bigfoot Field Researchers Organization. (March 14, 1999). Large human-like tracks were found in the snow and mud. Retrieved February 15, 2019 from http://www.bfro.net/gdb/show_report.asp?id=1349

[73] Powers, K.J. (n.d.). Overlapping and Underlapping Toes. Retrieved February 15, 2019 from https://bloomingtonpodiatrist.com/overlapping-and-underlapping-toes/

[74] No author. (1956). Case 42. In A. Rosales (Ed.), *1955 Humanoid Sighting Reports*. Retrieved February 5, 2014 from http://www.ufoinfo.com/humanoid/humanoid-1955.pdf

[75] Grabski, S. (July 7, 2016). #ThrowbackThursday: 'Saucer' sighting probed at Presque Isle. Retrieved February 16, 2019 from https://www.goerie.com/news/20160707/throwbackthursday-saucer-sighting-probed-at-presque-isle

[76] Keel, J. (2002). *The Complete Guide to Mysterious Beings*. New York, NY: Tom Doherty Associates, LLC. (Original work published 1970 as *Strange Creatures from Time and Space*)

[77] Guttilla, P. (2003). *The Bigfoot Files*. Santa Barbara, CA: Timeless Voyager Press.

[78] Lyttle, S. (December 30, 2010). Cleveland County man reports encounter with Bigfoot. Retrieved February 16, 2019 from https://www.charlotteobserver.com/news/local/article9037616.html

[79] Moore, M. (July 29, 2008). 'Bigfoot' sighted in remote Canadian forest. Retrieved February 16, 2019 from https://www.telegraph.co.uk/news/newstopics/howaboutthat/2468852/Bigfoot-sighted-in-remote-Canadian-forest.html

[80] Nunnelly 2011.

[81] Hirthler, M.A. & Hutchison, R.L. (December 2012). Polydactyly in the Southwest: art or anatomy—a photo essay. *Hand 7*(4), pp. 464-468.

[82] Naish, D. (August 30, 2012). The anatomy of sloths. Retrieved February 17, 2019 from https://blogs.scientificamerican.com/tetrapod-zoology/the-anatomy-of-sloths/

[83] Bigfoot Evidence. (June 13, 2012). Bigfoot and the Ground Sloth Connection. Retrieved February 17, 2019 from http://bigfootevidence.blogspot.com/2012/06/bigfoot-and-ground-sloth-connection.html

[84] Rohter, L. (July 8, 2007). A Huge Amazon Monster Is Only a Myth. Or Is It? Retrieved February 17, 2018 from https://www.nytimes.com/2007/07/08/world/americas/08amazon.html

[85] Ibid.

[86] Rose, C. (2000). *Giants, Monsters & Dragons: An Encyclopedia of Folklore, Legend, and Myth*. New York, NY: W.W. Norton & Company.

[87] Carlson, I.M. (November 13, 2013). *Notes on a demonic pantheon.* Retrieved February 17, 2019 from http://www.personal.utulsa.edu/~marc-carlson/history/demon.txt

[88] Guiley, R.E. (2009). *The Encyclopedia of Demons & Demonology.* New York, NY: Facts on File, Inc.

[89] Vernor, E.R. (2017). *Lilith: From Ancient Lore to Modern Culture.* Fort Wayne, IN: Dark Moon Press.

[90] Guiley, R.E. (2013). *The Djinn Connection.* New Milford, CT: Visionary Living, Inc.

[91] Ibid.

[92] Dash, M. (2000). *Borderlands: The Ultimate Exploration of the Unknown.* New York, NY: Dell Publishing.

*If you have a footprint, be happy, because
it means that you aren't a shadow.*
          - Mehmet Murat İldan

7 Trackways

Atypical circumstances can complicate the discovery of even the most mundane five-toed bigfoot tracks. Sometimes, they simply appear in nonsensical patterns. During the 1960s and early 1970s, witnesses in California's Mojave Desert sighted a tall, hairy creature they dubbed "Big Ben." One sighting left behind physical evidence in the form of various-sized footprints.[1]

"They put prints in a lot of places that didn't make any sense," the witness mused. "They were facing all different directions, and then a group of them would trek off into a flat area and then stop completely for no reason. There were footprints helter-skelter all over the place."[2]

Solitary Footprints

Every cryptozoological research organization around the country counts among its members at least one investigator who has found a single bigfoot track, completely alone, the surrounding earth untouched. As with oddly toed footprints, many detractors immediately jump to the conclusion such prints are hoaxed—without appreciating the fact that any hoaxer should leave additional evidence *somewhere* in the vicinity. Instead, solitary tracks should be appreciated for the true anomalies they are.

- In Spottsville, Kentucky in 1935, a young girl was washing dishes when a pervasive silence settled over the area, immediately followed by an enormous gust of wind that set her hair and all the curtains into a frenzy. Stepping toward the living room, she found a large, hairy creature doubled over, filling the building floor-to-ceiling. The creature's eyes glowed red and its eyes and mouth seemed to spew blue fire. She fainted. Hours later her mother and brother found her locked inside the home in a state of shock. In the center of the living room was a single, 24-inch long footprint. The family left the home the next day, but a similar creature would return four decades later to haunt the Nunnelly family.[3]

- In 1960, future sasquatch researcher Philip Spencer "found a large strange track in a plowed field" on his family farm in Alton, Kentucky. "It was a single track and only had three toes. It was near the middle of the field with no sign of any other track or the ground being disturbed anywhere in the field."[4]

- According to legend, a giant named *Aikanaka* lurks along abandoned Hawaiian roads and pineapple fields. In the 1960s, an irrigation crew member at the Dole Pineapple Company "suddenly tripped and fell into a shallow hole." It was allegedly a single, enormous footprint. "I swear we measured the thing," he said. "It came out to about three feet!"[5]

- A nine-foot tall, shaggy, gray-haired bigfoot was regularly spotted in Corona, California between 1964 and 1975. Dave Wilson and Tom McKelvy first sighted the beast in a lemon grove, where it emitted a "metallic screech" and lurched toward their pickup truck. The following morning the witnesses and a friend discovered a single footprint 18 inches long and 7 inches wide, with "three large and slightly pointed toes." To make matters even more peculiar, Corona resident Bob Houghton had his rabbits taken two days before another sighting… via a "perfectly round" hole drilled into their cage. The stench of rotten eggs permeated the scene.[6]

- A young man camping in Kentucky's Natural Bridge State Park in 1978 was wandering to the community lodge for some ice when an odor of decomposition hit him. "It was at that time that I stopped dead in my tracks, because right in front of me was the biggest foot print I'd ever seen," he recalled years later. "It was so big that there was only one of them, directly in the center of the soft muddy road. It was a bare footprint, complete with the impression of 5 toes... I couldn't figure how someone could only leave one footprint and why they weren't wearing shoes." Suddenly, he noticed "a dark figure" covered in "shiny, like greasy hair" 50 to 80 yards away across a stream. He ran back to camp to fetch his parents, and though the creature was gone the footprint remained. "It easily doubled my step dad's size 10 1/2 foot," he said.[7]

- In the winter of 1996, a Texas witness driving during an ice storm "saw a large ball of hair about the size of a large deer on the side of the road. I had my bright lights on the animal when it stood up, took two big steps, went over onto its knuckles and lunged into the woods." His passenger was slumped into his seat, and saw nothing. The witness revisited the location after most everything had melted and found "one single solitary footprint."[8]

- On April 27, 2003 Rick Fisher and members of the Pennsylvania Bigfoot Society found "a large track of something unknown... We tried to follow the track but interestingly it was the only one, a thorough search of the surrounding area could find no trace of another step. It just ended there." The print measured 15 x 5.5 inches.[9]

- A Missouri witness residing near Table Rock Lake began noticing odd howls and whoops in late 2003. Around the same time, a single barefoot track was discovered on the shore. "The distance between the print and either edge of the washout was about ten feet, yet there was [sic] no other prints in the mud of the washout."[10]

- A family hiking Colorado's Green Mountain Trail stumbled upon a possible single track 13.5-14 inches long in summer 2015. The surrounding dirt was untouched, yet the father was unable to duplicate the impression with his 6'7", 200 lbs. frame.[11]

Finding a solitary footprint is "not unusual if you've spent some time in the woods looking for the creature known as bigfoot," wrote Fisher. "In fact that is quite common. There are many bigfoot reports of only one track being found. Can anyone explain this?"[12]

Typical excuses for these anomalies include bigfoot's preternaturally long strides, incredible leaping abilities, or the surrounding media being too hard to transfer any footprints (despite the single track's existence in the first place). In summer 2003, two college students camping in Snohomish County, Washington discovered a tree break nine feet off the ground and one large, solitary footprint in the soil.

"I don't really have a problem with there only being one track since the discoverers were not specifically trying to find more," wrote Richard Noll of the BFRO, who felt the track was genuine. "Other pictures from the witness shows [sic] that there was [sic] even more forest leaves over the most likely spot for the next track. They just didn't clear them away to the soil underneath." Noll believes new leaf litter covered up subsequent tracks, which is entirely possible—but says nothing in his report of the direction from which the first track originated.[13]

It is also widely believed bigfoot are capable of incredible leaps (addressed later) or they are exceptionally discerning about where they step. This was the suggestion offered by an elk hunter and his friend in Chaffee County, Colorado after coming upon a single 15-16 inch long tridactyl track in the snow.

"We walked down the creek a little farther when we saw something we could not believe," the witness told the BFRO. "About 100 yards from the original track were about six or seven additional tracks in snow and mud. These tracks were in much better condition. They had the same dimensions of the first track and appeared to be just as old. Like the first track, they only showed three toes but one track showed four and one showed five. The only explanation I had for the tracks being so far apart was that what ever made the tracks must have used the rocks along the creek to walk on."[14]

These scenarios may well explain solitary footprints in some—but not all—cases. Recall the single pair of tracks found on a sandbar in Fred Beck's Ape Canyon story: "There we were, standing in the middle of the sand bar, and not one of us could conceive any earthly thing taking steps 160 feet long."[15]

Like tridactyl tracks, lone footprints are a hallmark of the paranormal, appearing in numerous poltergeist and haunting cases. For instance, in her book *The Hand on the Mirror*, author Janis Heaphy Durham detailed numerous after-death communications from what she believes is her husband, including evidence in the form of hand and footprints; one photo in her book shows a "very large... significantly oversize" footprint which materialized on the arm of a gold suede club chair. It looks astonishingly like a bigfoot print.[16]

Disembodied footprints appear in other paranormal cases. Betty Hill—who, alongside her husband Barney, participated in one of the earliest alien abductions of the modern era—led a life full of paranormal activity, including clairvoyant dreams. When a television host asked if she'd ever like to be taken aboard a UFO again, she replied, "They know where I live. If they want to see me they can come visit any time." Author Scott Carr wrote, "as if in acknowledgment of her stubborn humor, the next morning she went outside to discover a single, solitary footprint in the exact center of a yard of pristine, untouched snow."[17]

In his seminal work *The Mothman Prophecies*, John Keel spoke with a recurring witness to all sorts of High Strangeness who saw a strange, tanned man carrying "a box in his hand. Some kind of instrument." The witness thought it was a hitchhiker, but was shooed away after offering a ride; the next day, the man was still there. Keel and the witness discovered "huge dog tracks… so deep the animal who made them must have weighed 200 pounds or more," as well as "a single footprint of what appeared to be a large, naked human foot. This was planted in the center of a muddy section with no other footprints of any kind around it." Nearby, Keel also spotted "prints made by ripple-soled shoes" like astronaut moon boots, "a type of footprint that has appeared at many UFO sites around the country."[18]

In late 2017, Timothy Renner interviewed "Dave," a recurring sasquatch witness, for the *Strange Familiars* podcast. His earliest encounters were of a general paranormal nature, but his bigfoot sightings began when he saw a creature's face through a window the night before his eighth birthday. Dave's peculiar encounters escalated when he moved back into his childhood home. "I don't know how far out you want me to go but —I remember I used to see astral sasquatch there," he said. The creatures would appear around the house and move to and from a small patch of woodland.[19]

"Sometimes I'd see them *in* the house," he added. The beings appeared in "the shape of a bigfoot" and seemed semi-transparent, quickly darting into rooms and vanishing. Dave also heard disembodied voices, raps, and experienced telepathic communication with the creatures.[20]

On one particularly active evening, Dave heard the noise of a tortilla chip bag rustling in the kitchen, despite being the only one awake in the house, as well as an "incredible loud pop" and "something pulling or playing at the door from the garage into the house." The next morning, the accompanying door handle was "bent backward." Most peculiarly, Dave found a single 18-inch footprint in his basement carpet, which he photographed.[21]

"I did not make that, that was there," he said of the photo. "You can see an imprint in the rug, one singular right footprint... take it for what it's worth." On the way back out to his car, Dave found a small woven effigy of a humanoid figure with a stick waiting for him, which he also collected and documented.[22]

One-Legged Trackways

Single footprints may be of a piece with an even more peculiar bigfoot sign: one-legged trackways, where a path of prints exclusively depicts a left or right foot. While relatively rare, such tracks do appear from time-to-time. In 2016, mountaineer Steve Berry photographed what appeared to be a trackway along an impassable chasm in Bhutan.

"The local people said we were the first to ever set foot on that pass," said Berry. "I had always thought that stories about the yeti were a bit of old bunkum. But there is no denying these tracks existed." The indentations were uniform, yet did not represent a bipedal human gait: they formed a straight line, and did not exhibit any toes, suggesting a small mammal (e.g. rabbit) was responsible.[23]

Prosaic explanations aside, many legitimate bigfoot trackways display what can only be described as an "in-line gait," i.e. one foot is placed directly in front of the other. The author of the Bizarre Bigfoot blog directly asked Jeffrey Meldrum about this anomaly:

> Citing the clear paths that Mountain Gorillas leave in the areas they occupy, including nests and trampled vegetation, I asked him why a bipedal hominid of such large size doesn't leave any obvious evidence of passage? His answer wasn't very satisfactory, when he said, "Sasquatches have a very large range of territory and I've been in areas where entire herds of Elk have come through and when I went to look at the tracks, there was almost nothing there." Elk vs. Sasquatch... I'm not convinced. I got back to another question about in-line gaits and straddle and he elucidated, "The leg bones grow down into a 'v' shape, which allows the Sasquatch to be able to put one foot in front of the other." I didn't really understand this, when humans do not appear to have significantly different anatomy, but, he's the specialist. [24]

We are reminded of the true definition of Occam's Razor, that "entities [in this example, *variables*] should not be multiplied without necessity."

Like solitary footprints, critics and believers alike cite hoaxing for in-line *one-legged* prints, leading to their suppression in cryptozoological discussion. A group of bigfoot hunters escorted author Gregory L. Reece on an investigation near Paris, Texas; after discovering a trackway, one researcher immediately dismissed them as a hoax. "'Hell!' he says, 'anyone can tell those tracks were fakes,'" Reece wrote. "'Didn't they think we would notice that all the tracks were of the right foot!'"[25]

Joe Burcaw allegedly discovered a similar trackway in November 2012 near Litchfield Hills, Connecticut. The footprints "were single and had no pairing whatsoever." Burcaw later claimed a series of intense experiences with both sasquatch and extraterrestrials, sometimes together.[26]

Jeffrey Meldrum met a series of one-footed tracks discovered in Russia's Kemerovo region with extreme skepticism:

> Another piece to this problematic scenario was that as soon as Meldrum suggested he couldn't place any credibility in just one footprint, suddenly another one was found — another right footprint. When he looked a little further, he found a third print, "but it was also a right and I said it would be nice to find a left one, and I said facetiously, 'Is the Yeti playing hopscotch here?'"...
>
> "But my point was simply that if this was a spontaneous line of tracks, we'd expect to see both rights and lefts," he said. "And why is it that the tracks are only leading out and none are leading in?[27]

Meldrum goes on: "If an animal is occupying this cave..." This is a flawed approach: the assumption we are dealing with a flesh-and-blood creature.[28]

Another one-legged trackway featured in an article from the October 29, 1967 edition of *The Oregonian*:

> Back in 1924 this area had its own hairy ape scare. A terrified miner reported in Kelso, Wash., that he had seen great apes which threw rocks at his cabin in the Mt. St. Helens area. An ape-hunting safari, which included our L.H. Gregory, set out for the mountains armed to the teeth. They found giant footprints around the cabin but all of the right foot. The search was called off when it was discovered that a piece of board found at the scene, combined with the knuckles of a man's hand, made the perfect one-legged ape track.[29]

This must refer to the 1924 Ape Canyon encounter. While not an unimpeachable incident, ample evidence suggests the attack was simultaneously genuine and anything but normal—one-legged tracks would present merely another layer of High Strangeness.

The hoaxing explanation fails to answer a basic question: why fake lines of one-legged tracks? Hoaxing three-toed tracks seems quite rational by comparison (unless perpetrators are so foolish as to use a single mold for both strides). At least there is *some* biological precedent for mammalian tridactyl prints. Nothing natural hops around on one foot.

Unnatural things do, however.

The most explicit connection between bigfoot and single-footed trackways comes from a strange 1978 sighting near Cowley, Louisiana. A boy watched a "big ape" eating minnows directly from a stream. The broad-shouldered creature was entirely hairy, save its buttocks and the soles of its feet. Frightened, the witness tossed stones at the beast, causing it to hop away on one leg.[30] Is this a viable means of bigfoot transportation?

One of archaeology's enduring mysteries is the trackway left 20,000 years ago around Lake Mungo, Australia. From *National Geographic*:

> "All we could pick up was the right foot," Webb said, adding that each step left a very deep impression in the mud.
>
> "It's a very good impression," he said. "It's one of the best foot impressions there is on the whole site. But there is no sign of the left foot at all."
>
> The conundrum was solved with the help of five trackers from the Pintubi people of central Australia.
>
> "They looked at the ... track and said, 'Yes, it's definitely a one-legged man,'" Webb said..."So they see nuances of tracks in a way we have no skill in doing whatsoever"... The trackers believe the ancient man probably threw his support stick away and hopped quite fast on one foot.[31]

The Lake Mungo site also features what archeologists have dubbed "a 'bigfoot' set of prints, believed to belong to a 6ft 6in man, with [Australian] size 12 feet, who was pursuing an unknown prey, possibly water birds."[32]

A broad variety of folklore describes monopods, stretching all the way into antiquity. Ancient Greeks believed a race of one-footed men inhabited India or Ethiopia;[33] the *Kasa-obake* is a monopod Japanese umbrella spirit;[34] the Brazilian *Saci* is a one-legged dwarf;[35] Latin American countries harbor *la Patasola*, a monopod enchantress known for shape shifting and drinking human blood (*la Matlacihua*, a Mexican variant, is also known as *The White Lady*).[36] In keeping with the theme of tridactyl prints, some creatures feature a single bird foot: the Aymara of Bolivia believe in *Quetronamun*, a duck-footed monopod devil.[37]

Some traditions describe monopod giants. The Washo *Hanawiywiy* is varyingly described as a west coast Centaur, giant, or one-legged Cyclops.[38] The *Fachan* was a cycloptic Scottish wild man of enormous stature bestowed with a single hand and foot. Folklorist J.F. Campbell suggested the *Fachan* might have roots in Arabic traditions of *Nesnas* and *Shikks*, one-legged creatures described as "half of a human being."[39]

Penutian legends describe two one-legged wild men: the *Yayaya-ash* and a *Ste-ye-hah'mah* (bigfoot) variant. Of the latter, L.V. McWhorter wrote in 1916: "Their mode of locomotion is supposedly long leaps, since the foot impressions appear at a considerable distance apart. Some Indians contend that these enigmatical beings are possessed of two legs, the same as any other people, and the difference is in the foot alone. Both tracks (impressions) are identical, conforming to the right or the left foot exclusively."[40]

It is tempting to wonder whether Vikings encountered monopods when they arrived in Newfoundland circa 1000 A.D. *Eiríks saga rauða*, a 13th century saga chronicling the Norse exploration of North America, describes an encounter with an *Einfœting*, or one-legged person:

> One morning Karlsefni's people beheld as it were a glittering speck above the open space in front of them, and they shouted at it. It stirred itself, and it was a being of the race of men that have only one foot, and he came down quickly to where they lay. Thorvald, son of Eirik the Red, sat at the tiller, and the One-footer shot him with an arrow in the lower abdomen. He drew out the arrow. Then said Thorvald, "Good land have we reached, and fat is it about the paunch." Then the One-footer leapt away again northwards. They chased after him, and saw him occasionally, but it seemed as if he would escape them. He disappeared at a certain creek...
>
> Then they journeyed away back again northwards, and saw, as they thought, the land of the One-footers. They wished,

however, no longer to risk their company.[41]

While Newfoundland is not particularly well-known for bigfoot sightings, the general region (northern North America) and extant indigenous lore from the continent (where cannibal giants are described as monopods) leaves one wondering if Karlsefni's band did not encounter something simultaneously strange *and* genuine.

Nonexistent Tracks

One enduring cryptozoological mystery is why bigfoot sometimes fail to leave tracks where they clearly should. With weights often estimated upwards of 500 lbs., these creatures *should* leave tracks in all but the hardest media—yet many do not.

- **1962 – Ohio:** A couple parked near Big Indian Creek see a large figure walk through a barbed wire fence and approach the car. The creature is a seven-foot-tall, tan-colored bigfoot with fangs and claws, albeit sickly or "dead" looking. Snapping out of their daze, the couple rolls up their windows and drives away, but not before the beast crouches in front of the car, hops up, and disappears. They return the next day but find zero evidence of the event—including footprints.[42]

- **1969 – Alberta:** Guy L'Heureuse and Harley Peterson are building a pumphouse foundation by the North Saskatchewan River when Peterson spies "a tall, dark figure standing on top of a 300-foot-high bank about half a mile away and watching them." Both witnesses observe the figure for a half hour. When they finally investigate the area, they estimate the being's height around 15 feet—but find no footprints.[43]

- **1975 – Utah:** A couple in their mountain cabin 70 miles outside Cedar City notice a variety of strange noises, including "a motor running" every night. Early one morning, the husband hears "heavy footsteps" approaching the cabin accompanied by "a huge, dark form" moving outside the window. The witness opens the cabin door slowly, but sees no one outside and hears nothing retreating. "What puzzles me is there were no footprints of any kind and we have lots of snow here," he later told Alan Berry. "My Indian friends tell me it is *Newputz*, meaning ghost in their language, and only a few will dare stay in the area overnight."[44]

- **1975 – Kentucky:** During the Spottsville Monster sightings, a neighbor visits the Nunnelly family and tells them he encountered an eight-foot-tall bigfoot the previous summer. He fired his rifle sixteen times at the creature through his screen door. "It just walked off without makin' a sound," he tells them. The neighbor found neither blood nor footprints. "Not even a single footprint… and it had to weigh at least four or five hundred pounds."[45]

Perhaps the most famous sasquatch to never leave tracks is the large, hairy hominid that stalked a home in Roachdale, Indiana. Beginning in August 1972, Lou Rogers and her son Keith started hearing odd vocalizations on their property, beginning as animalistic growls and hoots before shifting to more human sounds.

"Whatever had made [the noises] seemed now to be breathing down her neck," wrote Jerome Clark of one early incident. "She turned around slowly but could see nothing. Thoroughly shaken, she and Keith fled into the house." Unbeknownst to Lou, her brother had observed "a luminous object" land in a nearby cornfield 90 minutes earlier—before disappearing in a flash. This cornfield would serve as ground zero for the Roachdale bigfoot.

The Rogers's home soon came under assault from slaps and taps on the siding and windows. Soon after, the six-foot tall creature began appearing nightly between 10 and 11:30 p.m. for three weeks. "You could feel it coming somehow. It's hard to explain," Rogers said. "The feeling would just keep getting stronger and stronger, and then when it got strongest so you knew something had to happen, the knocking would start."

The creature was sometimes seen peering through windows, giving the impression of a broad, bipedal gorilla with intermittently glowing eyes. It never left any physical evidence, however. Rogers said:

> What was weird was that we could never find tracks, even when it ran over mud. It would run and jump but it was like somehow it wasn't touching anything. When it ran through weeds, you couldn't hear anything. And sometimes when you looked at it, it looked like you could see through it.

The only footprints ever discovered were tiny three-inch tracks of "a foot and a stub." Other Roachdale residents began seeing the creature, and the strange activity started ramping up: Lou found a plastic "flying saucer" toy in her home which did not belong to Keith; the creature shrugged off shotgun blasts; animal pens and gardens were raided; livestock were exsanguinated. An officer told Jerome Clark he believed tracks were never found because "the ground was hard and the vegetation was high."[46]

Gliding Bigfoot

A Pennsylvania witness and his friend were gripped by abject terror when a hulking bigfoot crossed the road 15 feet from the bumper of their truck. The entire creature was impossibly black, especially its face—which was nonexistent, as if "imploding on itself." The creature continued across the road and into "a bunch of crabapples and things like that, going into the woods." Its locomotion was particularly unsettling, covering a hundred yards in 30-45 seconds, miraculously avoiding the thick, thorny underbrush.[47]

"If that was a man, that would cut you to shreds," the witness said of the undergrowth. "It was like it wasn't even touching the ground, I mean it was just so smooth, it was weird. I really can't explain it… Just the way it walked, it's like it shouldn't be that way, it shouldn't be… It wasn't natural. Everything about it, it wasn't right." Neither witness remarked on the incident until some years later, and could not recall anything about their return trip home.[48]

Missing time aside, similar reports abound where sasquatch are seen "gliding" across uneven terrain or through thick, uneven brush. Witnesses commonly remark upon the smoothness with which bigfoot move, so consistently it can be claimed a hallmark of encounters. F&BH advocates commonly cite biological mechanisms for bigfoot's smooth gait. From Meldrum:

> The overall dynamic signature of the sasquatch footprints concurs with numerous eyewitness accounts noting the smoothness of gait exhibited by the sasquatch. For example, one witness observed, "It seemed to glide or float as it moved." Absent is the head-bobbing or vertical oscillation characteristic of the stiff-legged human gait. The compliant gait on flexed knees and hips not only reduces the peak impact forces under the feet, but also avoids the focused concentration of pressure under the heel and ball of the foot. Recall that these pressures would be disproportionate in a sasquatch-sized biped. Instead, the broad foot is placed flat on

the ground, distributing weight more evenly across a large surface area and throughout a thick sole pad. The compliant gait also increases the period of double support, when weight is borne over both feet, simultaneously reducing the duration that an individual foot must bear the brunt of total body weight.[49]

This may well be the case—but bigfoot locomotion seems eerily unnatural to dozens of eyewitnesses.

- A wild man seen around Newfield, Pennsylvania in 1879 had a "silent, ghost-like manner" of moving about the forest. "Large and heavy as the wild man is, he glides so swiftly and silently that he frequently is at hand before his coming has been observed."[50]

- In 1968 the Allison family of Salem, Ohio came home to find a bigfoot in their driveway. It ran away "so fast it did not even seem to touch the ground, whereas a large person running at such a speed would inevitably stumble and trip over roots and rocks," one witness said. A large feline was also seen lurking about the property.[51]

- Two men near Germany's Hahn Air Force Base observed "an eight-foot tall, two-legged, hairy creature rapidly cross a 30-yard clearing in 'long gliding steps'" in January 1985. The creature bore dark red-brown hair, and was often blamed for "loud wailing sounds" emanating from the forest.[52]

- In June 1989 an eight-foot tall bigfoot was spotted at Fort Bidwell, California. "It seems like it just glides," the witness said.[53]

- A witness driving south of Candor, North Carolina in June 1990 saw "something big and black/brown come out of the woods" and cross the four lane highway in the blink of an eye. "It ran with a smooth, almost gliding movement."[54]

- In 2001 a couple rollerblading near Port Charlotte, Florida happened upon something large and hairy digging in the dirt. Though quadrupedal, they were adamant it was not a bear. "When the creature first started running, it 'drifted' into the road, and appeared to 'float' while running."⁵⁵

• On August 21, 2005 a family hiking in Mono County, California saw a large, dark figure crossing a meadow. "At first I thought it was a backpacker perhaps riding a bike, because it was moving so quickly across the meadow," the witness told the BFRO. "It was moving quickly and smoothly. It didn't make sense." The entire motion was fluid "despite the fact that these Sierra mountain meadows are generally strewn with a profusion of granite rocks and boulders hidden in deep vegetation."⁵⁶

Bigfoot's motion is commonly compared to cross-country skiers. In one 2012 case from Traverse City, Michigan, a snowmobile driver thought it *was* a cross country skier he saw crossing an adjacent hill… until he realized the figure was nine feet tall and moving without skis.⁵⁷ Another witness described a Louisiana bigfoot's "gait as being very smooth, and fluid-like, unlike how a human would walk, but more as if it were skiing."⁵⁸

Anyone familiar with cross-country skiing will get a good idea of bigfoot locomotion, and the efficiency with which they move. Even when the skier comparison is not explicitly evoked, descriptions hint at this stiff-legged, agile appearance. According to Alexander Porteous's *The Forest in Folklore and Mythology*, certain Native American tribes describe the *Smolenkos*, "one-eyed jointless fiends, who run along the mountain-sides swifter than the black-tailed deer."⁵⁹ In 2000, a Colorado family watching a bigfoot flee into the tree line said it moved in "either a fast walk or a slow run" and "didn't bend its knees much."⁶⁰

Author Chris Merola claims six encounters with bigfoot. During his first sighting, he caught a clear look at the creature's peculiar "goose step" gait:

> In the distance, I finally I [sic] saw the Beast and he saw me. We were actually face to face. My entire body was completely frozen in shock. All I was able to do was stare in disbelief at this long, slender black body as he ran towards me at what seemed like warp speed with unorthodox body movements.
>
> His arms were so slender and long, swaying back and forth like the German military high step. His long legs appeared almost straight, with hardly a bend in them as he raced through the ragged cliff tops as if he was on a newly paved road. He didn't make a sound as he was running.⁶¹

While plenty of bigfoot sightings describe a bent-knee gait, Merola's testimony, as well as the "cross country skier" comparison, seems to directly refute Meldrum's theory that bent knees are responsible for the smoothness of bigfoot's gait.

It appears something stranger is afoot.

Levitation and Speed: The Massless Bigfoot

Effortlessly gliding bigfoot—coupled with nonexistent footprints, as in the Roachdale incident—beg the question: *can bigfoot move above the ground?* The question sounds ludicrous, but would account for nonexistent footprints and the ease with which the creatures navigate dense forests. There is also no shortage of indigenous tradition and eyewitness testimony supporting the notion.

"There is your big man standing there, ever waiting, ever present, like the coming of a new day," said Pete Catches, an Oglala Lakota Medicine Man. "He is both spirit and real being, but he can also glide through the forest, like a moose with big antlers, as if the trees weren't there."[62]

"He said he couldn't see feet—and he hesitated to say this—but he said, 'It moved almost like it floated,'" Stan Gordon said of one 2018 witness who saw a wraithlike, muscular creature cross a road in Pennsylvania. "Over the years I've had other reports of various types of entities that are gliding or floating across fields or across roadways."[63]

Some encounters clearly describe levitating bigfoot, while others merely suggest this supernatural ability.

- Manuel Arias and Beatriz Turiella were drawn to a strange light in an Argentinian field one night in 1978. As they approached, two smaller lights broke off and floated toward some construction equipment before blinking out. A pair of large, hairy shapes with glowing red eyes appeared, floating in midair over fences and obstacles.[64]

- A pair of boys saw a black-haired bigfoot moving toward them down a path near Trafford, Pennsylvania on September 22, 1980. The creature appeared to glide, rather than walk, just above the ground.[65]

- Kirk Stewart and a friend were hunting in California's

Siskiyou Wilderness area in October 1990 when they encountered two sasquatch in a lake. The dark-haired creatures were splashing water at one another in a playful manner "like two children." When one of them caught sight of the hunters after five or six minutes, the pair "took off running across the water at an unbelievable pace." The animals seemed unimpeded by the water's resistance. "It almost appeared as though the creatures were running on water, they were moving so fast," wrote David Paulides in *Tribal Bigfoot*. Stewart's friend verified this impression, stating that the bigfoot were almost "running on the top of the water."[66]

• In 1997, children observed a large, hairy hominid near Bragança Paulista, Brazil. The beast "hovered just above the ground, moving very fast and stirring the leaves under its path."[67]

• A miraculous sighting of large, hairy hominids allegedly took place at a military installation in Russia's Chelyabinsk Oblast region, according to Vladimir P. Boyko. A cook supposedly spotted two hairy creatures trudging through the snow one morning in January 1997. The witness ran outside to pursue the creatures, which managed to stay just beyond his reach until they reached the perimeter fence. They then levitated into the air and over the fence. The tracks left behind gradually became shallower as the creatures had approached the fence, indicating their peculiar ascent.[68]

• In 2003, college student Clifford Marshall and a friend were driving along Highway 96 north of Hoopa, California when they spotted a tall, shaggy biped in their headlights. The creature crossed the road and leapt over the rail on the far side of the road. "Clifford said that he couldn't believe what he was watching. He stated that it was at least 200 feet straight down to the Trinity River in this area, and that no man could survive the fall," wrote Paulides in *The Hoopa Project: Bigfoot Encounters in California*. "The real question that I've always asked myself is, did the Bigfoot know it was jumping several hundred feet off a cliff when it made that leap? If Bigfoot is a creature that is eight feet tall and weighs 800 pounds, then its bone density must be much greater than a human's. It is still hard to believe that the creature could survive a fall of 200 feet unscathed."[69]

Anomalous fog often accompanies sightings of floating bigfoot. A 1975 sighting by a group of Pennsylvania witnesses described a floating bigfoot that disappeared into a strange mist,[70] while a 2001 Chilean case involved a littlefoot apparently travelling above the ground at a high speed, leaving a trail of grey smoke in its wake.[71] Fogs and mists occur in a variety of folklore where beings travel from our reality to the Otherworld, and are regularly reported in UFO and faerie encounters.

"It was noted by Stan Gordon during the 1973-4 Pennsylvania scare that [bigfoot] were most active at the time of the full moon and on humid, foggy nights," wrote Janet and Colin Bord in *Alien Animals*.[72] These features naturally bring to mind the attributes so often ascribed to ghosts. Stories of levitating spirits are legion; floating is also quite common in encounters involving extraterrestrials, faeries, ghosts, witches, and even various holy figures.

Just as the ability to hover above ground might account for single prints—or, as addressed later, abruptly ending trackways—it might also provide insight into how bigfoot can move so quickly. After all, friction is the primary adversary of acceleration. There is no shortage of bigfoot encounters where the creatures pace speeding cars, something few mammals (and no primates) can do. Bigfoot regularly move "faster than anybody I've ever seen," "faster than a man—faster than a bear in fact."[73]

The speeds reported in such cases are mind-boggling. In 1979 Jorge Villasana was driving 65 miles per hour near Gilroy, California when an odd feeling overtook him, as if he was being watched; from the corner of his eye he spotted a large, hairy figure fading away. The creature did this several times, and Villasana only lost his pursuer when he accelerated to 90 miles per hour.[74] In another sighting, a car was allegedly paced by a bigfoot while travelling between 75 and 80 miles per hour.[75]

Though it is difficult to be entirely accurate, the fastest land animal in the world is the cheetah, capable of bursts of 60-63 miles per hour (over long distances the pronghorn antelope of North America holds the record, with sustained speeds of 35-55 miles per hour).[76] The fastest primate is the patas monkey, also known as the wadi or hussar monkey. This species tears across the west and central African savannah at 34 miles per hour.[77] A larger species might theoretically be capable of faster movement, but it is a significant gap between the patas monkey's top speed and 80 miles per hour. Bigfoot's immense stride could account for *some* of the difference, but not all.

Apparitions pace cars at incredibly fast speeds in a variety of eyewitness accounts. Witnesses of dogman in America regularly report this feature. In Japan—where urban legends quickly synthesize into contemporary folklore—*Turbo Bachan*, or "Turbo-Granny," was allegedly first reported pacing cars around Mount Rokko in Hyogo Prefecture.[78]

"The general premise of these sightings involves a driver driving on the highway at night," according to one urban legend blog. "Suddenly, he/she will catch the glimpse of an old lady speeding [towards the car in] the rear mirror. In most stories, the driver could only catch a glimpse of her, before she dashes away." Variations on this being include impossibly fast businessmen and infants, some of which "purposely tail someone or knock on the windows. In these cases, the goal of *Turbo Bachan* is to cause an accident. In other times, it was said that only people going over speed limits will end up getting hurt during their encounters. In these interpretations, the legend acts as a parable to those who disregard traffic regulations while driving."[79]

"It just moved impossibly fast, it moved like a ninja, nothing can move this fast," a sasquatch witness told podcaster Wes Germer of his 2006 sighting. "Impossible speed. There's nothing out there living that can move that fast... I've seen cheetahs run, and this is way faster than that. 80 plus miles an hour from a standstill [to] one step."[80]

The witness also described the creature "so black that it seemed like it absorbed the light," akin to a black hole. While not a hallmark of every encounter, witnesses employ this description from time-to-time, and it is also frequently heard in UFO reports, particularly those involving large triangular or chevron-shaped craft.[81]

One witness from Newcastle, England claimed to see "a Yeti, but it was black, two-dimensional, and moving fast... It was like a man-shaped hole in reality. This was not a flesh-and-blood animal. It was something stranger."[82] It is interesting how closely this description resonates with tales of "shadow people," home-invading entities who—despite their description—typically appear *darker* than shadows. The "blacker than black" motif also applies to Nyarlathotep, an entity from the fictional H.P. Lovecraft Mythos (who, in turn, was inspired by an entity Lovecraft encountered in a nightmare).[83]

Levitating bigfoot... missing footprints... large, hairy hominids running at 80 miles an hour... creatures appearing as an absence of light. These factors "make you wonder how much mass there really is there," said Seriah Azkath, host of the *Where Did the Road Go?* podcast. Azkath wonders whether creatures like bigfoot might possibly be "manifestations of light, more than anything else. Because movement like that [means] physics would seem to get in the way, but they don't."[84]

Where the Footprints End

All the above anomalies are exemplified in the phenomenon of abruptly ending trackways, a pernicious thorn in the proverbial side of F&BH advocates. Also known as "disappearing trails," these occur when "whole sets of prints simply vanish in soil or muck that had not ended itself."[85]

From Stan Gordon:

> Some of the initial occurrences that caught our attention were cases where trails of odd footprints with large strides would be observed over a distance in various ground conditions, then just suddenly stop and vanish. Over the years, this has also been seen in fresh heavy snow. There were no other tracks around and no evidence of a hoax.
>
> There is a comment I recall from one witness from the 1973 Bigfoot wave. The man was a non-believer in Bigfoot until he had one standing only feet away from his mobile home. The witness was terrified when he called the state police to report the close encounter with the creature. The fellow had cut his lawn that evening and the creature left its 14-inch long tracks in the fresh cut grass, and on his patio where it was observed. In one area the tracks ended abruptly. The witness, after seeing that the tracks had just stopped, *asked me if these creatures could fly*, since what he saw was so unusual.[86]

In a world where these creatures share so much in common with faeries, extraterrestrials, witches, ghosts, and spirits, are flying bigfoot so absurd? Perhaps sasquatch *can* levitate.

A few examples of disappearing trails from around the United States:

- In January 1978 a bizarre set of footprints manifested on the Hilsmeier property near York, Pennsylvania. An astonishing 2,000 tridactyl tracks, each measuring 16 inches long and six inches wide, crisscrossed the family's farmland.[87] These terminated, in the words of the Hilsmeier patriarch, "in the middle of a field—the creature had to backtrack in its own steps."[88]

- Several trackways found during the Rome, Ohio sightings

of summer 1981 ended abruptly. "In many areas a human footprint could be found, as nobody had really been out up thru this area," wrote Dennis Pilichis. "Many of the 'creatures' footprints were on virgin ground, no other type of prints around for a great distance."[89]

- At 11:45 p.m. on March 28, 1987, Green Mountain Falls, Colorado resident Dan Masias observed "these creatures... running down the road in front of my house, which at one point is 30 feet from my front window." The hairy, apelike humanoids swung their arms "in a pendulum motion" as they trudged through the freshly fallen snow. News of Masias's sighting emboldened other area witnesses to speak up, many of them claiming the creatures' trackways through the snow "vanished in midstride."[90]

- During his tenure as a newspaper reporter in the late 1980s, Chas Clifton "interviewed a man who said two 'creatures' had walked past his house and left footprints in the snow... The large tracks just ended abruptly in the fresh powder."[91]

- In one example with complicated implications, researcher Peter Byrne was called upon to examine a trackway found by Paul Freeman. After examining approximately a hundred prints along a ridgeline, Byrne "determined that the tracks started and ended abruptly... Byrne sarcastically congratulated Freeman on his discovery of the first flying bigfoot." While Freeman remains a controversial figure, both Grover Krantz and Jeffrey Meldrum supported at least some of his finds, calling into question whether or not Byrne mistook genuine, if paranormal, footprints for a hoax.[92]

- In the 1990s a law enforcement officer from Box Elder County, Utah, allegedly followed a set of large, bare footprints into a farmer's field one winter. The tracks simply disappeared in the middle of the property, without any apparent turnaround.[93]

- In March 2014, investigators discovered a quarter mile bigfoot trackway near Crownpoint, New Mexico. Each print measured 18" x 6", with a five-to-six foot stride. "The Navajo Rangers and Navajo Criminal Investigations had previously examined the track line and noted that the prints abruptly ended," wrote Lon Strickler of the *Phantoms & Monsters* blog. "From the witness' statement, these officials were 'freaked out' when this irregularity was seen."[94]

• Southeastern researcher Jeffrey Teagle followed 16-18 inch tracks on multiple occasions in various locations where they abruptly ended. "The most memorable of these times was when I followed a set of prints into an alfalfa field [near Valley, Alabama]. It was a most beautiful day, the sun was out and I was on the chase. Near mid-field the tracks suddenly stopped without warning. So imagine my surprise when I am standing there with gear in hand looking a quarter of a mile in either direction at wide open space." (Valley has experienced its share of UFO sightings as well.) Some time later Teagle found a solitary track in Tennessee, only to find his camera suddenly sapped of power as a "large, black hulk of a thing" observed him.[95]

• Researcher Colleen O'Hara-Epperly described a bigfoot trackway found by two snowshoers near Scout Mountain, Idaho. "The couple followed the trail of tracks for several hundred yards. Then all of a sudden, the tracks ended without explanation." The couple was so frightened they abandoned camp "and snowshoed back to their vehicle in the middle of the night."[96]

• In January 2018, Stan Gordon was shown "a series of large footprints in fresh snow" from North Huntingdon Township, Pennsylvania, each 16 inches long with a four to five foot stride. "The family was startled because the tracks seemed to just suddenly appear in the yard with no entrance point, then continued on about 70 feet across the yard," Gordon wrote. "The tracks continued until they reached a play area for children and then suddenly just stopped and vanished."[97]

In *Bigfoot*, Ann Slate and Alan Berry described how one trackway curiously ended. While the footprints began among boulders and high brush, they terminated in the direction of a spring, where the soil "was soft and mushy… anything heavy should have left additional impressions— even allowing for the creature's apparent speed and gigantic step." There was, however, nothing to be found.[98]

Another story from Berry describes disappearing tracks of a different variety: *ones which literally vanished.* After locating "six of the most clearly defined footprints" they had ever seen at a location in southern California's Big Rock Campground, two researchers were ready to proudly share their discovery with a skeptical Forestry Service employee named Doc.

The researchers had been waiting for an exemplary set of tracks to share so they "wouldn't make jackasses" out of themselves. Upon reaching the site, "the tracks were gone, like bigfoot came back and picked them up," one researcher said. "Rich and I stared at the ground where they had been, feeling like a couple of jerks."[99]

F&BH advocates proffer a host of "rational" explanations for such tricksterish activity, outlined below. Students of folklore, however, will immediately recognize disappearing trails as a hallmark of Otherworld denizens: America's famed Jersey Devil was notoriously untrackable, because its footprints would simply stop; paths of faerie footprints mysteriously terminated; caped intruders and large wolves left behind disappearing trails in Point Pleasant, West Virginia[100] and at Utah's Skinwalker Ranch, respectively.[101]

One of the most famous cases of an abruptly ending trackway took place in England in February 1855, though it did not appear to involve any large, hairy hominids. Residents of East and South Devon awoke to discover a trail of hoof marks in the freshly fallen snow, all in a straight line. The trail was estimated to stretch between 40 and 100 miles, and mounted a variety of inaccessible locations: walls, roofs, enclosed courtyards, etc., in addition to open fields. The tracks would occasionally end abruptly and reappear some distance away. While not in the shape of a human foot, the in-line gait and ability to vanish and return is evocative of modern bigfoot trackways. Popular skeptical explanations include distorted tracks from rodents, badgers, an errant kangaroo, or shackles trailing from an escaped balloon, none of which seem particularly plausible.[102]

Thoughts on Abruptly Ending Trackways

When not blaming hoaxes, skeptics argue that abruptly ending sasquatch trackways are merely misidentification of a common wildlife narrative: a rodent, bounding along, leaves vaguely footprint-shaped tracks before being scooped up by a bird of prey, leaving the impression of a vanishing trail. This is a believable explanation for vague prints found in snow, but does little to explain the sudden termination of clearly defined tracks in other media.

This isn't to suggest F&BH advocates provide better explanations. A variety of scenarios, each less likely than the last, are deployed by anyone hoping to dismiss how trackways suddenly vanish. By far the most reasonable is that bigfoot use their immense stride—occasionally reported as large as ten feet or greater—to step onto media that does not transfer footprints, e.g. rocks, tree roots, streams, etc. This is a possible explanation in some cases, but what of tracks ending in the middle of a field, surrounded by identical, unsullied media?

Others suggest bigfoot take to trees when wishing to avoid detection. Though arboreal bigfoot sound odd, some have observed large, hairy hominids moving through the canopy. Once more, we are faced with an answer quite possible in certain circumstances, like old growth forests capable of supporting a 400-600 lb. primate, but less likely when trees are thin, branches appear weak or extremely high, or there simply are no trees nearby (a counterargument, focused on bigfoot's ability to leap preternaturally far, is discussed shortly).

From here, theories become more convoluted. Some actually argue bigfoot *tiptoe backwards through their tracks*, presumably to confuse investigators. Researcher Jeffrey Teagle, mentioned earlier, entertained bigfoot's flesh-and-blood existence until he encountered the Valley trackway. "Backtracking proved unfruitful as I realized that the creature did not reverse its path because the other prints left [behind] remained too defined and undistorted," he wrote. "So the creature did not backtrack to cover its whereabouts." In another instance, Teagle found a set of tracks ending in a gully of saplings, indicating the sasquatch did not jump into a tree.[103]

Perhaps the most laughable idea is that bigfoot deliberately brush away their tracks. One of the clearest descriptions of this came from controversial bigfoot habituator Janice Carter Coy, who said:

> They do drag branches to cover their tracks. They dust the tracks out with them. You asked me about the big guys covering their tracks with the tree branches. Anyway, they had some cedar branches and drug them behind them from the woods and field all the way into the barn...
>
> Once before this, they did this same thing when they crossed the dirt road that we had at that time in front of our house. It was a long time ago and I don't remember what they were after on the other side of the road. One morning, they just came to the edge of the woods and broke off these pine or some other type of tree limbs (can't remember which kind) and crossed the fence on our side and the fence on the other side...

> [One bigfoot] used a tree limb off of an old poplar tree to cover her tracks late one afternoon around maybe one or two when it was hot and in the summer time. She used it to sweep after herself while walking backwards. She walked backwards all the way to where she slept at under the two trees that were over the rock that we called her cave (even though it isn't a real cave). I don't know why she did this but it did make the grass stand back up where she had just stepped on it.
>
> By the way, when she walked backwards she didn't take long strides to do this. Her steps were a lot closer together and she went really slow… I don't think they are adept enough to walk backwards and watch where they are going at the same time. I don't remember her looking behind herself to see where she was going at all. She just sort of stepped on everything and anything and bumped into the trees and all. That was why I thought it was so funny at the time. It looked funny the way she was doing it.[104]

Coy also claimed to have seen bigfoot walking backwards in their tracks without brushing their footprints away. "They do this and I don't know the reason except they are trying to cover their tracks as to where they have been or that they are trying to cover their tracks up for the real direction they are going in," she said, speculating it might be "sort of like a fox backtracking on its own trail to cover its scent."[105]

The idea of *Gigantopithecus* or any other simple-minded "damned dirty ape" backtracking through their footprints, or brushing away tracks to obscure their destination, pushes the threshold of credulity. Coy's testimony is scoffed at by quite a bit of the F&BH establishment—rightly so, as she never provided any clear photographic evidence of her dramatic habituation—yet some of them still embrace such patently absurd theories.

On balance, some researchers argue animal populations in high-risk areas alter their behavior to avoid detection. After reestablishing populations in Colorado and Idaho, both bears and wolves began moving exclusively at night, decreased their territories, and avoided "leaving tracks that reveal their whereabouts and travel routes," according to Thom Powell. "If bears are clever enough to conceal their whereabouts by taking care not to leave obvious tracks, the same ought to be true for still smarter creatures such as bigfoots."[106]

If not to frustrate researchers, what other reasons might bigfoot walk backwards, or otherwise obscure their tracks? A variety of indigenous cultures place emphasis on walking backwards as a means of spiritual protection. Diné (Navajo) tradition dictates that, after burying the dead, "they walk backwards and brush out their tracks so that no evil spirits can follow."[107] In the Indian subcontinent, any cursed object can be disposed of at a crossroads, provided it is approached and left by walking backwards to confuse any attached spirits.[108] When harvesting ochre, Aboriginal Australians thwarted the *Mondong*, faerie-type creatures, by leaving mines backwards, "brushing away their footprints as they went."[109] These ideas certainly resonate with speculation that sasquatch may somehow be a magically operant race.

Plenty of creatures in folklore walk backwards, reflecting their inversion of the natural order. This extends to large, hairy hominids: the *Migoi*, a *Yeti* variant, is said "to become invisible and to walk backwards to fool any trackers."[110] Researcher Dmitri Bayanov writes of the Russian *almasty*, "having spotted people, [they] would stand still, sometimes for a long time and would never immediately run on a surprise encounter but would first step quietly backward."[111] Further complicating matters, both faeries and a variety of bigfoot analogues, including the Chinese *feifei*, display rear-facing feet.[112]

Perhaps the most popular explanation for disappearing trails cites bigfoot's ability to make superhuman leaps. According to some, bigfoot jump either to a distant tree, rock, or other hard media to avoid leaving footprints. This scenario is also employed to explain large gaps in trackways. While problematic, as discussed shortly, this talent does consistently appear in eyewitness reports worldwide.

- An 1875 newspaper article described a wild man seen near Swatara Gap in Berks County, Pennsylvania. The creature stood more than seven feet tall, was covered in hair, and leapt "ten feet at a time with apparent ease."[113]

- In 1941, numerous witnesses spotted a baboon-like creature near Mount Vernon, Illinois. It was noted for its ability to move "20 to 40 feet per leap."[114]

- A witness on Ben MacDhui, home to Scotland's Big Grey Man, found a series of 19 inch footprints in the snow on December 2, 1952. "At one point, the tracks jumped a road over a distance of 30 feet."[115]

- In 1964 Mr. and Mrs. Ahmed Bey were driving near a railroad track in Koyulhisar, Turkey when a UFO "the size of a house" descended, disgorging an "enormous hairy creature." The beast ran towards their car in "fantastic leaps," prompting Mr. Bey to grab his knife and confront the creature. When he tried to stab the beast it lifted him bodily, dropped him, and stepped upon him. Mrs. Bey ran to fetch the police, who allegedly found her husband's corpse at the site.[116]

- Lee Burnette, uncle to bigfoot researcher Tom Burnette, allegedly ran into a five-hundred pound "ape-man" in the North Carolina mountains "that could leap twenty to thirty feet in a single bound."[117]

- In April 1973, Mr. and Mrs. Henry McDaniel of Enfield, Illinois saw a short ape man with stubby arms and pink eyes cover 50 feet in three leaps.[118]

- During the infamous Noxie/Indianola bigfoot flap of 1975, a large, hairy hominid moved across the Oklahoma landscape via "startlingly long hops—rather like a kangaroo."[119]

- According to a 1992 article picked up by *The Daily Telegraph*, "two red-eyed abominable snowmen" were sighted on a Russian military outpost. The largest was 10-feet-tall, and both leapt over a nine-foot fence to escape pursuers.[120]

- Oddo Brunamonti was clearing brush near Scheggia e Pascelupo, Italy in May 1997 when he spied a figure watching him from the trees. Returning later with his vehicle, he found upon closer inspection it was a large, bipedal creature covered in reddish-brown hair. The creature covered the distance between them in one enormous leap and screamed at Brunamonti, who drove away as quickly as possible.[121]

- Beginning in 2001, a "monkey man" started harassing settlements throughout India. It was "variously reported as a monkey, a man with a monkey face, a man with a mask and helmet, or even an alien or robot" and could "jump 20 feet into the air from a crouching position."[122]

"It went across the road… it would probably take me 13 to 15 steps to cross this road—this thing does it in one leap," podcaster Wes

Germer said of his sighting. One of the creatures appeared to leap into the road, bounced off it as if it were a trampoline, and disappeared into the trees with an "otherworldy" gliding motion.[123]

The incidence of three-toed footprints takes on new meaning in light of bounding bigfoot, as there exists a mammalian correlation between tridactyl feet and enormous leaps. The kangaroo—whose family name, *Macropodidae*, literally means "big foot"—have three primary toes.[124] A similar configuration presents in certain hopping desert rodents. Indeed, people have even mistaken bigfoot *for* kangaroos because of their locomotion: in 1907, Pennsylvania's *Reading Times* wrote of a "strange wild animal… which was supposed to be a kangaroo, is a baboon."[125] Seven years earlier, an Oregon paper published a similar piece on a hairy "Kangaroo Man" spotted by miners that "with a few bounds was out of sight."[126]

If bigfoot exist, there is ample evidence for their ability to cross great distances through incredible jumps. But how far can they jump? 30 feet? 50 feet? 80? 100? In his excellent work *Mysterious Creatures: A Guide to Cryptozoology,* George M. Eberhart writes North American Apes (aka "Napes") "can leap 20-40 feet in a single bound."[127]

This is pushing, but not exceeding, the record distance for the largest leaps in the animal kingdom. Depending on the source, the snow leopard or klipspringer (a small African antelope) jump farthest, circa 50 feet horizontally.[128] Both max out at a 20-25 foot vertical leap.[129] Suffice to say, plenty of disappearing bigfoot trails end in soft media far exceeding a 50 foot radius. While leaping bigfoot might explain certain trackways, they fail to account for the most vexing circumstances.

Portals

Those more forgiving of the peculiarities surrounding bigfoot sightings endorse a host of other possibilities surrounding abruptly ending trackways. The idea of interdimensionality remains popular; presumably a dimension-hopping bigfoot would simply snap out of existence, or utilize a portal to phase into another reality, leaving behind a series of steps which simply end.

Such accounts are not unheard of: Tom Dongo wrote of a witness who fled after seeing multiple nine-foot-tall bigfoot guarding a portal that opened near Sedona, Arizona.[130] In 1995's *Merging Dimensions*, Dongo and Linda Bradshaw described "Big Girl," a large, white sasquatch who came and went from the Sedona area, materializing in conjunction with UFOs, petting horses, and leaving behind gifts and messages ("There in the sand was the empty plate turned upside down with a perfect triangle or pyramid drawn around it."). Big Girl's appearances were often accompanied by "a large beam of light… from an unknown source" that "encompassed the area," suggesting, in Bradshaw's words, "her interdimensionality." [131]

> All in all, Big Girl is a big part of the puzzle here. If indeed she is interdimensional, this explains why she remains close to the portal. Nothing, I feel, is by accident. I believe that she is serving a function here on Earth, and as far as I'm concerned, she's more than welcome here. Perhaps the day will come when we can meet formally without any hesitation. I would like that very much.[132]

Barton Nunnelly investigated another portal-hopping sasquatch. "Roy," a family friend, neighbor, and fellow witness of the Spottsville Monster episode confided in Nunnelly:

> One day he was walking along an old fence-line next to a field and noticed a strange area that looked like "heat waves rising from a hot, summer road." The area was only a few yards wide and to either side everything looked normal. According to Roy, as he was watching, one of the creatures stepped out of this strange wavy area like stepping out of a doorway. One second nothing, and the next… there it was looking right at him. It growled at him and at the same time, screamed inside his head to "leave me alone!" Then it turned around and took a step back into the strange-looking 'doorway'—and disappeared.[133]

Jim Urland, another sasquatch witness, described watching with several others as one of the creatures stepped through an aperture that manifested between adjacent copses of pine trees some 20 yards apart. "He went out into a clearing, and as he walked into the clearing, there was a shimmer that began in a circle," he later said. "As he kept walking, everything that was on the outside of the shimmer disappeared and it got to the center, and it just went away." The creature had simply disappeared. Urland carefully examined the area to see if the beast could have vanished in any other fashion, to no avail. "It was just a really life-changing experience for me," he said.[134]

Additional stories about bigfoot emerging from portals are touched upon in Chapters 3 & 7, Volume I of *Where the Footprints End*. Once again, while F&BH cryptozoologists scoff at such tales, indigenous traditions remain undaunted by interdimensional bigfoot.

"A medicine man, one time, he told me that, 'A lot of people don't believe it, but we live in [a] parallel world,'" recalled former Jicarilla tribal officer Tim Anderson, who claims to have seen, smelled, and tracked bigfoot. According to Anderson, this elder described "a parallel world next to us… Bigfoot lives in the other world, and sometimes it comes over. So when he lose[s] his track, he goes back to the other side."[135]

Urland and Anderson appeared in the 2020 documentary *The Bigfoot Alien Connection Revealed* alongside none other than the late Rosemary Ellen Guiley, who had this to say:

> We have what would be called a 'bilocation,' or rapid transport, and that's the ability to be here and then suddenly there without visual means of getting there. That has been described on many occasions where people will see a being in front of them, and then suddenly it's behind them, and they don't see it go behind them—how did it get there? It's just suddenly there… If a bigfoot seems to want to be material and tangible, it seems to have the ability to do that, and then to turn itself into something intangible, as though it's going through an interdimensional doorway.[136]

Anecdotes about bigfoot portals remain frustrating for their unfalsifiability, yet multiple chapters have flirted with the notion of "interdimensional bigfoot." It is a compelling notion: these creatures cannot be wholly intangible, for they leave a plethora of physical evidence, yet their elusiveness suggests a certain ephemeral quality. Still, the actual meaning of interdimensionality remains so ill-defined that it feels a bit like a reinvention of the old medievalist challenge, "How many angels can dance on the head of a pin?"

It is interesting how often trackways disappear in urban legends and folktales. Perhaps the most famous is the "David Lang disappearance," a rumor based off an 1888 Ambrose Bierce short story wherein a boy disappears, leaving behind a trail suddenly terminating in an open field. Variations—claiming names of Larch Thomas, Oliver Lerch, Oliver Larch, Oliver Thomas, and others—are likely fictitious, though contemporary accounts bearing none of Bierce's fingerprints are commonly presented as fact.[137] The very notion that abruptly ending trackways are embedded in popular culture raises a host of possibilities vis-à-vis bigfoot… if sightings of large, hairy hominids are a product of the collective unconscious manifesting the wild man archetype, could the "disappearing trail" be a similarly manifesting motif?

UFO abduction researcher and Harvard psychologist John Mack commonly evoked the concept of the "reified metaphor," the notion that supernatural phenomena employ symbolic manifestations to impart their true intentions in our reality. In Mack's work, paranormal phenomena utilized symbolic presentations to convey their meaning, e.g. human-alien hybrids don't represent actual, literal offspring but rather a *coincidentia oppositorum*, a union of opposites which denizens of the Otherworld wish to invoke.

Could abruptly ending trackways be a symbolic representation from another intelligence? If so, what message do they convey?

It seems plausible—if a meta-narrative is at play—that disappearing trails represent the futility of attempting to understand mysteries by following others. Everything about the paranormal experience —be it UFOs, ghosts, synchronicities, or bigfoot—appears intensely personal. It cannot be experienced second hand. Following others is an unrewarding fool's errand… it leads to literal dead ends. You must engage it yourself. In this sense, abruptly terminating trackways accomplish a goal shared with so many other paranormal phenomena: they imbue the world with meaning. They call us to engage with the unknown. To push boundaries, to sit with the messiness of the mystery.

To venture where the footprints end.

---

[1] Slate, B.A. & Berry, A. (1976). *Bigfoot*. New York, NY: Bantam.

[2] Ibid.

[3] Nunnelly, B.M. (2011). *The Inhumanoids: Real Encounters with Beings That Can't Exist*. Woolsery, UK: CFZ Press.

[4] The Bigfoot Forums Blog. (December 5, 2011). Interview with Author and Paranormal Investigator Philip Spencer. Retrieved February 26, 2019 from https://bigfootforums.blogspot.com/2011/12/interview-with-author-and-paranormal.html

[5] Grant, G. (2000). *Obake Files: Ghostly Encounters in Supernatural Hawaii*. Honolulu, HI: Mutual Publishing.

[6] Guttilla, P. (2003). *The Bigfoot Files*. Santa Barbara, CA: Timeless Voyager Press.

[7] Bigfoot Field Researchers Organization (December 14, 2000). While observing a footprint, youth looks off the path to see shiny haired creature looking at him. Retrieved February 17, 2019 from http://bfro.net/gdb/show_report.asp?ID=912&PrinterFriendly=True

[8] Bigfoot Field Researchers Organization. (July 29, 1998). Night time road side observation. Retrieved February 17, 2019 from http://bfro.net/GDB/show_report.asp?ID=2049&PrinterFriendly=True

[9] Fisher, R. (April 2004). Track to Nowhere. *Paranormal Pennsylvania 8*, p. 27

[10] Boles, R. (April 11, 2008). Possible track and vocalizations at Table Rock Lake. Retrieved February 17, 2019 from http://www.bfro.net/gdb/show_report.asp?id=23581

[11] Wick, E. (July 9, 2015). Hiking family finds possible track off trail outside Estes Park. Retrieved February 17, 2019 from http://www.bfro.net/GDB/show_report.asp?ID=49243&PrinterFriendly=True

[12] Fisher 2004.

[13] Noll, R. (June 24, 2003). Campers find a large track. Retrieved February 17, 2019 from http://bfro.net/GDB/show_report.asp?id=6527

[14] Bigfoot Field Researchers Organization. (March 14, 1999). Large human-like tracks were found in the snow and mud. Retrieved February 17, 2019 from http://www.bfro.net/GDB/show_report.asp?id=1349

[15] Reece, G.L. (2009). *Weird Science and Bizarre Beliefs: Mysterious Creatures, Lost Worlds and Amazing Inventions.* London, UK: I.B. Tauris.

[16] Durham, J.H. (2015). *The Hand on the Mirror: A True Story of Life Beyond Death.* New York, NY: Grand Central Publishing.

[17] Carr, S. (November 30, 2008). An Afternoon With Betty Hill, America's Most Famous Alien Abductee. Retrieved February 18, 2019 from http://weekinweird.com/2008/11/30/an-afternoon-with-betty-hill/

[18] Keel, J. (1975). *The Mothman Prophecies.* London, UK: Panther Books.

[19] Renner, T. (December 6, 2017). The Astral Sasquatch. Retrieved May 15, 2019 from https://strangefamiliars.podbean.com/e/episode-21-the-astral-sasquatch/

[20] Ibid.

[21] Ibid.

[22] Ibid.

[23] Macrae, F. (January 31, 2016). Are these the footprints of the yeti? Trekker believes mystery trail spotted in remote area of the Himalayas could come from the legendary beast. Retrieved February 18, 2019 from https://www.dailymail.co.uk/news/article-3425663/Are-footprints-yeti-Trekker-believes-mystery-trail-spotted-remote-area-Himalayas-come-legendary-beast.html

[24] S.A.R. (November 25, 2013). Sasquatch Summit 2013. Retrieved February 18, 2019 from http://bizarrebigfoot.blogspot.com/2013/11/sasquatch-summit-2013_25.html

[25] Reece 2009.

[26] Guiley, R.E. (2019). Interdimensional Paraphysical Sasquatch. In R.E. Guiley (Ed.), *FATE Presents: Planet Bigfoot.* (pp. 171-186). New Milford, CT: Visionary Living Publishing.

[27] Speigel, L. (November 22, 2011). Yeti Evidence Falls Flat: Scientist Says Local Officials Staged Siberian Snowman Hunt For Publicity. Retrieved February 20, 2019 fro https://www.huffingtonpost.com/2011/11/22/yeti-siberian-snowman-evidence_n_1100497.html

[28] Ibid.

[29] Rick. (July 3, 2013). Earliest documented Bigfoot Sighting in Pacific Northwest. Retrieved January 8, 2019 from http://hamell.net/earliest-documented-bigfoot-sighting-in-pacific-northwest/

[30] Bord, J., & Bord, C. (2006). *Bigfoot Casebook Updated: Sightings and Encounters from 1818 to 2004.* Enumclaw, WA: Pinewinds Press.

[31] Markey, S. (May 24, 2016). AUSTRALIA'S 20,000-YEAR-OLD HUMAN FOOTPRINTS. Retrieved February 18, 2019 from https://www.nationalgeographic.com.au/nature/australias-20000-year-old-human-footprints.aspx

[32] Marks, K. (December 23, 2005). Ice Age footprints hold outback's clues tell a touching tale. Retrieved February 19, 2019 from https://www.independent.co.uk/news/world/australasia/ice-age-footprints-hold-outbacks-clues-tell-a-touching-tale-520472.html

[33] Pursiful, D.J. (April 25, 2017). Wondrous Tribes: Monopods. Retrieved February 19, 2019 from https://intothewonder.wordpress.com/2017/04/25/wondrous-tribes-monopods/

[34] Seaburn, P. (October 9, 2018). Mysterious One-Legged Ghost Recorded Hopping Around Laos. Retrieved February 19, 2019 from https://mysteriousuniverse.org/2018/10/mysterious-one-legged-ghost-recorded-hopping-around-laos/

[35] Wickham, A. (2012). *The Dead Roam the Earth: True Stories of the Paranormal from Around the World.* New York, NY: The Penguin Group.

[36] Sloan, K.A. (2008). *Runaway Daughters: Seduction, Elopement, and Honor in Nineteenth-Century Mexico.* Albuquerque, NM: University of New Mexico Press.

[37] Roth, J. E. (1997). *American Elves: An Encyclopedia of Little People from the Lore of 380 Ethnic Groups of the Western Hemisphere.* Jefferson, NC: McFarland & Company, Inc.

[38] Van Winkle, B. (2006). Cannibals in the Mountains: Washoe Teratology and the Donner Party. In S.A. Kan & P.T. Strong (Eds.), *New Perspectives on Native North America* (pp. 395-413). Lincoln, NE: University of Nebraska Press.

[39] Campbell, J.F. (1890). *Popular Tales of the West Highlands.* London, UK: Alexander Gardner & Paisley.

[40] Rennard, A. (June 18, 2000). Pre-Columbian and Early American Legends of Bigfoot-like Beings. Retrieved February 19, 2019 from https://www.bfro.net/legends/penutian.htm

[41] Scammell, J.C. (1910). *The Library of Entertainment, Vol. IX.* Chicago, IL: Geo. L. Shuman and Co.

[42] Pilichis, D. (1978). *Bigfoot: Tales of Unexplained Creatures (UFO and Psychic Connections).* Rome, OH: Dennis Pilichis.

[43] Bord & Bord 2006.

[44] Slate, B.A. & Berry, A. (1976). *Bigfoot.* New York, NY: Bantam.

[45] Nunnelly 2011.

[46] Clark, J. (December 1974). Anthropoid and UFO in Indiana. *Flying Saucer Review* 20(3), pp. 17-18.

[47] Renner, T. (February 28, 2019). A Halloween Flannel Man and an Impossibly Black Bigfoot. Retrieved February 28, 2019 from https://www.strangefamiliars.com/e/a-halloween-flannel-man-and-an-impossibly-black-bigfoot/

[48] Ibid.

[49] Meldrum, J. (2006). *Sasquatch: Legend Meets Science*. New York, NY: Forge Books.

[50] Renner, T. (2017). *Bigfoot in Pennsylvania*. Charleston, SC: CreateSpace Independent Publishing Platform.

[51] Bord & Bord 2006.

[52] Guttilla 2003.

[53] Bord & Bord 2006.

[54] Pardue, D. (August 11, 2006). Road-crossing sighting by motorist on Hwy 220 north of Candor. Retrieved February 21, 2019 from http://www.bfro.net/GDB/show_report.asp?ID=15492&PrinterFriendly=True

[55] Familant, M. (May 25, 2014). Husband and wife have close encounter while roller blading outside Port Charlotte. Retrieved February 20, 2019 from http://www.bfro.net/GDB/show_report.asp?ID=45137&PrinterFriendly=True

[56] Fahrenback, W.H. (August 22, 2005). Hiking family has daytime encounter in Sierra. Retrieved February 21, 2019 from http://www.bfro.net/GDB/show_report.asp?id=12383

[57] Fleming, K. (February 8, 2013). Snowmobiler observes a large figure cross the trail behind him near Traverse City. Retrieved February 21, 2019 from http://www.bfro.net/gdb/show_report.asp?ID=39578&PrinterFriendly=True

[58] Betz, C. (January 27, 2008). Woman recounts childhood sighting behind her house near Lake Charles. Retrieved February 21, 2019 from http://www.bfro.net/GDB/show_report.asp?id=23018

[59] Porteous, A. (1928). *The Forest in Folklore and Mythology*. New York, NY: The Macmillan Company.

[60] Bigfoot Field Researchers Organization. (September 24, 2000). Teen and uncle chase reddish bigfoot in San Isabel National Forest. Retrieved February 21, 2019 from http://www.bfro.net/gdb/show_report.asp?id=348

[61] Merola, C. (2018). *The One Who Runs and Hides: A True Story*. USA: Merola.

[62] Franzoni III, H.J. (2008). *In the Spirit of Seatco*. Deer Island, OR: Ste Ye Hah Publishing.

[63] Strickler, L. (September 28, 2018). Stan Gordon - PA UFO / Anomalies Investigator - Arcane Radio. Retrieved February 20, 2019 from https://arcaneradio.podbean.com/e/stan-gordon-pa-ufo-anomalies-investigator-arcane-radio/

[64] Picasso, F. (n.d.). Case 304. In A. Rosales (Ed.), *1978 Humanoid Sighting Reports*. Retrieved February 5, 2014 from http://www.ufoinfo.com/humanoid/humanoid-1978.pdf

[65] Johnson, P.G & Jeffers, J.L. (1986). *The Pennsylvania Bigfoot*. Pittsburgh, PA: Johnson & Jeffers.

[66] Paulides, D. (2009). *Tribal Bigfoot*. Blaine, WA: Hancock House.

[67] Augusto, N. (n.d.). The Varginha Diary. Retrieved February 20, 2019 from http://www.thelosthaven.co.uk/VarginhaDairy.html

[68] Boyko, V.P. (n.d.). Case 26. In A. Rosales (Ed.), *1997 Humanoid Sighting Reports*. Retrieved February 5, 2014 from http://www.ufoinfo.com/humanoid/humanoid-1997.pdf

[69] Paulides, D. (2008). *The Hoopa Project: Bigfoot Encounters in California*. Blaine, WA: Hancock House.

[70] Johnson & Jeffers 1986.

[71] Ferrer, J. (n.d.). Case 156. In A. Rosales (Ed.), *2001 Humanoid Sighting Reports*. Retrieved February 5, 2014 from http://www.ufoinfo.com/humanoid/humanoid-2001.pdf

[72] Bord, J. & Bord, C. (1985). *Alien Animals* (2nd ed.). London, UK: Panther Books.

[73] Alley, J.R. (2007). *Raincoast Sasquatch*. Blaine, WA: Hancock House. (Original work published 2003)

[74] Villasana, J. (n.d.). Case 156. In A. Rosales (Ed.), *1979 Humanoid Sighting Reports*. Retrieved February 5, 2014 from http://www.ufoinfo.com/humanoid/humanoid-1979.pdf

[75] Shiel, L.A. (2006). *Backyard Bigfoot: The True Story of Stick Signs, UFOs, and the Sasquatch*. Lake Linden, MI: Slipdown Mountain Publications LLC.

[76] Carwardine, M. (2008). *Natural History Museum: Animal Records*. New York, NY: Sterling Publishing Co.

[77] Kennedy, A.S. & Kennedy, V. (2014). *Animals of the Serengeti and Ngorongoro Conservation Area.* Princeton, NJ: Princeton University Press.

[78] UrbanFolkores. (November 7, 2016). Monsterpedia: Turbo Bachan. Retrieved June 6, 2019 from http://urbanfolkores.blogspot.com/2017/04/urban-legends-turbo-bachan.html

[79] Ibid.

[80] Germer, W. (December 24, 2016). Sasquatch Chronicles Radio // SC EP: 284 The Christmas Show. Retrieved February 21, 2019 from https://sasquatchchronicles.com/sc-ep284-the-christmas-show/

[81] Ibid.

[82] Eno, P. & Eno, B. (2017). *Behind the Paranormal 2: Bigfoot, Mothman and Monsters You've Never Heard Of.* Woonsocket, RI: Barking Cat Books.

[83] Carter, L. (1972). *Lovecraft: A Look Behind the Cthulhu Mythos.* New York, NY: Ballantine Books.

[84] Azkath, S. (December 8, 2018). Strange Things in the Woods: Listener Stories – December 8, 2018. Retrieved February 26, 2019 from https://www.wheredidtheroadgo.com/show-archive/2018/item/563-strange-things-in-the-woods-listener-stories-december-8-2018

[85] Bizarre Bigfoot. (August 3, 2011). The Trouble with Tracks. Retrieved February 12, 2019 from http://bizarrebigfoot.blogspot.com/2011/08/trouble-with-tracks.html

[86] Gordon, S. (October 22, 2018). Large Footprints in Fresh Snow Suddenly Stop and Vanish (North Huntingdon, PA). Retrieved February 26, 2019 from http://www.stangordon.info/wp/2018/10/22/large-footprints-in-fresh-snow-suddenly-stop-and-vanish-north-huntingdon-pa/

[87] Guttilla 2003.

[88] Renner, T. (2018) The Company They Keep. In D. Weatherly (Ed.), *Wood Knocks: Journal of Sasquatch Research - Volume III* (pp. 31-46). NV: Leprechaun Press.

[89] Pilichis, D. (1982). *Night Siege: The Northern Ohio UFO Creature Invasion.* Rome, OH: Dennis Pilichis.

[90] Clark, J. (2012). *Unexplained!* (3rd ed.). Canton, MI: Visible Ink Press.

[91] Clifton, C. (October 14, 2011). Various Thoughts on Bigfoot. Retrieved February 27, 2019 from https://www.southernrockiesnatureblog.com/2011/10/various-thoughts-on-bigfoot.html

[92] Daegling, D.J. (2004). *Bigfoot Exposed: An Anthropologist Examines America's Enduring Legend.* Walnut Creek, CA: Altamira Press.

[93] Arave, L. (June 16, 2012). Bigfoot Isn't Cain, Yet He Is Supernatural. Retrieved February 26, 2019 from https://nighuntokolob.blogspot.com/2012/06/bigfoot-isnt-cainyet-he-is-supernatural.html

[94] Strickler, L. (March 27, 2014). Crypto 4 Corners Investigates 'Furry One' Track Line. Retrieved February 26, 2019 from https://www.phantomsandmonsters.com/2014/03/crypto-4-corners-investigates-furry-one.html

[95] Teagle, J. (February 6, 2009). Strange Places Where Things Do Go Bump In The Night... Retrieved February 27, 2019 from http://chattahoocheebigfootblog.blogspot.com/2009/02/strange-places-where-things-do-go-bump.html

[96] Ashby, D. (October 29, 2015). 6 most haunted outdoor places in Pocatello. Retrieved February 26, 2019 from https://www.idahostatejournal.com/outdoors/most-haunted-outdoor-places-in-pocatello/article_e9a517d6-b06d-58dc-a793-301b6b460344.html

[97] Gordon 2018.

[98] Slate & Berry 1976.

[99] Ibid.

[100] Keel 1975.

[101] Kelleher, C.A. & Knapp, G. (2005). *Hunt for the Skinwalker: Science Confronts the Unexplained at a Remote Ranch.* New York, NY: Pocket Books.

[102] Dash, M. (1994). The Devil's Hoofmarks. *Fortean Studies 1*, pp. 71-150.

[103] Teagle, J. (February 6, 2009). Strange Places Where Things Do Go Bump In The Night... Retrieved February 28, 2019 from http://chattahoocheebigfootblog.blogspot.com/2009/02/strange-places-where-things-do-go-bump.html

[104] Green, M., & Coy, J.C. (2002). *50 Years with Bigfoot: Tennessee Chronicles of Co-existence.* TN: Mary Green.

[105] Ibid.

[106] Powell, T. (2003). *The Locals.* Surrey, CA: Hancock House Publishers Ltd.

[107] Hassell, S.W. (1949). *Know the Navajo.* Estes Park, CO: Vic Walker, Indian Trader.

[108] Ghassem-Fachandi, P. (2015). Urban Thresholds: crevices, crossroads and magic remainders. In C. Bates & M. Mio (Eds.), *Cities in South Asia* (pp. 180-194). London, UK: Routledge.

[109] Monroe, M.H. (n.d.). Australia: The Land Where Time Began. Retrieved March 3, 2019 from https://austhrutime.com/ochre_mining.htm

[110] Redfern, N. (2016). *The Bigfoot Book: The Encyclopedia of Sasquatch, Yeti and Cryptid Primates.* Canton, MI: Visible Ink Press.

[111] Bayanov, D. (2011). *Bigfoot Research: The Russian Vision.* C.L. Murphy (Ed.). Blaine, WA: Hancock House Publishers.

[112] Ibid.

[113] Renner, T. (2017). *Bigfoot in Pennsylvania.* Charleston, SC: CreateSpace Independent Publishing Platform.

[114] Bord & Bord 2006.

[115] Eberhart, G.M. (2002). *Mysterious Creatures: A Guide to Cryptozoology.* Santa Barbara, CA: ABC-CLIO, Inc.

[116] Ferguson, J. (1977). *Les humanoides: Les cerveaux qui dirigent les soucoupes volantes.* Montreal, CAN: Lemeac.

[117] Burnette, T., & Riggs, R. (2014). *Bigfoot: Exploring the Myth and Discovering the Truth.* Woodbury, MN: Llewllyn Publications.

[118] Eberhart 2002.

[119] Brandon, J. (1983). *The Rebirth of Pan: Hidden Faces of the American Earth Spirit.* Dunlap, IL: Firebird Press.

[120] Short, B. (n.d.). The De Facto Sasquatch. Retrieved January 18, 2019 from https://static1.squarespace.com/static/596c0bae4c0dbfa1d26e86be/t/5b9bff06562fa7cfcdf1bfc8/1536950038606/The+de+facto+Sasquatch+premier+installment.pdf?fbclid=IwAR3763B1leKUEQofPRbPvzAItNH5K-RUVoKU-vOLW_iXvSFkdKSg4o4xBXw

[121] Tambellini, M. (n.d.). Case 132. In A. Rosales (Ed.), *1997 Humanoid Sighting Reports*. Retrieved February 5, 2014 from http://www.ufoinfo.com/humanoid/humanoid-1997.pdf

[122] Eberhart 2002.

[123] Germer, W. (November 3, 2013). Sasquatch Chronicles Radio // SC EP: 2 Class A Bigfoot Encounters. Retrieved December 8, 2018 from https://sasquatchchronicles.com/sc-ep2-class-a-bigfoot-encounters/

[124] McDade, M.C. (Ed.). (2004). *Grzimek's Animal Life Encyclopedia: Volume 13 – Mammals II* (2nd ed.). Farmington Hills, MI: Gale.

[125] Renner 2017.

[126] Nunnelly 2011.

[127] Eberhart 2002.

[128] Singha, J. & Moitra, A. (Eds.). (2018). *I Can't Believe It! 2*. New York, NY: DK Publishing.

[129] Davies, E. (August 26, 2016). The greatest jumper on Earth is probably not a flea. Retrieved March 3, 2019 from http://www.bbc.com/earth/story/20160825-the-greatest-jumper-on-earth-is-probably-not-a-flea

[130] Dongo, T. (1990). *The Alien Tide: The Mysteries of Sedona, Book 2*. Flagstaff, AZ: Light Technology Publishing.

[131] Dongo, T. & Bradshaw, L. (1995). *Merging Dimensions: The Opening Portals of Sedona*. Sedona, AZ: Hummingbird Publishing.

[132] Ibid.

[133] Nunnelly 2011.

[134] Megargle, A., Meyer, R.C. (Producers), & Megargle, A., Meyer, R.C. (Directors). (2020). *The Bigfoot Alien Connection Revealed*. USA: Centre Communications, Inc.

[135] Ibid.

[136] Ibid.

[137] Castle of Spirits. (2001). Strange Disappearances. Retrieved September 13, 2017 from http://www.castleofspirits.com/strangediss.html

Take nothing on its looks; take everything on evidence. There's no better rule.

- *Charles Dickens*, Great Expectations

Disappearing Evidence

Flesh-and-blood hypothesis bigfooters have one solid advantage over almost every other sector of the paranormal: physical evidence. UFOs occasionally scorch fields, or leave other physical traces at supposed landing sites. Ghosts bestow infrequent hand or footprints—though these often seem as ephemeral as the spirits themselves, appearing only on glass or in fine powder. Tangible evidence for these phenomena remains both scant and, in any case, far from incontrovertible.

By comparison, bigfoot leave robust trackways of evidence in their wake: various researchers have collected alleged sasquatch scat, hair, blood—and, above all, footprints. Leaving the problematic three and four-toed tracks for Chapter 6, it is worthwhile to note that five-toed tracks, replete with dermal ridges, mid-tarsal breaks, and even the occasional genetic defect are objectively the most convincing evidence for the existence of a relict hominid or undiscovered giant primate. Dr. Jeffrey Meldrum, a tenured academic at Idaho State University and specialist in primate foot anatomy, became convinced of bigfoot's existence based on footprint evidence alone. The proof, for Meldrum, lies in the details—and the best casts exhibit an array of features indicating something quite solid and heavy walks upright in our forests, leaving footprints for us to find.

In the end, however, all we have are plaster casts.

In some sense, our discussion of bigfoot evidence might be

rendered both more insightful and easier if we frame it in terms of religious artifacts: specifically, saints' relics in Christian tradition. *Primary relics* are parts of a saint's body—or their entire body—venerated by followers, often placed on display. Hair and bones are the most common primary relics, though sometimes things get a bit more bizarre (multiple churches claimed ownership of Christ's foreskin during the Middle Ages, for instance).

Secondary relics, on the other hand, are objects saints were believed to have come into contact with, such as clothes and possessions. Though often of dubious provenance, these articles still hold sway today over throngs of devout Christians, who believe they are imbued with a magnetic, spiritual power. (One can also draw obvious parallels to recovered "crash material" in Ufology, a comparison recently addressed in Diana Walsh Pasulka's excellent work *American Cosmic: UFOs, Religion, Technology*.)

Ergo, our best evidence for bigfoot correlates to secondary relics.

Primary Relics

Bigfoot's primary relics—all that hair, scat, and blood—remain inconclusive. Some studies, such as Dr. Melba Ketchum's Sasquatch Genome Project, claim to have sequenced bigfoot DNA but are fraught with controversy and are widely regarded as questionable. As yet, none of the studies asserting positive proof of bigfoot's existence have been universally accepted by mainstream science. Ketchum's own study is as contentious and skeptically attacked as anything else in the realm of the bigfoot phenomenon, yet supporters believe the mainstream has, for one reason or another, refused to accept her results. To date, no peer-reviewed scientific journal has agreed to publish Ketchum's study, resulting in her self-publishing the work under the banner of her own *DeNovo Journal* on February 13, 2013.[1]

Upon examining Ketchum's study, the scientific community was not kind. Leonid Kruglyak, a geneticist from Princeton University said:

> To state the obvious, no data or analyses are presented that in any way support the claim that their samples come from a new primate or human-primate hybrid. Instead, analyses either come back as 100% human, or fail in ways that suggest technical artifacts. They make the bizarre claim that the failures might be caused by novel, nonstandard structure of the DNA ("Electron micrographs of the DNA revealed

unusual double strand – single strand – double strand transitions which may have contributed to the failure to amplify during PCR.") which would mean this DNA was different from DNA in all other known species.[2]

(It is worth noting that, if Ketchum's study is valid, the existence of "novel" DNA—different from all known species—*would* indicate that bigfoot could very well be more than a simple relict hominid or undiscovered animal, supporting many of the suggestions made in these very volumes!)

Other shortcomings were cited. Ketchum included a phylogenic tree representing the evolutionary relationships of different organisms in her bigfoot DNA paper, to which Kruglyak commented, "The tree … is inconsistent with known primate phylogeny and generally makes no sense."[3]

Even those sympathetic to the bigfoot question were critical. Todd Disotell, a human origins expert from New York University with an interest in sasquatch study, was markedly *less* generous in his view of Ketchum's *DeNovo Journal* and the bigfoot DNA study: "It's clearly a fake Vanity Journal with lots of ShutterStock pictures, misspellings and it was only created on 2/4/13 [shortly before the publication of results]. I've only read the abstract and conclusion and neither makes any sense."[4]

A separate bigfoot/Yeti DNA study, headed by Oxford University genetics professor Dr. Bryan Sykes, was completed in 2014. Of the 57 samples received for this study from all over the world, 37 were deemed acceptable for testing. None of the results pointed to an undiscovered primate of any sort, nor any kind of "novel" DNA. The study wasn't without its curiosities—one sample apparently originated from an unusual and presumed-extinct Asiatic bear, while another represented an unspecified canid—but all other samples matched extant mammals.[5]

While such prominent DNA studies haven't exactly judged in their favor, some hair analyses have given the F&BH crowd a little more hope. Various hair samples, purportedly from sasquatch, have returned from examination with vague-but-enticing results like "unknown animal" or "unknown primate."

In her report on a sample submitted by Tobe Johnson from the Owl Moon Prints, hair analyst Cindy Dosen concluded, "The following has been determined from a microscopic hair examination. The sample may have come from a loose hair, last stages of resting growth. No postmortem banding on hair to indicate death. This was from a live animal. All other species have been ruled out. This is an UNKNOWN HAIR"[6] (see Case Study: Under the Owl Moon for further details).

In 1995, Paul Freeman—the man behind the legendary "Freeman footage," a video tape purportedly (but inconclusively, of course) showing a bigfoot—followed strange screams into the Blue Mountains of Washington along with former game warden Bill Laughery and another man, Wes Summerlin. The men came to a clearing filled with broken and twisted trees, dripping with sap—indicating fresh breaks. Caught on these trees were clumps of long black and brown hair.

The samples Freeman, Laughery, and Summerlin collected were sent to Ohio State University for testing. Upon examining the hair, Dr. W. Henner Fahrenbach's report "determined microscopically that the hair appeared to have come from two individuals of the same species, that it differed in color, length, and hair growth cycle between the two sets, had not been cut and was indistinguishable from human hair by any criterion."[7] Upon attempting to extract DNA from the samples, OSU scientists determined the "DNA extracted from both hair shaft or roots was too fragmented to permit gene sequencing."[8]

The question remains, then: why can't science agree on these primary relics? Given that we have what seems to be physical material left behind by bigfoot, why can't experts come to an acceptable conclusion of any sort? Something strange seems afoot with the evidence. It is almost as if the bigfoot phenomenon itself—or whatever intelligence is behind said phenomenon—is determined to keep evidence of bigfoot's existence *inconclusive*.

Disappearing Evidence

Finding a bigfoot print or trackway is an unusual thing indeed. Finding a "primary relic" of a bigfoot creature is rarer still. Given that so few primary relics exist—and presuming that great care is taken in both preserving the provenance and ensuring the safekeeping of said relics—we must ask why *so much* bigfoot evidence simply goes missing?

Cindy Dosen related the issue of disappearing hair samples to Tobe Johnson. When Johnson sent his sample to Dosen for analysis, he was advised to take special care in mailing the artifact: Dosen had noted a problem with previous samples sent her way disappearing in the mail, for whatever reasons.[9]

Vanishing hair samples were also a problem for Stan Gordon. In August of 1973, Pennsylvania was in the middle of a wave of bigfoot and UFO sightings which would keep Gordon and his team of investigators busy for years. One of Gordon's associates, identified as Ken R., responded to a bigfoot sighting in Monongahela, Pennsylvania and obtained two, foul-smelling hair samples. Ken let his dog sniff at the samples and saw it cower at the scent.

Ken R. mailed one hair sample, along with his report describing the incident, to Gordon and phoned to let Stan know the package was on its way. Ken had mailed the envelope *personally* from his local post office. The missive never reached Gordon. After a few days, Gordon telephoned Ken to inquire about the package. It should have arrived. Ken mailed a second copy of the report. This too, never arrived.

While they were discussing these events, another phone conversation between Ken and Stan was interrupted by a loud, metallic, electronic sound. The interference was loud enough to drown out the conversation. Gordon noted that this interference became somewhat common. It would happen whenever he discussed bigfoot creature sightings over the telephone.

Suspecting their mail was being intercepted, Ken R. eventually hand-delivered the second hair sample to Gordon. However, that isn't the last time bigfoot evidence gathered by Ken would go missing.

Ken R. kept all of his bigfoot reports and evidence in a filing cabinet at his home. In the same file, Ken also kept personal and family information. One day, around the same time as the mailed hair sample and reports went missing, Ken went to retrieve his bigfoot files from the cabinet. Anything concerning the creature was gone. All of Ken's reports and witness interviews had vanished. All other files—detailing personal and family information—remained untouched.[10]

Melba Ketchum herself suggested some of the Sasquatch Genome Project's evidence was effectively "disappeared" by other researchers. When taken to an independent laboratory to verify the results, the samples revealed a mix of DNA from opossum and other known animals. Ketchum alleged the samples "may have been switched."[11]

Various bigfoot investigators have claimed factions within the United States government, for unknown reasons, confiscate or destroy evidence of sasquatch. This provides a convenient excuse for missing evidence, tied up nicely in a conspiracy theory bow. The government *knows* bigfoot exist, these investigators assert; the reasons why authorities deny the creature's existence vary from individual to individual, ranging from bigfoot's existence negatively impacting the logging industry to the idea that people would fearfully avoid visiting National Parks if they knew bigfoot was "out there."

Exposing a vast government conspiracy covering up bigfoot's reality may be as difficult as proving the creatures themselves exist. For the sake of our argument, however, it really doesn't matter. Whether taken by the government and stored in some top-secret vault, or, instead, if the evidence disappears by some other, stranger means, the end result is the same: in both scenarios the evidence is gone.

The idea of a government cover up of giant creatures extends at least as far back as the 1800s. Newspapers from the 19th to the early 20th centuries frequently reported discoveries of giant—eight-foot tall plus—human skeletons throughout North America. These bones, in most cases, do not appear to be bigfoot remains (occasional photos and descriptions of the bones seem to indicate these skeletons came from a very tall race of humans). The giant skeletons were found, according to the articles, in various burial mounds and tombs throughout America, sometimes accompanied by large, heavy tools or weapons. Nearly without exception, the giant skeleton newspaper reports consistently mention that the bones will be taken to some institution, usually the Smithsonian Institution.[12]

These articles have fed modern day conspiracy theories that the Smithsonian has secret warehouses containing these giant skeletons, or, alternately, that the institution actually *destroys* these skeletons. Again, the motives for this cover-up vary according to the individual—but most often the reason provided is that these giant skeletons do not conform to "accepted science." Whether said conspiracy theories have any veracity is irrelevant here. Assuming these skeletons did exist, the fact remains they have been confiscated so only a select, chosen few may know the truth—or they have been destroyed. The reason for, and method of, the evidence's removal really doesn't matter. The end result is the same: it has disappeared.

Alleged bigfoot bones, another primary relic, meet a similar fate. Dr. Robert W. Denton was on a Boy Scout outing near Mammoth, California in July 1965 when a pack mule tethered in a boggy area near their camp kicked up a piece of a skull. The skull was humanlike, but extraordinarily large and heavy. It appeared unusually long with an occipital ridge higher than found on modern humans.[13]

Denton sent the skull to Dr. Gerald K. Ridge, a Ventura County pathologist, for identification. Ridge found the skull so unusual he wondered if it came from an "anthropoid species other than human."[14] He passed the skull along to two scientists at the University of California, Los Angeles, Dr. Bleibtreul and Dr. Prost, but by 1973 the skull had disappeared.[15]

Several inquiries were made regarding the location of the skull. "Apparently the specimen was never turned into the museum for cataloging: if it had been, we would have record of it," UCLA anthropologist professor Clement Meighan replied by letter. "I'm sorry we don't seem able to find this skull, but this is the first I have heard of it…."[16]

Clay Singer, the UCLA museum technician, followed up a few weeks later. "I have tried to be as exhaustive as possible in attempting to locate the skull fragment," he said. "I have personally questioned everyone in the department who might know something about it, including former museum technicians as far back as 1964. Nobody has seen it since mid-1965... I have also carefully checked every burial and accessioned skull in our collection without result."[17]

When Bleibtreul was questioned about the specimen he replied that he had no record, nor recollection of the skull. "I'm sorry, but I don't remember it," Bleibtreul wrote. Prost answered similarly, stating he had no memory of anyone giving him a skull of any kind while he was at UCLA —nor of even having such a skull in his lab.[18]

How does such an unusual, important, and potentially groundbreaking specimen as the Denton skull simply *disappear*? Why do so many of the parties involved have difficulty even remembering the skull, much less locating it?

Footprints? What Footprints?

Researcher William Jevning tells another story of alleged destruction of bigfoot evidence by government employees. On the November 6, 2011 episode of the *Bigfoot Tonight Show*, Jevning related a tale from the early 1990s of United States Forest Service employees destroying a bigfoot trackway.

After finding multiple large, human-looking tracks impressed in fine silt-like dirt in a remote area near Mount Adams, Washington, some unnamed associates of Jevning passed a Forest Service truck. When they told the Forest Service employees about the bigfoot trackway, one produced a camera and asked where he could find the prints. The researchers directed him to the location and asked if they could receive copies of the photographs. The photographer replied he would be happy to provide copies of the photographs and instructed Jevning's associates to just ask for him by name at the Forest Service.[19]

Jevning and his associates returned to the location later that day to examine the footprints. When they arrived, the entire area had been sprayed with water, destroying the trackway. After contacting the Forest Service about the photographer, they were told no such man worked at the agency.[20]

Stan Gordon reported a similar instance of bigfoot tracks being destroyed and other evidence being confiscated. In 1973, the Superior Mobile Home Court of Derry Township, Pennsylvania produced multiple encounters with bigfoot creatures. By mid-August residents of the mobile home park were reporting strange crying noises and sounds of something heavy walking around the trailer park. On August 24 at about 11:30 p.m., "Beverly Burns" (a pseudonym given by Gordon) heard scratching sounds at the back of her mobile home. She and her son also reported hearing what sounded like a baby crying outside of the trailer before their home's electricity began turning on and off by itself.[21]

Burns stepped outside into the darkness and observed a huge, black form which she described as "gigantic"—well over six-feet tall with a husky build. When the creature saw Burns it turned and ran off, disappearing between two other mobile homes and leaving a strong sulfur-like smell hanging in the air. Burns phoned law enforcement, who arrived to find strange footprints on the ground around the trailer. They also noted that the electrical service line running from the meter to the trailer had been pulled out—apparently by the creature. Scratches were also discovered on the back of Burns's trailer.[22]

Three days later at 6:50 a.m., another woman in the trailer park spotted a bigfoot in the woods above the community. The creature was covered in white hair and seemed to reach for something in a tree before turning and walking into the forest.[23]

On August 28, an unknown stranger with an interest in these bigfoot encounters visited the Superior Mobile Home Court. The man arrived at Beverly Burns's residence around 7:30 p.m. claiming to be an investigator from Ohio. He flashed Burns some sort of photo identification, including a badge which she later could only remember had the words "Ohio" and "UFO" printed on it. Burns could not recall any other details about the man's credentials. She described him as short and on the heavy side with brown hair and glasses. He was wearing grey work clothes and a belt with "some kind of face on it."[24]

The stranger proceeded to question Burns about her bigfoot encounter, asking if she was the woman who had the scratch marks on her trailer. He would not reveal to Burns how he knew her name. She told the stranger she had found some hair samples, presumably from the creature that molested her home on August 24, which she was trying to get to Stan Gordon. The man took the hair and said he would ensure Gordon got the samples.

Later, some residents from the trailer park gathered near the Burns home to look at the odd footprints left by the creature. One boy taking polaroid photographs of the tracks said to the stranger, "I have just made a picture."

The man replied, "You have just made us a picture," then took the photograph from the boy, crumpled it, and put it in his pocket. He wrote down the measurements of the creature's tracks before placing his shoe in the footprints and scuffing the ground—completely ruining the prints. The stranger then said aloud, "It has been destroyed."

The neighbors grew upset at the man's behavior and threatened to call the police. The mysterious stranger quickly hopped into his vehicle—a brown station wagon with Ohio tags—and sped away from the scene. He has never been identified.[25]

Plaid is the New Black

The behavior of this strange man at the mobile home park in 1973 recalls those odd arbiters of information from the UFO world, the Men in Black (MIBs). Though some researchers have made valid arguments that the MIB are just a modern expression of a far older phenomenon, proper MIBs began appearing to UFO witnesses in the 1950s. MIB typically appear in groups of two or three, dressed in a kind of timeless black suit and hat, driving large, anachronistic black cars. They often behave oddly, displaying little knowledge of basic social interaction, and sometimes exhibit strange physical features as well, including deathly complexions. MIB appear most often to witnesses a short time after their UFO sighting, intimating—or outright claiming—they belong to some sort of *official* organization, ending visits with threats that witnesses should keep silent about their sighting.

Unsurprisingly, the bigfoot community seems to have its MIB equivalent—not just in the stranger from the Pennsylvania trailer park above—but in cases from across the United States of America. These men, often claiming to be from the Department of the Interior, Bureau of Land Management, or some other government-affiliated agency, allegedly visit bigfoot witnesses who have experienced particularly intense encounters or people who have collected some kind of primary evidence. One of their earliest appearances took place in 1989.

A woman named Claire, on a business trip to America from the United Kingdom, had some spare time to sightsee near Carmel, California. While there, she followed a coastal path to a cove area with the intent of photographing sea otters. She was sitting on some rocks near the beach taking photographs when she began feeling frightened and cold, the hair on her neck standing up. Looking to the other side of the cove, she saw what she first assumed was a group of large cats—but soon realized they were too bulky to be felines. According to Claire:

> They came around the promontory. I have never seen anything like it in my life. Very, very large. Very hairy.

Moving on all fours. There were several of these creatures —one behind the other. It obviously wasn't a cat because it was moving in a very strange manner. The head kept popping up as if it was sniffing and then—it popped up. It stood up on two feet... It was bipedal. It must have been seven-to-eight-feet tall. It was followed into this cove by two others, maybe five-to-six-foot, maybe six-and-a-half-foot, and three much smaller ones.[26]

Claire watched a male, the largest of the creatures, wade into the ocean. The two six-and-a-half-foot tall creatures, females, and the three smallest creatures sat on the beach. The large male was tearing out seaweed and throwing it to the female creatures. Claire observed the females chewing at the roots of the seaweed, rubbing it on their chests and necks, and then draping the seaweed over their shoulders.

Claire observed the group of bigfoot for a time, stunned at the sight of the creatures. She reached for her camera, intent on getting a shot of the amazing scene when part of the lens kit fell and hit the rocks. The sound caused the creatures to turn their heads and stare at Claire, suddenly aware of her presence.

The male waded out of the water, moving toward Claire. "I have never seen anything move like that in my life," she stated. "It looked almost as if it was gliding across the beach." One of the two female creatures followed after the large male. The two bigfoot seemed to have an argument. "They were screaming at each other in gibberish," Claire recalled. The male turned back toward Claire, let out a bellowing howl, and pounded its fists into the sand. "The last thing I remember—I was feeling incredibly sick—was this thing, mouth wide open, big pink mouth. It was obviously male. It had an erection and it was urinating... and that is all I remember." Claire presumes she passed out at this point.[27]

She regained consciousness about 20 yards from her car with her jacket pulled around her head, black and blue with bruises on her left side and bad scratches on her face. The creatures had presumably dragged her back to her vehicle. Her camera and camera bag were missing. Claire returned to her hotel in a daze and, assuming she had been the victim of an assault, hotel employees sat her in a private room and called the police.

A police officer arrived and, after taking down the details of her encounter, asked Claire if she had been drinking. His attitude seemed rude and obnoxious. A second man entered the room: "If he was a police officer, well I've never seen a police officer like him. He had jeans on; what we refer to as a lumberjack shirt—so it was plaid—a white t-shirt underneath that. He was in his early-mid 40s; very, very wiry pepper hair; big beard; didn't say anything—just stood in the back of the room and listened to what I had to say."[28]

Claire related her story a second time while both men listened. When she finished, the man with the beard told her that what she had seen was a group of "bears" and that she was "lucky to be alive." Claire was emphatic what she had seen was *not* a group of bears, but the mysterious stranger insisted she was not to speak of the account except to tell people that she had run into bears—and she was not to return to the area of her sighting. Claire continued feeling ill for the rest of the weekend, canceled her remaining business plans, and returned home the following Tuesday.[29]

These strange MIB analogues appeared again to a man named Travis in 1997. Travis was employed at Glacier National Park in Montana doing maintenance and cleanup work. On July 30, after being called to cleanup a campsite area in the park, Travis and another park employee were greeted by a horrible smell—"like dead skunk." The two men were making their way up the trail when one exclaimed, "Oh my God! There's a bigfoot!" They witnessed a huge creature, lying on its side, tearing apart a rotting tree. At the sound of the man's voice, the creature leapt to its feet and looked at Travis, who immediately felt nauseous. At that moment, a radio the men were carrying crackled with static, apparently upsetting the bigfoot. The creature began shaking all over and let out a ferocious roar, prompting the witnesses to run.[30]

Travis was cautioned by some Forest Service employees to not discuss his encounter. He was told no one would believe him, that people would just make fun of him. However, Travis persisted in sharing his encounter, telling other employees and asking questions about bigfoot. On August 2, a black Ford Explorer with government plates arrived at the park. A large, bearded man exited the vehicle and asked to talk with Travis who, at 6'4", said he had to look upward to talk to this man.

The large man started speaking loudly so that everyone around could hear, accusing Travis of not being able to differentiate between a bear and a mule deer, adding Travis was fabricating ridiculous sasquatch stories. When one of the workers called this man "Gary," he insisted they call him "Bear." Travis believed this man had come specifically to intimidate him and prevent him from further discussing his bigfoot encounter.[31]

A very large man who just happens to show up and intimidate bigfoot witnesses—telling them again and again to say that they have only seen a bear—then indicates he is to be called "Bear"! It seems layers upon layers of strangeness envelop every aspect of the bigfoot mystery.

Another encounter with the Man-in-Plaid occurred after a November 26, 2003 sighting in Tazewell County, Virginia. A hunter, who wishes to remain anonymous, encountered two bigfoot creatures after happening upon a large, bare, human-like footprint in the snow. Thinking it was a prank or an anomaly, he dismissed the track until he found a second print—the opposite foot—on a far creek bank. The hunter measured the stride between these prints, and found it was equal to three of his own steps.[32]

The footprints led to a trackway through the woods, which he followed for 150 yards to a small laurel thicket. As he drew closer, he heard a low grunt and assumed it was a bear. Something was moving in the thicket, but he could not identify what. As he circled the thicket for a better view, he heard another grunt.

Still thinking he was tracking a bear, the hunter shouldered his rifle and prepared to fire. At this point another sound erupted to his left, which he described "like a bear climbing a tree. It sounded like something was really grabbing the tree." He turned to his left and, in the tree, about 30 yards away, saw a five-and-a-half foot tall, hair-covered bigfoot. The hunter continued:

> It's maybe 15 feet into the tree—and it's in a V-part of the tree. His right arm is wrapped around part of the tree and his left arm is out. I can see his whole chest and legs, and he's only holding onto the tree with one arm. He's got one foot in the V of the tree and his left foot is kinda just pressed against the tree. I can see this individual as plain as day. He's black—black fur—long hair on him. I was so scared that I came close to vomiting. It scared me that bad.[33]

After noticing small protruding breasts on the creature in the tree, the hunter determined it was a female. He started backing away from the scene, when, from the laurel thicket, another bigfoot stood up. This creature was much larger, its head protruding above the eight-foot tall thicket.

"He looked like a man," the hunter said. "His head was bigger than a basketball. He had three or four wrinkles at the bridge of his nose... His nose looked like a man's nose... I saw no white in the eyes. His eyes were completely brown. I saw no pupil... His mouth was extremely wide. It almost looked like he was smiling because his mouth was so wide."[34]

The hunter was still backing away when the creature in the tree grunted. Alarmed, he turned, aimed his rifle at the chest of the female creature, fired, and began running back in the direction he had come. He looked behind him and saw the bigger creature lifting the female off the ground.

"It picks it up like it's a rag doll—grabs it by its arm—and this thing probably had to weigh 500 pounds," he said. "The big one, I would guess, weighed 800 pounds, 900 pounds maybe. It was just a beast of an animal. Shaquille O'Neal looks like a kid to this thing." The creature turned toward a sheer cliff, scaling the rock face with ease and carrying the dead or wounded female in one arm.[35]

The hunter sped from the woods and returned home. Troubled by the events of the day, he described the incident to his wife, who convinced him to call a game warden. The witness was an experienced bear hunter who insisted to the game warden that whatever he shot was *not* a bear.

"The bigfoot part is strange," the hunter said, "but this part is even stranger." A game warden arrived the following day at his home to discuss the sighting. Incredulous about the hunter's claims that he had shot a bigfoot creature, the game warden asked to see where the incident occurred. After relocating the tracks, and retracing them out of the snow and into mud where they were very clear, the game warden declared, "This ain't right."[36]

The two proceeded to the shooting location and discovered heavy puddles of blood in the snow where the hunter shot the creature, samples of which were collected by the game warden in a plastic bag. They also found a bloody handprint on the cliff face as well. After returning to the hunter's residence, the game warden departed, but warned the hunter someone from "another government agency" might contact him.

About a week later, two individuals showed up at the hunter's place of employment and asked to speak with him. They arrived in a grey minivan with a government license plate and were described as follows:

> One of the gentlemen was clean-cut—had a suit and tie on. Nice and polite. The other individual was a very large man—probably 6'8" or better. He did not look like someone who would work for the government—had long hair, kind of a scruffy beard—wasn't clean-shaven at all. [He] didn't look like a government employee would look.[37]

The hunter inquired why these men wished to speak with him, and they replied it pertained to the incident he had reported to the game warden. The men asked to speak in private and the hunter offered that, as the workday was almost finished, they could follow him home.

Arriving at the hunter's residence, the men asked him to recount his experience on November 26. When he was finished, the larger of the two asked, "Do you think what you saw was really a sasquatch?" This was despite the hunter specifically noting he had not once called the creatures "sasquatch" in his testimony—only "bigfoot."

"I am 100% sure that I saw a sasquatch," the hunter replied, adopting the term.

The large man then stated bluntly, "No, you didn't."

"I know what I saw," the hunter retorted. "I'm pretty confident that is what I saw."

"No, you're not understanding me," the large man replied. "You did not see what you think you saw and it would be in your best interest not to tell anyone else about what you think you saw. It would be in your best interest to forget the incident ever happened."

Following this exchange, the two men departed. For ten years the hunter remained silent about his bigfoot encounter, only sharing details with his wife and his father before eventually speaking out under strict promises of anonymity. "The strangest thing about me shooting a bigfoot was what the government done [sic] to try to suppress what I saw," he reiterated.[38]

In 2015 a police officer named Jack encountered "Bear." Jack was investigating several bigfoot encounters reported in his jurisdiction. The reports ranged from creatures harassing farmers to a "gorilla" which chased a 15-year old boy riding his bike at night. During his investigation, Jack was confronted by two "feds" from an unnamed government organization. One of these men was clean-cut and nicely dressed. The other, Jack noted, was larger and more unkempt—with a beard, messy hair, and a "ratty button-down shirt". The two men told Jack to stop talking to witnesses and filing reports on bigfoot encounters. In a meeting with the district's chief of police, the large, bearded man became aggressive and tried to intimidate Jack. After verbally confronting the big man, Jack was suspended for two weeks.[39]

When he returned to duty, one of Jack's first calls was an investigation of a disturbance outside a local residence. As Jack searched outside the house, he came face-to-face with a bigfoot creature.

> I got called out on a prowler call…turned around the corner and there it was. It was looking at me. It was about ten feet away. I got [sic] a tac light on my sidearm—and my tac light hid it right midriff—and I started going up—and as soon as that light hit its face—that's when it threw an eighteen-inch-by-four-inch log at me—and just barely missed my head. He wasn't happy to see me.[40]

Startled, Jack aimed his firearm at the creature. As he did so, he heard a noise behind him, causing him to briefly take his eyes off the bigfoot and glance in the direction of the sound. When he looked back to the creature it was loping away into the night.

From out of nowhere, the large, bearded "fed" walked up behind Jack.

"Couldn't shoot, could you?" he asked.

"No," Jack replied.

The big man put his hand on Jack's shoulder and said, "Good man."[41]

Wes Germer, host of the popular *Sasquatch Chronicles* podcast, has arguably heard more bigfoot encounters than anyone else on the planet over the course of the program's nearly-700 episodes. Germer stated in 2015 that he had been getting calls from police officers who didn't necessarily want to come on the podcast, but wanted to relate their stories to Germer privately. Policemen from all over the country were describing the same two men: one large, bearded, ill-tempered fellow, and another of slighter build, neatly dressed and well-mannered. This odd couple seemed to show up whenever officers collected evidence of bigfoot creatures. They confiscated any evidence and warned the officers not to pursue the topic of bigfoot.

"It's always the same two guys," said Wes's then-cohost, Will Jevning.[42]

While the large, bearded man and his well-dressed partner may in some way function as the bigfoot community's own MIBs, a man who collected bigfoot evidence in Ochopee, Florida encountered more traditional MIBs. Multiple encounters with tall, hairy hominids were reported in the area in 1997. One of the witnesses, Dave Shealy, collected hair samples and made plaster casts of the creatures' footprints. At about 9:30 p.m. on July 28, 1997, Shealy heard a knock on his door. When he opened his door he was confronted by two tall men wearing sunglasses and "English style felt hats." They flashed identification, but Shealy was unable to see any agency on the badges. The two men began asking questions about the bigfoot sightings in the area and requested to see Shealy's casts and hair samples. When Shealy produced the hair samples, the two men said they would take them to have them analyzed, then left the premises. The next day at about 3:00 a.m., Shealy was awakened by the sound of helicopters. He saw eight, large helicopters circling the area over the nearby Turner River Swamp.[43]

"We Don't Want to Be Hurt"

Perhaps related, and often conflated with MIBs, is the Black Eyed Kid (BEK) phenomenon: stories of creepy children, often in groups of two or three, who show up outside people's homes or vehicles and, with persistent knocking and even more persistent begging, ask to be let inside vehicles or residences. The odd behavior of the BEKs often echoes that of the MIBs—they seem socially awkward, somehow out of time and place, and often fail to recognize everyday items like doorbells. However, the most disturbing feature of the BEKs is their eyes. Reported to be solid black in color, their ebony oculi inspire fear and panic in witnesses.[44]

A series of events from early 1974 includes repeated bigfoot activity along with an encounter with something very much like the BEK phenomenon. Andrew Stone, along with his wife, Hilda, and their 20-month-old son, Michael, had recently moved into their new home in Littlerock, California. They soon noticed that Michael disliked being placed in his crib under the bedroom window. "He went into hysterics," said Hilda, "screaming and crying, and Andy and I would rock him and he'd quiet down until we tried to put him back under that window. He had never acted this way at bedtime before. It was like he sensed something outside the window and we finally had to put his crib in another part of the room."

The family dog was the next to act up, acting wildly and scratching at the door to be let out. After the canine refused to let up, the Stones relented and let the dog out of their home. They found the poor animal's dismembered body a short time later. "He was torn apart, torn to shreds, his head way over there, his tail yards away. Coyotes don't do that! They eat the remains!" Hilda recalled in horror.

Next, several fish Andrew had tied on a stringer, twelve feet in the air, disappeared. Around the pole where the fish were tied, leading into a nearby thicket, were huge, three-toed footprints. On several evenings, the Stones noticed an eerie quiet about their home—even the nighttime insects would not chirp—then the silence would be broken by what Hilda described as "a crying, horrible noise like a woman screaming."

One night these cries grew louder as if something was approaching. The dogs in the neighborhood were highly agitated—frantically barking—and sounded as if they were trying to break their leashes. The Stones then heard something hit the wall of their house with a powerful blow.

In March 1974 the Stones were returning home in their car when they saw a large figure, covered with black hair, standing in a shallow stream. "He looked like he was scooping something out of the water, maybe fishing," Hilda said. "It looked about twelve feet tall," Andrew added.

The creatures continued to intrude on the Stones' property with regularity. Often Andrew would hear a clanging sound as the bigfoot slammed something against the water tank in his backyard. Shining a flashlight in the direction of the sound, Andrew regularly caught sight of red eyes staring back from the darkness. The next day, he could see tracks around the tank. The footprints were three-toed and measured as long as 19 inches. Almost nightly, the Stones' cabin was pelted with rocks, preceding the horrid wailing of the creatures—a sound which would, in turn, awaken Michael who, himself, then cried in fear.

One night, as Andrew was watching television, he had the sensation of being watched. He turned toward his open window to see a bigfoot peering in at him. "I could see the color of its face," said Andrew. "His skin was a sandy brown. Now, I'm six feet tall and my window stands higher than me. He was bending over to peek in, so I estimate he was about nine feet tall, built like a barn." The bigfoot's huge hand was on the window screen—strangely, it only had four long fingers, each topped with a black claw. It did not appear to have a thumb.

The Stones made plans to move, fearing for the safety of Michael and Hilda, but in late June other strange visitors appeared on their property. Having fallen asleep watching television, Andrew was awakened by Hilda at about 3:30 a.m. She held her finger to her lips, indicating Andrew should remain quiet. The knob on the front door was turning. Someone seemed to be trying to open it from the outside.

Andrew grabbed his shotgun while Hilda slowly unlocked the door. Andrew concealed the gun behind the door and cautiously pulled it open. Two dark-haired young men stood in their front yard. They were clean-cut, and the Stones estimated them to be in their late teens. In unison, the teens said, "We don't want to be hurt!"

Andrew recalled the disconcerting moment: "Most people, when they walk up to your house at night, would say something like 'Gee I hate to bother you,' or something like that. And you'd think they would knock instead of jiggling the door." The teens could not have seen Stone's shotgun, as it was hidden out of sight. Andrew felt it was odd that the first thing they said was that they did not want to be hurt.

The Stones' new dog, a replacement for their previous canine so horribly dismembered, usually barked loudly at the approach of any people. On this occasion the animal cowered in silent fear—a reaction she also manifested when the bigfoot creatures were nearby.

The strange teenagers related a story of their car running out of gasoline seven miles away. They asked the Stones to borrow a dime so they could use a payphone and call for help. Andrew noticed, though the boys claimed to have walked seven miles on rural roads, their clothes looked new and clean. "Have you ever seen spanking new clothes out of the store? Like that! And their shoes were a shiny black patent leather with round toes—but without a speck of dust on them!" Andrew continued, "I'm wondering how they could have walked seven miles down a filthy, dusty road without getting their shoes dirty?"

Nevertheless, Andrew fetched the teenagers a dime. He placed the coin into the palm of one of the boys, "and I didn't feel his hand!" Andrew said. "I was very deliberate to get it right into his hand as I didn't want it to drop in the dirt and get lost because it was the only dime I had. There was nothing there! Like I hadn't even done it!"

After closing the door, Andrew realized the phone booth, which was some 200 yards down the hill from his cabin, did not have a light. He grabbed a flashlight and went outside, intent on offering it to the teenagers. They had disappeared. Stone walked down the road, trying to find the boys. "They were nowhere around," said Stone. "Nowhere. There were no cars, no noise, the crickets weren't going, the frogs weren't croaking, and I got the eeriest feeling I ever felt!" Hilda added, "It sounds like we were dreaming, but we were wide awake! And Andy doesn't drink! And they never brought back our dime!"

While he recalled in detail what the teenagers were wearing and the other events of the night, Andrew Stone was troubled by two things. First, the faces of the boys were a blur in his memory—and perhaps most disturbing of all, Stone could not recall seeing the *eyes* of his visitors.[45]

Threats from the Unknown

One of the best documents of an ongoing paranormal investigation, and the odd synchronicities and bizarre happenings they attract, is John Keel's *The Mothman Prophecies*. This book captures the disorienting, confusing, sometimes claustrophobic High Strangeness which appears to be a symptom, or at least a side effect, of dealing with The Other. In *The Mothman Prophecies*, Keel details multiple incidents of strange phone calls from unknown sources, weird letters from nowhere, MIBs, and other mysterious contacts from someone or something which seems to have knowledge of the investigation.[46]

Bob Garrett, a Texas bigfoot researcher, seemed cursed with the modern equivalent of Keel's landline phone calls and postage from unknown sources. After posting a video on his YouTube channel of a campsite which Garrett referred to as "the torn-up camp"—a location he believed might be the site of a bigfoot attack on campers—he began receiving threatening text messages from random numbers: "Remember the torn up camp? Should have been you," read one such threat. Garrett also believed someone was accessing his computer remotely as files were opening on their own and his cursor would move without anyone touching the mouse.[47]

Bodies of Evidence

Over the years, many people have claimed possession of a bigfoot body, or at least knowledge of where a bigfoot corpse is located. Many of these claims have proven to be hoaxes (see Chapter 9). However, every case seems to share one thing in common: these bodies, in one way or another, *always* disappear.

Researchers claim various methods of the bodies' removal—from mysterious unmarked black vans and helicopters to living bigfoot creatures reclaiming the corpses of their brethren. As with the giant bones mentioned above, the method of the bigfoot corpse removal is inconsequential, as the end result remains the same: the body is missing.

An early tale of hunters killing what sounds like a bigfoot creature appeared in *The Los Angeles Times* on April 8, 1888. The story details two hunters who tracked an "immense" hair-covered, upright-walking creature through a canyon in San Diego County known as Dead-Man's Hole. As the creature climbed a rock face, one of the hunters fired his rifle. "With a cry like that of a human being, the beast instantly fell in a hideous heap across a boulder."[48]

While some assert the Dead-Man's Hole account was an April Fools' Day hoax, the article provides anatomical details of the creature from the hunters, features strongly matching reports of bigfoot from modern witnesses. A separate article claimed the creature was loaded on a wagon and hauled to San Diego for public exhibition. There is no record of this exhibition. When curious onlookers arrived at the police station to view the remains, they were told to come back for next year's April Fools' Day.[49]

Doug Tarrant, former member of rock band Bill Haley and the Comets and one-time deputy sheriff, related a tale of a captured "Yeti." According to Tarrant, Fred Bear (of "Bear Archery" fame) told him the Clyde Beatty Circus had captured a live Yeti in 1925 and planned to bring the creature on their stateside tour. Upon learning of the captive Yeti, the Smithsonian Institution dispatched three professors to examine the specimen. The scientists found the Yeti was "too close to a human" and advised the circus to release the creature, rather than bring it on tour with the circus.[50]

The Smithsonian strikes again! This story is problematic for many reasons, not the least of which is that the Clyde Beatty Circus did not exist in 1925.[51] At that time Clyde Beatty was employed by the Hagenbeck-

Wallace Circus.[52] Even so, suggestion that a circus at that time would have had *any* problem showcasing a creature that was *close* to a human is laughable; this was the age of sideshows and human "freaks," after all. A Yeti specimen would have been worth an incredible amount of money, even in 1925. It is extremely doubtful a few "professors" from The Smithsonian could convince a circus to give up profit in favor of "doing the right thing." Circuses didn't exactly have the best track record in that department. Whatever the facts are regarding this captured Yeti, if there is any truth at all to the story, the end result was the same as every other case of someone who has claimed possession of a large, hairy hominid's body: it disappeared.

Perhaps the most famous body of a bigfoot—or something like it—is that of the Minnesota Iceman, detailed at length in Chapter 9. As with all things bigfoot, experts on both sides have weighed in on the original specimen's possible authenticity. Even those fiercely clinging to the idea that there was a real specimen initially—an actual corpse of some kind of bigfoot-like hominid—admit that, at some point, the original Minnesota Iceman body was replaced by a model. The original has disappeared to some anonymous "cold storage warehouse," or perhaps lies in the possession of some wealthy "collector."[53]

In 1996, a man named "Bugs" declared on the *Coast to Coast AM* radio program that he had shot and killed two bigfoot in the 1970s. He claimed to have Polaroid photographs of the creatures and, later, provided then-host Art Bell with a map to the creatures' bodies. Bell was instructed not to use the map—or release it to the public—until after Bugs's death. He was, he said, afraid of being prosecuted for murder if it was determined that said creatures were hominids.

It was later revealed that "Bugs" was none other than Ed Hale, owner of Plains Radio and friend of Art Bell. Hale admitted he was the man who had called *Coast to Coast*, but insisted that the bigfoot shooting story was true. He also claimed that federal agents had discovered his identity, showed up at his door, and forced him to take them to the burial site. The bodies were exhumed and confiscated by the federal agents. Hale's polaroid photographs of the creatures have, to date, never surfaced.[54]

Justin Smeja, an experienced California bear hunter, claimed he shot two bigfoot in October of 2010. While out hunting with a friend, Smeja encountered a large female bigfoot, along with two smaller creatures, assumed to be juveniles, in the Sierra Mountains. Smeja described the female creature as a "monster," seven-to-eight-feet tall and weighing about 600 pounds. Smeja shot the female in the torso, causing the creature to fall. His friend then called his attention to the two smaller creatures—each three-and-a-half-feet tall and 35-40 pounds.

Smeja claimed he and his friend observed the smaller creatures for 10-15 minutes before shooting one of them in the neck. He then walked over to it and picked up the body. "It was bleeding all over me," Smeja said. Despite being faced with the find-of-the-century, neither man took photographs nor thought to bring the body of the smaller creature with them.

After reporting the incident on a hunting website, Smeja was contacted by Derek Randles, a bigfoot researcher with the Olympic Project who convinced Smeja to return to the scene of the shooting and collect whatever evidence he could find. Though the bigfoot bodies were gone (of course), Smeja managed to recover a piece of flesh from the site and returned home, placing it in his freezer.[55]

Part of the flesh was sent to Melba Ketchum and became part of her problematic DNA study, detailed above.[56] Smeja's boots, upon which the smaller creature bled, were sent to Dr. Bryan Sykes, as part of the Oxford University DNA study. The blood was determined to have come from a bear.[57]

Another Bigfoot was reportedly shot and killed on April 25, 2013 by a man named Brian who claimed to have repeated bigfoot encounters around his property in southern Ohio. After seeing a bigfoot in the area when he was a teenager, Brian heard long, loud howls around his property, mysteriously lost full bags of dog food overnight, and eventually sighted multiple creatures.[58]

On the day in question, Brian was dressed in heavy camouflage and sounding a turkey call when a bigfoot stepped out of the woods. He described the encounter:

> It was probably about 40 yards—and I tried to scare it off because I didn't want to shoot it... When it seen [sic] me move, it took an aggressive stance and it just kept coming closer... When he got about 15 yards away and looked at me and made this gargling growl sound I just hit the trigger. I made up my mind, "Well, it's either gonna be him or me and goddamn sure it ain't gonna be me"—because I had five rounds in that 12 gauge and I would have put all five in him —but one done [sic] it. He went straight back and did not move. I literally blew half his head off... It was gargling, shaking trees, growling, making all kinds of weird sounds. And it got too close so I blowed [sic] its head off...He was probably about nine-feet tall—probably about five-feet wide —had arms the size of tree trunks. The thing was a monster...

I mean, it kinda looked like King Kong staring me down it was so damn big... He wasn't a bit afraid of me—so, I shot it.[59]

Brian began inspecting the corpse, but believed he heard other creatures making noise nearby, so he left the area. Once safe, Brian called a few of his friends who agreed to accompany him back to the site of the shooting. Brian continued, "We went back up there with AK-47s and something had drug the body at least 300 foot [sic]. We followed the drag marks up a real [sic] steep hill and then we finally found it and I said, 'Right there's what I shot'—and they couldn't believe it." The men began hearing what they believed were more creatures, so they once again fled the scene.[60]

Brian said he called the Bigfoot Field Researchers Organization (BFRO), who sent an investigator the following day. However, when he arrived the investigator refused to accompany Brian to the site of the shooting for some reason. "The very next day, three blacked-out SUVs pull up—and a game warden truck pulled up," Brian said. "I told them what had happened."

The vehicles' mysterious occupants informed Brian he had broken federal law by killing an endangered species. Brian, upset, led the men to the scene of the shooting, where they took photos and collected hair and blood evidence. The bigfoot corpse had disappeared. The men left Brian with a warning not to shoot another bigfoot.[61]

Witness accounts of bigfoot display a consistent pattern of appearance and behavior manifesting in stories across centuries. Some of the newspaper "wild man" accounts from the 1800s read very much like modern bigfoot accounts, for instance. Many witnesses report some very strange things, besides ape-men. Strange things are what much of this book concerns, after all... is it so much more outrageous, then, when a witness claims to kill or capture a bigfoot?

While some of these reports are likely hoaxes, one has to wonder if it is not simply in the nature of this phenomenon for evidence to just disappear. For reasons unknown, it seems we are simply not *allowed* to have a bigfoot body. There are no exceptions. In every single case, one way or another, the bodies go missing.

Copies of Copies

As far as bigfoot evidence goes, few video recordings have bolstered the F&BH more than the famous Patterson-Gimlin film. Shot at Bluff Creek, California in October 1967, the film shows either a large, upright-walking, hair-covered creature… or a man in a suit.

Yards of verbiage have been written on the footage. Hours of frame-by-frame analysis have been conducted. Hollywood special effects artists and costume designers, zoologists, primate locomotion specialists, and all manner of experts from various fields of study have critiqued the film. Is it a hoax? Or does it actually show a real creature? Like all things bigfoot, layman and expert alike weigh in passionately on both sides of the debate.

Whatever the Patterson-Gimlin film shows, it is unlikely costume designers in 1967 would have been capable of making such a convincing fake. The locomotion of the creature is very unusual, and its proportions do not seem to match those of a human. To reinforce this argument, the contemporary "Gold Standard" for ape-man effects was used in the motion picture *Planet of the Apes*, released the following year. Even modern attempts to reproduce the film have fallen short.

Hoax or not, the Patterson-Gimlin footage is extremely important. If it is legitimate, it could be the single most important piece of bigfoot evidence ever collected. The original film would be invaluable. Yet, like so many other pieces of bigfoot evidence, it has disappeared. What remains are copies of the original film—and copies of those copies.

The provenance of the film, as well as the legal rights to the footage, is a long and winding saga involving various "big names" in the bigfoot phenomenon, multiple film and television production companies, lawyers, and individuals who all claimed some financial interest in the film. It is as messy as it sounds. Somewhere, amidst the legal tug-of-war, the original film canister vanished. A number of locales purportedly harbor the priceless footage: one film warehouse or another, a lawyer's office, or the private colection of one of the many "interested parties". Whatever the case, the original film cannot be found.[62]

In 2004, a man named Bob Heironimous claimed that the Patterson-Gimlin film shows a man in a gorilla suit and, indeed, he was that monkey-suited man. If true, neither Heironimous nor anyone else has been able to produce the costume used in the famous footage. It's an interesting twist to our *disappearing evidence* theme.[63]

The one thing that could prove—once and for all—whether the Patterson-Gimlin footage was real or fake, is also missing… if it ever existed at all.[64]

[1] Ketchum, M. S., Wojtkiewicz, P. W., Watts, A. B., Spence, D. W., Holzenburg, A. K., Toler, D. G., Prychitko, T. M., Zhang, F., Shoulders, R., & Smith, R. (Feburary 13, 2013). DeNovo – Special Edition. Retrieved February 24, 2019 from http://www.denovojournal.com/denovo_002.htm

[2] Berger, E. (February 14, 2013). What do geneticists think of the Bigfoot paper? Retrieved February 24, 2019 from https://blog.chron.com/sciguy/2013/02/what-do-geneticists-think-of-the-bigfoot-paper/

[3] Ibid.

[4] Ibid.

[5] Sykes, B.C., Mullis, R.A., Hagenmuller, C., Melton, T.W., & Sartori, M. (August 22, 2014). Genetic analysis of hair samples attributed to yeti, bigfoot and other anomalous primates. *Proceedings of the Royal Society B*. 281: 20140161.

[6] Dosen, C. (April 26, 2018). Hominidae Enigma Unknown / Sasquatch Hair Analysis report - Client: Toby Allen Johnson.

[7] Wagner, S. (May 24, 2019). The Best Sasquatch Evidence. Retrieved February 24, 2019 from https://www.liveabout.com/sasquatch-best-evidence-2593656

[8] Ibid.

[9] Johnson, T. (February 24, 2019). Personal correspondence.

[10] Gordon, S. (2010). *Silent Invasion: The Pennsylvania UFO-Bigfoot Casebook*. R. Marsh (Ed.). Greensburg, PA: Stan Gordon Productions.

[11] Campbell, A. (July 3, 2013). Bigfoot DNA Tests: Melba Ketchum's Research Results Are Bogus, Claims Houston Chronicle Report. Retrieved February 24, 2019 from https://www.huffpost.com/entry/bigfoot-dna-test-results_n_3541431

[12] The Tri-Weekly Herald. (April 11, 1876). The Remains of a Giant. *The Tri-Weekly Herald (Marshall, TX)*, p. 1.

[13] Slate, B.A. & Berry, A (1976). *Bigfoot*. New York, NY: Bantam.

[14] Ibid.

[15] Ibid.

[16] Ibid.

[17] Ibid.

[18] Ibid.

[19] Bigfoot Tonight Show. (November 6, 2011). William Jevning. Retrieved February 24, 2019.

[20] Ibid.

[21] Gordon 2010.

[22] Ibid.

[23] Ibid.

[24] Ibid.

[25] Ibid.

[26] Germer, W. (February 15, 2019). Sasquatch Chronicles Radio // SC 515: I Shouldn't Be Alive. Retrieved May 19, 2020 from https://sasquatchchronicles.com/sc-ep515-i-shouldnt-be-alive/

[27] Ibid.

[28] Ibid.

[29] Ibid.

[30] Germer, W. (January 11, 2015). Sasquatch Chronicles Radio // SC 72: Down the rabbit hole Part 3 [Members]. Retrieved May 19, 2020 from https://sasquatchchronicles.com/sc-ep72-down-the-rabbit-hole-part-3-members/

[31] Ibid.

[32] CryptoWatch. (October 9, 2013). Bigfoot Encounter - Bigfoot Shot - Exclusive! Never Told Until Now! Retrieved May 19, 2020 from https://www.youtube.com/watch?v=uYPMU5wEcvw&feature=youtu.be

[33] Ibid.

[34] Ibid.

[35] Ibid.

[36] Ibid.

[37] Ibid.

[38] Ibid.

[39] Germer, W. (January 8, 2015). Sasquatch Chronicles Radio // SC 70: Down the rabbit hole. Retrieved May 19, 2020 from https://sasquatchchronicles.com/sc-ep70-down-the-rabbit-hole/

[40] Ibid.

[41] Ibid.

[42] Germer, W. (January 11, 2015). Sasquatch Chronicles Radio // SC 71: Down the rabbit hole part 2. Retrieved May 19, 2020 from https://sasquatchchronicles.com/sc-ep71-down-the-rabbit-hole-part-2/

[43] Grootveldt, R. (n.d.) Case 224. In A. Rosales (Ed.), *1997 Humanoid Sighting Reports*. Retrieved February 5, 2014 from http://www.ufoinfo.com/humanoid/humanoid-1997.pdf

[44] Weatherly, D. (2017). *The Black Eyed Children* (Revised 2nd ed.). AZ: Leprechaun Press.

[45] Slate & Berry 1976.

[46] Keel, J. (1975). *The Mothman Prophecies*. London, UK: Panther Books.

[47] Germer January 8, 2015.

[48] Renner, T. (2018). *Bigfoot: West Coast Wild Men*. Charleston, SC: CreateSpace Independent Publishing Platform.

[49] Crawford, R. (October 31, 1991). Old Skeletons. *The Los Angeles Times (CA)*, p. 2.

[50] Jevning, W. (2016). *The Minnesota Iceman.* William Jevning. Charleston, SC: CreateSpace Independent Publishing Platform.

[51] No author. (2013). Clyde Beatty Circus. Retrieved May 15, 2020 from http://www.circusesandsideshows.com/circuses/clydebeattycircus.html

[52] No author. (2013). Clyde Beatty. Retrieved May 15, 2020 from http://www.circusesandsideshows.com/owners/clydebeatty.html

[53] Jevning 2016.

[54] Coleman, L. (January 7, 2009). Bugs Bigfoot Legend Begun By Radio Freakazoid. Retreived March 4, 2019 from http://www.cryptozoonews.com/bugs-freakazoid/

[55] Woolheater, C. (January 4, 2012). Update: Sierra Kills Shooter Talks. Retrieved March 4, 2019 from https://cryptomundo.com/bigfoot-report/sierra-kills-shooter/

[56] Ketchum et al. 2013.

[57] Sykes et al. 2014.

[58] Merkel, T. (August 19, 2017). Episode 31: I Killed Bigfoot. Retrieved March 4, 2019 from https://www.theconfessionalspodcast.com/theconfessionals/episode-31

[59] Ibid.

[60] Ibid.

[61] Ibid.

[62] Long, G. (2004). *The Making of Bigfoot: The Inside Story*. Amherst, NY: Prometheus Books.

[63] Lei, R. (March 7, 2004). The Reliable Source. Retrieved March 4, 2019 from https://www.washingtonpost.com/archive/lifestyle/2004/03/07/the-reliable-source/87511230-07b8-4c97-9424-602dbd413da3/

[64] Long 2004.

I can believe things that are true and things that aren't true and I can believe things where nobody knows if they're true or not."

- *Neil Gaiman,* American Gods

The Trickster

Loki. Brer Rabbit. Coyote. Anansi. Puck. Reynard the Fox. Till Eulenspiegel. All are variations on a powerful, universal archetype winding its way through a diverse array of cultures: The Trickster. Trickster figures are found in every indigenous mythology on the planet, each presenting a consistent set of attributes best described as anti-structural, taboo-violating, and playful.

The Trickster archetype also commonly manifests in paranormal research. This concept was no better studied than in George P. Hansen's masterwork *The Trickster and the Paranormal.* This landmark text so excellently, comprehensively illustrates how both witnesses and investigators alike fall prey to the trickster archetype that it would be not only impossible, but ill-advised to summarize its contents here. Still, a basic overview of Hansen's talking points is necessary before demonstrating how the trickster appears in bigfoot research, an aspect of paranormalia Hansen's masterwork fails to address in any significant way.

Anomalists new to Hansen's work erroneously seize upon "The Trickster" as a discrete entity, akin to a god or minor deity. This is not only a misreading of Hansen's work, but also displays a lack of understanding of fundamental Jungian and Platonic concepts. William Anderson wrote in *Green Man: The Archetype of our Oneness with the Earth:*

> An archetype can be thought of according to the older use of the term as one of the eternal ideas of Platonic and Neo-Platonic philosophy and therefore as an ever-living, vital and conscious force, or in the sense in which Jung made use of it as an image from the Collective Unconscious of humanity. According to both these theories an archetype... will recur at different places and times independently of traceable lines of transmission because it is part of the permanent possession of mankind. In Jung's theory of compensation, an archetype will reappear in a new form to redress imbalances in society at a particular time when it is needed.[1]

There are a plethora of archetypes, from the Crone to the Mother to the Warrior, each manifesting their salient features not only in folklore but also in social structures, individual psyches, and institutions (as alluded to dozens of times, the wild man is a cross-cultural archetype in its own right). The Mother archetype, for example, with its emphasis on care, nurturing, and security, appears not only in the lives of new parents but also manifests in the healthcare and hospitality industries as patterns of behavior. Moms, Dads, nurses, doctors, hoteliers, etc. all unconsciously express The Mother. Archetypes are ancient, powerful motifs shared by every human being at a fundamental level.

The Trickster is no exception. The hallmarks of a trickster character are well-defined, if difficult to articulate. Their primary role is to challenge order and structure, violating natural laws, cultural taboos, and convention. In their mission to usurp order, tricksters become explicit and transgressive, embracing gender fluidity, sexuality, and excrement. Despite this "inappropriate" behavior, tricksters are nonetheless possessors of profound secret knowledge, and maintain a fundamentally playful or mischievous attitude, even when their antics end in calamity. Many tricksters are self-negating in their behavior, undermining their own interests. Because of this, they are universally disreputable, yet—being an embodiment of contradictions—still highly valued for the roles they play, often delivering supernatural knowledge to mankind. In their quest to challenge authority, tricksters also generate *communitas* (i.e. societal leveling, where individuals are rendered equal despite socio-economic disparities).[2]

Because tricksters display a propensity to push, cross, and break boundaries, they are universally regarded as *liminal* figures, gods of thresholds and transitions. Writes Hansen:

> [Cambridge anthropologist Edmund Leach's] 1962 essay

"Genesis as Myth" notes that God-man is a major opposition, and he explains that "'Mediation' (in this sense) is always achieved by introducing a third category which is 'abnormal' or 'anomalous' in terms of ordinary 'rational' categories. Thus myths are full of fabulous monsters, incarnate gods, virgin mothers. This middle ground is abnormal, non-natural, holy. It is typically the focus of all taboo and ritual observance." This middle ground is the liminal, the interstitial, the betwixt and between, the anti-structural; it provides contact with the supernatural realm.[3]

Many tricksters, including the Norse god Loki, display gender fluidity. They thrive in the liminal middle ground: it is for this reason trolls live under bridges (a classic zone of liminality and transition), the devil appears at crossroads, monsters relish twilight, and faeries abduct unbaptized children (infants born into the world but not yet "born" into the church). With few exceptions, all paranormal entities exhibit some form of liminality, of being neither one thing nor another… ghosts are dead yet still roam the land, UFOs act as a bridge between earth and sky, bigfoot are neither men nor apes, but somewhere in between.[4]

It is easy to see how The Trickster manifests in our lives: most families have a proverbial "black sheep" who is disreputable, yet speaks the truth when no one else will; governments regularly fall into self-parodies of their authority; paranormal reports and the larger communities attempting to study these phenomena are rife with similar difficulties. Large-scale research organizations are constantly plagued by infighting and scandals. In addition to their fundamentally liminal nature, whatever lies behind ghosts, UFOs, and bigfoot seems to possess secret knowledge, though it only ever reveals a few tantalizing tidbits. All paranormal phenomena violate "laws," laughing in the face of both physics and logic.

Like trickster archetypes, sexuality runs rampant through these topics: aliens and faeries kidnap and molest their abductees, bigfoot steal virginal brides to interbreed, etc. Supernatural entities themselves gravitate towards individuals leading anti-structural lives, such as artists or transients. Because of this—and the self-negating aspect of The Trickster archetype—the paranormal is relegated to ridicule and derision. Paranormal celebrities, when not outright charlatans (tricksters in their own right), can attest to how distinctly *un-glamorous* their vocation is: scrounging together a meager income to supplement their day jobs, headlining at dingy basement conference rooms in airport hotels. At these events, the high are brought low due to their interest in such absurd "fringe" topics—*communitas*.

"In short, the paranormal and supernatural are ambiguous and marginal in virtually all ways: socially, intellectually, academically, religiously, scientifically, and conceptually," Hansen wrote. "They don't fit in the rational world."[5]

Social leveling and self-negation—two hallmarks of tricksterish behavior—are no more apparent than in the robust world of hoaxes. Throughout *The Trickster and the Paranormal*, Hansen deftly illustrates how frauds are not outliers of some paranormal reality, but in actuality a fully-functioning facet of how the trickster archetype manifests itself.

Of hoaxes in Ufology—equally applicable to bigfoot study—Hansen writes:

> Hoaxes are liminal productions. They lower the statuses of the victims, and loss of status is one of the defining characteristics of liminal conditions. Marginality is another trickster quality, and hoaxes help marginalize not only the victims but the whole field of ufology.
>
> Hoaxes assist the rationalization and disenchantment of the world. They help consign the paranormal to the realm of fraud and gullibility, so that the phenomena receive little serious study. With the taint they induce, hoaxes protect the paranormal from close examination.
>
> Anti-structure is a trickster quality, and it manifests in ufology's inability to effectively institutionalize its research. The failure is not a shortcoming of the leaders in the field, but rather it is a direct consequence of the phenomena studied.[6]

This overview of how The Trickster archetype appears in the paranormal is a pale reflection of Hansen's intensive work, which remains essential to anyone dissatisfied with conventional beliefs that UFOs are extraterrestrial spacecraft, or bigfoot is a relict hominid. Despite the insight with which Hansen wrote, *The Trickster and the Paranormal* only mentions bigfoot in passing. However, applying a Hansenian approach to some of the greatest bigfoot hoaxes reveals that The Trickster is alive and well in cryptozoology.

The Trickster and Bigfoot

During the Corona, California bigfoot flap of 1964-1975—a series of sightings largely regarded as legitimate—police officers "found a monster costume on the ground near the area where they had received one of the reports of the 'Foothill Monster.'" Regarding this discovery, Alan Berry and Ann Slate cheekily added, "The name of the six-foot adolescent said to have worn the costume was not released. The authorities did not press charges."[7]

This is a fine example of how disreputability and doubt engulf any serious discussion of bigfoot. Despite the genuine fear reported by earnest eyewitnesses, pernicious inconsistencies undermine serious discussion of the phenomenon. Even in the absence of specific case studies—examined shortly—broader trends support the assertion that The Trickster archetype is embedded in bigfoot culture.

This is perhaps no more obvious than how bigfoot witnesses, researchers, and enthusiasts are commonly portrayed in media. While UFO buffs are consistently regarded as paranoid conspiracy theorists, those with an interest in bigfoot are universally and regularly deemed backward rural rubes, despite evidence to the contrary. Reinforced by unflattering reality television programming, the quintessential "'Squatcher" is an overweight, conservative, gun-toting, country-dwelling white male (an overgeneralized stereotype), the very embodiment of disreputability in the 21st century and worthy of mockery. Countless comedians joke that alien abductees are invariably "trailer park residents"—living conditions still bearing a shockingly negative stigma, even in today's progressive society—and bigfoot witnesses are no different in the eyes of the public.

In *Paranormal America: Ghost Encounters, UFO Sightings, Bigfoot Hunts, and Other Curiosities in Religion and Culture*, professors Christopher D. Bader, Joseph O. Baker, and F. Carson Mencken handily demonstrate through various surveys that, to a degree of statistical significance, bigfoot enthusiasts are "remarkably normal, everyday people. The average Bigfooter was married and above average in education and income (with a four-year degree from a college or university and earning $50,000 a year or more)." The only true deviation from conventionality was in religion: less than half of American bigfoot conference attendees identified as Protestant, and attended church less frequently than the national average.[8]

This being said, the bigfoot community *is* simultaneously white male-dominated *and* obsessed with scientific legitimacy, telling features when viewed through Hansen's work. While paranormal phenomena repeatedly emphasize the role of the feminine—a detail not lost upon Spiritualists, witches, or Neo-Pagans—those seeking to study, codify, and harness it are mostly male. They are, in Hansen's words of criticism aimed at skeptical organizations, "large, male-dominated, status conscious, hierarchical institutions." The research of Bader et al. found that "women are more likely to believe in *enlightenment*-related paranormal topics than men," (e.g. the New Age, psychics, mediums, etc.), while "men are more likely to believe in *discovery*-related paranormal topics than women, with higher levels of belief in Bigfoot and UFOs."[9] Exceptions, of course, prove rules; Thom Powell astutely observed, "Bigfoot is considered paranormal by the general public. Only in the Bigfoot community do we distinguish between Bigfoot and the paranormal."[10]

Though groups like the North American Wood Ape Conservancy (NAWAC) and Bigfoot Field Researchers Organization (BFRO) are firmly ensconced in the "true believer" camp, the rigidity with which they pursue Materialist validation of bigfoot is on par with skeptical organizations. They are obsessed with scientific credibility and, as such, are status conscious.[11]

(As a side note, the term "Materialism" can more or less be used interchangeably with "Physicalism." Regardless of its name, it remains a central tenet of modern science, wherein the only things extant are based upon matter. Within the Materialist paradigm, psychic phenomena, spirits, archetypes, etc., are mere fancy.)

In Hansen's model, even skeptical organizations are susceptible to The Trickster archetype, insofar as their efforts to disenchant the world, i.e. remove mysticism from the human experience. "The sheer volume and intensity of the debunkers' activities suggests something other than dispassionate inquiry; rather, one suspects the operation of some energetic, unconscious, archetypal process," he wrote. "The trickster figure Prometheus illuminates this, and he has much in common with the skeptics. Prometheus was not a god, but a titan, who stole fire from the gods for the benefit of humanity."

Hansen further argues Prometheus's suspicious, intolerant, anti-deity tendencies are manifest among skeptics. It can be easily argued that dogmatic adherents of the flesh-and-blood hypothesis, who believe bigfoot is solely reducible to an uncatalogued primate, embody this anti-deity (e.g. anti-magical, anti-supernatural) trickster urge.

The very fact that skeptics are susceptible to The Trickster emphasizes the archetype's contradictory, nonsensical, nature. Hansen draws the comparison to the Christian Reformation. Utilizing the Aristotelian format, we can express Hansen's views as *Disenchantment : Protestantism :: Enchantment : Catholicism.* If we were to amend this analogy to encompass sasquatch studies, *Disenchantment : Cryptozoologists :: Enchantment : Paranormalists.* Though cryptozoologists regularly rail against academe, their goal is to enroll rather than restructure; instead of wishing to dismantle Materialism, they yearn for its embrace.

Researchers' "focus on proving Bigfoot's existence appears largely motivated by vindication, and they dream of the day that the scientific community is forced by the weight of evidence to announce to the world that Bigfoot is real," wrote Bader et al. "They think of themselves as normal people who just so happen to have seen or believe in Bigfoot." This is evidenced in the rebranding of organizations like NAWAC, who dropped "bigfoot" from their name because, "In the minds of many, 'Bigfoot' remains a solitary, presumably magical creature along the lines of the Tooth Fairy or Jack Frost." NAWAC researchers told Bader et al. that "Bigfoot ain't no unicorn" and that the organization "is very careful to avoid getting caught up in 'that UFO nonsense.'" It is implied that the aversion to these possibilities is because "to believe in such things is a threat to [one's] self-image as a normal guy who just happens to hunt Bigfoot."[12]

Advocates of the F&BH wish to, as Hansen puts it, "put the phenomena in frameworks, and some structure and limitation are thereby imposed. Action can be taken. Gods can be propriated, dangerous humans avoided. Outsiders may see such beliefs as paranoid or as a crackpot religion, but it is not unreasonable to adopt such perspectives when confronted with strong manifestations of autonomous intelligent power."[13]

The number of bigfoot witnesses who sight the creatures while camping further supports Hansen's assertion that The Trickster archetype is drawn to anti-structure. Few things are as diametrically opposed to modernity and all its conveniences as camping. There is also a liminal component to camping: it is a home away from home, where certain (but not all) belongings are brought, neither shelter nor wilderness, but somewhere in between.

More obviously, The Trickster archetype can be directly applied to bigfoot itself, whatever its true nature may be. In addition to the sexuality embedded in bigfoot legends and the creature's liminal nature as "the Missing Link," sasquatch are commonly described as pranksters, playing what essentially amount to games of hide-and-seek with researchers, exchanging items, and remaining one step ahead of verifiable scientific fact. In indigenous lore, they are commonly regarded as thieves and gluttons, stealing food at night. Tricksters are typically fundamentally male, and most bigfoot witnesses—if genitalia is noticed at all, perhaps another nod to the archetype's gender fluidity—report males. Because tricksters commonly engage in deception, it comes as no surprise that impersonation and mimicry (both reflected in modern bigfoot reports) are central to their mythos. There is also the pernicious problem of disappearing evidence, as covered in Chapter 8, which smacks of deception.

Among the Muckleshoot of Washington, Stick Indians are thieving tricksters who, while exhibiting kleptomania, nonetheless return items to where they were taken.[14] Tricksters are commonly shape shifters, another ability occasionally attributed to bigfoot. Some even assert *Iktomi*, "the trickster or double face" of the Sioux, is actually a bigfoot creature.[15]

According to Jack "Kewaunee" Lapseritis, the Chippewa regard bigfoot as tricksters. "They pull all kinds of stuff with me," he told Stephen J. Spignesi in *The UFO Book of Lists*. "They will startle me, and then laugh, and that will get me laughing."[16]

Of Eurasian relict hominids, Dmitri Bayanov writes:

> [Hairy demons] also love dancing and merrymaking, especially all kinds of pranks, so that Russian peasants called them "jokesters" and "pranksters." A favorite prank of *rusalkas* was to catch wild geese on the river and entangle the feathers of their wings so that the birds could not fly. Or they would let the fish out of the fishermen's net and fill the latter with slime and water-plants, or divert themselves by putting out a fishermen's or hunters' campfire with the water dripping from their hair covering.[17]

Indeed the Green Man, whose ties to the wild man are explored in Chapter 3, Volume I of *Where the Footprints End*, has a certain association with The Trickster archetype. Depictions of the Green Man sometimes show "a foliate fool's cap," with "a cup and bauble. At a deeper level the Green Man shares with the Fool [i.e. Trickster] the qualities of unexpectedness, of unconventional wisdom, of the joker," wrote Anderson.[18]

The affinity for bigfoot to commune with and imitate birds—addressed at length in Chapter 3 of this volume—also finds precedent in trickster lore. "St. Francis was renowned for his communion with nature, particularly with birds," Hansen wrote. "Tricksters and liminality also share this feature... St. Francis' association with birds is very well known, but medieval fools were also frequently connected with birds, as were novices in liminal periods."[19]

Consider as well the matter of unnatural fear, commonly ascribed to infrasound, which marks bigfoot encounters. Witnesses commonly describe a terror both profound yet irrational, a hallmark of contact with the Otherworld. Hansen aptly defines this as "the wrath of God" and, citing the work of Rudolph Otto, calls it an "incalculable, arbitrary," and "grisly" fear of the divine, coupled with awe and fascination.[20] Such psychological possibilities render concepts like infrasound quaint.

The setting in which bigfoot are observed demands equal consideration. The wilderness, archetypally, is commonly regarded as a place of spiritual awakening, be it in Christian tradition—see Jesus's 40 days and nights in the Judaean Desert—or indigenous belief, as exemplified by walkabouts in Australian aboriginal culture. Cemeteries and graveyards, another common location of bigfoot sightings, are also liminal zones, bringing together both the living and the dead.

Fake It 'Til You Make It

Bader et al. wrote:

> Frustrated Bigfoot advocates point to a mountain of evidence. Thousands of supposed Bigfoot footprints have been cast in plaster by researchers. There are an abundance of photographs and enough purported films to warrant their own book-length listing. Bigfoot hunters have collected samples of claimed Bigfoot hair and feces. Most scientists, however, are simply not convinced of the *quality* of this evidence. The films, photos, and foot castings are obvious hoaxes, they argue. The feces and hair samples must be from known animals; the many sightings are simply misidentifications of bears, if not outright hoaxes themselves.[21]

"Charges of fakery, lies, and hoaxing are leveled at all paranormal phenomena," wrote Patrick Harpur. "I prefer to see hoaxing as a daimonic quality inherent in, and continuous with, anomalous events—which are neither 'genuine' nor 'fake' but, in a deeper sense, *both*." The rationalist, uncomfortable with ambiguity, will undoubtedly regard such a statement as nonsense. It is an understandable objection—yet, framed within the confines of the paranormal as a whole, Harpur's contention begins to make sense. There is no shortage of individuals who have, to put it colloquially, "faked it until they made it" regarding paranormal evidence. For instance, while many (if not most) crop circles are manmade, hoaxers regularly report strange occurrences and lights while working in the fields they select.[22]

Perhaps the most famous example is the Philip Experiment, implemented by Canadian parapsychologists in 1972. Psychologist Joel Whitton oversaw the affair, which involved the creation of an elaborate—

albeit fictional—character named "Philip Aylesford." Philip was given a robust, detailed backstory, born in 1624 and participating in historical events like the English Civil War and spying for King Charles II. After initial attempts failed to contact the fictional spirit, Philip finally made his presence known during more traditionally-staged séances including dimmed lighting. In addition to eyewitness accounts, audio and video recordings documented vibrations, table levitation, echoes, felt presences, and raps, the last of which *correctly answered questions about Philip's fictional life*. The group apparently, through some manner of psychic ability, fashioned paranormal phenomena from whole cloth simply by acting as though it were real.[23]

Something similar may have happened with controversial bigfoot researcher Paul Freeman. In June 1982, Freeman claimed he observed an eight-foot tall bigfoot in the Blue Mountains of the Pacific Northwest. He collected footprint casts afterward. Because Freeman was employed as a watershed patroller, the Forest Service became involved and, following a detailed investigation, deemed the tracks a hoax, "but in true bureaucratic form the Service withheld the findings from the public."[24] This widened existing schisms among researchers like Grover Krantz—who, being privy to the details, maintained Freeman's casts were authentic—and other researchers like Rene Dahinden who argued they were "absolutely fakes."[25]

Regardless of the original casts' veracity, subsequent evidence from Freeman was embraced by none other than Jeffrey Meldrum, who invested a significant amount of time in examining the tracks. Freeman consistently impressed Meldrum with casts of hands, knuckles, and buttocks, as well as his compelling, if low resolution, sasquatch footage shot in 1994.[26] Did Freeman, like crop circle hoaxers or participants in the Philip Experiment, draw the attention of genuine anomalies by presenting fakes as fact, almost akin to a magical ritual?

Perhaps such questions are immaterial, for even Freeman advocates like Meldrum notice The Trickster archetype creeping into the scenario. Upon first meeting Freeman at his home, Meldrum was asked to examine a newly discovered trackway, an invitation he saw as both highly compelling—because his visit was unannounced—yet simultaneously suspicious.

> Freeman joined me and described how it seemed that the tracks began about where he had parked the truck, made a hairpin loop in the soft soil of the adjacent plowed field, and ended once again along the side road precisely where the truck was parked… Again I thought to myself, how convenient for a hoaxer—simply don false feet in the back of

the truck, jump onto the muddy road, trot out a truncated trackway, jump back into the back of the truck, doff the muddy false feet, and away you go.[27]

In another example, an Alabama hoax may have well attracted legitimate phenomena. In October 2001, Neal Williamson admitted to starting the "Choccolocco Monster" sightings of 1969 near Anniston. Williamson claimed to stand alongside deserted country roads between May and June wearing a full-length black coat, waiting for automobiles to pass by. Whenever they did, he would dance along the tree line, brandishing an old cow skull over his head, just long enough for motorists to catch a glimpse.[28]

Despite Williamson's insistence he acted alone, one of the earliest witnesses, Johnny Ray Teague, claimed to have observed multiple creatures. Teague and several friends were driving through the area when their car stalled. As they examined the engine, a monster "the size of a cow, gray to black in color, humped similarly to a camel" came crashing through the brush, a description confirmed by his companions. Everyone loaded into the car, which started without incident—yet a half-mile away, saw three or four additional creatures even larger than the first.[29]

Did Williamson's antics draw in something genuinely anomalous?

Make It 'Til You Fake It

More commonly, hoaxes present themselves alongside genuine paranormal evidence in an inversion of the "fake it 'til you make it" scenario, i.e. a genuine event occurs and the eyewitness receives intense scrutiny, after which they feel pressure to deliver further results. This naturally discredits the initial encounter, allowing paranormal phenomena to evade objective proof and continue operating in the shadows.

Some Ufologists have adopted this position regarding the UFO contactees of the 1950s and 1960s: an individual would report an authentically anomalous, pseudo-religious revelation and, to satisfy eager followers, later fabricate claims of further interaction with their "Space Brother" contacts. This allegation finds claim among other paranormal witnesses: the 1917 Cottingley Fairy photographs, which so infamously fooled Sir Arthur Conan Doyle, are obviously artificial, yet their creators claimed "they had actually seen fairies" and "faked the photographs to get back at adults" who disbelieved them.[30] Similarly, many leading parapsychologists regard England's Enfield Poltergeist of the 1970s as a case "that involved trickery along with some evidently genuine phenomena."[31]

The self-negation of The Trickster is equally prevalent in bigfoot sightings. Ray Wallace's discovery of the 1958 Humboldt County, California prints, widely regarded as bigfoot's first true moment in the limelight of American popular culture, came, in cryptozoologist Loren Coleman's words, "in two forms":

> Apparently an authentic bigfoot left real prints, from August through October 1958 (and beyond). Sometime during that period, Ray and his associates allegedly started putting down another series of imprints from wooden fakes that looked much different than the actual bigfoot footfalls…
>
> After a few months of workers finding the tracks, finally taxidermist Bob Titmus taught Jerry Crew how to make a cast, to prove to people they weren't crazy. It was after that, not until October, when Crew took that one now-famous "Bigfoot" cast to a local newspaper editor that the media took notice.[32]

This deception retroactively tainted the initial discovery to the extent that many today incorrectly regard the entire affair as a hoax. Figures like Wallace occupy a liminal space: they are tricksters, positioned halfway between legitimacy and fakery.

Another recurring figure in paranormal research—the individual who emerges years later to claim they hoaxed a well-regarded case—is yet another trickster manifestation, serving to blur boundaries between the real and artificial. For an example of how this presents itself in bigfoot research, one only needs to do a cursory amount of research on the number of claims surrounding the Patterson-Gimlin film; if every account is to be believed, it was a dozen individuals wearing a suit made by another dozen costumers. All the whistleblowers cannot be telling the truth, so the entire film is demeaned and dismissed by the general public regardless of its authenticity.

Hansen draws a clear parallel between con artists (trickster figures) and mystics (paranormal intermediaries). Both Eastern and Western spiritual figures exhibited grotesquery, deception, and madness.

"Mystics have also displayed some of the most extreme manifestations of the trickster," Hansen wrote. "A number of them had ambiguous sexual orientations; some sexually abused their devotees; some simulated paranormal phenomena in order to lure followers. This association between mysticism and deception is long-standing, and many times it is difficult to tell the difference between a holy man and con artist, or even if it is meaningful to speak of any such distinction."[33]

Genuine phenomena attract enterprising hucksters trying to make a quick buck. In the wake of the Bossburg, Washington (aka "Cripplefoot") tracks, a gentleman named Joe Metlow claimed to not only hold a bigfoot captive in a local mineshaft, but offered a genuine frozen sasquatch foot for a paltry $50,000.[34]

Also present at Bossburg was Ivan Marx, a man who predicted (and failed) he would capture a bigfoot within a year. Like the Wallace incident, some feel Marx's presence casts a shadow over the Bossburg tracks' authenticity. In any case, Marx mentored the most controversial figure in bigfoot research: Tom Biscardi.[35]

Biscardi—self-proclaimed "greatest hunter of Bigfoot in the United States"[36]—has consistently overpromised and underdelivered on providing objective proof for bigfoot's existence, to the extent that many in the community level accusations he is an outright hoaxer whose association with any case is an immediate red flag. Between 1973 and 1981 he told the media multiple times he "was going to capture a bigfoot," possessed footage of the creature he refused to sell, had sighted a sasquatch, etc.[37]

Biscardi was also involved with one of the most prominent bigfoot hoaxers of the 21st century: Rick Dyer.

Case Study: Rick Dyer

The timeline of the 2008 Georgia Bigfoot Hoax is a bit convoluted and is therefore presented in truncated form for efficiency's sake. Anyone seeking to parse out the exact details will find no greater resource than Loren Coleman's excellent summary "The Ultimate Georgia Bigfoot Hoax Timeline," posted September 14th, 2008 on the *Cryptomundo* website.

In mid-2008, Rick Dyer and police officer Matt Whitton claimed to stumble upon the body of a bigfoot in the north Georgia woods. The creature, they said, was so immense it took them and six other men a day-and-a-half to transport it out of the forest, all while followed by several other creatures (which they purportedly captured on film). They then preserved the body on ice.[38]

The ensuing media circus burned through the summer news cycle, gaining the pair national attention, fueled by online videos claiming absolute proof of bigfoot's existence and deriding mainstream cryptozoologists. Amidst the fervor, radio host (and former Tom Biscardi employee) Steve Kulls hosted Dyer and Whitton on his Internet program.[39]

"During the show, Dyer says the pair would welcome only three Bigfoot researchers to their location—Steve Kulls, Tom Biscardi, and another individual (CH) who has little to do with this fiasco other than to have been trying to seriously investigate it," wrote Coleman. Kulls facilitated communication between Biscardi and the pair, and while the former expressed interest, Dyer and Whitton informed him the body had been sold to the *National Enquirer*.[40]

After this proved untrue, the three individuals partnered together, with Biscardi flying to Georgia to oversee collection of DNA samples from the specimen. Staying in contact with Biscardi throughout the summer, Kulls allegedly expressed suspicions of fakery, but was assured by his former employer that Biscardi was "right there when the DNA was cut off the body… This thing has incredibly thick skin" (he later changed his story, saying he was handed the sample).[41] Around August 10, 2008, Biscardi further described the bigfoot in detail to Kulls, including the creature's eyes, teeth, and genitals.[42]

Assuring everyone of the specimen's veracity, "Biscardi generates wild rumors that the filming of the autopsy of the 'body' is being sold for 11 million dollars, that two Russians are flying in to conduct the autopsy, and that other side deals or contracts are in the works," Coleman wrote. Biscardi also claimed that "the DNA amplification size was consistent with human/ape and was going to be sequenced."[43]

On August 11, Whitton and Dyer released a video flashing an image of the corpse, which was subsequently posted to Loren Coleman's website *Cryptomundo*. What followed was an exchange between Biscardi and Coleman where a clearer photo was released with an August 15 embargo, but "Biscardi's own organization… prematurely released it themselves," prompting a once "skeptically optimistic" Coleman to post the new photo online. Shortly afterward, a reader sent evidence highly suggestive that the "body" was an off-the-shelf costume.[44]

A flurry of activity ensued, with cryptozoologists analyzing the photograph and Coleman expressing caution, dismissed by mass media. Major news networks ignored the warnings and covered the story anyway, including Biscardi's planned news conference, after he purchased the "body" for $50,000.[45]

"The DNA results that are 'released' and 'read' by Biscardi are inconclusive and confusing, while the two pictures released do not show anything compelling either," Coleman wrote. "Biscardi is abrupt and confrontational with the media, at one point saying that he wanted to get as much money as possible and saying Jeff Meldrum 'wasn't an anthropologist.'"[46]

Finally in the presence of the specimen, several researchers began thawing the body and discovered what so many suspected all along: Biscardi paid $50,000 for what was indeed revealed as a costume stuffed with hog intestines. When informed of this, Kulls said Biscardi was "unusually calm."[47]

Biscardi attempted to return the "body" to Dyer and Whitton and, according to Kulls, placed a gag order on the whole affair. Kulls objected, instead asking the pair for Biscardi's money to be returned, but Whitton said they no longer had it, and would deal with Biscardi personally.[48]

"Biscardi calls Kulls back and claims that Whitton & Dyer will sign a promissory note and a confession the next morning before they leave for home," Coleman wrote, but the pair quietly returned to Georgia. They eventually presented a televised confession of the hoax on August 18, though two days later claimed Biscardi and Kulls coached them, a statement denied by the latter. Kulls then appeared on national television where he spoke of "the deceptions of Tom Biscardi" and his belief Biscardi was "complicit in the hoax."[49]

A few points beg Hansenian analysis and reveal manifestations of The Trickster archetype in the 2008 Georgia Bigfoot Hoax. Obviously, as in all hoaxes, deception played a crucial role. More subtle aspects can also be pinpointed.

- **Liminality.** On July 3, 2008 Whitton was wounded in the line of duty and placed on medical leave.[50] Ergo, during almost the entire time of the hoax, he was in a liminal state between employment and non-employment. Following the incident, Dyer began working as a tow truck driver and used car salesman. Both can be seen as liminal occupations: tow truck drivers make their living in liminal spaces (roads) hauling vehicles that are designed to travel yet cannot; used car salesmen trade vehicles that are neither new nor obsolete (moreover, the occupation is often regarded as contemporary shorthand for modern tricksters).

- **Loss of status.** Prior to his leave, Whitton was "given heroic media coverage." By the end of August, his police department had fired him, meaning this liminal period culminated in a complete loss of status. Dyer also experienced a loss of status from the hoax as well: according to Kulls's website, Dyer was charged with numerous crimes between 2008 and 2012.[51] The hoax itself also caused a loss of status for cryptozoology (whatever little bit of reputability it had in the mainstream).

- **Communitas.** Like Whitton, Dyer was also employed for

a time in law enforcement as a corrections officer[52]—yet some of the earliest YouTube videos posted by user RDYER678 describe "a felon" who killed the bigfoot. Law enforcement fraternizing with felons is the very definition of communitas or social leveling.[53]

- **Challenges to the natural order and inversion.** Dyer and Whitton's videos challenged and mocked many prominent bigfoot researchers, including Coleman, Meldrum, and Matt Moneymaker.[54] At the same time, the pair obtained a degree of national recognition and attention many "famous," reputable cryptozoologists never attain. The 2008 GA Bigfoot Hoax also inverted the typical roles of cryptozoologists and the mainstream media: the cryptozoological community was more skeptical than mainstream news networks about the hoax, a reversal of typical stereotypes.

- **Ambiguity.** Who was the true mastermind behind the entire hoax? Did Biscardi *ever* believe the body was real? Why did Biscardi tell conflicting stories about the DNA collection? What motivated Dyer and Whitton to lie about the *National Enquirer* sale? Was there any truth to the rumors Biscardi started?

- **Anti-structure.** The entire 2008 GA Bigfoot Hoax exhibited systemic disorganization at every level, an observation which speaks for itself.

- **Shifting alliances.** Kulls was formerly employed by Biscardi, but ended the summer of 2008 opposed to him. Dyer and Whitton were once in Biscardi's favor, a partnership that also ended poorly.

Since the 2008 Georgia Bigfoot Hoax, Dyer has continued to present fabricated evidence of large, hairy hominids, including an eight-foot tall bigfoot "corpse" named Hank he toured around the country. However, Dyer no longer denies his fakery, thus embodying another aspect of The Trickster: disenchantment.

From a 2014 Huffpost article:

> I was one of the people who did the Bigfoot hoax in 2008, and got worldwide notoriety... And it turned out to be a hoax with a lot of money off this hoax. I, myself, made a ton of money.

We are now looked at as the black sheeps [sic] of the Bigfoot community, and let me tell you something: We don't care.

[My website] Bigfoottracker.com is back for one reason only: To convert people who believe in Bigfoot to Bigfoot haters. We are tired of seeing people give their money away for something that's not real.

There's no more evidence for Bigfoot than the Tooth Fairy or the Easter Bunny. And that's what people have to get through their heads. I have taken people out to hunt for Bigfoot, and all the time I was thinking in my head, 'Why would someone pay to go out to hunt for something that does not exist?' But people do.

It's really easy to trick people. People that believe in Bigfoot are not idiots—they're just really naïve and they're missing something in their lives, so they want to believe in something that they know deep down inside, it does not exist.[55]

Case Study: The Minnesota Iceman

Dyer may have drawn inspiration from the Minnesota Iceman, a complex and circuitous case which—in an embodiment of The Trickster's contradictory duality—simultaneously represented the best bigfoot evidence *and* the greatest hoax ever documented. Again, we are forced to oversimplify a complex narrative; for the complete story, consult Bernard Heuvelmans's exhaustive firsthand account of the saga, specifically *Neanderthal: The Strange Saga of the Minnesota Iceman*, a new translation from Anomalist Books featuring an afterword by Loren Coleman.

Described as a six-foot tall humanlike creature covered in dark brown hair and entombed in a block of ice, the Minnesota Iceman was brought to cryptozoology's attention by college zoology major Terry Cullen, who first saw the specimen at a traveling exhibit in Milwaukee, Wisconsin in late 1968. Cullen contacted Fortean investigator Ivan T. Sanderson, who in turn enlisted the help of zoologist Bernard Heuvelmans. Together, they obtained permission to examine the body from its owner, Frank Hansen.[56] (Presumably no relation to George P. Hansen—but, to avoid confusion, hereafter referred to as "Frank.")

Heuvelmans wrote of his initial reaction:

> I would be lying if I claimed to have felt a shock, or some intense emotion, when suddenly faced with this escapee from prehistory. After all, I still had no idea of what lay under my eyes, and I was content with examining it with extreme attention, understandable mistrust, and, I must admit it, increasing amazement...
>
> It was undoubtedly a man, tall and well muscled—a little over 1.80 m [nearly 6 ft] tall—a man who, at first glance, appeared to have the same proportions as you and I, but a man as hairy as a gorilla or a chimpanzee!
>
> He was lying flat on his back, his head tilted back, his left arm raised over his head, his right hand seeming to protect his lower belly, in the familiar pose of a sleeping man. However, he was definitely not sleeping and undoubtedly dead. His head was stained with blood and his eye sockets were empty and bloody. His left arm was strangely curved like that of a rag doll: actually, it was certainly broken because halfway between the wrist and the elbow the ulna was sticking out of an open wound. His right foot, bent upwards while the knee was also bent, seemed in an abnormal position, resulting from a muscular spasm, a disability, or a wound. This mutilated corpse was embedded in an icy shroud.[57]

After carefully examining the specimen through its icy, rectangular tomb, both investigators were convinced the specimen was genuine, for a host of reasons Heuvelmans comprehensively detailed in his book. Among the most visceral clues was "the nauseating smell of a rotting corpse" emanating from a broken seal in the refrigeration unit, a detail Heuvelmans found especially compelling.[58]

Despite its apparent authenticity, Frank acted suspiciously from the very beginning, eschewing the allure of publicity when confronted with the magnitude of his exhibit. Equally problematic was the body's provenance: over time, the story shifted numerous times to include a Soviet trawler or Japanese whaler discovering the creature entombed in ice, floating off Kamchatka; a purchase from "an import-export specialist" in Hong Kong; and, in an eventual "confessional" published in *Saga Magazine*, a hunting casualty by Frank's own hand in Minnesota.[59] Other stories, each varyingly attributable to Frank, included a "Helen Westring" who killed the beast when it tried to sexually assault her,[60] a Siberian hunter who felled the creature, and a mysterious benefactor who met with Frank in Arizona in

1967, all of whom passed the corpse to Frank.[61]

The last story may be closest to the truth. Frank regularly stated a mysterious millionaire was the *actual* owner of the specimen, though the benefactor remains unidentified.[62] Jimmy Stewart was often cited as a possibility, though little real evidence has surfaced to support the claim. (Though it should be noted, as a minor synchronicity, that Stewart starred in *Harvey,* a popular 1950 film depicting a *pooka*—an Irish faerie trickster.)

When Sanderson confronted Frank about taking the Minnesota Iceman for publicity and further examination such as x-rays, he categorically refused. "Deeply disappointed, Ivan then played his trump card," Heuvelmans wrote. "He told [Frank] that I was about to publish a report of my examination of the specimen in a European scientific journal." Sanderson also published an article in *Argosy Magazine.*[63]

"[Frank's] problems began with the publication of the Heuvelmans article and escalated when Sanderson's piece hit the newsstands," wrote author Troy Taylor. "To make it worse, Sanderson, who was a well-known nature personality for television, mentioned the Iceman during an appearance on *The Tonight Show*. Soon, newspapers, television shows, radio stations and magazines from all over the world began trying to verify the existence of the creature."[64]

Frank claimed this enraged the owner, who retrieved the specimen and left in its stead "a replica created earlier at great cost and difficulty 'just in case he had problems some day.'" (Frank later claimed this replica functioned as a sort of "insurance policy," should ownership of a corpse become problematic.) This was the official story presented to the media.[65]

At this juncture, a number of other interests chimed in, from the Smithsonian, which cited academic interest, to the Federal Bureau of Investigation, which was interested in any criminal implications the body might present.[66] Some contend this push came at the behest of Sanderson, who "decided that getting [Frank] busted for breaking some law would be the easiest way to do this." Wrote Brian Dunning of *Skeptoid*:

> Sanderson alerted the Bureau of Customs, Department of Agriculture, Department of the Interior, and the Department of Health, Education, and Welfare. He also brought the case to his contacts at the Smithsonian Institution, whereupon its secretary, Dillon Ripley, reported to the FBI (in fact he wrote J. Edgar Hoover personally) that [Frank] was transporting a corpse across state lines, and that a scientific journal had identified the corpse as a human who had been shot."[67]

Regarding the "replica," some believe—based upon increased clarity of the ice and consistency of the body—that Frank merely thawed and refroze his exhibit, changing it somewhat to throw off Heuvelmans and Sanderson. This new version was accompanied by the humorous signage: *SIBERSKOYA CREATURE (a Siberian creature) A MANUFACTURED ILLUSION, AS INVESTIGATED BY THE F.B.I.*[68]

Even if this was still the original body, it is apparent that Frank indeed employed a replica at some point. In his afterword to Heuvelmans's memoir, Coleman described his impressions of the exhibit from August 8, 1969:

> I took photographs and sent them to Sanderson, Heuvelmans, and Hall. The four of us worked closely together to determine the differences between the hominid-like body that Sanderson and Heuvelmans had seen and photographed in December 1968, and the obvious fake that Hall and I saw a few months later in 1969. The toothy model that is often shown as the "Real Iceman" is one of the photos taken of the acknowledged fake being shown in 1969…
>
> Sanderson and Heuvelmans discussed 15 specific differences they noticed between the original Minnesota Iceman and the model. They include known details for the original body, such as vegetable material apparent in the teeth, parasites on the skin, and other items mentioned by Heuvelmans in his book, which were not there on the model.[69]

The above summary pales in comparison to the intricacies of the entire Minnesota Iceman affair, but the case presents a quaint postscript. In 2013 the model resurfaced and was subsequently purchased by Austin, Texas's Museum of the Weird, where it can still be viewed today.[70]

The entire Minnesota Iceman saga embodies the self-negating aspect of these phenomena; what sounds like an unambiguously genuine specimen is undercut by the appearance of an equally unambiguous hoax in its place. There is also an aspect of self-negation to Sanderson. When asked to defend the exhibit's legitimacy, he bafflingly stated "even if that specimen had been a fake, which it couldn't be for a variety of other reasons, it would necessarily have been constructed from parts taken from living beings. And he went on to explain, in that tone of his that bore no contradiction, how he would have proceeded to make such a fake…"[71]

This led to, in Heuvelmans's words, skeptics declaring: "Since

Sanderson, one of the discoverers of the specimen, admits that it would be quite possible to make one just like it, it's obviously a fake."[72]

Heuvelmans described the entire affair at least once as "seamy," a telling description entirely fitting with Hansen's model of The Trickster. More trickster attributes appear upon closer inspection:

- **Trickster imagery.** The Trickster has longtime associations with both the circus (clowns) and sideshows, the latter of which accurately describes the Minnesota Iceman exhibit, even in its "genuine" form. Carrying The Trickster archetype further, Sanderson "had given [the body] a code name: Bozo, which was also unfortunately that of the most famous clown in the US."[73] The Minnesota Iceman was definitively a sideshow attraction. Finally, we cannot ignore, from a synchromystic standpoint, the coincidence of a trickster figure being named "Hansen," the same surname of the gentleman who would author such a seminal, scholarly book on the paranormal.

- **Liminality.** Throughout its entire investigation, the authenticity of the Minnesota Iceman was mired in liminality, duality, and ambiguity: first it was presented by Frank as an authentic specimen, perceived as authentic by cryptozoologists; then presented as a fake, perceived as authentic; then presented as a fake and perceived as a fake. Whether or not the specimen was man or animal, in addition to being itself a liminal condition, left the legal ramifications of the exhibit in a sort of limbo as well. Additionally, much of Heuvelmans's book is occupied with the issues of transporting corpses across borders—getting the Iceman into America, transporting it across state lines, and, in one dramatic incident, Frank's 24-hour detainment at the Canadian border—all zones of liminality.

- **Loss of status and communitas.** The premise that a travelling carnival curiosity might yield one of the 20th century's most profound scientific discoveries juxtaposes low and high status. The Minnesota Iceman also facilitated the appearance of a cryptozoologist on *The Tonight Show*. While such publicity is not unheard of—David Letterman, for example, interviewed John Keel in 1980[74]—it is nonetheless a *mainstream* presentation of a *fringe* topic. There is also an element of "odd couple" communitas in the pairing of Sanderson, an increasingly fringe personality, and Heuvelmans, a legitimate scientist. "I had not failed to notice that because of the rather undiscriminating interest [Sanderson] had shown over the past few years to everything that was fantastic and unexplained, the naturalist and author of many well-received works had gradually acquired a wretched scientific reputation," Heuvelmans wrote. "While acknowledging his originality, I had many times chided him in a friendly manner for the excessive enthusiasm with which he sometimes blindly welcomed marvelous events without verifying their authenticity."[75]

- **Ambiguity.** Of Frank's deliberately noncommittal *Saga Magazine* confession, Heuvelmans wrote the owner's "usual strategy" was designed to "keep them guessing, maintain the ambiguity. A specimen is henceforth to be shown. The real one? The fake? Maybe yes, maybe no. A specimen that is presented as false. Yes, but is it? Finally, it can be anything."[76]

- **Anti-structure.** Frank's lifestyle travelling around the countryside showcasing the frozen corpse of a hairy hominid is by definition anti-structural: every day, setting, and lodging was different. Similarly, even Sanderson and Heuvelmans's small, two-person confederation was plagued by infighting, as evidenced by how the latter wrote of publication disputes between the two: "This certainly didn't improve our relationship, which was already somewhat strained from our divergent views on how to proceed in this affair."[77]

- **Deception.** Frank's ever-changing origins for the Minnesota Iceman are self-evident in their ambiguity and deception. Moreover, consider the mysterious owner of the specimen—who may or may not have existed.[78]

- **Social leveling.** In early 1969, in an effort to gain "the support of influential colleagues as well as publicity in reputable publications," Heuvelmans found himself wandering the streets of New York City, presenting his portfolio of Minnesota Iceman photos around town. "Hating as I did to beg for anything, I nevertheless found myself acting like a travelling salesman for Science, going from door to door to sell my merchandise," he wrote. Additionally, while many in the United States Air Force left the service for prestigious occupations as airline pilots, Frank Hansen (a veteran of both the Korean and Vietnam Wars) began showcasing a frozen bigfoot. In Heuvelmans's words, "How does one go from piloting combat aircraft to the chatter of a carny?"[79]

While not every bigfoot hoax fits George P. Hansen's trickster criteria, the above examples demonstrate the profundity of his observations… observations which, if not explicative in their power, at least grant researchers new lenses through which to view the phenomenon. For too long, cryptozoologists have held the subjects of their scrutiny immune to such effects, factors that plague every other aspect of paranormalia: ghosts, UFOs, psi effects, magic, etc. If bigfoot are a part of a larger super-reality—as *Where the Footprints End* argues—then perhaps it is time to begin embracing, and accounting for, the tricksters in our midst.

---

[1] Anderson, W. (1990). *Green Man: The Archetype of our Oneness with the Earth.* San Francisco, CA: HarperCollins Publishers.

[2] Hansen, G.P. (2001). *The Trickster and the Paranormal.* Bloomington, IN: Xlibris.

[3] Ibid.

[4] Ibid.

[5] Ibid.

[6] Ibid.

[7] Slate, B.A. & Berry, A. (1976). *Bigfoot.* New York, NY: Bantam.

[8] Bader, C.D., Backer, J.O., & Mencken, F.C. (2017). *Paranormal America: Ghost Encounters, UFO Sightings, Bigfoot Hunts, and Other Curiosities in Religion and Culture* (2nd ed.). New York, NY: New York University Press.

[9] Bader et al. 2017.

[10] Ibid.

[11] Hansen 2001.

[12] Bader et al. 2017.

[13] Ibid.

[14] Sailor, C. (September 30, 2018). Before 'Smallfoot' and Bigfoot, native tribes told stories of child-stealing creatures of the woods. Retrieved March 30, 2019 from https://www.thenewstribune.com/news/local/article219134245.html

[15] Prescott, T. (January 2018). Sasquatch: The 'Myth' That Won't Go Extinct. Retrieved March 30, 2019 from https://atlantisrisingmagazine.com/article/sasquatch/

[16] Spignesi, S.J. (2000). *The UFO Book of Lists*. New York, NY: Citadel Press.

[17] Bayanov, D. (2011). *Bigfoot Research: The Russian Vision*. C.L. Murphy (Ed.). Blaine, WA: Hancock House Publishers.

[18] Anderson 1990.

[19] Hansen 2001.

[20] Ibid.

[21] Bader et al. 2017

[22] Thomas, A. (1998). *Vital Signs: A Complete Guide to the Crop Circle Mystery and Why It is NOT a Hoax*. Berkeley, CA: Frog, Ltd.

[23] Owen, I.M., & Sparow, M. (1976). *Conjuring Up Philip: An Adventure in Psychokinesis*. New York, NY: Harper & Row.

[24] Dennett, M. (June 2003). Bigfoot Proponent Comes to the End of the Trail. *Skeptical Briefs 13*(2), pp. 1-2.

[25] Dennett, M. (September 2006). Experiments Cast Doubt on Bigfoot 'Evidence.' Retrieved April 1, 2019 from https://www.csicop.org/sb/show/experiments_cast_doubt_on_bigfoot_evidence

[26] Meldrum, J. (2006). *Sasquatch: Legend Meets Science*. New York, NY: Forge Books.

[27] Ibid.

[28] Creamer, M. (October 31, 2001). The Choccolocco Monster: Jokester reveals 32-Year-Old Prank. *The Anniston Star,* pp. 1, 4A.

[29] Clark, J., & Coleman, L. (1978). *Creatures of the Outer Edge*. New York, NY: Warner Books.

[30] Guiley, R.E. (2007). *The Encyclopedia of Ghosts and Spirits* (3rd ed). New York, NY: Facts on File, Inc. (Original work published 1992)

[31] Ibid.

[32] Coleman, L. (April 30, 2006). Media Watch: Wallace Again, Wrong Again. Retrieved April 1, 2019 from https://cryptomundo.com/cryptozoo-news/wallacewrong/

[33] Hansen 2001.

[34] Coleman, L. (2008). The Ultimate Bigfoot Hoax Timeline. Retrieved April 1, 2019 from http://www.cryptozoonews.com/ultimate-timeline/

[35] Ibid.

[36] Wheeler, C. (May 22, 1973). Bigfoot "Migration" through Valley nearing end according to specialist. Retrieved April 1, 2019 from http://www.bfro.net/gdb/show_article.asp?id=102

[37] Coleman 2008.

[38] Coleman, L. (September 14, 2008). Ultimate GA Bigfoot Hoax Timeline: 2008. Retrieved April 1, 2019 from https://cryptomundo.com/cryptozoo-news/hoax-tl-08/

[39] Ibid.

[40] Ibid.

[41] Ibid.

[42] Ibid.

[43] Ibid.

[44] Ibid.

[45] Ibid.

[46] Ibid.

[47] Ibid.

[48] Ibid.

[49] Ibid.

[50] Ibid.

[51] Kulls, S. (December 26, 2012). Since everyone is pointing out an old arrest of Dyer... let me point out something rather new... Retrieved April 2, 2019 from https://squatchdetective.wordpress.com/2012/12/26/since-everyone-is-pointing-out-an-old-arrest-of-dyer-let-me-point-out-something-rather-new/

[52] McKinley, J. (August 14, 2008). Two Georgians Say They Have Bigfoot's Body. Retrieved April 2, 2019 from https://www.nytimes.com/2008/08/15/us/15bigfoot.html

[53] Coleman September 2008.

[54] Ibid.

[55] Speigel, L. (February 27, 2014). Bigfoot 'Killer' Rick Dyer: 'It's Really Easy to Trick People.' Retrieved April 2, 2019 from https://www.huffpost.com/entry/rick-dyer-bigfoot-traveling-tour_n_4827104

[56] Heuvelmans, B. (2016). *Neanderthal: The Strange Saga of the Minnesota Iceman.* (P. LeBlond, Trans.). San Antonio, TX: Anomalist Books.

[57] Ibid.

[58] Ibid.

[59] Ibid.

[60] Taylor, T. (2003). The Minnesota Iceman. Retrieved April 3, 2019 from http://www.prairieghosts.com/iceman.html

[61] Benedict, A. (August 18, 2018). Cryptid Profile: The Minnesota Iceman. Retrieved April 3, 2019 from https://pinebarrensinstitute.com/cryptids/2018/8/18/cryptid-profile-the-minnesota-iceman

[62] Heuvelmans 2016.

[63] Ibid.

[64] Taylor 2003.

[65] Ibid.

[66] Ibid.

[67] Dunning, B. (May 16, 2017). Thawing the Minnesota Iceman. Retrieved April 3, 2019 from https://skeptoid.com/episodes/4571

[68] Heuvelmans 2016.

[69] Ibid.

[70] Ibid.

[71] Ibid.

[72] Ibid.

[73] Ibid.

[74] Admin. (April 10, 2011). David Letterman Interviews John Keel. Retrieved April 3, 2019 from http://www.johnkeel.com/?p=640

[75] Heuvelmans 2016.

[76] Ibid.

[77] Ibid.

[78] Ibid.

[79] Ibid.

Case Study: Out of This World

While most researchers naturally embrace clear, concise hypotheses—sasquatch is an ape, sasquatch is interdimensional, a spirit, an archetype, etc.—no one proposal satisfies all criteria without dismissing countless other sightings. Many case studies serve not only as reminders of our collective ignorance regarding reality, but also present humbling, teachable moments advocating the virtue of agnosticism. The experiences of credible witnesses can present themselves as complex Gordian Knots, fantastic tales best understood by admitting they are *impossible* to understand.

Such is the life of Ron Johnson, a 65-year-old retired heavy equipment and diesel mechanic from East Carbon, Utah. Johnson has experienced a lifetime of peculiar events, including what many would qualify as "alien abductions"—a detail most traditional researchers would employ to discount his claims. For the true Fortean, however, or any open-minded researcher aware of the interconnected nature of the paranormal, the ongoing, repeated nature of Johnson's interactions strengthens, rather than weakens, his testimony.

In 2005, Johnson (who has maintained a healthy interest in bigfoot for some time) went to Salt Lake City to attend a lecture presented by researcher Darrell Smith. The two not only became fast friends, but began embarking on field expeditions together in search of Utah's undiscovered large, hairy hominids. Tragically, an ALS (amyotrophic lateral sclerosis, aka "Lou Gehrig's disease") diagnosis circa 2009 meant Smith could no longer accompany Johnson on his expeditions.

"Just before he died, I interviewed [Darrell Smith] on video," Johnson said. "He told me that, 'When I die… I'm going to learn, I'll know the secret to sasquatch. And if there's any way I can come back to see you and tell you about it, I'm going to do it.' And I told him, 'I wouldn't expect any different from you.' About two weeks after that he died."

Smith's passing came two years after his diagnosis.

Premonitions

Approximately three months after his friend's funeral, Johnson experienced a profoundly vivid dream featuring Smith, who told him, "Ron, I know all about bigfoot. When you die, you will know the secret." Smith also imparted a cryptic warning: "Be very careful, be prepared, something wonderful is going to happen to you. Something just totally out-of-this-world is going to happen to you, and you need to be prepared."

Johnson was perplexed. Was this merely a dream, or something more? If so, what could it mean? Prepare for what? The topic remained at the forefront of his thoughts for a full month. Then something truly unexpected occurred.

> I was watching TV one night, and it was the strangest thing. And I still don't know if this happened, or if it was a dream. But this light appeared in my living room… it was a ball of light and it turned into a pillar. It was really weird, this kind of a "bigfoot type" creature appeared in my living room.
>
> And [it] says, "Ron, your friend Darrell Smith wanted me to come and see you." And then I started thinking: is this what I was supposed to be prepared for? [The creature] says, "I want to take you to meet my family. Will you go with me?"
>
> And I said, "Yes."

Johnson rose from the couch, finding himself immediately transported with his guide to a dark cave inhabited by 12-14 other bigfoot, one of whom was eviscerating a deer carcass. The sasquatch offered Johnson some of the venison, but he politely declined.

The guide began speaking telepathically to his family. "This is my brother, Ron," he said. "His friend Darrell, who died, wanted me to bring him to meet you." This marked the end of the experience, and the duo returned to Johnson's living room.

"I know this sounds crazy," Johnson said. "Before he left, he told me the same thing [as Darrell]: be very, very careful, Ron. Something really wonderful is going to happen to you, and it's going to be very soon. Be prepared." His sasquatch guide vanished.

Many will argue this clearly represents a dream, a criticism Johnson fully embraces. "I still don't know if it was a dream or if it really happened," he said in hindsight, while simultaneously noting that the encounter was identical in feel to his "alien abduction" experiences. "I knew when I reported this to the BFRO… they weren't going to think too highly of it," he added.

Several months later, on May 4, 2012, a friend of Johnson's reached out to him about a recent sighting near a local coal mine. The witness was leaving work when, approximately three miles from the mine gate, he saw what he initially believed was a bear. Exiting his vehicle, he immediately realized he was looking at a nine-foot-tall bigfoot. Johnson's friend hopped back in his car and fled the scene.

(Though not pertinent to the current narrative, another sighting from the witness bears mentioning in a collection of strange sasquatch sightings. In November 2013, the same individual saw another sasquatch standing beside a boulder behind a barbed wire fence, mimicking the sound of a cow in distress. When he later investigated where the creature stood, Johnson's friend found a series of stones laid out in a giant "C" pattern. The location was Utah's "C Canyon.")

Since the sighting occurred within five miles of Johnson's home, it naturally piqued his interest, and the following morning he found himself hiking the area with his camera, which he keeps on his person religiously. However, several days in the bush yielded absolutely nothing: no sightings, no footprints, no signs at all.

The Event

On May 12, Johnson stopped by his cousin's home in Price on a whim—meaning, for once, he had none of his equipment on his person, including his camera. After talking for a while, Johnson asked, "Do you want to go up and see where the bigfoot sighting was?" His cousin agreed and, on the spur-of-the-moment, drove to the site of the encounter, stopping at a high point overlooking the area.

Seeing nothing, the pair decided to leave after a time—but a quarter mile from the main road, a figure caught Johnson's eye.

"My cousin said, 'What's the matter?' and I said, 'I've seen something,'" Johnson recalled. He threw the car into reverse and, to their surprise, saw a tall, hairy biped staring at them from a clearing. The being was standing completely still.

"Very carefully get out of this jeep," Johnson told his cousin. "But be very careful, don't make any sudden moves or noise." Johnson got out, quietly shutting his car door… but, frustratingly, the creature was nowhere to be seen.

"Do you think we should go down there?" his cousin asked. Johnson enthusiastically agreed.

"So we started walking down towards where we saw this thing," Johnson said, "And right then I got this telepathic message, and it says, 'Stop. Stay back. Do not approach. Stay back.' And it was real blunt." The voice was "real deep, rough," distinct from his inner monologue. Johnson compared it to his abduction experiences: "It wasn't my voice. I've never heard an inner voice like this before."

A wave of fear washed over Johnson, comparable to the anxiety of encountering a bear in the wilderness. He relayed the telepathic warning to his cousin, and the pair froze. Once the sense of unease diminished, Johnson's cousin dropped to the ground.

"There's two more over here in the trees!" he whispered. "I'm looking at their feet!"

Before Johnson could verify his cousin's sighting, he heard "this *thump-thump, thump, thump-thump*, like something real heavy running away." He took up a vantage point, but saw nothing. The only evidence was aural: heavy footsteps and a loud grunt.

As Johnson arose, he was again telepathically assaulted.

"I grabbed my cousin and I said, 'I'm getting that message again,'" he related. "So we kind of stayed there a moment, and then after a couple minutes, when the uneasiness went away, I told my cousin, 'Let's continue.'"

The pair pushed deeper into the forest, reaching a vantage point from which they could see a gently declining bench (long, narrow rise of land) perhaps 1,500 feet distant. The tops of three furry heads were bobbing and disappearing behind the rise.

"I can't really say if they were bigfoot or not," Johnson said. "It was just for a split second that I noticed them." Before investigating the bench, the pair briefly returned to the original clearing to look for footprints, but found none save a few vague exceptions (it is worth noting Johnson ascribes this to the number of rocks in the ground, rather than any supernatural reason).

Once they reached the distant rise, Johnson and his cousin found a handful of likely tracks descending the opposite side. The bench also hosted a peculiar structure made from dead limbs leaned together, creating a crude hut six to six-and-a-half feet tall. It appeared too simple to be manmade, yet too organized to be random. The two stood for a time, looking and listening for further evidence, but nothing occurred. Johnson later speculated the bigfoot(s) had retreated into the steep washes lining the bottom of the valley, but the encounter left a lasting impression.

Was this sighting the "wonderful" event to which both Darrell Smith and Johnson's sasquatch guide had alluded? Like his vivid dream encounter, Johnson speculates that might be the case, but stops short of any absolute declarations. His caution and self-doubt are essential to his account's believability, and both are virtues possessed by far too few researchers. If his encounter and its surrounding details are what they appear to be, Johnson's case represents a number of anomalies associated with bigfoot: alien abductions, the dead, strange lights, spirit journeying, glyphs, mimicry, mindspeak, and, of course, trickster phenomena—as evidenced by Johnson's sighting coinciding with the one time he failed to bring his camera.[1]

---

[1] Johnson, R. (2019, May 20). Personal communication.

Case Study:
Under the Owl Moon

March 30, 2018: Tobe Johnson and his research partner, Darrell Adams, are making their way along some backroads near Curtin, Oregon when Tobe spies something by the roadside:

> ... a set of what looked like deep appendage impressions. It almost looked like someone took a basketball and bounced it in the clay mud—and there were these nice, rounded-out divots next to these elk tracks... I immediately turned on my camera and started filming because they were just curious-looking.[1]

These curious indentations were later dubbed the "Owl Moon Prints": impressions from something large, kneeling in the mud. Tobe continues:

> It turns out when we leaned in on these impressions there was two of them—there was a left and a right—and they were relatively close to the gravel bank, and separated about 18 inches apart... They had hair sticking out of them—little black hairs, very human-looking—and they were coming out of what looked like bone structure, and they

looked like kneecaps that had plunged into the red clay.[2]

Tobe and Darrell spend the next five to six hours documenting the find: filming and photographing, carefully extruding hair from the mud, and, finally, casting impressions.

> So, we have these plaster knees that show anatomy. They show patella, bone structure, skin folds—and they still have hair sticking out of the kneecaps. The right one in particular is very impressive.[3]

A sample of the hair is sent to Cindy Dosen in British Columbia. Dosen runs the Hominidae Enigma Program, specializing in the investigation of hair—with a particular interest in verifying the existence of unknown hominids (i.e. bigfoot) through microscopic hair analysis. Dosen determines the hair sample is similar to human hair and comes from the lower extremity of a creature. From Dosen's report on the Owl Moon hair:

> The following has been determined from a microscopic hair examination. The sample may have come from a loose hair, last stages of resting growth. No postmortem banding on the hair to indicate death. This was from a live animal. All other animal species have been ruled out. This is an UNKNOWN HAIR.[4]

Dosen notes that the hair collected from the Owl Moon impressions matches only one other sample in her database: a hair collected from Ocean Shores, Washington. The matching hair is thought to come from a juvenile sasquatch.[5]

Tobe enlists the help of another expert to determine the weight of whatever made the Owl Moon impressions. An engineer by trade, Washington's Scott Taylor crafts impressions of Tobe's own knees—created under similar conditions as the Owl Moon prints. Whatever produced the impressions Tobe and Darrell cast was determined to weigh between 1200-1400 pounds.[6]

The evidence presented above seems like an open-and-shut case for the F&BH bigfoot enthusiast: deep impressions in the mud, left by something of great weight and large stature, exhibiting apparent primate anatomy; hair samples collected and, scientifically analyzed, determined to come from an unknown creature. However, things surrounding both the Owl Moon Prints and Tobe evolved in shorter— and stranger—fashion.

Reporting the paranormal is often a difficult task. The nature of writing requires that tales be told in a somewhat linear narrative: one thing happens, then the next, etc. The nature of the paranormal, however, commonly runs contrary to linear causality. One thing happens... then perhaps a dozen other things occur before something else, seemingly related to the inciting incident (either directly or through some kind of synchronistic symbolism) takes place. These paranormal happenings, when mapped out, look perhaps more akin to a spider's web than a neat, clean line.

Such is Tobe's story, a tangled web of strangeness, twisting deep into bigfoot and its attendant mysteries: unexplained lights, poltergeist activity, psychics, ghosts, and more.

Murphy is a Bigfoot

Tobe's involvement with the bigfoot phenomenon started some years earlier with the discovery of a single track in the town of Thurston, Oregon, during the winter of 2008—a lone, bare footprint, 12-inches long, which left a deep impression in the ice-covered mud.[7]

On February 12, 2012 a man named Max Roy found a series of large footprints while walking his dog alongside London, Oregon's Cottage Grove Reservoir. At the time, Roy recalled seeing a parked automobile, covered with bigfoot stickers, which he had noticed elsewhere locally. Thinking the series of prints might be of interest, Roy reported it—and presented photographs of the trackway—to the vehicle's owner, who amazingly happened to be Tobe's ex-wife (Tobe had previously owned the bigfoot sticker-emblazoned car). The information soon found its way to Tobe who proceeded to the location of the trackway.[8]

This set of prints, known as the London Trackway, consisted of over 100 individual footprints tracing the reservoir, into—and back out of—the water. It is considered an important, if controversial, find in the bigfoot world.

As this is not a story of the London Trackway *per se*, we will leave further research of this find to the interested reader. However, given the scope of these volumes it seems pertinent to note a statement made by Cliff Barackman, BFRO researcher and noted F&BH proponent, concerning his own involvement with the London Trackway, the difficulties surrounding documenting the prints, and bigfoot research in general:

> Not only do I believe that "Murphy's Law" is real, but I also believe that "Murphy" is a bigfoot. Strangely [sic] bad luck often surrounds bigfoot encounters, and apparently this

footprint find was no exception.[9]

A Paranormal, Supernatural Phenomenon

After finding the Owl Moon Prints, the bigfoot phenomenon's paranormal aspects manifested more readily around Tobe, yet he appeared unsurprised by this strange turn of events. On connecting sasquatch with the paranormal, Tobe stated:

> I always did... it was just intrinsically put inside my brain that this was a paranormal, supernatural phenomenon... This is a layered subject and it has all of this connective tissue of the paranormal that's kind of attached to the whole.[10]

The Owl Moon Prints were placed in a garage on Darrell Adams's property. Once Tobe and Darrell went "public" with the prints, they were somewhat worried about security—both from curious bigfoot believers and those strange, unknown agents so intent on making bigfoot evidence disappear (see Chapter 8). Little did they suspect this unassuming garage would become a focal point of paranormal activity on the property—an area Tobe eventually dubbed "The Owl Moon Lab," due to their ongoing experiments and interaction with multiple strange phenomena.

Tobe related, "As soon as we brought those knees and housed them here it seemed like a giant welcoming committee said, 'Oh, ok, you got something. You like it, we like it. Maybe we'll come visit more often.'"[11]

As if in confirmation of their fears, the garage door was found open one morning shortly after the casts were stored in the building. A series of footprints were found (shoe prints, not bigfoot prints) leading to the Owl Moon cast. Upon the cast itself, Tobe and Darrell found a toothbrush. Tobe related:

> That toothbrush [being there] was kind of indicative to me that someone was trying to mess with my head because I always put that little excavation device away in its proper drawer... It was sitting right on the right kneecap—and here's the muddy sneaker prints walking up to it. And then they moved a couple other things around—and then they undid the deadbolt—and just walked out the door.[12]

Echoing some of the issues endured by Stan Gordon and other paranormal investigators in the 1970s (see Chapter 8), Tobe and Darrell began experiencing telephone troubles after discovering the toothbrush on the Owl Moon cast. "Then our phone started acting up," Tobe stated. "That lasted about 48 hours. Anytime we talked, our phone would do a very strange high pitched buzz—and then it would shut down."[13]

Around the same time, Tobe began constructing a life-sized bigfoot model in the garage at the Owl Moon Lab for display at conferences and other events. About a month after they found the doors opened the first time, the intrusion happened again.

> One day, the garage doors went flying back up again. In the morning Darrel walks out here and sees the garage doors opened and, sitting between these plaster hands I'm making for this sasquatch structure, is a little blue [toy] dinosaur... it's just sitting there on top of the desk where I'm molding these hands. I couldn't believe it.

Who would walk in here and put a little blue dinosaur?[14]

Gifting Exchanges

Tobe eventually moved to the Owl Moon Lab, residing in a camper on the property. This triggered a series of bizarre gifting exchanges during which *something*—presumably bigfoot—left items that not only sparked curiosity but also suggested a deeper *meaning* to Tobe, Darrell, and Darrell's wife.

> When I moved into this property, things just really started to amp up as far as—we'll call it "gifting"... Immediately, when I put my camper up, little things would appear on the awning. Now they weren't just sticks and stones. One of the first things that appeared was just a pebble—a little tiny rock—and it was just sitting there. It certainly didn't belong on the canopy but we kind of just played it off. Maybe a leaf blower did it. Maybe it fell out of a tree—I don't know....
>
> Then we took my son fishing one day... Right before we left, we look on top of the canopy. There was this piece of wood sitting on top of the canopy... It was this little chunk of wood and it looked like a piece of Palo Santo incense... so there's this chunk of little, tiny—maybe two-inch long—piece of wood sitting up there. So we knock that down and take a look at it. Then we go out fishing and we're talking

about that piece of wood. We get back home—now, we've only been gone about two hours—and here's when things start to really amp up as far as what I think they [bigfoot] are trying to get across to us—that they can read our mind.

I've heard time and time again from long-term witnesses that they want you to know that you can't trick them. So they let you know how out-played you are by telling you, "Hey, we can read your mind." The way they did that was they put a carnelian stone—a beautiful fiery orange agate, about the size of a half dollar—on top of the canopy. ...

We see this thing sitting on the canopy. As soon as we see it's a carnelian stone, I said, "Darrell, that's the one stone you told me that was worth money. You mentioned that in the garage."... Out of all the rocks sitting on this canopy—six-and-a-half-feet off the ground—they put that one?[15]

This "mind reading" continued. Darrell's wife, Cindy, had open-heart surgery a short time later; when she returned home, she found a little glass heart placed beneath their hummingbird feeder. She picked up the "gift" to look at it and set it back down where it was found. Two hours later the glass heart had moved—found this time hanging from a tree branch at eye level.

On another occasion, Tobe discovered a dead rabbit, freshly killed, with a stone lodged in its skull. After finding the rabbit, Tobe, who has no affinity for serpents, exclaimed, "Thank God they are not leaving snakes!" Three days later—in the same spot where the rabbit was found— Tobe found a decapitated red garter snake.

The gifting continued with various items, stick glyphs, and dead animals being left for Tobe or Darrell to find. A short list includes a seven-foot honed walking stick; a green plastic disc; a blue action figure; a red pipe; a metal flange; a pebble (found inside the camper, on Tobe's bed); a bronze bracelet; a fishing bobber (found after going fishing); a rifle casing from the 1800s (found after Cindy requested gold from the creatures—while not made of gold, the casing had a gold-like hue); and dead moles and voles, appearing with some frequency—often beheaded or pinched in half.[16]

An Apport

While away from the Owl Moon Lab property one day, Tobe received a phone call from Darrell. A piece of white agate stone had appeared at one of their gifting areas. At Tobe's request, Darrell sent him a photograph of the rock. A short time later, Tobe was speaking on the phone with his son, Jude, when (in the course of their discussion) Jude asked, "I wonder if bigfoot will ever bring me anything?"

Afterward, Darrell phoned Tobe a second time to inform him that the white agate had disappeared. Tobe called Jude back:

> I said, "Jude, grab your camera, put it on FaceTime, don't ask me any questions. You're going to be ok. If this is what I think it is, it's going to be really cool"... I said, "Jude, what you're looking for is an orange rock." I kind of fibbed to him [about the color of the stone]—because I wanted this to be a true test...
>
> And so here he is looking around on the floor of his living room. He walks into the bathroom and at the threshold of the bathroom is this little white rock—and it's sitting right dead center on the threshold. It's the same rock. You can see it in the picture. So, that rock had aported, I guess is the technical term—from 45 miles away in the matter of a half hour or so—on its own, into a locked house with my son.
>
> Now that rock, it disappears periodically. It's locked inside a little metal tin can and we have this game with it where we go shake the can. Sometimes the can is empty. Then you'll shake the can and sometimes the rock is back.[17]

Unexplained Phenomena

Other unexplained phenomena began plaguing the Owl Moon Lab. Large hand prints appeared on rain gutters, 12 feet in the air. Greasy handprints were found in the bed of a truck and on the outside of the garage. Inside Darrell's home, small, white, chalky handprints appeared in one of his bedrooms.

They later learned that when the house was occupied by previous residents, that particular bedroom belonged to a child who had since passed away; the hand prints were found on the day of the child's funeral. In the same room, Tobe and Darrell recorded an example of EVP (Electronic Voice Phenomenon—anomalous voices caught on recordings, often unheard until playback, and believed by many to be the voices of ghosts or other paranormal entities). The EVP sounds like a voice saying, "I'm dead."[18]

Additionally, neighbors of the Owl Moon Lab regularly report unexplained aerial phenomena and mystery lights. Darrell himself captured some strange lights on his cell phone camera:

> I brought my dog out about 11:00 at night and right above that tree-line there, I saw something that appeared to be fireworks going off. So, I thought maybe there was some kids up in the woods doing fireworks...
>
> As I stood there for a minute, the thing started coming this way—and it wasn't fireworks... It would just flash— looked like a jellyfish or something—flash, expand, flash, go off—vanish for a minute and then it would come right back in a little different area. It just kept doing that—and then it got right over me and it just went out. It was gone. I stood there for a while and it never came back.[19]

Adams's admittedly shaky video seemingly shows something which changes shape and moves in a way inconsistent with fireworks or known aircraft.

Psychic Impressions

In May 2018, Tobe took a hair from the Owl Moon cast and traveled to the McMinnville UFO Festival in McMinnville, Oregon. His intention was to give the hair to reporter, author, and part-time host of *Coast to Coast AM*, George Knapp, who was appearing at the event. Before he could deliver the hair to Knapp, Tobe's journey took another strange detour, as he related:

> I'm walking around this festival and this gal says, "Hey you!"—I mean there's thousands of people at this festival. It's one of the biggest in the country. So this gal sitting at the outdoor restaurant with her friend yells, "Hey you! You've got a story to tell."
>
> I was like, "What?" She flagged me over, so I came over and

introduced myself. I said, "What do you mean I have a story to tell?"

She said, "I've seen you walking around here. What are you talking about?"

The woman claimed to be a psychic medium. Tobe explained that he had a sample of sasquatch hair he wished to give to George Knapp. Tobe sat down with the psychic and handed her the envelope containing the bigfoot hair.

"I just want you to know, I'm a skeptic when it comes to bigfoot," the psychic told Tobe, elaborating that she considered sasquatch the pursuit of "machismo men with monster fantasies." The medium took the hair from Tobe. Her eyes rolled back in her head and she exclaimed, "Oh my fucking God, they *are* real!" She imparted numerous revelations about bigfoot, including their hierarchy amongst the faerie folk—she declared them holy beings, akin to the Dalai Lama.

"They are very profound creatures," she said. The psychic also related that the hair belonged to a female creature who was very afraid when the impressions were left.[20]

Messages from Beyond

Back at the Owl Moon Lab, Tobe and Darrell continued their experiments. They recorded multiple EVPs and banging sounds coming from the garage, including a 30-minute long chorus of loud pops, clacks, and clanks (after which nothing was found disturbed). Weird popping sounds, strange voices, guttural growls, howls, screams, and other unknown sounds were recorded elsewhere on the property.[21]

Just outside of the garage, Tobe began communicating with wooden blocks upon which were written letters. On one occasion he left the message, "Thank you for gifts" spelled with the blocks. Tobe described a reply received three days later:

> ... spelled out with letters and numbers—because they didn't have enough letters to spell out this word, they used numbers—underneath "Thank you for gifts" was spelled "Welcome" [w3l4ome]—and they used the letter [sic] "three" to make an "E" and the number "four" to make a "C" because they ran out of letters.[22]

It Follows

Though the strangeness at the Owl Moon Lab continued in all its varied expressions, eventually both Tobe and Darrell moved from the property. Tobe has since relocated to Washington state, onto land he has dubbed "The Owl Moon Altar."

The attendant strange phenomena, to some extent, seem to have followed Tobe—he continues to exchange gifts with some type of nonhuman intelligence. At several designated "altars" around his property, Tobe finds objects moved or changed, even discovering new, never-before-seen items. As before, these totems typically hold a personal symbolism for Tobe, who continues to discover stick glyphs and the occasional dead animal—just as he and Darrell found previously at the Owl Moon Lab.[23]

It is worth noting that other researchers claim the bigfoot phenomenon "follows" them from one location to another. Lisa A. Shiel's *Backyard Bigfoot* documents a series of strange events attributed to bigfoot creatures—including stick glyphs and horse mane braiding—which followed the author from Texas to Michigan.[24]

The Web

Unwinding the tangled web of Tobe and Darrell's various experiences proves a difficult, if not impossible, task. There are no neat boxes for any of these strange events. The F&BH bigfoot theorist would likely be just as happy to separate the Owl Moon Prints from the catalog of oddities which followed their discovery. Likewise, many Ufologists would be happy to extricate Darrell's encounter with the flashing, shape-changing, flying object from bigfoot and the poltergeist-like phenomena happening around the Owl Moon Lab property. Most ghost hunters would likely be satisfied to say the house was haunted and disconnect it from all of the attendant paranormal phenomena happening outside of the house.

Webs, however, tend to be sticky. Tugging on the bigfoot strand, one inevitably pulls the UFO and poltergeist cords as well. Where does one end and another begin? To separate these things into individual events becomes a fruitless pursuit. Instead, it seems necessary to consider the web as a whole, however twisted and, at times, nonsensical it may be.

If the bigfoot phenomenon is communicating with Tobe, some part of the message seems to be the interconnected nature of these various paranormal phenomena. Where the footprints end (or in this case, knee-prints), poltergeist activity begins; UFOs appear; a mind-reading presence starts leaving gifts; and all manner of oddities follow.

Though noted in Volume I of this collection, it seems pertinent to reiterate: what strange company bigfoot keep!

---

[1] Renner, T. (August 11, 2018). Strange Familiars Episode 42: Paranormal Bigfoot with Strange Brau. Retrieved July 12, 2020 from https://www.strangefamiliars.com/home/paranormal-bigfoot-with-strange-brau

[2] Ibid.

[3] Ibid.

[4] Dosen, C. (April 26, 2018). Hominidae Enigma Unknown / Sasquatch Hair Analysis report - Client: Toby Allen Johnson.

[5] Ibid.

[6] Renner 2018.

[7] Johnson, T. (August 7, 2020). Personal correspondence.

[8] Barackman, C. (2013). London Trackway History. Retrieved July 12, 2020 from https://cliffbarackman.com/bigfoot-prints/the-london-trackway-2/the-london-trackway/

[9] Ibid.

[10] Renner 2018.

[11] Megargle, A., Meyer, R.C. (Producers), & Megargle, A., Meyer, R.C. (Directors). (2020). *The Bigfoot Alien Connection Revealed.* USA: Centre Communications, Inc.

[12] Renner 2018

[13] Ibid.

[14] Ibid.

[15] Ibid.

[16] Ibid.

[17] Ibid.

[18] Ibid.

[19] Megargle et al. 2020.

[20] Renner 2018.

[21] Renner, T. (October 3, 2019). Strange Familiars Episode 120. Retrieved July 12, 2020 from https://www.strangefamiliars.com/home/owl-moon-echoes-in-pandemonium-swapcast-with-strange-brau-radio

[22] Megargle et al. 2020.

[23] Renner 2019.

[24] Shiel, L.A. (2006). *Backyard Bigfoot: The True Story of Stick Signs, UFOs, and the Sasquatch.* Lake Linden, MI: Slipdown Mountain Publications LLC.

Afterword

Joshua and I have had an ongoing discussion about just how to *end* this collection. It is a difficult problem, for the information we have gathered is a mere sampling of a phenomenon which is growing (and possibly changing) as the culture grows and changes around it. Does the bigfoot phenomenon influence culture or does the cultural lens color our view of bigfoot? It may be a "chicken-or-the-egg" scenario or, perhaps, both things are true.

For all of the ideas we have put forth; for all of the strange bigfoot cases we have collected; for all of the connections we've made between sasquatch and various folkloric traditions; for all of the common ground we've shown that is shared by bigfoot and other paranormal phenomena; we are left, at the conclusion of two volumes, with just as many questions as we had when we started.

Our answer to the question, "What is bigfoot?" in truth remains: *We don't know.*

If pressed, I will say I think it has something to do with the archetype of the *wild man*—those strange beings that have walked beside us through the forests for as long as mankind has been walking. Bigfoot certainly act like *genii locorum*—spirits of place—and may indeed fulfill that role.

The danger, however, in talking about spirits and archetypes is that they tend to evoke ethereal forms in the minds of many. To the general populace, such words equate to non-physical or even *unreal* beings. It is important for me to be clear that I believe, whatever bigfoot are, they are real. They are physical beings—or at least they *can* be physical.

I have talked to many bigfoot witnesses in person, often at the location of their encounters. I myself have experienced some powerfully strange things in the woods. Whatever is out there is *not* all in the imagination of the witnesses. Bigfoot is real.

Unfortunately for the F&BH crowd, bigfoot is also undeniably weird. Too weird to simply be an undiscovered primate or a relict hominid.

With two heavy volumes dedicated to the *weirdness* of bigfoot, I feel it is important to note that there are far more accounts of oddities surrounding hairy hominids than those we documented. For each topic we covered, we took a sampling of reports as illustration of the points at hand. We found—and we keep finding—one report after another demonstrating how these strange things are woven into the bigfoot phenomenon. (Josh was fond of using the metaphor "drinking through a firehose"). Were we to attempt to document every case of High Strangeness associated with bigfoot, I am doubtful ten volumes would be enough.

The bigfoot phenomenon is, no pun intended, a living tradition. Reports of new bigfoot encounters surface weekly thanks to podcasts like *Sasquatch Chronicles* and other online resources. If we have added anything to this tradition with *Where the Footprints End*, I think it may be in the connections we've made between the bigfoot phenomenon and these other traditions and areas of study. These connections are just one more footprint in a very long trackway. We were not the first, nor will we be the last. Others will expand upon our work—and find more connections that we never realized.

Here at the end of our journey, I would point the readers to another book—a volume which more thoroughly and eloquently addresses the notion that things can be both apparitional *and* physical. It is a book from which we quoted at length in this volume. While it is not a bigfoot book *per se*, it is a book that everyone interested in bigfoot should have on their shelf. So, dear reader, I implore you to run and find a copy of *Daimonic Reality* by Patrick Harpur. Through Harpur's keen insight we gain a sharper focus to many of the ideas explored herein.

Finally, I will note that, at the beginning of this project, I stated publicly that *Where the Footprints End* would be my bigfoot "mic drop." I believed I had little more to say about the phenomenon. Standing now at the end of our shared path I can see that, while I thought I was done with bigfoot, bigfoot is not done with me.

The trackway may stop... but the footprints never end.

- Timothy Renner
Somewhere in Pennsylvania, August 2020.

Index

A

ABC (see *Alien Black Cats*)
Abominable Snowman (see *yeti*)
Aborigines (people, Australian), 46, 82, 106, 185, 236
    Kamilaroi, 153
Acadian (language), 64
Accord, Russell, 118
Adams, Cindy, 265
Adams, Darrell, 260-261, 263-265
Aeneid, 95-96
Africa, 119, 140, 177, 187
    Congo, 124
    Ethiopia, 169
    Middle East, 51, 169
    Senagambia, 119
agate, 265, 266
Aikanaka, 162
Ainu (people), 82
AK-47 (see *firearm*)
Akin, Jim, 58
Al, 4
Alabama (see *United States*)
Alaska (see *United States*)
Albany (Kentucky), 145
Alberta (see *Canada*)
Albuquerque (New Mexico), 141
Alexander, Colette, 43
alfalfa, 181
algae, 101, 116
Alien Black Cats (see also *cat*), 97-98
aliens (see *extraterrestrials*)
all-terrain vehicle, 96, 117
Alley, J. Robert, 123
alligator, 152
Allison family, 173
almasty, 89, 185

ALS (see *amyotrophic lateral sclerosis*)
Alton (Kentucky), 162
Amanita muscaria (see *psychedelics*)
Amazon (region), 80, 152
America (see *United States*)
Amish (see *Pennsylvania Dutch*)
amyotrophic lateral sclerosis, 256
Anclote River, 6
Anderson, Tim, 189
Anderson, William, 228, 235
Andes (mountains), 53
Angeles National Forest, 86
Anniston (Alabama), 238
Ape Canyon Incident, 102-103, 164, 168,
apple (see *fruit*)
Arab (culture), 4, 62, 64, 169
Argentina (see *South America*)
Argosy Magazine (publication), 246
Arias, Manuel, 175
Arizona (see *United States*)
Arkansas (see *United States*)
Arundel Mills Mall, 9
Asbjørnsen, Peter, 3
Asia (see also *Russia*), 64-65, 83, 140, 203
    Bhutan, 166
    Cambodia, 52
    China, 4, 42, 46, 153, 185
    Hong Kong, 150, 245
    India, 4, 98, 124, 153, 169, 185
    Indonesia, 42
    Iran/Persia, 4, 62, 64
    Japan, 63, 64, 81, 82, 124, 139, 169, 177-178, 245
    Kyrgyzstan, 15

Malaysia, 46, 63
Mongolia, 29, 82
Nepal, 53, 147
Scythia, 136
Tajikistan, 54
Tibet, 53, 82, 147
Turkey, 185
Athens (Greece), 62
ATV (see *all-terrain vehicle*)
Audubon Society, 48
Austin (Texas), 247
Australia, 13, 41, 46, 54, 82, 98, 105, 106, 140, 147, 153, 168, 185, 236
Austria (see *Europe*)
automobile, 1, 6, 8, 13, 16, 28, 33, 34-35, 53, 54, 55, 92, 97, 100, 101, 102, 142, 148, 149, 150, 166, 170, 177-178, 186, 209, 210, 216, 217-218, 238, 242, 257, 258, 262
    Explorer, 211
    truck, 53, 57, 162, 172, 207, 222, 237-238, 242, 266
    van, 34
ayahuasca (see *psychedelics*)
Aylesford, Philip (see *Philip Experiment*)
Aymara (people), 169
Azkath, Scriah, 20, 178

B

Baba Yaga, 153
baboon, 185, 187
Bacon, Brad, 56
Baddour (witness), 54-55
Bader, Christopher D., 232-233, 234
Bahr, Ehrhard, 51
Baker, Joseph O., 232
Baltimore (Maryland), 140
Baltimore Zoo, 140
bamros, 147
Barackman, Cliff, 2, 262
barbarous words, 61-62
Bartra, Roger, 62
Battle of the Trees, 120
Bayanov, Dmitri, 53-54, 83, 89, 185, 235
BB-gun (see *firearm*)
beagle (see *dog*)
bear, 2, 6, 42, 46, 56, 65, 82, 84, 124, 129, 139, 143, 149, 150, 153, 154, 173, 177, 184, 203, 211, 212, 213, 220, 221, 236, 257, 258
Bear, Fred, 219
Bear/Gary (Man-in-Plaid), 209-215
Beatty, Clyde, 219-220
Beaudoin, Jeff, 117
Beaver (Pennsylvania), 15
Beck, Fred, 102-103, 164
beetle, 101
BEK (see *Black Eyed Kids*)
bell, 45, 53-54, 216
Bell family, 32-33
Bell Farm, 32-33
Bell, Art, 220
Belsnickel, 119
belt, 29, 208
Bem, Daryl, 87
Ben MacDhui, 54, 185
Benzie County (Michigan), 116
Beowulf, 4
Bering land bridge, 65
Berks County (Pennsylvania), 12, 185
berry (see *fruit*)
Berry, Alan, 17, 61, 81, 95, 137, 138, 140, 149, 170, 181, 232
Berry, Steve, 166
Betelgeuse, 126
Bethlehem (Israel), 153
Bey, Ahmed, 185-186
BFRO (see *Bigfoot Field*

Researchers Organization)
Bhutan (see *Asia*)
Bible (see *Christianity*)
Bierce, Ambrose, 189
Big Ben, 161
Big Girl, 187-188
Big Indian Creek, 170
Big Red Eye/Old Red Eye, 5
Big Rock Campground, 181-182
Big Thicket, 52, 89
Bigfoot Discovery Museum, 48-49
Bigfoot Field Researchers Organization (BFRO), 44, 45, 47, 56, 57, 87, 94, 101, 164, 174, 222, 233, 257, 262
Bigfoot Tonight (podcast), 207
Bill Haley and the Comets, 219
bioluminescence, 2-3
bird (see also *owl*), 11, 42, 46-52, 54, 57, 84, 99, 128, 146, 147, 152, 153, 168, 169, 182, 235, 265
    blue jay, 42, 46
    catbird, 46
    chicken, 48, 52, 55, 98, 153, 272
    Cooper's hawk, 52
    crow, 48, 52
    duck, 64, 169
    finch, 52
    Gray-crowned babbler, 46
    hummingbird, 84, 265
    loon, 48
    lyrebird, 54
    ostrich, 146
    parrot, 41, 47-48
    partridge, 48
    ptarmigan, 53
    sparrow, 42
    swallow, 52
    toucan, 49
    turkey, 42, 48, 221
    woodpecker, 48

bird trap fetishes (see *devil nets*)
Birnam Wood, 120
Biscardi, Tom, 240-243
Bishop, Dave, 148
Bishop, Greg, 103-104
Bishopville (South Carolina), 116, 153
Bizarre Bigfoot Blog (website), 118, 139, 166
Black Eyed Kids, 215-218
black giant, 46
Black Mass (magic), 61
black widow spider, 11
Blair Witch Project, The (film), 125
Blanco, Antonio, 97
Bleibtreul (researcher), 206-207
Blessed Virgin Mary, 34, 84
Block Island (Rhode Island), 13
blood samples, 94, 201, 202, 213, 221, 222
blue jay (see *bird*)
Blue Mountains, 116-117, 204, 237
Bluff Creek (see also *Patterson-Gimlin Film)*, 222
Bolivia (see *South America*)
Boneyard, The, 19
Bord, Janet & Colin, 177
Bossburg (Washington), 137, 240
Box Elder County (Utah), 180
Boy Scouts, 206
Boyko, Vladimir P., 176
Bozo the Clown, 248
Bradley, Julie & Allen, 92
Bradshaw, Linda, 187-188
Bragança Paulista (Brazil), 176
Brandon, Jim, 63, 96, 146
Brazil (see *South America*)
Brer Rabbit, 228
Brian (witness), 221-222
Britain (see *England*)
British Columbia (see *Canada*)
British Natural History Museum, 11

Brittany (France), 4
Brooksville (Florida), 12
Brown, Albert, 123
Brown, Brian, 100
Brownie, 3,4
Brunamonti, Oddo, 186
Buddhism, 4, 82, 147, 153
Buenos Aires (Argentina), 34-35
Bugs (see *Hale, Ed*)
Buk'wus, 63, 147
bumblebee, 84
Burcaw, Joe, 167
Burnette, Lee, 186
Burnette, Tom, 45-46, 64, 89, 101, 186
Burns, Beverly, 208-209
Burton, Wayne, 19
bushman, 46
buzzing, 14, 34, 81-86, 264
BVM (see *Blessed Virgin Mary*)
Byhalia (Mississippi), 98
Byrne, Peter, 180

C

C Canyon, 257
California (see *United States*)
Cambodia (see *Asia*)
Campbell, J.F., 169
Campbell, Keri, 90
Canada, 84, 103, 123, 143, 149
    Alberta, 97, 170
    British Columbia, 84, 96, 143, 145, 261
    Manitoba, 142
    Newfoundland, 169-170
    Ontario, 50, 151
Candor (North Carolina), 173
canid/canine (see *dog*)
Cape Coral (Florida), 95

Cape Fear River, 142
car (see *automobile*)
Caracas (Venezuela), 28
Caribe State Forest, 34
Carmel (California), 209
carnelian stone, 265
Carpenter, Scott, 82-83
Carpenter's Knob, 151
Carr, Scott, 165
Cascade County (Montana), 15
Cascades (mountains), 81
cat (see also *Alien Black Cats*), 49, 98, 173, 209, 210
    cheetah, 177-178
    cougar, 43-44
    leopard, 42
    lion, 5
    panther, 98, 127
    snow leopard, 187
catbird (see *bird*)
Catches, Pete, 175
Catholicism (see *Christianity*)
Caucasus (see *Russia*)
Caufield, James, 84
Cedar City (Utah), 170
cedar tree, 17, 118, 123, 183
centaur, 81, 169
Central America
    Guatemala, 43
cephalopod (see *octopus*)
Chaffee County (Colorado), 150, 164
Charles II, 237
Charlie, Willie, 98
Charlotte Observer (publication), 151
Chatham County (North Carolina), 142
Chatham Township (New Jersey), 142
cheetah (see *cat*)
Chehalis (people), 98

Chelyabinsk Oblast (see *Russia*)
Cherokee (people), 62, 64, 98, 116
cherry tree, 119
Chesterfield (Idaho), 148
Cheyenne (people), 42, 147
Chicago (Illinois), 47
chicken (see *bird*)
Chihuahua (see *dog*)
Chile (see *South America*)
chimpanzee, 9, 46, 245
China (see *Asia*)
Chippewa (people), 235
Chiu, Law, 150
Choccolocco Monster, 238
Choctaw (people), 88
Christianity (see also *Jesus Christ*), 6, 31, 100, 128, 149, 153, 202, 232, 233, 236
Christ (see *Jesus Christ*)
Christmas, 119, 128,
Claire (witness), 209-211
Clallam (people), 46
Claremont (California), 12
Clark, Barry, 32-33
Clark, Jerome, 145, 146, 171, 172
Clelland, Mike, 50
cleromancy, 128
Cleveland County (North Carolina), 151
Clifton, Chas, 180
clinodactyly, 150, 151, 152
Clyde Beatty Circus (see *Beatty, Clyde*)
Clydebank (Scotland), 149
Co-Creation Hypothesis, 103-104
Coast to Coast AM, 88, 220, 267
Cochno Stone, 149
cockroach, 101
Cole Hollow Road, 141
Cole Hollow Road Monster (see *Cohomo*)
Cohomo, 141

Coleman, Loren, 144-145, 146, 239-244, 247
Collier, Wren, 61
colobus monkey, 140
Colorado (see *United States*)
communitas, 229, 230-231, 242-243, 248, 249
Congo (see *Africa*)
Connecticut (see *United States*)
contact calls, 43, 49, 51
Cooper's hawk (see *bird*)
Corona (California), 162, 231-232
Corrales, Scott, 35
Cottage Grove Reservoir, 262
Cottingley Fairy Photographs, 238
cougar (see *cat*)
Courtney, Stan, 42, 45, 48, 130
cow, 6, 44, 53, 54, 83, 146, 238, 257
cowbell (see *bell*)
Cowley (Louisiana), 168
Coy, Janice Carter, 183-184
Coye, Lee Brown, 125
coyote (see *dog*)
Coyote (trickster), 228
Crick, Francis, 80
cricket, 218
Cripplefoot tracks, 137, 240
crow (see *bird*)
Crownpoint (New Mexico), 180
Cryptomundo (website), 240, 241
Curtin (Oregon), 260
Curupira, 46
cyclops, 169
cypress bush, 43

D

Dahinden, Rene, 138, 145, 237
Dahl, Vladimir, 83
Daily Colonist (publication), 65

Daily Telegraph (publication), 186
Dalai Lama, 268
Daly, D., 148
Darkness Radio, 12
Dave (witness), 165-166
David (*Qur'an*), 51
David Lang disappearance, 189
Davies, Adam, 118-119
Davis Lake, 96
Davis, Richard, 94-95
Dead-Man's Hole, 219
deer, 1, 9, 17, 43, 57, 94, 97, 163, 174, 211, 256
Denmark (see *Scandinavia*)
DeNovo Journal, 202-203
Denton skull, 206-207
Denton, Robert W., 206-207
deoxyribonucleic acid (see *DNA*)
Derry Township (Pennsylvania), 8, 32, 207
devil nets, 125, 126
Devil's Creek, 57
Devil's Footprints, 182
Devon (England), 182
Dhinnabarrada, 153
didgeridoo, 82
Die Zauberflöte, 51-52
Diné (people), 42, 180, 185
djinn, 153
DMT (see *psychedelics*)
DNA, 80, 128, 202-204, 205, 221, 241, 243
Dodds, E.R., 51
dog, 3, 5, 6, 7, 8, 9, 13, 14, 15, 30, 31, 42, 44-46, 47, 48, 50, 54, 57-58, 99, 122, 130, 140, 144, 149, 151, 165, 177, 203, 205, 216, 217, 221, 262, 267
    beagle, 45
    Chihuahua, 58
    coyote, 42, 45, 56, 216
    fox, 184
    German shepherd, 6
    golden retriever, 50
    Newfoundland, 5
    wolf, 4, 45, 98, 121, 127, 182, 184
Dole Pineapple Company, 162
domovoy, 83
Dongo, Tom, 187
donkey, 44
Dosen, Cindy, 203, 204, 261
Dover, Daniel, 116
Doyle, Sir Arthur Conan, 238
Drudenfuss (see *elhaz rune*)
duck (see *bird*)
Dunn, Patrick, 62
Dunning, Brian, 246
Durham, Janis Heaphy, 164
Dutch (see *Netherlands*)
dwarf, 28, 169
Dyer, Rick, 240-244
Dyson Perrins Folio, 147

E

East Carbon (Utah), 255
Eberhart, George M., 145, 187
Ebu gogo, 42
Ed (witness), 28-29
Eight Dollar Mountain, 149
Einfæting, 169-170
Eirik the Red, 169
Eiríks saga rauða, 169
el Chupacabras, 153
elder futhark, 127
Elder Kamooh, 94
electronic voice phenomena (EVP), 63, 267, 268
elephant, 124
elhaz rune, 127
elk, 147, 164, 166, 260
Elkins Creek, 58

Enfield (Illinois), 186
Enfield Poltergeist, 238
England (see *United Kingdom*)
English Civil War, 237
entheogens (see *psychedelics*)
Escambia River, 64
Ethiopia (see *Africa*)
Europe (see also *Russia*), 38, 48, 50, 51, 59, 65, 97, 119, 121, 147, 149, 246
    Austria, 43, 137
    France, 4
    Germany, 61, 119, 124, 127, 173, 174
    Ireland, 4, 246
    Latvia, 63
    Lithuania, 5-6
    Mediterranean, 51
        Greece, 51, 62, 81, 169
        Israel, 153
        Italy, 95, 97, 186
        Judea, 236
    Moldavia, 136
    Netherlands, 53
    Romania, 50
    Scandinavia, 51, 119, 124, 127
        Denmark, 119, 124
        Norway, 3, 84, 119, 101, 123, 124, 127, 169, 230
    Scythia, 136
    Spain, 15, 59
    Switzerland, 53, 137
    United Kingdom, 121, 209
        England, 11, 27, 30, 120, 153, 154, 178, 182, 238
        Scotland, 4, 54, 99, 120, 149, 169, 185
Evarts (Kentucky), 150

EVP (see *electronic voice phenomena*)
Explorer (car; see *automobile*)
extraterrestrials, 26-39, 81, 83, 84, 86, 87, 89, 94, 104, 165, 167, 177, 179, 186, 190, 230, 231, 232, 255, 257, 259

F

Fachan, 169
faeries (see also *Brownie, domovoy, dwarf, Kelpie, Mondong, Nain, Norn,* ogre, *Orang buni, pixie led, pooka,* Puck, troll, *Yûñ'wi Tsunsdi'*), 3, 4, 11, 12, 47, 48, 51, 60, 62, 80, 81, 83, 84, 86, 89, 97, 104, 106, 119, 121, 124, 127, 131, 152, 153, 177, 179, 182, 185, 230, 238, 246, 268
Fahrenbach, W. Henner, 204
Fan (Congo), 124
Faroe Islands (Denmark), 124
Fate magazine (publication), 53
faun (see also *Pan, satyr*), 96, 153,
Fawn Grove (Pennsylvania), 7
Fay, James "Bobo," 16
FBI (see *Federal Bureau of Investigation*)
Federal Bureau of Investigation, 246
feifei, 185
feline (see *cat*)
finch (see *bird*)
Finding Bigfoot (television program), 2, 16
fir tree, 119, 124, 128
firearm, 8, 14, 15, 31, 49, 54, 57, 65, 82, 89, 100, 130, 213, 214, 215, 217, 220, 221, 222, 232, 246
    AK-47, 222

BB-gun, 34
shotgun, 6, 28, 172, 217
pistol, 7, 94
revolver, 95
rifle, 8, 30, 65, 117, 171, 212, 219, 265
fish, 2, 8, 11, 13, 28, 33, 35, 41, 53, 57, 85, 96, 99, 125, 216, 235, 264, 265
    flatfish, 41
    lionfish, 41
    minnow, 168
    salmon, 57
    sole, 41
Fisher, Rick, 163
Fitiev, Sasha, 92
flatfish (see *fish*)
Flores (Indonesia), 42
Flores, Delia, 34
Florida (see *United States*)
Fluorescent Freddie, 6, 117
fly, 84
fly agaric (see *Amanita muscaria*)
flying saucer (see *UFOs*)
Foothill Monster (see *Corona (California)*)
Fort Bidwell (California), 173
Forth, Gregory, 97
Fouke (Arkansas), 143
Fouke Monster, 143
Four Corners, 152
fox (see *dog*)
France (see *Europe*)
Frank, Otis, 42
Franzoni, Henry James, 88, 139
Freeman, Paul, 180, 204, 237-238
French Lick (Indiana), 6, 117
Fresno (California), 5
Fresno County (California), 85
frog, 4, 44, 84, 146, 218
fruit, 55, 92
    apple, 92, 95, 172

    berry, 5
    pineapple, 162
Fulton, Charles, 7
Fusch, Ed, 83

G

Gage (witness), 104-105
Galveston (Indiana), 33
Garden Grove (California), 34
Garrett, Bob, 116, 218
Gary (Man-in-Plaid; see *Bear/Gary*)
Genonsgwa/Genoskwa, 116 147
Geof (witness), 122
Georgia (see *United States*)
Georgia Bigfoot Hoax (see *Dyer, Rick*)
German Shepherd (see *dog*)
Germany (see *Europe*)
Germer, Wes (see also *Sasquatch Chronicles*), 17, 52, 53, 58, 98, 178, 187, 215
Gessner, Conrad, 137
ghillie suit, 101
giant ground sloth (see *Megatherium*)
gibbon, 140
Gibsonia (Pennsylvania), 141
Gigantopithecus blacki, 64, 184
Gilbert, Dallas, 19
Gill, Sam, 147
Gilroy (California), 177
Gimlin, Robert "Bob," 130, 222, 223, 239
Glacier National Park, 211
glossolalia, 61
Glue-keek, 83
Goat, 44, 62
golden retriever (see *dog*)
Gordon, Stan, 6, 27, 32, 140, 175,

177, 179, 181, 204-205, 207-208, 263
gorilla, 2, 27, 28, 105, 123, 128, 131, 143, 150, 166, 171, 214, 223, 245
Graham, D. Douglas, 53
Grand Junction (Colorado), 100
Grants Pass (Oregon), 148
grasshopper, 3
Graves, Robert, 81
Gray-crowned babbler (see *bird*)
Greece (see *Mediterranean*)
green bigfoot, 6, 117
Green Man (see also *Wodwose*), 116, 125, 228, 235
Green Mountain Falls (Colorado), 180
Green Mountain Trail, 163
Green, John, 27, 137-138
Greensburg (Pennsylvania), 30
Greenwater (Washington), 65
Gregory, L.H., 167
Grendel (character), 4
Gross, Hanns, 43, 49
Gross, Harvey, 44
Guaraní (people), 46
Guatemala (see *Central America*)
Guffey (Pennsylvania), 14
Guiley, Rosemary Ellen, 61, 153, 189
Gul, 83
gumbo tree, 7
gun (see *firearm*)
gunas, 153
Guttilla, Peter, 151
Gwich'in (people), 46

H

Hackney (England), 153

Hagenbeck-Wallace Circus, 219-220
Hahn Air Force Base, 173
Hairy Biped, 145-146
Hale, Ed, 220
Hall, Mark A., 149, 247
Hanawiywiy, 169
Hancock, Graham, 79
Hanna, Jon, 81
Hanover (Maryland), 9
Hansen, Frank (see *Minnesota Iceman*)
Hansen, George P., 51, 228-229, 231-235, 239, 242, 244, 248, 249, 250
Hantu sikai, 46
Harford County (Maryland), 14
Harpur, Patrick, 37, 38, 236, 273
Harris, Brenda, 42
Harrison (British Columbia), 84
Harrison, Edgar, 31
Harry & the Hendersons (film), 138
Harvey (film), 246
Haverigg Beach (England), 27
Hawaii (see *United States*)
HB (see *Hairy Biped*)
Healy, Susan, 59
Hebrew (see *Judaism*)
Heindel, Ned D., 122
Heironimous, Bob, 223
Henkins, Dawn, 56
Heracles, 136
Herodotus, 136
Hertel, Lasse, 58
Hesperia (California), 148
Heuvelmans, Bernard, 244-249
Hexenkopf Rock, 122
Hill, Betty, 165
Hillsboro (Oregon), 104
Hilsmeier family, 179
Himalayas (mountains), 53
Hinduism, 4, 98, 153

hobo, 129-131
Holland, Ranae, 16
Hominidae Enigma Program, 261
Homo ferus, 137
Honey Island Swamp Monster, 116, 141
Hong Kong (see *Asia*)
Honobia (Oklahoma), 58
Hoopa/Hupa (people), 64, 99, 118, 176
Hoover, J. Edgar, 246
horse, 3, 4, 7, 16, 42, 44, 52, 62, 99, 122, 142, 146, 187, 269
Houghton, Bob, 162
Howard, Pat, 31
Huffpost (website), 243
Huildad (Chile), 10
Humboldt County (California), 239
hummingbird (see *bird*)
Huntington, Roger & Sheila, 148-149
Huse, Doug, 54
hussar monkey (see *patas monkey*)
hydrogen sulfide, 85
Hyogo Prefecture (Japan), 178
hypnosis (see also *meditation*), 83-86, 91, 95, 102, 104, 152

I

iboga (see *psychedelics*)
Idaho (see *United States*)
ignis fatuus (see *lights*)
Iktomi, 235
Illinois (see *United States*)
in-line gait, 166-167, 182
Inda'cinga, 48
India (see *Asia*)
Indiana (see *United States*)
Indonesia (see *Asia*)
infrasound, 43, 81-83, 235-236

Inker (guide), 118
Iowa (see *United States*)
Iran/Persia (see *Asia*)
Ireland (see *Europe*)
Israel (see *Mediterranean*)
Italy (see *Mediterranean*)

J

Jack (witness), 214-215
Jack Frost, 234
Jack-o-Lantern, 3
Jackson, Al, 123
Jackson Demonstration State Forest, 65
Jacobs, David, 94
Janson, H.W., 52
Japan (see *Asia*)
Jasper County (Texas), 56
Jeff (witness), 11
Jeffries, Anne, 84
jellyfish, 37, 41, 267
Jephcott, Sydney, 147
Jeremy (witness), 9-10, 12, 15
Jersey Devil, 182
Jesus Christ (see also *Christianity*), 153, 236
Jevning, William, 207, 215
Jicarilla (people), 189
Jimmy B. (witness), 17
Johnson, Jude, 266
Johnson, Larry, 44
Johnson, Lewis, 18
Johnson, Matthew, 119
Johnson, Ron, 255-259
Johnson, Tobe, 203, 204, 260-270
Johnson, Warren, 18
Jones, Kevin, 116-117
Jordan, Robert, 86
Journey to the West, The, 4
Judaism, 62, 64, 153

Judea (see *Mediterranean*)
Jumping Frenchman Syndrome, 60
Jung, Carl, 36-37, 228-229

K

Kachuba, John B., 98
Kaiser, George, 29, 148
Kamchatka (see *Russia*)
Kamilaroi (people; see *Aborigines*)
Kamoss, 99
kangaroo, 90, 152, 182, 186, 187
Kangaroo Man, 187
Kankakee (Illinois), 28
Kansas (see *United States*)
Karlsefni, 169-170
Kasa-obake, 169
Keel, John, 11, 20, 53, 57, 150, 165, 218, 248
Kelley, Laura, 59
Kelpie, 99
Kelso (Washington), 167
Kemerovo (see *Russia*)
Ken R. (researcher), 205
Kennedy, Lynda, 91
Kensinger, Kenneth, 80
Kentucky (see *United States*)
ketamine (see *psychedelics*)
Ketchum, Melba, 202-203, 205, 221
Kheyak, 83
Kindell, Vanessa, 129
King of the Forest, 119
Kirk, John, 87
Kirlin, R.L., 58
Klamath (people), 48
Klamath River, 48, 82
Klawock Lake/Mountain, 123
klipspringer, 187
Knapp, George, 267-268
Knobby, 151
koala, 59

Kodama, 124
Kolchak: The Night Stalker (television program), 98
Kootenai (people), 98
Korean War, 249
Koyulhisar (Turkey), 185
Krantz, Grover, 45, 180, 237
Krashnikov, Yuri, 54
Kruglyak, Leonid, 202-203
Kulls, Steve, 240-243
Kushtakaa, 98
Kutchin (see *Gwich'in*)
Kwakiutl (people), 63, 147
Kyrgyzstan (see *Asia*)

L

L'Heureuse, Guy, 170
ladybug, 11
Lae ho'a, 42
lake monster, 99
Lake Mungo, 168
Lake Pairon, 54
Lakota Sioux (people), 129
Language of the Birds (magic), 51-52
Lapseritis, Jack "Kewaunee," 94, 138, 235
Latrobe (Pennsylvania), 14
Latvia (see *Europe*)
Laughery, Bill, 204
laughter, 49, 53, 61, 63
laurel, 212
law enforcement (see *police*)
Leach, Edmund, 229-230
Ledford Hollow (Kentucky), 149
Leischi (see *Leshy*)
lemur, 2
Lenape (people), 122
leopard (see *cat*)
Leshy, 46-47, 121

Lesnik/Lesovik/Lesovoi (see *Leshy*)
Levittown (Pennsylvania), 90
Lewisberry (Pennsylvania), 17
lights (anomalous; see also *UFOs*), 1-40, 50, 51, 55, 84, 97, 99, 101, 102, 104, 117, 119, 122, 124, 127, 142, 148, 150, 175, 188, 236, 256, 259, 262, 267,
Lilith, 50, 153
limestone, 31
liminality, 51, 60, 229-231, 234, 235, 236, 239, 242, 248
Linnaeus, 137
lion (see *cat*)
lionfish (see *fish*)
Lister, Lew, 97
Litchfield Hills (Connecticut), 167
lithoboly (check stone throwing!), 6, 14, 19, 52, 55, 86, 91, 149, 167, 217
Lithuania (see *Europe*)
little owl (see *owl*)
Littlerock (California), 216
Lizardman, 116, 153
locomotive, 53, 54, 130-131
Loki, 228, 230
London (Oregon), 262
London Trackway, 262
Lookout Mountain (Georgia), 5
loon (see *bird*)
Lord of the Rings trilogy, 120
Los Angeles (California), 51, 206, 219
Los Angeles Times (publication), 219
Losa, Hector R., 34-35
Lossiah, Lynn King, 62-63
Lou Gehrig's disease (see *amyotrophic lateral sclerosis*)
Louisiana (Missouri), 4, 31, 144
Louisiana (see *United States*)
Lovecraft, H.P., 125, 178
Loyalhanna Creek,

LSD (see *psychedelics*), 8
Lugar Penamoa (Spain), 15
lumberjack, 60, 210
Lummi (people), 90
lyrebird (see *bird*)
lysergic acid diethylamide (LSD; see *psychedelics*)

M

macaque, 139
Macbeth, 120
Mack, John, 84, 190
MacLeod, Susan, 50-51
Macropodidae (see *kangaroo*)
Madison (New Jersey), 12
magic mushrooms (see *psilocybin*)
magical practice, 38, 51, 61-62, 120-129, 128, 185, 237
Magonia, 37
Magraner, Jodi, 59
Maine (see *United States*)
Malaysia (see *Asia*)
Mammoth (California), 206
Mamu, 98-99
Man-in-Plaid (see *Bear/Gary*)
Mangano, Jim, 86-87, 89
Manitoba (see *Canada*)
Manley, Paul, 100
Mann Brook (New York), 125
Mapinguary, 116, 152
Marian apparitions (see *Blessed Virgin Mary*)
Marinelli, Mark, 56
Marshall, Clifford, 176
Martin, Jeff, 33
Martinez, Emelino, 28
Marut, 124
Marx, Ivan, 240
Maryland (see *United States*)
Marzolf Hill, 31, 144

Masias, Dan, 180
Mason County (Kentucky), 7
Materialism, 38, 80, 88, 106, 146, 233
Matlacihua, 169
Maxemista, 147
Mayor, Adrienne, 136
McChesneytown (Pennsylvania), 141
McDaniel, Henry, 186
McIntyre, Willard, 14
McKelvy, Tom, 162
McKenna, Terence, 80
McMinnville (Oregon), 267
McTaggart, Lynne, 87
McWhorter, L.V., 169
meditation (see also *hypnosis*), 50, 79, 86, 89
Mediterranean (see *Europe*)
Megatherium, 152
Meighan, Clement, 206
Meldrum, Jeffrey, 137, 166, 167, 172, 175, 180, 201, 237-238, 241, 243
Melkoy, 91
Men in Black (MIB), 209, 211
Mencken, F. Carson, 232
Merola, Chris, 174-175
Metlow, Joe, 240
Mexico, 42, 169
Mi'kmaq (people), 50
Miami (Florida), 90
MIB (see *Men in Black*)
Michigan (see *United States*)
Middle East (see *Africa*)
Middlebrook (Virginia), 13
Migoi (see *Yeti*)
Mike (researcher), 130
Milazzo (Italy), 97
Miller, Carl, 28
Millrace Park (Indiana), 117
Milne, Linda, 30

Milner, Robert, 81
mindspeak (see *telepathy*)
Mineral Point (Pennsylvania), 30
Minnesota (see *United States*)
Minnesota Iceman, 220, 244-250
minnow (see *fish*)
Misaabe, 99-100
Mississippi (see *United States*)
Mississippi River, 58, 143
Missouri (see *United States*)
Möbius strip, 38
Modoc (people), 46
Mojave Desert, 161
Moldavia (see *Europe*)
Momo, 4, 31-32, 55, 143-144
Mondong, 185
Moneymaker, Matt, 55, 243
Mongolia (see *Asia*)
monkey, 8, 28, 48, 49, 98, 140, 145, 146, 147, 148, 177, 186, 223
Monkey Man, 186
Mono County (California), 174
Monongahela (Pennsylvania), 6, 141, 204
monopods, 169-170
Montana (see *United States*)
Montana Santa (Puerto Rico), 34
Moody, Raymond, 87
Moon, Henry, 46
Morehead, Ron, 17, 44, 53, 59, 61, 90,
Morris County (New Jersey), 142
Moscow (Russia), 90
moth, 101
Mount Adams, 207
Mount Rokko, 178
Mount Vernon (Illinois), 185
mouse, 18
Mozart, Wolfgang Amadeus, 51
Mt. Hood (Oregon), 91
Mt. St. Helens (Oregon), 167
Muckleshoot (people), 235

Mullis, Kary, 80
Murphy's Law, 252
Murray, John, 96
Museum of the Weird, 247

N

N, N- dimethyltryptamine (see *DMT*)
Nage (people), 42
Nain, 4
Nakani, 83
Napes, 187
Napier, John, 137, 146
National Enquirer (publication), 241, 243
National Geographic (publication), 168
Natural Bridge State Park, 162
Navajo (people; see *Diné*)
Navajo Times (publication), 42
NAWAC (see *North American Wood Ape Conservancy*)
Neanderthal, 59, 128-129
Nebraska (see *United States*)
Ned (witness), 129
Nelson, Scott, 61, 64
Nepal (see *Asia*)
Nesna, 169
Netherlands (see *Europe*)
Nevada City (California), 44
New Canton (Illinois), 31
New Jersey (see *United States*)
New Mexico (see *United States*)
New York (see *United States*)
New York City (New York), 249
Newcastle (England), 178
Newfield (Pennsylvania), 173
Newfoundland (see *Canada*)
Newfoundland (dog; see *dog*)
Newkirk, Greg & Dana, 19-20

Newputz, 170
Ngoi rung, 52
Niagiusar, 124
Noah, 153
Noël, Christopher, 43, 57, 126
Noll, Richard, 164
Norg, 119
Norn, 127
North America (see also *Canada, Central America, Mexico, & United States*), 9, 38, 42, 64, 65, 140, 146, 147, 149, 169, 170, 177, 187, 206
North American Apes (see *Napes*)
North American Wood Ape Conservancy, 100, 233, 234
North Carolina (see *United States*)
North Huntingdon Township (Pennsylvania), 181
Norway (see *Scandinavia*)
Noxie (Oklahoma), 186
Nun'yunu'wi, 98, 116
Nunnelly, Barton, 139-140, 162, 171, 188
Nyalmo, 147
Nyarlathotep, 178

O

O'Hara-Epperly, Colleen, 181
O'Neal, Shaquille, 213
Occam's Razor, 166
Ocean Shores (Washington), 261
Ochopee (Florida), 215
octopus, 41, 81
Odin, 127
Oester, Dave & Sharon, 91
Oglala Lakota (people), 175
ogre, 4, 119
Ohio (see *United States*)
Ojibwe (people), 99-100
Oklahoma (see *United States*)

Old Red Eye/Big Red Eye, 5
Olympic Project, 221
Ontario (see *Canada*)
Orang Buni, 63
orangutans, 27, 41
Oregon (see *United States*)
Oregon Bigfoot Group, 98
Oregonian (publication), 167
Orion, 126
ostrich (see *bird*)
Otto, Rudolph, 235
Ottosen (Iowa), 56
Ouachita National Forest, 92
overtone singing, 81-82
Owens, Zollie, 64
owl (see also *bird*), 9, 42, 48-52, 56, 104, 119
Owl Moon Altar, 269
Owl Moon Lab, 263-269
Owl Moon Prints, 203, 260-263, 269
Oxford (England), 30, 57, 203, 221

P

Padilla, Anthony, 97
Paiute (people), 46
Palmdale (California), 95, 150
Palo Santo incense, 265
Pamir Mountains (Kyrgyzstan), 15
Pan (see also *satyr, faun*), 81, 95-96
panther (see *cat*)
Papageno (character), 51
Paris (Texas), 167
parrot (see *bird*)
partridge (see *bird*)
Pasulka, Diana Walsh, 202
patas monkey, 177
Patasola, 169
Patterson-Gimlin film, 130, 222-223, 239

Patterson, Roger, 130, 222-223, 239
Patterson, T.W., 65
Paulides, David, 43, 64, 99, 138, 176
Pearson, Clara, 88
Peeler, Tim, 151
Pennsylvania (see *United States*)
Pennsylvania Bigfoot Society, 163
Pennsylvania Dutch, 43, 90, 119
Pennsylvania German (see *Pennsylvania Dutch*)
Penrod, Clyde, 32
Pentecostal church (see *Christianity*)
Peoria (Illinois), 141
Perchta, 122
Perseus, 136
Persia/Iran (see *Asia*)
Peru (see *South America*)
Peterson, Harley, 170
peyote (see *psychedelics*)
Philip Experiment, 236-237
Phillip (witness), 27
Physicalism (see *Materialism*)
Piaui (Brazil), 9
Pierce County (Washington), 84
pig, 145, 148, 242,
Pike County (Georgia), 58
Pilichis, Dennis, 142-143, 180
pineapple (see *fruit*)
pistol (see *firearm*)
pixie led, 63
Planet of the Apes (film), 223
Point Isabel (Ohio), 97
Point Pleasant (West Virginia), 182
police, 35, 54-55, 58, 117, 125, 141, 145, 148, 172, 179, 180, 186, 189, 208, 209-210, 214-215, 219, 232, 240, 242, 243
poltergeist, 60, 164, 238, 262, 269
Ponce (Puerto Rico), 91
pony, 42
pooka, 246
poplar tree, 184

Poplar River (Manitoba), 141
porcupine, 53
Port Charlotte (Florida), 173
Porteous, Alexander, 48, 63, 174
Powell, Thom, 140, 184, 233
presentiment (see *psi phenomena*)
Presque Isle (Pennsylvania), 150
Price (Utah), 257
Prince of Wales Island (Alaska), 123
Procyon, 126
Prometheus, 233
pronghorn antelope, 177
Prost (researcher), 206-207
Protestantism (see *Christianity*)
Provid, Katie, 11
psi phenomena, 80, 87-88, 102-103, 105, 250
    presentiment, 87, 165
    psychic, 14, 36, 89, 90, 233, 237, 262, 267-268
    telepathy, 19, 86-95, 165, 257, 258
psilocybin (see *psychedelics*)
psychedelics, 79-81, 83, 85
    Amanita muscaria, 79, 81
    ayahuasca, 79, 80
    DMT, 81
    iboga, 79
    ketamine, 81
    LSD, 80
    peyote, 79
    psilocybin, 79, 80, 81
psychic (see *psi phenomena*)
ptarmigan (see *bird*)
Puck, 228
Puerto Rico (see *United States*)
Puget Sound, 83
Puzzo, Thomas, 34
Pyle, Robert Michael, 81

Q

Quay, Ray, 148
Quetronamun, 169
Quinault (people), 83
Qur'an, 51

R

rabbit, 44, 162, 166, 265
raccoon, 42
Radin, Dean, 87
Rain, Bianca Ester Cardenas, 10
rakshasa, 4, 98
Randall (witness), 12
Randles, Derek, 221
Raudive, Konstantin, 63
Ravenna (Nebraska), 6
Raymond (Washington), 57
Reading Times (publication), 187
Red Cap Creek, 148
Redfern, Nick, 42, 56
Reece, Gregory L., 167
Renner, Timothy, 82, 165
Rennie, James Alan, 143
revolver (see *firearm*)
Reynard the Fox, 228
rhinoceros, 152
Rhode Island (see *United States*)
Ridge, Gerald K., 206
rifle (see *firearm*)
Riggs, Rob, 45-46, 52, 84, 88, 89, 101
Ripley, Dillon, 246
Rising Sun (Indiana)
river monster (see *lake monster*)
River Road, 31
Roachdale (Indiana), 171-172, 175
Robbins, Freddie, 144
Rockaway Township (New Jersey),

142
Roger, Lou & Keith, 171-172
Rolfing, Charles, 29
Romania (see *Europe*)
Rome (Italy), 95,
Rome (Ohio), 7, 142, 146, 179
rooster (see *chicken*)
Rooster Rock State Park, 91
Rosales, Albert, 102
Roth (zoologist), 140
Roy (witness), 188
Roy, Max, 262
Rugaard (Denmark), 124
Rugg, Mike, 48
Ruppelt, Edward J., 36
rusalka, 235
Russell (Pennsylvania), 5
Russia, 42, 53, 64, 83, 89-90, 92, 119, 121, 153, 167, 176, 185, 186, 235, 241
    Caucasus, 90
    Chelyabinsk Oblast, 176
    Kamchatka, 245
    Kemerovo, 167
    Siberia, 64, 82, 83, 245, 247

S

S'cwene'y'ti, 83
Saci, 169
Saga Magazine (publication), 245, 249
Saint-Hilaire, M.H. & J.M., 60
Salem (Ohio), 173
Salish (people), 83
salmon (see *fish*)
Salt Lake City (Utah), 255
Salzburg (Austria), 137
Sam Houston National Forest, 9
Samkhya (see *Hinduism*)
Samurai chatter (see also *Sierra Sounds*), 60-66
San Diego County (California), 54, 219
San Juan (Puerto Rico), 13
San Juan National Forest, 44-45
San Lorenzo River, 43
Sanderson, Ivan T., 244, 246-249
Sandy Hook (Kentucky), 101
Santa Lucia del Mela (Italy), 97
Sarjeant, William, 136
Sartori, Penny, 87
Sasquatch Chronicles (podcast; see also *Germer, Wes*), 9, 17, 129, 215, 273,
Sasquatch Genome Project, 202, 205
Satan, 153
Satus Pass (Washington), 100
satyr (see also *Pan, faun*), 62, 81, 96, 121, 153
Sawin, Brenton, 85
Scandinavia (see *Europe*)
Scheggia e Pascelupo (Italy), 186
Schiller Woods, 47
Schneck, Robert, 138
scops owl (see *owl*)
Scotland (see *United Kingdom*)
Scott, Dave, 96-97
Scout Mountain, 181
Scranton (Pennsylvania), 5
Scythia (see *Asia* and *Europe*)
sea snake, 41
Seattle (Washington), 103
Sedona (Arizona), 187
Seeahtik, 46, 83,
Sehlatik, 81
Senagambia (see *Africa*)
Seneca (people), 116, 147
Shaanxi province (China), 42
Shade family, 31-32
Shade, Louis, 31-32
shadow people, 50-51, 92, 142,

175-178
Shakespeare, William, 120
shape shifting, 60, 65, 90, 95-102, 116-117, 142, 169
Shawano (Wisconsin), 65
Shealy, Dan, 215
Shedim, 153
Sheehan, W.J., 96
sheep, 54
Sheldrake, Rupert, 87
Shenandoah (Virginia), 13
Sherman, Jim, 44
Sherry, Sam, 8
Shiel, Lisa, 16, 127, 128, 269
Shikk, 169
Shingkyong, 147
shingleback lizard, 41
Short, Bobbie, 46, 83, 139
shotgun (see *firearm*)
siamang, 140
Siberia (see *Russia*)
Sierra Camp, 17-19, 53, 58
Sierra Mountains, 220
Sierra Nevada Mountains, 17
Sierra Sounds, 17, 61, 63
Sigurdson, Kirk, 87
Simpson, Frank, 91
Singer, Clay, 207
Sioux (people), 48, 129, 235
Sirius, 126
Sisemite, 43
Siskiyou Wilderness, 176
Site 7 (Seven), 11, 12
Skamania County (Washington), 47
Skeptoid (podcast), 246
Skidaway Island State Park, 44
skinwalker, 98
Skinwalker Ranch, 182
skunk, 47, 137, 211
slalocum, 98
Slate, Ann, 137, 138, 140, 149, 181, 232

Sleepy Hollow (Pennsylvania), 8
sloth, 101, 116, 152
Smarr, Jack, 101
Smeja, Justin, 220-221
Smith, Darrell, 255-256, 259
Smithsonian Institution, 151, 206, 219, 220, 246
Smolenko, 174
snake, 41, 99, 146, 265
Snohomish County (Washington), 164
snow leopard (see *cat*)
Snow Mountain (California), 5
Snowy Mountains (Australia), 46
sole (see *fish*)
Somerset Hills (New Jersey), 142
Soucie, David, 28
South America, 38, 46, 53, 65, 116, 140, 147, 149, 169
    Argentina, 34-35
    Bolivia, 169
    Brazil, 9, 169, 176
    Chile, 10, 177
    Peru, 152
    Venezuela, 28
South Carolina (see *United States*)
Spain (see *Europe*)
Spanish (language), 64
Sparks, Cliff, 6
sparrow (see *bird*)
Spencer, Philip, 162
Spenser, Edmund, 62
Spignesi, Stephen J., 235
Spink, Jim, 7
Spottsville (Kentucky), 162, 171, 188
Spottsville Monster, 162, 171, 188
spruce tree, 117
St. Francis, 235
Ste-ye-hah'mah, 169
Stevenson, Ian, 87
Stewart, Jimmy, 246

Stewart, Kirk, 175-176
Stick Indians, 83, 235
stick structures, 120-122, 124-131, 166, 265, 269
Stikine River, 44
Stillwell (Oklahoma), 55
Stone Coat/Giant (see *Nun'yunu'wi/Genoskwa*)
Stone, Andrew, Hilda, & Michael, 215-218
Stonke, Madesta, 5-6
Stover, Steve, 14-15
Strain, Bob, 100
Strange Familiars (podcast), 9, 82, 165
Strassman, Rick, 80-81
strigoi, 50
Stroud, Les, 89, 118, 123
succubus, 153
Suddarth, Bill, 32, 144
Suleiman/Solomon (*Qur'an*), 51
Sullivan, Brian "Duke," 116
Sullivan, Irene, 147
Summerlin, Wes, 204
SunBôw True Brother, 94
Superior Mobile Home Court, 207-208
Survivorman – Bigfoot (television program), 118
swallow (see *bird*)
Swatara Gap, 185
Sweden Valley (Pennsylvania), 63
Switzerland (see *Europe*)
Sydney (Australia), 105
Sykes, Brian, 203, 221
Sykesville (Maryland), 14
Sykesville Monster, 14
Sylla, 62
syndactyly, 140, 151-152

T

Tabasco (Mexico), 42
Table Rock Lake, 163
Tailem Bend (Australia), 13
Tajikistan (see *Asia*)
Taliesin, 120
tapetum lucidum, 1-2
Tarrant, Doug, 219
Taylor, Ashley P., 47
Taylor, Scott, 261
Taylor, Troy, 144, 246
Tazewell County (Virginia), 211
Teagle, Jeffrey, 181, 183
Teague, Johnny Ray, 238
Teale, Sarah, 101
telepathy (see *psi phenomena*)
Tenacious D in the Pick of Destiny (film), 52
Tennessee (see *United States*)
Tenney, John E.L., 136
Texas (see *United States*)
Thompson, David, 149
Thompson, Lucy, 48
Thorvald, 169
Three Jewels, 153
Thunder (giant), 88
Thurston (Oregon), 262
Tibet (see *Asia*)
Till Eulenspiegel, 228
Tillamook (people), 88
Titmus, Bob, 239
Tlingit (people), 98
Toad Road, 117
Tolkien, J.R.R., 120
Tonight Show (television program), 246
Tooth Fairy, 234, 244
torn-up camp, 218-219
Toronto Star (publication), 98
toucan (see *bird*)

toys, 172, 264
Trafford (Pennsylvania), 14, 175
train (see *locomotive*)
trance (see *hypnosis*)
Traveling Museum of the Paranormal and the Occult, 19
Traverse City (Michigan), 174
Traverspine (British Columbia), 143
Traverspine Gorilla, 143
Travis (witness), 211
Trent (Pennsylvania), 30
Trinity (see *Christianity*)
Trinity River, 176
troll, 115, 230
truck (see *automobile*)
True Detective (television series), 125
true giants, 149
Tsiatko, 83
Turbo Bachan (see *Turbo-Granny*)
Turbo-Granny, 177-178
Turiella, Beatriz, 175
Turkey (see *Asia*)
turkey (see *bird*)
Turner River Swamp, 215
Tutosel/Tut-ursel, 48
Tuvan throat singing, 82
Twin Peaks (television program), 49
Tyras River, 136

U

UFOs (see also *lights (anomalous)*), 20, 26-40, 50, 51, 53, 55, 57, 83, 84, 87, 99, 101, 103, 104, 127, 136, 138, 141, 142, 145, 146, 150, 153, 165, 177, 178, 181, 185, 187, 190, 201, 202, 204, 208, 209, 230, 231, 232, 233, 234, 238, 250, 267, 269
unicorn, 234
Unidentified Flying Object (see *UFOs*)
United Kingdom (see *Europe*)
United States, 3, 13, 130, 137, 144, 145, 151, 182, 209, 232, 239, 248
    Alabama, 181, 238
    Alaska, 44, 123
    Arizona, 187, 245,
    Arkansas, 52, 143
    California, 5, 12, 28, 34, 43, 44, 48, 51, 64, 65, 85, 86, 92, 95, 99, 118, 138, 148, 150, 161, 162, 173, 174, 175, 176, 177, 181, 206, 209, 216, 219, 220, 222, 231, 232, 239
    Colorado, 44, 84, 100, 123, 150, 163, 164, 174, 180, 184
    Connecticut, 167
    Maryland, 140
    Florida, 6, 7, 12, 64, 90, 95, 126, 140, 173, 215
    Georgia, 5, 44, 58, 240, 241, 242, 243
    Hawaii, 162
    Idaho, 53, 137, 148, 181, 184, 201
    Illinois, 28, 31, 42, 45, 47, 130, 141, 185, 186
    Indiana, 6, 29, 33, 117, 148, 171
    Iowa, 56
    Kansas, 57
    Kentucky, 7, 101, 145, 149, 150, 153, 162, 171
    Louisiana, 116, 141, 168, 174
    Maine, 60, 117
    Maryland, 9, 14, 140
    Michigan, 43, 44, 56, 61, 97, 116, 127, 174, 269
    Minnesota, 56, 245

Mississippi, 98, 140
Missouri, 4, 31, 44, 45, 55, 143, 163
Montana, 15, 116, 211
Nebraska, 6
New Jersey, 5, 12, 142
New Mexico, 56, 80, 141, 180
New York, 6, 92, 125, 148, 203, 249
North Carolina, 45, 47, 57, 142, 151, 173, 186
Ohio, 7, 44, 94, 97, 142, 146, 148, 170, 173, 179, 204, 208, 209, 221
Oklahoma, 49, 55, 58, 85, 92, 186
Oregon, 5, 16, 91, 92, 104, 140, 148, 187, 260, 262, 267
Pennsylvania, 5, 6, 7, 8, 11, 12, 14, 15, 17, 30, 32, 63, 90, 91, 96, 117, 119, 122, 123, 126, 140, 141, 145, 150, 163, 172, 173, 175, 177, 179, 181, 185, 187, 204, 207, 209
Puerto Rico, 13, 34, 91, 153
Rhode Island, 13
South Carolina, 116, 153
Tennessee, 89, 93, 181
Texas, 9, 12, 15, 43, 47, 52, 56, 64, 89, 101, 127, 163, 167, 218, 247, 269
Utah, 91, 170, 180, 182, 255-259
Virginia, 13, 47, 57, 211
Washington, 17, 29, 47, 57, 65, 84, 85, 90, 100, 101, 103, 117, 137, 164, 204, 207, 235, 240, 261, 269
West Virginia, 19
Wisconsin, 49, 65, 244,
United States Air Force, 36, 249
United States Bureau of Customs, 209
United States Department of Agriculture, 209
United States Department of Health, Education, and Welfare, 209
United States Department of the Interior, 209
United States Navy, 61
Urglaawe, 122
Urland, Jim, 188-189
Ursula (see also *Tutosel/Tut-ursel*)
Utah (see *United States*)

##

Valley (Alabama), 181, 183
van (see *automobile*)
van Lommel, Pim, 87
van Manen, Johan, 53
Venezuela (see *South America*)
Ventura County (California), 206
Vertex Correlation, The (film), 126
Vietnam War, 7, 249
Viking (people), 169
Villasana, Jorge, 177
Vilnius (Lithuania), 6
Virgil, 95
Virginia (see *United States*)
vocal cords, 59
Vogel, Bill, 29

##

wadi monkey (see *patas monkey*)
Wagner, Karl Edward, 125
Wallace, Ray, 239, 240

Wanchun, Yang, 42
Wantage Canal, 30
Warren, Lorraine, 93-94
Washington (see *United States*)
Washo (people), 169
water-horse (see *Kelpie*)
Wayne National Forest, 44
Webb (researcher), 168
Weird Tales (publication), 125
Welsh Mountain (Pennsylvania), 12
Wendigo (see *Windigo*)
West Virginia (see *United States*)
Westring, Helen, 245
Where Did the Road Go? (podcast), 20, 178
White, Gordon, 105
Whitehall (New York), 6
Whitney (Ohio), 94
Whitton, Joel, 236
Whitton, Matt, 240-243
Wild Hunt, 48, 122, 124
Will-o-the-Wisps (see *lights*)
Williams Township (Pennsylvania), 122
Williamson, Neal, 238
Williamson, Robin, 120
Willis, Connie, 88
Willow Creek, 92
Wilson, Dave, 162
Windigo, 143
Winnipeg (Ontario), 151
Winter Triangle, 125
Wisconsin (see *United States*)
witch, 12, 13, 50, 51, 60, 61, 83, 86, 97, 115, 120, 122, 125, 128, 129, 152, 153, 177, 179, 232
witch's foot (see *elhaz rune*)
Wodwose, 116
wolf (see *dog*)
Wood-wife, 124
woodpecker (see *bird*)
Woodwose (see *Wodwose*)

woolly spider monkey, 140
Worley, Don, 101
Wrangell (Alaska), 44

Y

Yacolt (Washington), 17
Yagmort, 42, 53
Yah-yahaa, 46
Yahoo (see *yowie*)
Yakama (people), 29, 81
Yakima (people; see *Yakama*)
Yakima (Washington), 103
Yakima Reservation (Washington), 29
Yayaya-ash, 169
Yeti, 7, 102-103, 166, 167, 178, 185, 186, 203, 219-220
Yggdrasil, 119, 127
York (Pennsylvania), 179
York County (Pennsylvania), 11, 117
Young, Katie, 57
YouTube (website), 9, 218, 243
Yowie, 13, 46, 140, 147,
Yukon territory (see *United States*)
Yûñ'wi Tsunsdi', 62-63

Z

Zoobies, 54-55
Zorth, 119

About the Author

In addition to writing, Joshua Cutchin is a published composer and maintains an active performing and recording schedule as a tuba player based out of Atlanta, Georgia. He has appeared on dozens of programs including *Coast to Coast AM*, and is regularly invited to speak at paranormal conferences about his books. Joshua contributed to Robbie Graham's 2017 essay collection *UFOs: Reframing the Debate*, as well as David Weatherly's 2018 collection *Wood Knocks: Vol. 3*. Cutchin has also appeared on the hit History Channel television show *Ancient Aliens*. He is a recurring guest on *Where Did the Road Go?*, and maintains an online presence at JoshuaCutchin.com.

Other Books by Joshua:
A Trojan Feast (2015)
The Brimstone Deceit (2016)
Thieves in the Night (2018)

With co-author, Timothy Renner:
Where the Footprints End, volume I (2020)

Photo of the author by Nicole Eason

About the Author

Timothy Renner is an author, illustrator, and folk musician living in Pennsylvania. His illustrations have appeared in the pages of various books, magazines, fanzines and comics as well as on many record and CD covers. Since 1995, Timothy has been making music both solo and with his band, Stone Breath. Timothy is the creator of *Strange Familiars*, a podcast concerning the paranormal, weird history, folklore, and the occult. He makes regular appearances on the paranormal radio show, *Where Did the Road Go?*, and has appeared as a guest on many other podcasts and radio programs, including *Coast to Coast AM*.

Other Books by Timothy:
Beyond the Seventh Gate (2016)
Bigfoot in Pennsylvania (2017)
Bigfoot: West Coast Wild Men (2018)
Don't Look Behind You (2018)
Apparitions: Illustrations of The Other (2020)

With co-author, Joshua Cutchin:
Where the Footprints End, volume I (2020)

Photo of the author by Alison Renner.

Made in the USA
Monee, IL
23 May 2021